MARILLION   SEPARATED OUT ... REDUX

MARILLION
SEPARATED OUT ... REDUX

JON COLLINS

Foruli
Classics

Foruli Classics

Published by Foruli Classics

First published by Helter Skelter Publishing 2002
This revised & expanded edition published by Foruli Classics 2012

ISBN 978-1-905792-40-5

A CIP catalogue record for this book is available from the British Library

Cover & design by Andy Vella at Velladesign

Typeset in Palatino

Foruli Classics is an imprint of Foruli Ltd, London

www.foruliclassics.com

CONTENTS

ACKNOWLEDGEMENTS

Once again I'd like to thank all the fans who have contributed to this book, both directly and through forums and online reviews. For this edition I'd specifically like to thank Mike Ainscoe, Rick Armstrong, Ian Atkins, Carla Barros, Krys Boswell, David Brown, Simon Clarke, Dave Clarke, Jason Cobley, Dave and Christine Cooper, Anthony Craig, Steve Craig, Joe del Tufo, Michel Drolet, David Esquivel, Mark Frater, Sascha Glück, Rich Harding, Gary Hardman, Mark and Vanessa Kennedy, Mariusz Krauze, Mike Kuntz, Tuula Maenpaa, Pete Manning, Andy McIntosh, Liz Medhurst, Stuart Mitchell, Steve Moss, Darren Newitt, Erik Nielsen, Andy Rotherham, Joe Serge, Stuart and Richard Sharples, Peter Tornberg, Fabian Vinet, Ian Walford, Laura Warrickand forum members AndyS, Azdirkmore, Becca, Bulletproofmask7, Chesterbear, Elephant, Essexboyinwales, FinnFreak, Froggy, Frurken, Geol76, Gianfranco, Grendels pet frog, Hawkfanatic, Hillviewdavid, ICGenie, Jlindeman, Lostmarbles 2005, Malcolm, Marc1701, Mephisto, Musicaljim, Nathan797, Pieman73, River, RobEastUSA, Rotherrie, Salyerdk, Shoggz, Sstein, The 100th Night, Toteaux, Uxter and Yoooreds for their help and contributions; Paul and Lisa Walmsley for their sterling work reviewing the new content and Fraser Marshall for, once again, going beyond the call of duty with the album descriptions. I'd like to give another mention to Hugh Dorey, Gordon Gillies and Karin Breiter, without whom this book may never have existed. And then some names that were left out of the first edition – Mark Campbell, "He who should not be named" Crispin Bateman, Julie Hanlon, thank you.

Direct and heartfelt thanks also to Lucy Jordache, Stephanie Bradley, Rich Lee and Simon Ward at Racket Records, to all the wonderful Web UK team, to collaborators and colleagues Mike Hunter, Darryl Way, David Hitchcock, Colin Woore, Dave Meegan, Eric Blackwood, Richard Barbieri, John Arnison, Hannah Stobart, John Ireland, Howard Jones, Egbert Derix, Paul Rowlston, Antonio Seijas, Tim Sidwell and Colin Price. Best of luck to Rod Brunton! Apologies to anyone I have forgotten this time around, I owe you a beer.

Thanks to all at Foruli including Matt, Mark, Karl and Andy. In memoriam publisher, mentor and friend Sean Body who died of leukaemia in 2008, aged only 42.

My biggest debt is to my long-suffering wife Liz, who seems once again to have accepted my explanation that this is 'just work'. Thank you Ben and Sophie, my wonderful children, just for being there.

As ever, a final thank you to the members of the band – Pete Trewavas, Steve Rothery, Ian Mosley, Mark Kelly, Steve Hogarth – as well as Fish and all other past members including, this time, Neil Cockle, plus Jonathan, Mick, Diz, Brian, Doug, Martin and Andy. This is your story; I hope I've done it justice.

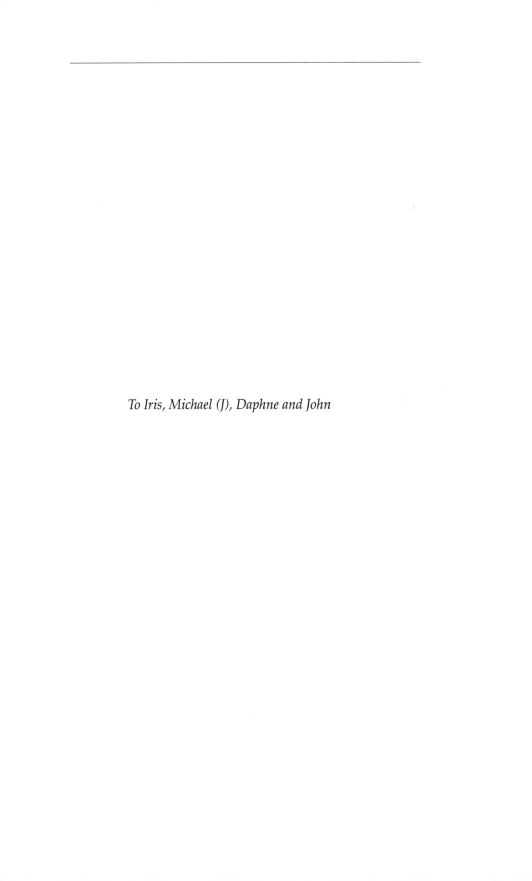

To Iris, Michael (J), Daphne and John

For the record, I have tried to use the past tense for quotes I have referenced from elsewhere, and the present tense for my own interviews.

I should also comment on names. To work for Marillion, it appears you have to have a name that is impossible to spell or impossible to pronounce (Mark Kelly is the exception). I have tried to be as accurate as possible, for example I am sure it is Jelleyman rather than Jelliman, Irvine rather than Irving(!), Marter rather than Martyr. I have quite deliberately said H rather than h for Steve Hogarth, simply because it stands out better in the text.

For hundreds of thousands of people worldwide, Marillion are alive and kicking, continuing to push their artistic boundaries, refusing to compromise or accept the adopted wisdom. Marillion have turned their back on the fashions of the time, the expectations of the mass market, and indeed the accepted practices of the industry. Who else has financed their own album through sales advances negotiated directly with their fans; who else then had the audacity to pick up a major label signing for the album's distribution?

Separated Out First Edition, 2002

Ten years have passed since this book was first released, during much of which time it has been out of print. Its cautionary ending – "the band's biggest challenge lies in the future, as they attempt to sustain their growing popularity and build their image, while keeping true to their ideals..." – was long ago superseded by the knowledge that Marillion have gone from strength to strength, releasing five studio albums and building their profile even while, through tours, conventions and direct contact, they have further cemented their relationship with a worldwide fan base.

The idea of adding a new chapter was first mooted back in 2006, and the question of a new edition has come up regularly ever since. As part of the exercise, I have reworked the original text as I knew it could be improved. At the same time I have fixed a handful of minor errors and resolved one glaring error, caused by the omission of the word 'publishing' next to the word 'income'.

Readers will note some changes to the format and structure of this edition, notably that the chapters are shorter and re-arranged, and that box-outs and fan stories are now integrated into the text. The reasons are simple: first that the single narrative needs to work just as well in an e-book edition as a printed volume, and second the hard reality of working within a word count limit. Adding half as much information again without significantly increasing the book's length has been quite a challenge!

I hope you enjoy this edition.

Jon Collins, October 2012

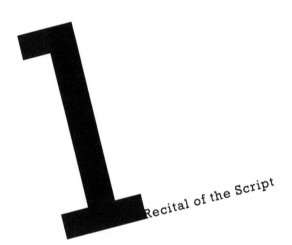

Recital of the Script

Where did it all start? 1977 is remembered as the year that anarchy ruled in the UK. Punk started as an anti-fashion movement, a deliberate revolt against the pomp and glamour of the music of the time, and the dreary grey of a Britain plagued by strikes and civil unrest. On October 3 of that year, striking undertakers left 800 corpses unburied in London; three weeks later, *Never Mind The Bollocks, Here's The Sex Pistols* was released to the faux-horreur of the establishment press.

While punk took a disproportionate share of the headlines, other musical styles refused to roll over and play dead. This was also the year of disco, of Abba, David Soul and Leo Sayer, of Stevie Wonder and the Jacksons. New Wave bands such as Elvis Costello and the Attractions, XTC and Talking Heads offered an intelligent counterpoint to punk's cynicism, even as The New Wave of British Heavy Metal forged a rebellion against the rebels, with Iron Maiden, Saxon and a host of others signalling a resounding return to rock and roll.

Elsewhere, the likes of progressive rock bands such as Pink Floyd, Genesis, Rush and Yes continued to draw strong support wherever they went. And outside of the media glare, in pubs and clubs across the country, bands formed and played, performers emulating their own heroes and upholding traditions. Largely oblivious of the fashion-conscious musical obsessions of the London scene, they created the music they wanted to play, for those who wanted to listen.

One such band was Electric Gypsy, whose line-up included the band's founder Doug Irvine on bass, Alan King on vocals, guitarist Andy Glass and a drummer whose name is long since forgotten. "We played rock, along the lines of Hawkwind," says Andy. Sparking a tradition that would be upheld for a good five years, the drummer did not last long. Fortuitously, Andy's fiancée heard someone practising in a shed next door to her parents' house on Brae Road, in the village of Brill in Buckinghamshire. That "someone" was Mick Pointer.

AN UNEXPECTED PARTY

The timing was perfect for Mick, then in a band called Stockade, formed eighteen months before with old classmate Martin Butler. Feeling that Stockade was going nowhere, Mick agreed to an audition with the Gypsies. He got the gig, left Stockade on amicable terms and joined Alan, Andy and Doug with high hopes. Mick's optimism was short-lived, however: "They spent less time doing music, and a lot more time talking crap and smoking dope all day," he says. The Gypsies did play a few times, "Our big gig was at Stone Free Festival near Aylesbury," says Andy. "Magic!"

By early 1978, Mick and Doug decided to leave the Gypsies and form an instrumental ensemble, recruiting local lads Neil Cockle on keyboards (From Starlight Cruiser, who had supported Electric Gypsy) and Martin Jenner on guitar. Rehearsals took place on Tuesday nights at Neil's place and Fridays and Saturdays at Mick's, a run-down cottage on Station Road in the village of Long Marston. "The place was a complete mess. The only food on offer was the dead mice brought in from the fields by the cats," Mick recalls. It was here that the four-piece sought inspiration for a name. "We went through hundreds of names, I saw the *Silmarillion* book on the shelf and said, 'Hey, how about that?' The name stuck."

The fledgling band had high aspirations for its musical style, drawing upon such bands as Camel and Genesis. Explains Martin Jenner, "Neil had a string synthesizer and played this to good effect on some of the slower segments and also to give that nice filling sound behind the stronger riffs. The Genesis influence came with things like song construction and most notably, off-beat timings." The band then added its own stylistic preferences - Martin describes himself as, "A die-hard rock guitarist who likes to play Gary Moore-style solos," while Mick sought to emulate his drumming hero, Neil Peart of Rush.

Following several months of rehearsals ("I really wanted to go out and gig but we spent the whole time practising," says Neil Cockle), the Sils used a studio in Amersham to write and rehearse an hour-long, largely instrumental set with Doug adding the occasional vocal. Finally, on April 22 1978, at the Hambrough Tavern in Southall, London, the band was ready to play. The gig was in support of punk band Robert and The Remoulds: Neil, Martin and the Remoulds' drummer (also called Martin) all worked for the same company. "We played instrumentals only, all band compositions," recalls Martin Jenner. "We had no strong vocalist in the band and hadn't yet auditioned a lead vocalist."

Despite a successful gig it was not the most auspicious of starts - the next day signalled the start of the 1978 Southall riots, made notorious with the death of protester Blair Peach following a baton charge by the police. It was also the last time that the four played together. Neil and Martin both left not long after the gig, with Martin the first to go. "We started auditioning soon after the gig and tried some, I thought, very good vocalists," says Martin, "Doug and Mick were not happy with them, seemingly knowing exactly what they wanted. It was this slow forward motion to accept a vocalist and get out playing regularly that helped me decide to leave the band."

Following Martin's departure, Mick and Doug placed an ad in *Melody Maker* for a guitarist. Despite numerous auditions with a good twenty hopefuls,

15

nobody fitted the bill. Until, that is, a young player and his mate arrived one Sunday morning in August. "I had called but they'd forgotten," reminisces Steve Rothery. "I'd got up at six in the morning to drive down in my Renault 5, and when I got there they were still in bed." After the 250-mile journey from Whitby, Steve was keen to show the somewhat hung-over Sils what he could do. Reluctantly, Doug and Mick agreed to listen to Steve's demo tape, but that didn't help matters. "It wasn't especially good," admits Steve, "I'd made it when I was playing with a chap called Edwin Hart; he was a huge Beatles fan. They weren't too impressed."

Mick and Doug felt enough sympathy to let Steve come in and have a jam. "He set up his gear in the living room while we all sat there, bleary-eyed," recalls Mick. "He was very impressive. We sat there and watched as he played to us, and we gave him the job there and then." Steve headed back up North to consider his options before deciding to accept the invitation a week later, on August 19 1979. "I just moved down," he recalls. "It was obvious I was in a similar area of music to them. Pink Floyd, Genesis, Camel - but not Rush. I gave everything up for a bass player and a drummer." Note the absence of keyboardist: Rothers' arrival coincided with the departure of Neil Cockle, who, like Martin, had also been frustrated with the lack of live outings. The final straw was seeing the rest of the band help themselves to equipment out of his car. "I'd left the car unlocked. Doug took his Micromoog out to make a point," says Neil, who wasn't too pleased at the time. Recalls Steve, "After a blazing row between Neil, Doug and Mick we were a three-piece."

Help was at hand as a friend of Doug's, Brian Jelleyman, had already expressed an interest in joining the fledgling line-up. Brian was no mean pianist, acknowledges schoolmate and future band member, Pete Trewavas. "He'd had classical lessons and I think he was Grade 8 - he was good." Following another audition in the front room of the cottage, a newly formed line-up started developing a set. Concerned about copyright, and besides, the name was "too Tolkien" according to the new guitarist, they also decided to change the name of the band. "Doug had Silmarillion painted on his guitar case - all he had to do was paint out the Sil," explains Steve. With a flick of a brush, Marillion was formed.

Following a few rehearsals in Hemel Hempstead, at an old music shop and The Queen's Head pub which was a few doors down ("the main venue for band meetings," says Brian), in February 1980 the band tramped off to The Enid's studio in Hertford with barely concealed delight. "We were big fans, we knew they had a studio and did their own recording," says Mick. Agrees Steve, "It was quite exciting, my first recording experience!" Also present was Chris 'Privet' Hedge, a Long Marston resident and the band's self-appointed roadie. The session included 'Lady Fantasy' and 'Alice' (which would later become part of 'Forgotten Sons'), recorded on a two-track demo tape for the band's own use.

Heartened by the studio session, the freshmen pushed forward, playing their first gig as an ensemble in the Berkhamsted Civic Centre on March 1 1980. It was not the most comfortable of settings, remembers Brian, "I know it was cold, as the fog from the dry-ice machine didn't stay on the ground where it was supposed to be." The material included 'Close', 'The Tower' and a couple of long-forgotten tracks, 'Herne The Hunter' and 'The Haunting Of Gill House', with Privet providing explosions to accompany the latter. "One of the flashes didn't go off, so he scraped the contents into another one," recalls Steve. "When he let that one off there was a huge sheet of flame up my back that nearly blew me off the stage. That was quite a first gig." Privet, who was in an upstairs booth "doing the lights" was oblivious to the goings-on below. "I'm not sure if I blew Steve Rothery up, but I'm inclined to think not," he says, a little dubiously.

Of the performance itself, perceptions vary. Mick remembers little other than the reaction. "Some guy came up and said, 'You guys are really excellent, you should be playing in London.' I thought, if he says that on the first gig... well." Rothers' rosy memories include no fewer than six encores. "Mind you," he says, "That could have been because they were all stoned out of their heads!" Early fan Mike Eldon remembers the onlookers as being less than receptive... but then numbers were not huge. Also in attendance was a youthful Steven Wilson, who had gone with friends to see local punk band, the Chiltern Volcanoes. "We heard that they were supporting another local band called "Marilyn" [sic]. When we got there Marillion were handing out some flyers and among other things mentioned some T-shirts for sale and the fact that Geddy Lee from Rush had one. When Marillion came on most of the punks departed, which left about 25 people. Consequently my friends and me had a pretty good view of the show. I don't know what we were expecting but it certainly wasn't what we got. Being a 'normal', rebellious 11-year-old, I was listening to Heavy Metal at the time, but also starting to discover more sophisticated rock music, so I was pretty amazed to see something that wasn't in the standard punk/metal anyone-can-play-guitar fare in a local venue. I recall that in one song Mick Pointer came to the front of the stage and played some flute..."

After Berkhamsted, Marillion played 14 dates between March and November 1980. All offers to play were accepted, including a 'Battle Of The Bands' at the Horn Of Plenty in St Albans, the Students Union in High Wycombe (where

Doug's girlfriend was president), a mental home in St Albans and a street traders' fair in Watford which also included a magician with a flair for sticking six-inch nails up his nostrils. Very early on, the band were keen to build rapport with the people attending the gigs. T-shirts were printed, and before the performance the band handed out flyers saying, "We hope you enjoy the gig and will come and see us again," including a phone number so that budding fans could find out where the band were playing next. Not the actions of a typical pub band. "We made the point of going out to the front, signing autographs and so on," says Mick. "You've got to have that contact."

BASSIST/VOCALIST REQUIRED

As autumn came to a close, Mick and Steve had moved to Quainton Road in Waddesdon and Steve was sharing another quaint little place with Privet, on Weston Road in Aston Clinton. Diz Minnitt later described it as "a tiny little Rothschild cottage," with three rooms downstairs and two above. It was no palace - Priv called it "the bear pit" and Brian simply referred to it as "a filthy, disgusting dive" but as the initial tenant at least Steve had a room to himself. Also resident was Guy Hewison, who shared the second bedroom with Priv. Guy met the band through his sister, Claire, who frequented the Queen's Head in Long Marston, one of Rothers' favoured haunts. Guy mucked in as driver – "I was over 21, so the only one who could drive a transit," he recalls, referring to 'Margaret', an unreliable green Commer van. Guy also acted as crew, booking agent and, before long, remembers Steve, "He fancied himself as our manager."

As Guy rented the house by this time, nobody was about to complain – and besides, it was just a band, wasn't it? Most band members had day jobs - Brian worked at the local benefits office, Doug was a photocopier engineer and Mick was a joiner and kitchen fitter. Steve drove a van for Shaw's Pet Products, situated ten doors down on Weston Road. Besides Shaw's, Rothers worked his way through a number of jobs including driving a baker's van for a day ("I found I had to get up at 5 every morning..."), a caravan factory ("A lady had a finger sliced off. I thought *this is no place for a guitarist.*") and giving some guitar lessons. One job application was for the National Film Archive in Aston Clinton. "Fortunately I didn't get it. It could have proved to be something I'd find hard to give up."

Not that there were any plans to dispense with day jobs, not at that stage – all the same, material was coming together and working well live. By November the time seemed right to capture the compositions on tape, so the band booked a session at Leyland Farm in Gawcott near Buckingham, a studio in a converted stable owned by Wild Willy Barrett. "I think we got free studio time there because Mick worked a deal where they used his microphones in exchange," recalls Diz, who experienced Leyland Farm during his own time with the band. The layout was not ideal, recalls Brian: "The studio was in the lower part of the stable, with the mixing desk in the room above." This had the unfortunate effect of not being able to see the person you were recording. Says Diz, "There was no direct connection with whoever was mixing. You couldn't see them." Nonetheless, it was serviceable and the first session was deemed a success.

It was just as Marillion were planning to record 'Close' at Leyland Farm that Doug Irvine announced his resignation from the band. "He had always said that if the band hadn't made it by the time he was 25 he would leave," explains Mick. So he did, heading for the relative simplicity of his day job as a photocopier engineer and taking the only Silmarillion demo tape with him. Mick, Brian and Steve fell back to the local pub and regrouped. "We were even more determined to continue," says Mick. The recording session for 'Close' took place soon after, with Steve playing the bass line.

On December 6 1980 another advert was placed, in the weekly paper *Musicians Only*. It read, "Competent bassist/vocalist required for established Progressive Rock group with own material in Aylesbury." To a couple of unemployed, would-be musicians living in Scotland, it couldn't have been better timed. Money and options were running out for Derek William Dick and William Roberts Minnitt, known to their friends as Fish and Diz (short for Dizzy, and as in, "Come here diz minitt!"). Explains Fish, "I'd had a bit of savings from my time in the Forestry Commission and we were getting a little bit of money from my parents but it was very tough. We were nicking turnips out of fields and stuff." The requirement was for one fellow, not two, so a bit of fancy talking was needed. Remembers Mick, "Diz phoned me and said, 'I'm a bass player, but I don't sing. I know a guy who does. How about I send you something with his voice on?' Fish and Diz sent a tape and received the Leyland Farm demo of 'Close' by return post, as well as an invitation to audition. So far, so good.

The plan was to head down on New Year's Day 1981. Despite getting rather lost on the way, the pair eventually arrived at Weston Road. "They all came out, thinking that we'd come for an audition," remembers Diz. "We said, 'Bugger the audition, we're here and that's that!'" Mick remembers thinking, "a big, loud, tall, arrogant Scotsman, just what we needed..." At least the band allowed the van to be unloaded – the sight of a paraffin heater helping to thaw the initially frosty reception. Mark Kelly, who would later join the residents at Number 64, recalls how, "We used to put it in the middle of the room and called it central heating." Then it was all down to the Rothschild Arms, a few doors away, for some equally ice-breaking beers.

Over the days that followed the ensemble returned to Leyland Farm where Fish performed a handful of songs by Genesis (notably 'I Know What I Like') and Yes before recording some of his lyrics over the top of the 'Close' demo tape. Everyone was delighted by the close fit between Fish's voice and the feel of the music, as well as his ability to mimic both Jon Anderson and Peter Gabriel. "We could see the potential in Fish; he had a really interesting voice," recalls Steve. Despite minor reservations about Diz's bass playing, the two were recruited into the fold. "I was self-taught and I'd only been playing for a couple of years," says Diz. "Fish said we came as a package."

The final seal on the contract was made between Fish and Priv, who went out on the razz the first evening. "We got blatted and fell into a ditch," laughs Priv. "We walked back with no trousers on. It was all a bit weird and crazy." The weeks that followed continued the theme, remembers Diz, "One morning after we had been up all night taking various things and drinking black tea we heard the milkman. Imagine being confronted by five guys totally off their faces at that time in the morning. Then we realised how bizarre it must look so we cracked up and ran back inside."

With the band up to full strength again, the newly completed line-up spent their daytime hours reviewing, revamping and refreshing the material, either at Leyland Farm or Anthony Hall studio. A proper vocalist enabled new possibilities - not just meandering instrumentals but real songs. Commented Mick Pointer at the time, in an interview with Hugh Fielder of *Sounds*, "Before they joined, the style was similar but it was more pretentious. We would drag out an idea for about five minutes when it was really only worth about 30 seconds. When Fish and the others joined, it added that bit of punch." Speaking of which, the first rehearsal at Anthony Hall gave the incumbents their first experience of Fish's wrath. "We hadn't used the PA for ages, so it took a while to get it working," says Priv. who had graduated to doing the band's sound. "Fish started throwing his toys out of the pram. A roaring hangover from the night before didn't help."

The much-required creative injection started to yield tracks such as 'Garden Party', 'He Knows, You Know' and 'Charting The Single'. Fish's ambitions went way beyond the music, however. "We immediately became a lot more professional," explains Steve, "Fish was so ambitious, ruthlessly so. All the qualities that made him difficult to work with also gave him his drive." Guy concurs: "Without Fish's pushiness, the band wouldn't have had the measure of success it had. It probably wouldn't have amounted to anything." After all, most of the band had started with day jobs, adds Fish, "Apart from Steve, we were the only ones who had given up a lot to come down. Steve really came through, but in the rest of the band there was still this weekend gig atmosphere."

THE EARLY CIRCUIT

With Fish and Guy manning the phones, it was only a matter of time before the new line-up were ready to go out and play. The first gig was on March 14 1981, in the back room of the Red Lion, Bicester. "It was a bit of a squaddies' pub," remembers Mick, "I remember walking round these streets wearing these bloody ridiculous costumes trying to drum up support." The technique didn't work: despite Guy's fly-posting around the town, only about fifteen people turned up. In the audience were members of local band Toad The Wet Sprocket. Remembers Diz, "They came over to give us fatherly advice. Bastards!" Despite the poor turn-out, the five were savvy enough to realise that success would not come easily with their chosen style of music: a definite, deliberate and distinctly unfashionable throwback to the progressive styles of ten years before. Instead, recalls early fan Mike Eldon, came the active decision "to swamp every possible venue within a fifty-mile radius with demands to book them." Bicester was one of the last appearances that Guy would book, as Fish took over and started to manage the bookings himself.

Marillion played several dates at The Britannia Pub, Aylesbury, including one attended by future band mate Pete Trewavas. The set list included 'Madcap's Embrace' graced by a flute solo from Mick. "I bet everybody likes to forget that," says Pete. "Mick had his flute moment 'cos I think at that stage Fish hadn't been in particularly long, and it was still very much Mick's band." Not that Fish didn't make an impression. Continues Pete, "The ceiling was very low so he had to stoop. He had blood capsules and all that kind of stuff and they put on a good show considering it was a pub. I could see they needed a bit of work on them, but I thought they had something. Fish certainly had a presence, you couldn't stop watching." In part this was down to Fish's own visuals, as he painted his face in ever-more dramatic styles. On the band's third ever gig he sported his first 'full facial' - a Union Jack mask. "I thought the Union Jack looked really good," comments Steve. "Some of the others looked a bit naff, though."

The band became a regular draw at The Wheatsheaf in Dunstable, which was soon-to-be-fan Mike Eldon's local. "It was a typical two-room pub," recalls

Mike. "By the time they got their equipment in I was standing about two feet from Fish. That was quite an experience." Not that Mike was daunted. "They were absolutely excellent, it was music I was into, from people of my own age." Stories of the early gigs are legion, like the band's "triumphant" return to the Students Union, High Wycombe - slightly marred by a crowd of skinheads who decided to trash the place. The implacable Fish was not having any of it, remembers Privet: "Fish went after them with a mic stand. He was rock-hard and scared the crap out of them. I'm surprised they didn't come back though - he looked ridiculous in a cape!" On another occasion Fish confronted a local chapter of Hells Angels who were making too much noise. Recalls Priv, "Fish gave them some verbal... then, while the band were playing, one of them rode his motorbike through the front door. It started getting a bit dodgy, then the next thing I saw was Fish having a drink with them. They became fans after that!"

With money still tight for the lead singer, about six months after Fish joined, Brian found him a job in Aylesbury's faceless, depressing benefits office. "He was very popular with everyone, but not really a civil servant," laughs Brian. It was here that Fish penned the lyrics to 'He Knows, You Know', as he came down from an acid trip. Recounts Diz, the trip didn't just inspire the lyrics to a song: "Some bloke came to sign on while Fish was completely off his face. Instead of getting him to sign the form, he made him do four circles and six signatures on this piece of paper. The guy went home thinking that he had signed for his benefit. At one point Fish wouldn't come out of the toilet because he was convinced there was an enormous spider, about six foot across, sitting on the ceiling. Straight after this he wrote the song."

Being of a generous disposition, Brian also invited Fish to share a flat at Winchester House in Aylesbury, with himself and his girlfriend Fran (who paid the rent). Fran was a nurse at Stoke Mandeville Hospital, and it wasn't long before the lads were patronising the nurses' accommodation. "We used to sneak there for parties," says Priv. One such nurse was Kay Atkinson, who moved in with Fish for a few months before she moved to Earls Court in London, the backdrop for a number of scenes that would one day lead to her immortalisation in a song.

Before long the pattern of phone calls, bookings and live gigs attracted the attention of David Stopps, manager of Aylesbury's Friars Club. "Fish was a larger than life character," recalls David. "His presence was felt in the town as soon as he moved down." David booked Marillion to play the Aston Hall, a small venue in Aylesbury's Civic Centre, as support to John Cooper Clarke during the town's annual arts week. As it happened, the northern poet's manager was the well-connected, London-based impresario, John Arnison.

By July, the collective band members had saved enough pennies to record a demo tape to send to gig promoters, club managers and record labels. Fish had been introduced by David to Les Payne, an established local performer who was training as an engineer at Roxon Studio in Watlington, near Oxford. Fish proposed that Les produced the session, so one Saturday morning the band headed to Roxon. "It was a grey industrial kind of building, with no sign of it looking anything like a studio on the outside," remembers Diz. "It reminded me of my father's piggery." When the engineer fell asleep at the desk having been up the night before, Les stepped into his shoes despite never having engineered in anger. The session included 'He Knows, You Know', 'Charting The Single' and 'Garden Party', the latter introduced by the popping of corks. "It was Mick Pointer's girlfriend Stef Jeffries' birthday," recalls Diz. "We had all this Asti Spumanti - it's no wonder the recordings went so smoothly." The final mixes were laid to tape on the Monday night. "It was surprising to hear the finished result," comments Rothers. "It sounded pretty good."

When the tape failed to cut any ice with the record companies in London, despite being sent to every major label, it was almost inevitable that the band turned to developing its already sizeable fan base. "We were defiant, we knew we'd get somewhere with it," says Mick. "When you're young, you can't believe you could possibly fail." Fish concurs: "We thought, fuck it, it's going to happen. It was absolute, total youthful arrogance!" As he noted in a 1983 interview with Jay Williams of *Sounds*, "Every record company was saying, 'We don't want a band like you, we want singles,' and the only way we could sit opposite them and not be dictated to was to build up a big live following."

And so they did. Promotion of the band continued relentlessly. Clubs were sent copies of the demo, along with a clutch of posters designed by Diz. "I wanted to use an eye as part of the Marillion logo for a long time," Fish wrote later. "We played around with Egyptian designs, Diz drew the eye crying into the palm of the hand and feeding the root of the stem from which the eye grew, indicating a sort of self-sufficiency or symbiotic relationship." The "Saliva Tear" design would be the mainstay of the band's image right up to its signing with EMI.

FRYING TONIGHT

By the summer of 1981, the band were playing at least weekly, and when they weren't out gigging they were calling venues, developing new songs and trying to hold down jobs. When Fish could stand his job at the benefits office no more, he packed it in and trudged the streets with Diz, putting up posters and looking for new places to play. Rehearsals continued at Leyland Farm and Anthony Hall before resorting to the tin-roofed Scout Hut in Aston Clinton. Remembers Diz, "The acoustics were appalling, but it was very cheap. I think we did a skeletal version of 'Three Boats Down From The Candy'."

New tracks were being added to the set all the time, including the crowd-swayer 'Margaret', which had started life even before Fish joined the band. Brian happened to play 'Scotland The Brave' in the studio, and Steve and Mick started jamming around it. It was originally tagged 'Scotch Porridge', then 'Margaret Gets Her Oats' in homage to the band's green Commer van. It was fortuitous indeed that the band now had a towering Scot to sing it. More controversial was the 19-minute 'Grendel', with lyrics based on an adaptation of *Beowulf*. With its origins in 'The Tower', the song evolved to be structurally similar to Genesis's 'Supper's Ready', a worry to some. "We were concerned," Fish agreed, "But it all flowed and the fans loved it." Laughs Steve, "We were showing our influences maybe a little too clearly - it was clumsily done, but it was sincere, it wasn't done to be pompous. Something set us apart though; I don't know what it was. Somehow we had more of an edge."

Despite a clear lean to the progressive, Marillion were never exclusive about either their influences or their audiences - all were welcome, and the rougher edge of punk played into the live performances. "I've got pictures where there are about 40 or 50 Mohicans down the front pogo-ing away," Fish recalled later. Meanwhile, crowds in army towns such as Bicester were inevitably military. Comments Mick, "We used to play to a lot of drunken, crew-cut squaddies. God knows what they made of it!" Unfortunately the audience diversity was not to last, as increased media attention led to pigeon-holing of the band. Commented Fish, "As soon as the Genesis tag came in, the Yes/Floyd audience came to see us along with a lot of metal and heavy rock aficionados and it shut out a lot of the fans I'd liked to have seen at the gigs."

Genesis were undoubtedly an influence, at least on Marillion's approach to music. "I can see why people said it - look at 'Grendel' and the face paint - but the music was more aggressive," says Mark Kelly. Comments David Stopps, whose club played an integral part in Genesis's own story, "Fish felt there was room for another band of that ilk. With the advent of punk, bands like Genesis had become uncool at street level, but there was a huge audience waiting to come out of the shadows." Long-time fan Steve Woods was one such aficionado. "I started noticing mention of a Genesis/Prog-influenced band called Marillion.

Being a devout Genesis follower it caught my attention. Genesis was public property, meanwhile here was a band we could call our own," he recalls.

The collective Marillion had a number of objectives to achieve before they could start to tackle finding a label or getting airplay. One was to headline at the Friars Club, considered by all as the most important venue in the region. Fortunately, having seen them in action, David Stopps was quick to book them again, offering the band their first "proper" gig in the Aston Hall in support of US band Spirit. With the date set as August 1, Les Payne suggested they wore costumes of some sort, so off Fish went to the Hammer House Of Horror TV studios at Hampden Woods. "The studios were closing down and Fish bought loads of stuff in the sale. The stage was crammed with the stuff," remembers Les. Indeed it was - a full-graveyard setting, complete with gravestones and dry ice.

The night of the gig went as smoothly as a *Spinal Tap* outtake. The performance started with the tolling of a bell, the band walking up to the stage from the back, through the audience. According to Steve, "We wore these long monk-style gowns without trousers on. We had some floor level lighting shining up. During the gig I turned around to see Diz. As I did, the lights came on and the material became transparent. So, there he was stood in his undies. I thought, well if I can see him... I couldn't help but feel a bit exposed after that." An undaunted Fish reeled out some of his favourite party tricks, such as the ketchup-filled cucumber for 'Garden Party' and the blood capsules for 'Forgotten Sons' (during which he wielded the microphone stand as a rifle).

By the end of the gig the band had the audience exactly where they wanted. Recounts Diz, "We had about four hundred people crammed into this tiny hall. You couldn't physically move." Agrees fan and Aylesbury resident Darren Newitt, "The band was contagious, they generated excitement. Utterly amazed and astounded by the performance and the audience's response, my belief in, and appreciation of Marillion was infinitely reinforced." Indeed, Darren's adrenalin was running so high, he decided to blag his way backstage: "I managed to casually sneak past the security guards into the after-show party, And yes, my dream came true... I got to meet and talk to Marillion. What struck me the most about the band was how normal and down to earth they were. For a young, naive schoolboy meeting his musical idols, this was quite unexpected. I had elevated Marillion to 'musical gods' but there were no Prima Donnas here. Marillion made me feel very appreciated and special. I think I smiled for at least a week."

Despite the costume drama, everyone that attended Marillion's Friars debut recognised they had witnessed something special. "It was a bloody amazing gig," remarks Priv. "One of those things where you don't realise how important it is until afterwards. More people came to see us than to see the gig in the main hall." Unsurprisingly, Marillion were invited back. Before long the band had moved up the Friars rankings, playing support to a number of acts (including virtuoso blues guitarist Rory Gallagher) before becoming a regular headliner. This led not only to bigger gigs elsewhere, but also to increased media focus on the band's steady progress, hampered only by the occasional disaster: the 101 Club in Clapham on November 12, where four people turned up and the band ended up paying for the PA, or eight days later at the reggae-based Caribbean Club in Oxford. Recalls Mick, "We were the only white faces there. They asked us to stop. It was the kindest thing to do."

In general however, both the size of the audiences and the optimism of the travellers were growing. Fish's charisma turned many a crowd, not least at the White Hart in Bletchley, recalled Diz: "A handful of disinterested drunks in the audience were offering low-level grumbling abuse. Fish dealt with it by using the opportunity to accentuate the inclusive nature of his stage performance and percussively beat time on one of their heads with the tambourine. Needless to say the verbal abuse stopped." To capitalise on the vibe, 400 more copies of the Roxon tape were made and advertised in the small ads and various fanzines, one of which was picked up by fan Anne Bond's older sister. "Jan saw an advert in the Genesis magazine for some demo tapes of a band who sounded like early Genesis," remembers Anne. "She sent off for them but they were very poor quality." Whatever the quality, the music was enough to hook Jan and another few hundred followers.

The second prong of Marillion's promotional attack was to ensure its message reached the higher echelons of Soho. Fish employed PR agent Keith Goodwin to ensure as wide coverage as possible. According to fan and early chronicler Claus Nygaard, "Fish just stormed into his office in London one day and almost forced him to be Marillion's PR agent." It would have been rude not to accept.

2

Going to London

London is a beacon, the true starting place for any aspiring southern UK band, not only because of the potentially larger audiences, but also because most record companies are based in the West End. Reps from the major labels already have their work cut out sifting through the bands that have taken the trouble to move to the capital, so there is little chance of being spotted outside the M25. And so it was, like many bands before (and after) them, that Marillion followed the Watling Way and headed for the lights.

The boys were not travelling alone. Structures were already in place to support the band's ventures, not least a newly-implemented telephone hotline linking fans with the band's movements. By the end of the summer of 1981, the ripple effect of Marillion's relentless self-promotion (supported by Keith, who got the band its first listings in *Sounds* and *Melody Maker*) reached the heart of the city, so much so that by October they were booked for a gig at the renowned Marquee. In parallel, some operational details needed settling. Not everyone in the band was as fully committed, devoted, even obsessive as the other members. It was time to unsheathe the long knives.

KELLY THE HERO

Marillion's debut at the Marquee on October 20 1981 was a riot. "The place had a real vibe but it was disgusting - you'd stick to the floor," recalls Steve. Supporting US glam-rock outfit Girl, the band left nothing to chance and, in now-habitual style, booked a coach from Aylesbury for its growing entourage. The result, according to a gig review in *Sounds*, was to "give the Aerosmith rip-off merchants a bit of a scare - it's not often a support act gets an encore at the Marquee." Fortunately, as Fish later said, "Girl had a good attitude about it, they gave us congratulations afterwards." The *Sounds* review gives an insight into the more devoted elements of the early fan base, which it described as "rather a large contingent of ageing hippy 'eadbangers. No denim and leather here mate, more like kaftans and loonpants." Hmm...

The following month saw Marillion embark on their most extensive touring programme yet, christened the 'Saliva Tears Tour' after Diz's posters. It was not as glamorous as the name would suggest, "We used to chuck everything in the back of the van and go off somewhere and play," recalls Mick. The first 'official' date (Marillion had already played 15 times in October) was at the Red Lion in Gravesend on November 1, and 20 further dates were planned.

Brian Jelleyman did not survive to the end of the tour, however. Though handy with the keys, to the others it was clear that his heart and soul were not in the band, at least not to the extent required. Says Guy Hewison, "Brian didn't feel that he could give up his job." "I never really put the practice in," says Brian, "I can understand the frustration Fish and the others felt at the time - I knew my attitude wasn't right. I knew the band was destined for success but I couldn't become what was needed. Everyone needed to be as totally dedicated to the band as Fish was, and I wasn't." Brian carried on playing, hoping things would sort themselves out, while (encouraged by Fish), the other band members kept their eyes open for a replacement.

The moment came on November 11, when Marillion supported Chemical Alice at Chadwell Heath. On keyboards was Mark Kelly, a competent player who, as luck had it, had been bored with his own band for some time. "The guitarist was into all this cosmic stuff from groups like Hawkwind," remembers Mark. "All he wanted me to do were silly synth noises." Even before the support band approached him, Mark was sold. "I watched their set and decided that I really wanted to play with them, so when they asked me to join them at the end of the night, I said yes." And the deal was done - well, nearly.

Without telling Brian (though "it didn't come as a total surprise," he says), Mark was invited to attend Marillion's 69th gig at Chesham's Elgiva Hall, a performance held in aid of Amnesty International. Brian played that night, but Mark went back to Aston Clinton with Fish. The pair stayed up all night talking (Mark on adrenaline, Fish on acid), then the following morning Mick and Diz arrived. "They all went round to Brian's house to sack him," recalls Mark. Brian comments, "I was a bit upset at first, but we parted company as friends. Once it was over it was quite a relief. Mark had been waiting in the wings and to be fair, he did a much better job." Mark joined the band a week later on November 27, the day after which Marillion played Aston Village Hall as a 4-piece without the new, as-yet-unrehearsed player. Time was short: Steve went to collect Mark from Romford on November 28, following which he spent a few days in intensive rehearsals at Leyland Farm, before playing his first gig at the Great Northern in Cambridge on December 1. "I didn't know any of the songs. 'Grendel' was the main one. I had to write all the chords down to jog my memory." Mark was even playing for two bands at once for a while. "There was a bit of a cross-over period," he recalled. "I said to the guys in Chemical Alice that I was leaving, but I'd play the gigs they had already booked. There was one week where Marillion were playing in Chadwell Heath and then Chemical Alice were playing in Chadwell Heath. That was a bit strange."

Mark's welcome included sharing the absence of warmth offered by the cottage in Aston Clinton with Fish and Guy: Steve, Diz and Privet had already left for better accommodation at Ingram Avenue in Aylesbury. "The shampoo used to freeze in the bottle," says Mark, who used to wash his Mellotron in the shower. "It was quite old, it was always chewing up tapes. I used to take it apart before every gig to clean the heads. I would clean the whole frame by swinging it into the shower and washing it down with soap and water." Mark's stay didn't last long; two months later he relocated to Victoria Street, Aylesbury, a house rented by Diz's girlfriend Helen Main (now Mrs Minnitt). "We had to move out because Guy wasn't paying the rent," recalls Mark. "We were paying him though - when we found out, we were already six months in arrears with no way of paying it again."

With Mark on board it was back to business as usual - gig, write, rehearse, record (a cover of the Genesis song, 'I Know What I Like' survives from this period, recorded at a Scout Hut in Aston Clinton village). The first new song that Mark was involved in was 'Three Boats Down From The Candy': he wrote the music for the second half of the song in the front room at Weston Road. Its title was based on Fish's shenanigans on a beach in Brighton that year. "The boat had a number and the nearest with a name was the Candy. I looked on that as being a symbol of how far away I was from a genuine fulfilling relationship at that time," he said. 'Market Square Heroes' was written shortly after, the first melodies being composed in the garage at Victoria Street and lyrics penned by Fish at St Mary's Church, Aylesbury as he came down from yet another acid trip. Mark's impact was a double-edged sword, remembers Fish, "His arrival made everyone aware of the limitations of the others." Not least in terms of commitment – all but Mick agreed to 'go professional' when Mark joined. Turning professional was a stark choice, says Mark, "It meant giving up jobs and signing on."

Much of the promotional activity was being handled by Fish, who could talk anybody into anything, remembers Mark, "Nobody wanted to book us - if you didn't play dance music, punk, or new wave, forget it; you couldn't get a gig anywhere. But Fish would spend all day on the phone, ringing up different clubs. Eventually we were doing three or four gigs a week, which was pretty good for a band that nobody wanted to book." Mick Pointer concurs, "Fish had a much more clued-up idea of publicity and marketing. He was a massive asset in the start."

Christmas Eve 1981 saw the band's 75th performance, at the Starting Gate, Milton Keynes, "A notable gig" according to the soon-to-be-released *The Web* fanzine and the first time out for 'Three Boats' and 'Institution Waltz'; Marillion also performed covers of Genesis songs 'I Know What I Like' and part of 'The

Lamb Lies Down On Broadway'. In the Friars Club annual poll ("We were accused of being a monopoly, so we tried to be a bit democratic," laughs David Stopps), Marillion were voted best local band and best support band, as well as gaining an honourable 18th position as best band of all time (Genesis came 5th!). Little did anyone know that Marillion would be voted best new UK band by the readers of *Sounds* magazine less than a year later.

Marillion's first date of the new year was back at the Marquee, supporting Spider. The Marquee's then-manager Nigel Hutchings was so impressed that he offered Marillion a headline later the same month, the first in a series. "Word spread quite quickly. Before long we were packing it out," says Mick. More serendipitous still was the presence (unbeknown to the band) of Tony Wilson, producer of the BBC Radio 1's *Friday Rock Show*. Radio 1 had a reputation for discovering and showcasing new music, particularly on the late night shows of DJs John Peel and Tommy Vance. Whilst John Peel tended to focus on the indie and punk scene, Vance's *Friday Rock Show* played music from rock bands old and new. According to Mark, Spider's manager was Maggie Farren, Tony Wilson's girlfriend at the time. A fortunate coincidence, which led directly to the offer of a slot on the show.

The following day, the band rolled up at the BBC Studios on Delaware Road, London to record a session for Tommy Vance's show. With Tony Wilson at the production helm, the recording capturing old favourite 'The Web' and two newer tracks - 'Three Boats Down From The Candy' and 'Forgotten Sons'. As the session was broadcast on February 26, Marillion's music left the Thames Valley for the first time and reached the furthest points of the United Kingdom. Regular listener Steve Wood heard the session and found plenty to whet his appetite. He admits, "I was slightly disappointed with the music, but there was something there that made me continue to follow them. I also knew they wouldn't stay unsigned for long." It also proved to be Diz's last recording, though he didn't know it at the time.

The fan base was growing fast, drawn to the resurgence of a genre that had largely been forgotten. Recalls early fan and band chronicler Claus Nygaard, "Marillion had a storyline; they demonstrated rare musical talent with their unique compositions; they played with craftsmanship rather than machines; and they allowed the listener more than 12 straight bars. Here, finally, was a band to sit down to, to listen to, to drink to, to think to, to cry to. Simply a band to experience and grow with. A new, up and coming band even in the early days of 1982. A lot of us die-hard fans experienced Marillion in our early teens and grew up with them, so they hit a part of a generation right on the spot, and these youngsters would follow the band over the years to come."

To respond to such levels of interest, the first issue of Marillion's official fanzine, *The Web*, was released that same month. Little more than a few stapled sheets of A4, it was written by Tim Hollings , who had met the band for the first time the previous September. Its first words were, "Hi, this newsletter is designed as a means of expression for both the band and you, the people who have supported Marillion in the past and we hope, the future." Little did anyone know that it would still be in print over 30 years later! *The Web* proved its worth early on, as a request in an early edition encouraged fans to request the 'Friday Rock Show' session again. "Write to the Beeb and ask them to play the track again SOON; it's the thing to do," implored Tim. It was indeed, setting the scene for three decades of fan power. The BBC was inundated with requests, leading to a repeat of the session in May "by popular demand". As the band's audience continued to grow, Mick's girlfriend Stef was brought in to help write the mag.

On March 7, six weeks after their first headline, Marillion made a "triumphant return" to the Marquee, supported by Solstice whose line-up included former Electric Gypsy Andy Glass on guitar. This signalled the beginning of a 13-gig marathon at the Marquee, some of the later dates previewing the title track of the planned new album.

Did someone mention an album?

NOT DIZ WAY

The executioner's axe was sharpened a second time shortly after the Radio 1 session, this time for Fish's long-time friend, Diz. "We couldn't have a band with passengers," explains Fish. "The band had come to me and said he wasn't good enough. I couldn't argue my corner: I don't think the band would have happened like it did with Diz still in it. That was tough for me, he was one of my best friends." Meanwhile Guy, who was not so much passenger as driver, also realised that his own journey with the band had reached the end of the road. "With the number of gigs I was finding it difficult to get time off," explains Guy. "Besides, once the band had found an agent (and then a manager), I was becoming more and more side-lined." And that was that for Guy, well almost: he went on to perform a similar role for Andy Glass's band, Solstice.

Fish had heard about a local pop band called the Metros who were on their last legs, but who had a pretty good bassist, named Pete Trewavas. He turned up at a Metros gig at The King's Head in Aylesbury, a leaving party for the bar staff before the place shut down for refurbishment. Remembers Pete, "There was quite a big occasion being made of it, we did an evening of rock and roll which seemed to go down quite well." The stout Scot chatted to the diminutive bassist about Marillion's predicament, playing it cool as a 'Garden Party' cucumber. "He told me that they'd held some auditions but he wasn't sure how it was going to go. They had a tour coming up and he was asking me if I knew of anyone," says Pete, who had already seen Marillion play and who quite fancied the job. "I'd been into pop and new wave as that's where the work was, but Marillion were very different." Pete had also played in prog band Orthi with his old chum Robin Boult. Despite being unsure if he would be taken seriously (or indeed, if Marillion would be taken seriously, as he remarks, "I wasn't sure there was room for it in this day and age,"), Pete asked for an audition. "I felt they were going places, just purely because of the way they acted and put themselves across," he says.

Whilst Diz holidayed with his girlfriend Helen, Pete was quietly auditioned in the garage at the back of Victoria Street. The audition was a bit uncomfortable - remembers Pete, "I had very short, slightly red hair at the time and I was wearing white trainers which was a bit of a no-no. They asked me what music I was into, I told them that I'd been listening to Haircut 100 and their eyes got wider and wider. If I'd said that I had a load of Caravan, Pink Floyd and Genesis in my collection, maybe they would have taken me a bit more seriously..." He pressed on regardless, plugged in (he recalls being told, "You can use Diz's amp, he won't mind,") and tuned up. "We were so impressed by his tuning up that we gave him the gig there and then," remembers Mark. Nearly true - the boys had one more person to see, but Pete was pretty much a done deal. The final decision was made in a well-concealed pub at the end of an alley off Market Square, known as The Dark Lantern. "We decided to go to a pub we'd never been to before so we wouldn't meet anyone we knew," recalls Mark. Funnily enough, it was here that Mark bumped into Suzy Coleman, who would become his future (ex-)wife - "She came over 'cos she recognised Fish," he says.

Diz's last gig was at Dacorum College in Hemel Hempstead on March 25, attended by student Mark Frater. "I was asked to help hump the band's gear in, which was going well until Mark's piano that I was carrying - I think it was a white baby grand - slipped and was cushioned by my little finger. I also remember that I had to scrounge some lighting as theirs either didn't turn up or didn't work. I managed to find a few red spots that were directed at Fish for the whole gig." Mark Frater, like Diz, was oblivious of the fact that matters would come to a head less than 24 hours later, at a return gig at the Starting Gate in Milton Keynes. Unbeknown to Diz, the band had invited another bassist along to check them out. Diz got wind of it, asked Rothers what was going on and things quickly unravelled. Fish broke the news gently, but Diz did not take it well. "He said, 'You can hit me if you like,'" says Diz. "I was devastated, but having been involved in Brian's departure I couldn't say I had no blood on my hands. As an observer I can see why they did it, my standard of musicianship and my style did not fit, but I'd poured all my energy into it, emotionally and physically." Asking the others to ensure his equipment was returned (it was already on stage), Diz went home before the performance. The remaining four covered for the missing bass line, coping admirably for a one-off.

To further complicate matters, Fish, Mark and Privet were still sharing a house with Diz and Helen. While Priv stayed on - "I was still there even after 1983 when we went to America for the first time," he laughs - before long Mark and Fish moved to Rothers' place on Ingram Avenue in Aylesbury. Steve describes it as, "A semi-detached house on quite a nice estate. The locals saw it as some sort of hippie commune. Someone threw a brick through the window once. The drug squad raided it, but luckily I was on tour at the time." Privet, who moved in later, recalls trying out the PA on the front lawn: "Someone said, 'Let's put *The Wall* on.' I said, 'OK, you get the ice-creams and I'll get the PA.' That didn't make us any friends. The landlord was always trying to kick us out. We kept paying the rent so I think it proved to be more trouble than it was worth for him."

The worst was yet to come for Diz, when he found himself being written out of history, 1984-style. He never claimed to be an artistically key player in the band, but when he found that his contribution was to be annulled (as well as any financial rewards), it was more than he could bear. "Fish told me they'd rewritten the bass tracks with Pete and I wasn't going to get anything. Knowing I did contribute to various tracks I felt totally abused; my trust was violated completely. That was the bit I found the hardest." It would be four years before an out-of-court settlement recognised both Diz's and Brian's input. "The driving force was never financial, it was to get a co-writing credit," says Diz, "They said I was there as a passenger, that always galled me."

SALIVA TEARS

The concept of a Scottish tour had been long in the planning for a multitude of reasons, from there being few (if any) examples of English bands touring north of the border and the fact that Fish himself was a Scot, to the sublimely illogical 'Hell, why not?' This was not some lip service to the North - rather than nip up to Edinburgh and Glasgow and say 'done that', the band had a total of 29 dates planned, both across Scotland and en route. As Mark Kelly confirms, "We thought it was better to get everywhere and really do a proper tour." Not all dates were set in concrete before the Commer van left Aylesbury, so the gig guide in Issue 2 of *The Web* requested fans to "check all venues before travelling."

The tour had to work, not least because it meant waving goodbye to a specific source of income. Explains Mark, "We had to sign off when we went to Scotland, we were away for five weeks. There was no way they were going to let us claim without signing for that long without realising we were working." Pete received the same baptism of fire that Mark had experienced - with a mere two weeks to get up to speed before heading North. "It was quite hard work, I definitely put the hours in," he says. Fortunately, Pete's previous prog band experience helped him through. "The music had a definite structure that reminded me of Orthi," Pete recalls. "It was snappy and hooky, I could just jam along." With Pete on board, the rehearsals yielded a complete 'Chelsea Monday', which had been played live for the first time only three weeks before he joined.

Pete may have had the bass chops but given his pop background, his band mates weren't about to give him an easy ride. "It must have been weird for him joining us lot fresh from a pop band, and me and Mick were both a bit mouthy I expect," say Priv. Adds Mick, "I'm a piss-taking bastard! Harmless, but I do love banter." Pete wasn't so sure about the 'harmless' bit. "He used to go on about wearing white shoes or whatever, which used to get me a little bit upset at times," says Pete. "Priv did as well, but it wasn't as meant." Pete got on immediately with Steve Rothery, but he wasn't so sure of Mark ("It felt like him and Fish were best mates") and as for Fish, well, "I didn't trust him an inch, I thought anyone who can sack his best mate could sell his grandmother," he says. Nonetheless, the mood was up: with the addition of Pete, Marillion had become a band that could face the world. Fan Paul Gates notes, "I have several recordings from 1981 and it's pretty obvious when Pete replaced Diz and Mark replaced Brian the quality and complexity of the music leaped forward!"

On April 2 Marillion played the General Wolfe in Coventry, Pete's first live date. It was also Priv's first 'performance', as he recited the prayer in 'Forgotten Sons' while Fish 'mixed'. "He sat by the desk drinking beer," says Priv. "I was utter crap, the reviews were scathing." A week later Mark celebrated his 21st birthday, and seven days after that, the band had played Bathgate, Bannockburn and Edinburgh. On April 22, at the Inverness Ice Rink, the travelling players met a young fan called Avril Mackintosh. "I'd won a competition on the Tony

Ferry show on Radio Scotland," says Avril. "The boys were really friendly, but Fish was a bit funny." Avril took the opportunity to seek some advice from Mr Hedge, who was on no mean learning curve himself. "I asked, how do I become a sound engineer?" recounts Avril. Whatever he said, it triggered the first step of a journey that took her to Advision Studios six years later where she assisted in the mixing of *Clutching At Straws*. It's a funny old world.

As they toured, the troupe drew attention from both local and national press. Not all reviews were favourable: while the May 2 gig at the Mayfair in Glasgow was reputed to be the best night of the tour, Andrea Miller wrote in *Melody Maker* a few weeks later that, "the band sound like early Genesis without the wit... going on and on, they do about five numbers but make them last an hour." Clearly not a fan in the making. Phil Bell of *Sounds* was kinder. "Mark my words," he said, "Critics may choke and chuckle en bleeding masse, but when action's sizzling at grass roots level, to ignore it would be tantermount [sic] to dodging our duty." Other reviews, though positive, demonstrated early signs of the potential for rifts within the band. Fiona Dempster wrote in Scottish newspaper *Gaudia* that Marillion's support of Pallas at The Venue was "A shining performance - it would be difficult to say who was better... The rest of the band took a back seat to Fish's eccentric appearance. This is not to say that the others are not accomplished musicians - they just lack the charisma of Fish."

For now there was no time to worry about such trivia. By May the band headed south again, playing Glasgow before crossing the border to play Penrith on the 8th. There was a detour through Wales, notably a gig at Bangor University attended by local lad (and later, Jump front man) John Jones. "They were dynamic in the extreme, and Fish was compelling in the extreme," remembers John. "I walked up the road with my then-drummer and said, 'They'll be famous.'" He made up his mind despite Priv's dubious attempt to join the band on harmonica.

The intensive tour achieved all of its major objectives, sowing the seeds for a huge following. "Everywhere we went the people were so friendly and responsive, we all had an amazing time," wrote Mick in *the Web* fanzine. Concurs Priv, "The enthusiastic anorak fan thing started on the Scotland tour. There were some lads from Luton who just kept showing up and the Scottish fans increased by the gig. It was a great vibe with just our little team." What was more, the tour had firmly cemented Marillion as an outfit. "After Scotland, I felt that we weren't playing at rock bands any more, it was a profession... except for the getting paid bit! It was about that time that I knew that the band was going to make it. A truly golden time."

FINDING A MANAGER

With the lands of the North receding fast in the band's collective memory, it was time to regroup and prepare for what would hopefully be The Big Time. Housing arrangements reshuffled once again, as Steve, Pete, Mark and his now-girlfriend Suzy moved into Grafton Road, Aylesbury. Not that it lasted - six months later, Mark and Suzy moved to Willow Road following the birth of Freya (an event he missed - "We were playing Bournemouth that night, I must have been mad," says Mark), and Pete moved to Mount Pleasant, having finally enough credit to get a mortgage.

Highly positive articles appeared in the mainstream music press: Dave Dickson wrote in *Kerrang!*, "When did you last get really excited about a band? When was the last time you saw a band and realised you were seeing the birth-pangs of something potentially devastating?" If that wasn't effusive enough, he went on: "Marillion generate a real passion. The chemistry is there waiting to be unleashed: the effect could be explosive. Catch them while they are still in their infancy." Such reports went straight to the heads of the band members - the cool, calculating bits that is. A record deal was so close it could be smelled (according to fan Mike Eldon, "It became quite usual for representatives of various record companies to appear at gigs,"), and a good manager was being sought as a matter of urgency.

First to try on the managerial shoes was Marillion's long-time friend and ally, David Stopps. Clearly experienced in running clubs such as Friars, David had frequently been approached by Fish to take on the role of band manager. "He was the big fish in a small pond," remarks Fish. "I was very reluctant, but I could see they had potential. It was quite an honour to be asked," adds David. "The band were quite organised, this was a train that was already moving. I was impressed with how the band (and in particular Fish) were getting things together. They had a loyal following and it was obvious it was growing." By the end of May 1982 David finally gave in and got to work. He contacted 15 recording companies and sent them copies of the demo recording, posted out numerous press kits, fixed meetings with agencies and generally put his back into the thing. He also offered to put in some money to buy a PA, rental of which was a major expense for the band.

Despite David's best efforts, success wasn't handed on a plate. Most of the labels returned the requisite rejection letters, but one did not: EMI (in the shape of Ashleigh Goodall , who had seen the band play at the Marquee at the beginning of July) agreed to let the band record a demo or two. Rumour has it that two A&R men at EMI drew lots for the privilege: recounts Pete, "Ashleigh had just changed jobs, leaving Dave Ambrose and Hugh Stanley-Clarke. They tossed a coin and Hugh lost!" Demos of 'Market Square Heroes', 'He Knows, You Know' and 'Chelsea Monday' were recorded on July 26 and 27 in the basement of EMI's Manchester Square studios. "They were quite happy with the results, though they would have liked more time," Tim reported in *The Web*. He was being polite - according to Pete, "They weren't very good."

It was a busy time for David, who was also seeing Friars grow from strength to strength. "I think Fish expected me to drop everything but I couldn't," he comments. With events like a 3,000 ticket gig at Stoke Mandeville stadium with the Clash, and a string of gigs at Friars already in the pipeline including The Police and Joe Jackson, David could not give Marillion 100% of his time. "We had a lot going on. It was a very busy, magical time," continues David. "My intention was to cut back on Friars and make a slow transition." Maybe so; meanwhile there was an impetuous band gagging to take on the world and it didn't want to hang around. Comments Fish, "We became concerned that we'd put on an anchor rather than wings." Concurs Mark, "We panicked, we thought he was being too relaxed and we were getting nervous."

Just five weeks after his recruitment, with plenty of regret on both sides, David was asked to give back his horsewhip. The spokesperson was, of course, Fish. "He came and saw me, he said he'd talked to the other guys and Marillion didn't want me to be manager any more." Following a heated debate (according to his notes, "A manager has to be able to manage, and not be a tea boy,"), the relationship was over. "I was really annoyed that I'd been fired, as I knew I could do really well for them," says David. "David was very upset," recalls Mark. "He went on to manage Howard Jones. We thought it was to prove to us that he had the ability to break an act." The band not only lost a good mate, but also an important promoter - it wasn't until March of the following year that the fivesome would play Friars again.

In stepped John Arnison, a young manager who had previously worked for Quarry Management, which represented Status Quo and Rory Gallagher. Quarry was based on Wardour Street, directly opposite the Marquee Club where John was a regular in the bar – he was also manager Nigel Hutchings' wife's cousin's husband! "There was nothing quite like it, it was where all the agents and music company people used to hang out," recalls John. A few months before, he had gone to the club to meet with Sony about signing John Cooper Clarke, when a new band was taking the roof off the place. What most surprised him was the crowd - "These weren't old Genesis fans, this was a new band with a new audience." he recalls. John stopped for a chat with Marillion's press officer Keith Goodwin. "I said, 'Listen, you know my numbers, any help or advice, give me a call.'"

That was that, until a few weeks later. "There was a phone call from Fish, out of the blue. He said, 'I understand you'd be interested in managing us, do you want to meet?'" says John, who met the band at the Prince Of Teck pub on Earls Court Road. "They all got up and went to the loo together, but came back without having made a decision. I don't know who wasn't sure." Assuming that the band would go with Peter Mensch, a more established manager who had bands such as AC/DC under his belt and who also had Marillion in his sights, John went home with low expectations.

To the band, however, John was a no-brainer. Having already determined that Marillion weren't going to be a mainstream act, to be represented by the manager of off-the-wall performers such as John Cooper Clarke, Pauline Murray and The Invisible Girls, as well as regular acts like Rage seemed ideal. "I've never been an out-and-out pop manager," laughs John. In addition, as John had followed the band himself for some months, he had an idea of where they could go and how he could get them there, bringing to bear his many contacts with the Soho elite. "I liked the music first and foremost," comments John. The next day the call came through from Fish - "Congratulations, you're Marillion's manager - if you want to be of course."

John's impact was, according to Fish, "dramatic". He was quick to pursue the relationship with EMI, first proposing new demos, so the band went to a house in Hayes, Middlesex for another try. The second batch was still pretty mediocre according to John, "They were made in a shed in the back garden, the band played live and nobody was producing them so it's no wonder they weren't very good." An alternative plan was agreed with Hugh Stanley-Clarke - to fill out the Marquee and invite the senior executives to attend. "They'd already spent money on us so they came along," remarks Pete. "They saw us at a packed venue and decided they'd be mad not to sign us."

According to John Arnison, "Everything moved unbelievably fast from that point on." The first gig John participated in was at the Liverpool Warehouse, which happened to coincide with the stag night of his friend and tour manager, Paul Lewis. Present was one of John's other signings, Rage. The relationship between the two bands was understandably cool, at least initially. "There was a bone of contention between us," recalls Pete. "We thought John was giving them too much attention, and they thought the same back." Everyone got on OK in the end - "We used to go drinking together and they supported us on a few shows."

Within the band, the excitement was building to unprecedented levels: Fish got his picture in the July 1982 issue of *Kerrang!* (Tim wrote in *The Web*, "He has been hell to live with ever since,"). The potential for head-swelling was kept in check by continued live appearances, which added a certain unpredictability - when Marillion played its first Manchester gig at a venue called The Gallery, somebody forgot to turn the telly off. A fan called Simon remarked in *The Web* that Mark appeared hesitant and nervous - unsurprising as Clint Eastwood's *High Plains Drifter* was showing above his head. "It was something of a triumph that the band got the enthusiastic response they thoroughly deserved," commented Simon. Another attendee, Dave Rogers concurs - "It was so refreshing to see guys actually playing - after all, this was the pop-driven early 80's, where pre-programmed 'product' was very much the flavour. Yet here was a band with a distinctive sound - each musician displaying a style that was both individual and skilful."

EMI were not the only label to show an interest in Marillion: Charisma Records, represented by Tony Stratton-Smith, was also keen – 'Strat' also included non-mainstream Van Der Graaf Generator, Rare Bird and the Bonzo Dog Doo-Dah Band on his books. As he was about to go on holiday however, he left a subordinate to negotiate the deal. Recalls Mark, "He came along and offered us a two-single contract but we weren't going to sign that." EMI then offered the band a five-album deal on what appeared to be reasonable terms... well, which would you have picked? When Tony came back from holidays he thought the band would be signing to Charisma, and nobody was around to put him right. The train was rolling on meanwhile: on Wednesday August 25 1982, a deal was agreed with EMI; in the afternoon, John drove up to Liverpool to attend Paul Lewis's wedding; on the Thursday, the band played at The Warehouse in Liverpool.

The success that Marillion had been nurturing over the many months of hard graft arrived as a double whammy. Not only did the boys finally pick up a recording contract with EMI, but just a few days later they played an exultant performance to their biggest audience to date. It was festival time.

STAGE BY STAGE

The Reading Festival was renowned as being the live outdoor stage for Marquee bands, and on Sunday August 29 it was to be Marillion's turn, alongside musical giants of the day, the Michael Schenker Group and Dave Edmunds.

"We were really low on the bill," recalls Mark. Hearing of the Theakston Music Festival being held at Nostell Priory in Wakefield the day before, Fish proposed to play there as well, in support of Jethro Tull and Lindisfarne. Headliners Jethro Tull thought it was a good idea, so off they went. Remembers Mark, "It was a nightmare! Ian Anderson was standing at the side of the stage watching us, and half the gear wasn't working." Despite everything, Marillion were enthusiastically received by fans old and new. "Nostell Priory was a fantastic summer's day, and one act just grabbed me," says fan Dave Rogers. "They rose to the task of playing to a much larger audience superbly: resplendent in stage costume and make-up, Fish had the audience captivated." For the band at least it provided an opportunity to try out the festival thing and fix any technical issues before climbing onto the Reading stage.

Show time came the next day, at Reading's Thameside Arena. Fish announced the new recording contract with EMI at the start of the set, triggering jubilant applause from the 35,000-strong crowd that continued throughout the performance. However, this was not only premature (the ink was still firmly in the pens, and would not reach the paperwork for a good few weeks), but also big news to Tony Stratton-Smith, who had booked a marquee at the festival in anticipation of the signing. "He was horrified," remarks John Arnison. Thinking on his feet, Tony asked whether a deal had been signed for the publishing. Continues John, "He immediately wrote out a cheque for five thousand pounds, and said, 'Whatever you get offered from anybody, I'll pay that plus five thousand.'" Through a sense of guilt as much as good business sense, Strat was given the publishing deal.

Marillion's festival performance was genuinely well received. "Marillion provided a marked contrast with what everyone had secretly desired for the whole weekend - a dose of keyboard rock," reported *Kerrang!* As Tim wrote more bluntly, "Marillion's set was a breath of fresh air on what was a dire diet of heavy metal." Among the audience was future fan Mike Palmer, whose soft-edged memories (largely due to the alcohol) were rendered crystal clear by Steve's fretwork. "This glorious, soaring guitar solo kicked in, and that was it - I stood up and couldn't believe this guy's guitar playing."

The recorded sounds of Reading were enough to reel in new fans across the globe. Remembers US fan Bubba, "Back in 1983 I was stationed in West Germany, I made friends with the German heavy metal people. I was looking through one guy Eddie's record collection - he had a live double LP called *Reading Fest*, featuring bands that I had never heard of like Budgie, Twisted Sister and Marillion. We played the record and 'Three Boats Down From The

Candy' came on. I fell in love with Marillion's music and had Eddie play the song over and over. He ended up giving me the LP. I still have it to this day."

Kerrang!'s final word on the gig is a fair indication of what was going down - the key turning smoothly in a lock and a door swinging open to reveal a brave new world of rock stardom. Not so much a compliment but a fact - "The piece de resistance, 'Forgotten Sons', resulted in one of the loudest ovations of the weekend." Considering who else was in the line-up, the members of Marillion knew that they had arrived.

3

Market Square Heroes

The official signing with EMI, a month or so after Reading, was a mundane affair - at least if you ignore the alcohol and the fact that Steve Rothery fell asleep during Hugh Stanley-Clarke's inaugural speech. According to Pete, "After the signing, we went around the corner to a burger bar. It was weird. I felt no different - there was a real anti-climax about it." Nonetheless the advance cheque for £20,000 may have helped the chips go down more easily?

Not every Marillion follower was comfortable with their newly-found major label status. "People wanted us to be their little secret," explains Steve. Mark agrees: "We did get some stick from the hard core; people like to have a band nobody's heard of." So was the plan to build a following dropped the moment the band achieved greater success? At the time, some said so. "It was disappointing," says fan Mike Eldon. "We'd got into local bands rather than watch the stadium players go through their paces, but things were going full circle for Marillion." The next five years were to be a roller coaster for the band, which wouldn't help. "It started off that we cared about the fans," agrees Pete. "But once we had signed with EMI, there wasn't time to care about our families, never mind the fans." Another casualty was the trusty van Margaret, which almost symbolically chose to run its last journey that month. An obituary was placed in the *Bucks Herald*, entitled 'Sad Times'. "In loving memory of our hard working friend and companion. May she rust in peace," it said.

The rewards of working for a major label quickly started to come through. The band picked up new equipment, and Priv was officially named as the guys' sound engineer. "We got budget: proper lights and real PA systems," says Priv. "Oh, and catering. And wages!" A fellow called Gary Townsend was brought in as production manager, to the dismay of the other two members of the entourage who were more than the deal could afford. Gary didn't stick around, according to Priv: "At the last count he was selling cars to big companies - he got sick of touring in the end. It happens a lot." Then it was show time: Marillion went back to EMI's studios once again. Only this time the recordings were to be for real.

CHARTING THE SINGLE

Given the head of steam building behind Marillion's live act, it was no wonder that EMI wanted to get its new signing into the studios at the earliest opportunity. The first planned release was a 12-inch, extended play single, as Fish later explained, "...to satisfy the album demand generated over nearly 18 months of touring." It included a selection of tried-and-trusted live material:

'Three Boats Down From The Candy', 'Grendel' and the title track, 'Market Square Heroes' – "an obvious choice - with a message and a chorus," remarks Pete. The song started out as a commentary on Fish's own live experiences. "I'd get images of the 1937 Nuremberg rallies," Fish later commented to *Sounds*. "It used to be that after I'd sung the line, 'Are you following me?' They'd go, 'YEAH!'"

The day before heading to Park Gate Studios in Battle, near Hastings, on September 25, Marillion played a final headline at the Marquee, a thank-you-to-the-fans gig entitled the 'Garden Party For Forgotten Sons'. "It was packed and the atmosphere was electric, an amazing night indeed!" Tim wrote. Peter Gee of Pendragon, who played support on the night, remembers the atmosphere as being, "Very exciting, very powerful. Much of that was due to the charisma of Fish, and the atmosphere of the Club packed with 700 or 800 people, when the capacity was meant to be something like 500!"

Then it was all hands to the pumps. The band had eight days of recording time before Mark was due to get married to Suzy (Fish had already suggested to John Arnison that the marriage was a bad idea: "That was a bit of a blow to our friendship," says Mark). With time being so short, the first task was to select a producer who would fit the bill. We hadn't any experience in a proper studio, so we had to find someone we could get on with," says Mick. Enter affable producer David Hitchcock, who had produced the Genesis album *Foxtrot* ten years before as well as seminal bands such as Caravan and Camel. This was a double-edged sword: although Marillion's sound tipped a hat to the glory days of progressive rock, the boys wanted to develop their own musical style, and David was only too happy to help. "I always regarded my job to bring out the sound of whatever band I was working with," he says. Concurred Fish in an interview, "He said he would do anything to avoid getting a sound like Genesis or Camel."

Following a number of recording sessions at the studio in Battle, band and producer moved to Wessex Studios in London for overdubs and mixing of the three tracks. Pressure was high, particularly on the unfortunate David Hitchcock. "I went straight from an all-night mixing session there to Trident in Soho to master the recording with Ray Staff, who was one of the two mastering engineers that I almost invariably used by then," he recalls. "I had worked for 48 hours non-stop to get the recording finished and mastered in time for EMI's marketing schedule." Sleep-deprived and mentally drained, he crashed his car on the way home. "He fractured his neck, bust his legs, he was a hell of a mess and we were told he was out for three months," Fish recalled at the time. "I feel incredibly bad - the reason he had the smash was because he was exhausted."

In parallel with the mastering, EMI brought in Jo Mirowski's company, Torchlight, to produce the artwork - which took its own time. "EMI wanted a similar formula to the Iron Maiden logo and character. Each time EMI accepted a design they were happy with, the band were not keen." Eventually Fish was able to circumvent the record label. "He called me from a gig in Brighton. He asked me to give a softer feel to one of the designs, a little bit of Yes logo in feel," continues Jo. "The next attempt, everything finally fell into place." Not for everyone, however: "I hated it!" says Mick. "It looked like the designer had been eating a bar of Old Jamaica chocolate and thought, I know, I'll do that!" Adds Pete, "It was only years later that we realised it was exactly the same as Barclay James Harvest's logo." You can guess who designed that one!

With the logo complete, it was time to work on the cover. Jo visited the band with an A2 folder packed with ideas from different artists and the young Marillos selected an artist they thought appropriate. Having talked to the band however, Jo thought aspiring airbrush artist Mark Wilkinson would be a better choice. "I phoned EMI and convinced them that Mark would be by far more suited," says Jo. Recalls Mark Wilkinson, "'Market Square Heroes' was done by proxy through Jo, it was not until the second single that I met the band." Adds Pete, "Jo was very workmanlike - he didn't want us to speak to Mark at all: he was the conduit." There could have been a reason for that... the artwork was accepted without criticism, and it only became apparent to the band years later that Mark had not, in fact, been the artist that the band had selected.

The single was dedicated to David Stopps and Friars, both in recognition of his help and "through a sense of guilt," says Mark. "We liked him and he really helped us, and we repaid him by a sacking!" It was released on October 25 to audiences old and new. Recalls fan Peter Gifford, "I'd been intrigued by articles I read in *Sounds* and *Kerrang!* and after speaking to a bloke in the local post office, I bought the single. I remember him commenting on a gig T-shirt I was wearing and asking if I'd heard of Marillion. I told him what I'd read and he suggested I check out the single. He particularly liked this 20-minute track on the B-side!" That would be 'Grendel', then. "Funnily enough, I actually preferred 'Grendel' to 'Market Square Heroes'," laughs fan Rich Dowson. He wasn't be the only one, as notes Steve Wood, "The 12-inch version gave me my first listen to 'Grendel', a track I had been reading about for months, and which gives me goose-bumps to this day."

'Market Square Heroes' achieved a No.60 slot in the UK charts - a respectable start, prompting a slot on the teenybopper show, *Top of the Pops*. John Arnison postponed his honeymoon with the long-suffering Ginny to attend this first TV appearance. "In hindsight, I must have been mad. But I wanted to be on that roller coaster, everything was moving so fast." Fish made a subtle change to the lyrics, replacing "antichrist" with "battle priest" - antichrists were so 70's, after all.

All was well that ended well, for everyone apart from David Hitchcock who became a casualty in more ways than one. While the plan was to use David again for the album (with *The Web's* Tim requesting, "Please get better by December!"), by the time he had recovered sufficiently, he found that EMI had deemed his services surplus to requirements. "It was incredibly important to me at the time that I got to do that album. I actually got my doctor at the hospital to discharge me early, on the condition that I wore an all-encompassing head support," says David. "I didn't find out I wasn't doing it until I got home after being discharged in November and called EMI's A&R man. He told me they had got someone else." A remorseful Fish commented at the time, "A lot of people think we ditched Dave. It looks that way, it looks very like that way." With reason - it was that way. "We've never spoken to him since," Fish noted a few years later, a little glumly.

REHEARSAL OF THE SCRIPT

In parallel with the single release Marillion hit the road again, kicking off with a warm-up gig at City University on October 26: the social secretary at the time was (now long-time fan) Dave Cross, who had got into the band a couple of months before. "I found a box of demo tapes that my predecessor had discarded, including a Marillion tape. I thought it was really good and decided that I'd like to book them, but thought that as they were getting so much press attention they'd be too big to play a small student union bar, so I thought no more about it. A few weeks later I was speaking to an agent about some other bands and one of us mentioned Marillion in passing. It turned out that he was either their agent or a colleague of their agent and knew that they were looking for somewhere to play a low-key, warm up gig just before their first major tour. He asked if I'd be interested and I leapt at the chance."

Even though the single had just been released, Marillion still had their work cut out. "The turnout was pretty small, there were maybe twenty people in the audience," Dave recalls. "To be honest, I can't remember what they played that night - I didn't know very many of their songs. I'd been sent a copy of the single so I recognised all of those tracks, plus 'Garden Party' from the demo tape. The few people who came all had a great time. A few weeks later their agent rang me again, to tell me that they were playing an extra gig at the Venue and to ask if I would like to be on the guest list. It was lucky that I said yes as that gig was a huge sell-out. It was great to see them again - this time with a massive and appreciative audience!"

In November the band members moved into an EMI-rented flat in Fulham, ready to record an album at the Marquee studios on Wardour Street, in the heart of Soho. The first practicality resulted from David's ill-concealed sacking, recalled Fish, "We thought, *Shit!* We had to start looking for producers again!" The band settled on Nick Tauber - again a rushed decision. Nick had produced *Anthem* by Toyah Willcox, as well as albums by Thin Lizzy and Girl. The boys hit it off immediately. "He was cynical and sarcastic enough to be another member of the band," Fish commented.

Another challenge was a lack of songs. Some of the best material had already been used on the EP, so the band found themselves a bit short in the writing sessions. By the time the band arrived at the recording studios, the intended title track still lacked several sections, a particular problem as it was intended to set the scene for the whole album, linking a number of pieces developed over many years into a coherent whole. A couple of the sections were written relatively quickly, while the band was in the studio. "It's amazing what a bit of pressure can do for the creative juices," Mark Kelly commented.

Nick had a methodical approach to recording, capturing the drums first and layering the other instruments and vocals on top, which immediately impressed the players. "I'd spent a fair amount of time in studios, but I'd never given this much attention to detail," comments Pete. Concurs Steve, "It was an amazing experience. Being in London, working in Soho, going next door to watch bands at the Marquee Club, there was never a dull moment!" Simon Hanhart, who was brought in as sound engineer, had the time of his life. "I was in a similar band when I was a teenager," says Simon. "I'd only been engineering for eight months, it was a big break for me!" One challenge was to accommodate Fish's desire to include a personal message to his girlfriend Kay: Nick reluctantly agreed but endeavoured to hide it in the mix. It's still there, playing backwards, as a whisper before the line "a scream that's borne from sorrow."

The opening section to the title track was written on the last day of recording, with time pressure acting in the band's favour. "If I'd had a bit more time to play with it I probably would have made it more complicated and ruined the atmosphere," said Mark. With final nips and tucks in place (Fish's idea of a spoken soliloquy to open the album was dropped at the last minute due to

Nick's fears of "commercial suicide"), band and management knew they had a winner. For Mick, it was the culmination of five years' work "finally realised with the release of an album." Recalls Fish on the sleeve notes to the remaster, "One EMI executive was actually in tears at the end of the playback." So much for cool, calculating record execs.

Mark Wilkinson's artwork on 'Market Square Heroes' was more than enough to ensure he was brought in for the album cover, as Fish would write, "Mark's style paralleled our musical and lyrical vision." It was agreed early on that the album sleeves would cover themes and concepts in parallel with the lyrics, from the chameleon and Punch on the TV set, to the central character - Fish's crying jester, his childhood alter ego and a powerful symbol of love and loss.

Before the album release, EMI planned a second, 'taster' single taken from the album. The initial cover idea for 'He Knows, You Know' came primarily from Mark Kelly, giving Mark Wilkinson a chance to meet the band for the first time. He recalls, "I'd heard the first single by then, it sounded tinny on the radio and the vocals were trebly and light, so I assumed the singer was a small guy." Little did he know: "Wearing a leather tasselled jacket, boots with strides tucked in, clanking silverware, studiously positioned kerchiefs hanging every-which-way, every inch the perfect model of the perfect Scottish rock star. He was huge in every way, exuded bonhomie and grabbed my hand to shake the bejeezus out of me!"

While Mark enjoyed the imagery, he wasn't so keen on the music."It left me stone cold, I'm afraid," he says. "I was given a coupla tickets for a show one evening and went along for my first glimpse of the band live. I was astonished that it could exist... The bastard child of Genesis and *Beowulf* was not my idea of a fun night out! But I was in a minority of one that night. Some time later I went to see them at the Hammy Odeon with Jo Mirowski. Jo leaned over halfway through, when the crowd had reached the 7th plane of Nirvana and said 'They're gonna be huge!' I wasn't so sure. I couldn't see that they had a shelf life beyond an album or two."

With significant support from EMI, as those who remember the massive posters will testify , 'He Knows, You Know' entered the UK charts at No.35 and was also released in the US, the first time that Marillion's now-signature sound had left the UK. With a video including Mark's three-week-old daughter Freya ("It was a spur of the moment, cool thing," he says), the single achieved instant recognition and a transatlantic fan base. "I was hooked on Marillion when I first heard 'He Knows, You Know' on KSHE-95," remarks US fan John Chudy. "This was, at the time, the premier rock station in St Louis." Oh, the advantages of major label backing! Not everyone liked it: Edwin Pouncey in *Sounds* declared, "The pomposity on this record is astounding! Marillion think the Peter Gabriel incarnation of Genesis was shit hot, so much so that they feel compelled to hobble into a recording studio to transfer their necromantic urges to record." Careful now, Edwin... you never know what might be around the corner.

OH PLEASE DO COME

Script For A Jester's Tear was released on March 14 1983, shooting past expectations as it climbed to No.7 in the UK charts in the first week of release. The album received numerous excellent reviews, not least a five star rating from Phil Bell of *Sounds*, the first time he had ever given such an accolade. The press were not unanimous in their praise, however - another *Sounds* reviewer declared the album to be "a clichéd load of humbug." Much of the negative press reaction was down to Marillion being perceived as unfashionable (which they were) and unoriginal (which they weren't). Comments Peter Gee, whose own band Pendragon suffered similar criticisms, "Not many of the press took them seriously. There was this big Gabriel/face-paint/voice rip-off thing being levelled at Fish. Many journalists' attitude was, *We buried all that Genesis stuff in the '70s, the last thing we want is for it to come back*. There was the anti-long-song lobby, and the fact that Marillion were themselves and not trying to be overly commercial."

Fans far and wide were delighted with the debut. "In those days you'd see people walking around at school with an album under their arm, *Script* was one of those," says fan Simon Clarke. "It created a bit of a buzz," recalls Dan Sherman, "I checked out *Script* because I was intrigued by the artwork and loved it immediately. I was a big Rush and Jethro Tull fan at the time and thought it had elements of both, punchy rhythms, skilful keyboard and guitars, and interesting lyrics."

Poor Edwin Pouncey was forced to eat his own words on February 19 1983, when *Sounds* readers voted Marillion the Best New Act. In the same mag, Edwin consented to interview Fish and Mick, understandably hesitant as his previous reviews had been far from generous. The journalist later admitted he didn't have a clue what Gabriel-era Genesis sounded like. *Sounds* was not the only rag to recant its opinions, as Fish remarked, "I can see we're going to start getting hip now, the *NME* want to do us now! They're apologising practically for ignoring us, it's hysterically funny: we're going to make this unfashionable music become so sickeningly fashionable, no one will believe it!"

Genesis comparisons may have filled column inches, but they didn't discourage anyone who actually listened to the band. To admit influences was in no way unique to Marillion, besides which there was a harder-edged sound that was distinctly their own and a vocal and lyrical angst that was unmistakably Fish. As fan Tony Wood recalls, "I loved all of it - Fish was without doubt the most passionate vocalist that I'd heard, the guitar tone was great and the music was intelligently put together. It tugged at the heart strings ('Script', 'The Web'), it made you laugh ('Garden Party'), and it made you angry ('Forgotten Sons')." Some fans saw very little association between the two bands. "I liked Peter Gabriel's voice but didn't like Genesis," says fan Jonathan Mock. "Enter Marillion. The singer sounded similar to Gabriel, but the music was more modern and just so different to everything else out there. I was hooked in an instant. *Script* was a revelation to me and I still maintain it's one of the best albums ever recorded by anyone."

With money rolling in, Fish purchased a house in Albert Street in Aylesbury, just round the corner from Victoria Street. The purchase took place with a little nudge from other band members. "We were trying to get him to settle down 'cos he would come off tour and carry on touring," says Pete. "Before he bought the house he didn't have anywhere to live, so he'd try and crash round at various people's houses and drive them mad." When Fish split up with Kay he stayed in Blackheath with John and Ginny Arnison, who had just got married. Fish didn't think much of Ginny and the feeling was mutual. "They used to argue all the time," remembers John. "One day, she accused him of lifting his words from various books, while he was saying it was there he found his inspiration." Fish later vented his spleen in a number of lyrics on *Fugazi*: the walls of the cell were indeed enticingly thin, as Fish slept in the living room of The Arnisons' one-bedroom flat. "John was Fish's playmate, he was never really forgiven for getting married," comments Mark. "Fish liked to have a drinking partner, someone as debauched as he was," explains Steve. "There were lots of tensions in the early days; Fish didn't like to lose his drinking partners, and he did some despicable things in the process." Indeed, Fish had even suggested to Ginny that John had been having an affair, before they were wed and before the first album had been recorded.

In early 1983 the band returned to what it was best at, heading on tour to play live and starting a pattern that continued, virtually unbroken, for the next four years. The tour manager was Paul Lewis, a colleague of John's who had just returned from a two year stint with Van Halen; the production manager was Gary Townsend; and Mick's drum roadie was Andy Field, who later became production manager. On the mixing desk was the unstoppable Priv. "Gary and Andy taught us young lads so much," he says. "Patient, charming gentlemen. I was more than happy to take any advice offered, particularly by Gary, who was a fine sound engineer himself." Touring started with barely a pause for breath after the release of the album. "I felt we had to keep working to increase the fan base, after *Script* came out," explains John.

Mo Warden remembers her first encounter with Marillion's motley-attired fans, at the Birmingham Odeon. "We were in the queue... what an unusual bunch of people waited with us, some face-painted and costumed, some in painted black leathers, some in corduroy and 'Cornish pastie' shoes - a wide mix." Mo was quickly to find that the fans were mere shades compared to the giant ball of energy that was Marillion's front man. "I remember this huge, painted demon at the front of the stage, he acted like a natural. I was near the front and watched him on one knee at the edge of the stage, leaning forward to sing, six inches from one girl's rapt face. With one light finger under her upturned chin, greasepaint sweat dripping from him, he sang into her eyes. I also remember clearly, the impression that the guitarist and the keyboard player had on me. I came away thinking, *This is one amazing band*. The rest of the gig is a blur but within a month I'd joined the Web fan club."

Indeed, the band's devotion to live duty ensured a constant stream of new fans, as well as a certain constancy of adrenalin, fatigue, distance from loved ones, alcohol and other substances - but that's getting ahead of ourselves... more urgently in need of treatment was the last remaining weakness in the line-up, which one occasion indicated all too clearly. On March 16 1983 at the Reading Top Rank auditorium, the band launched into 'Charting The Single', but something didn't seem quite right: it transpired that Mick was playing the beats the wrong way round. "Nobody changed, Fish couldn't work out what was wrong but got increasingly frustrated as he couldn't work out where to come in," recalls Mark. An honest mistake maybe, but Mick's days were numbered from that point. By the Scottish dates a month later, things came to a head: "Fish and I had our first blazing row in a hotel in Glasgow," recalls John. "He told me the band thought Mick had to go, but I felt he still needed a chance to grow; I was worried as Mick had formed the band, and because his wife, Stef was running the fan club."

Despite such hiccups the larger gigs continued to attract an expanding audience. One attendee was Kim Waring, who saw Marillion play at Bristol's Colston Hall on March 28 1983. "My boyfriend dragged me along," says Kim. "It was very loud, and there was an awful lot of strange people! At first it was quite daunting. By the end I was overwhelmed - by the show, the sound, the atmosphere... I went to as many concerts as I could after that!" A couple of weeks later, fan Chris Lewington had his first opportunity to see the band, in Aberdeen. "I had just relocated and I was staying in a hotel called the Treetops. I was looking for something to do when what was obviously a band checked into the hotel. I asked at reception who they were, and was told they were playing at the Capitol Theatre on Union Street that night. I called the venue and they had a few tickets, so off I went. They were Marillion and they were bloody brilliant!" As Chris was staying in the same hotel, he found himself in the same bar as the after-show party. "I remember a couple of the roadies taking bets on whether the barmaid was wearing stockings or not, and a serious cocktail drinking competition when one of the band took on a bet that he couldn't drink 10 blue bombers. I gather he was sick down the corridor later on that night. John Arnison was obviously in a good mood as he was buying Champagne and Guinness for everyone." What an introduction! Four days later, on April 15 it was fan Peter Gifford's turn, at Manchester Apollo. He recalls, "I was absolutely blown away. Fish made his entrance through the crowd, which I thought was fantastic. I've got a tape of the show somewhere; the highlight is hearing myself shout for 'Grendel' only to be shot down by Fish."

The tour closed at the end of April with a number of sold-out dates at the Hammersmith Odeon. Some journalists were surprised how the band managed to fill such a venue after only one single: Fish patiently reminded them of the 200 gigs that had gone previously. "I took a gamble," remembers John. "I wanted to get out of clubs and into theatres as soon as possible." It paid off: Marillion remain one of the few bands that sold out the Odeon before releasing an album. Fish was in no doubt of the fans' importance, making frequent forays into the audience. As he explained in an interview, "to communicate with the audience on an eye-to-eye level, you have to be prepared to go out on a limb now and again, just to see what happens."

As the tour came to an end, band members and management agreed to part with Marillion's remaining founder member, Mick. While Fish has affirmed his role as knife-wielder-in-chief, the decision was not his alone. "The person I went to for 100% confirmation was Steve Rothery," says John Arnison. "He told me, 'Sorry, he's going to have to go.'" This was not only following the incident at Reading: while the others had improved substantially over the months, in their eyes Mick had not. "Mick was a good drummer but not always accurate," says Neil Cockle. "He sometimes got a bit excited and would come out with the wrong beat or speed up a bit." Comments Pete, "Fingers were pointing at the rhythm section, but Diz had been a better bassist than Mick was a drummer, and Diz had already been sacked so it was only a matter of time." It was all a bit messy: Mick wasn't the roll-over-and-accept type, and Fish did not let him down gently. "Mick thought Fish had joined his band as a singer," remarks Steve. "Fish vented his anger, he ripped into him!" John recalls. Concurs Steve, "It was just unnecessary, he didn't want to sack him, he wanted to destroy him!"

The situation was difficult for all members of the band: Mark had been rooming with Mick on tour, so Mick thought Mark was conspiring against him. Meanwhile Rothers, who had been closer to Mick than Fish, felt a little betrayed. As he recalls, "It ended up a fait accompli that Mick was being sacked. I was very angry at the time as it had all happened behind my back. In a band, you have camaraderie, a family feeling, but there were too many things happening for me to call Fish a friend. I could never really relax with him after all that." Mick's feelings were of shock and disbelief. "I was playing Hammersmith Odeon one night and two weeks later I was standing in the dole queue," he says. "It took me an incredibly long time to realise how much of an effect it had on me. I had my dream taken away from me, then I watched them go on and achieve more."

And with that, Marillion entered its revolving drummer phase.

SCRIPT FOR A JESTER'S TEAR

Ambitious, varied moody, dramatic, lyrical, accomplished...

People simply weren't meant to be making debut albums like *Script* in the early 1980s. Later described by Fish as an album of bedsit thoughts, it recounted a series of stories "relating to a character in a particular situation, and reflecting the different moods that the character will go through."

Though never mentioned explicitly, that character was the jester, the hedonistic alter-ego of Derek Dick or, as we would come to know him, "Fish". The persona was one the big man had originally taken on to protect against the taunts of the schoolyard and latterly, to enable a stage presence that Derek could not sustain by himself.

"So here I am once more..." A whispered, attention-grabbing vocal line is trailed by a solitary piano. Slowly we're drawn into the depths of the title song. Introspection gives way to anger, then frustration boils over as the band soar into a showpiece of Marillion musicianship.

Of the meaning behind the title track, Fish confessed, "Only one person has ever truly understood." Its origins lie in the first song that he ever wrote, 'The Crying Jester'. "It was a total rip-off of a Jon Anderson song. It was written on the night that Keith Moon died; he was a jester, the crying jester."

There were other influences: Peter Hammill's song 'Lost and Found' inspired many of the lyrics. Additional emotional input was Fish's breakup with girlfriend Kay. It's no wonder that he remarked, "When I was doing the vocal I actually cried in the studio, it hit me that bad. It's probably the heaviest song we've ever done."

The second track would offer little respite. 'He Knows, You Know' was about, "someone who went from nervous exhaustion, through depression then full-scale drug abuse," explained Fish, who witnessed the experience through his own excesses and those of a friend. "He ends up in a hospital bed and someone comes up to him and says, 'I told you so.' Which helps him damn all."

The maudlin and brooding 'The Web' is one of Marillion's oldest performance pieces having started life as an instrumental, way before most of the recording line-up had ever heard of Marillion.

Fish's tale of ambition vs. creature comforts, it took inspiration from the tale of Penelope, wife of Odysseus. Claiming she would choose a new husband once she had finished making Odysseus's death shroud, she would unpick her work at night, allowing herself time to procrastinate. Fish's take on the song sees him assume the role of the jester once again, torn between mourning his lost love and getting out there and getting on with his life. Mark Kelly is singled out for credit for having given considerable assistance in the arrangement of the song. The midsection is worthy of comment, contrasting Pete Trewavas's fluid bass with Mick Pointer's drumming limitations.

Side Two opened with the upbeat 'Garden Party', a musical cousin of 'Market Square Heroes'. With biting, satirical lyrics originating from Fish and Diz's Cambridge days in the winter of 1980, 'Garden Party' upset many of the people it was written about; after all, it's an attack on the class system of hereditary privilege, encapsulated in a Cambridge University Garden Party. "It's our most Genesis-y song," Fish was later to comment.

Nevertheless, this Kelly-led rocker was a huge live favourite for many years. Unlike the delicately sung version on the LP, crowds delighted in bellowing 'I'm fucking!' at the tops of their voices.

'Chelsea Monday' was a product of bohemian days spent at the flat in Fulham. "Early morning walkabouts gave me examples of so many wannabes and could-be's and I wrapped them all up in a female character drowning in romanticism, unable to cope with reality," Fish explained.

Not only about the vocalist's ambitions for the band, it concerned "the fear of failure I went through," fear manifested through a girl performing an outrageous and deadly act in order to achieve some recognition. It asks, "How far would you go to achieve fame?" How far, indeed? As Fish screams the words 'Chelsea Monday', Steve Rothery launches into a long guitar interlude, sealing his reputation as he does so.

To close the debut, 'Forgotten Sons' was a masterpiece, a grand finale that transcended its subject matter. "It's about government manipulation," remarked Fish. Set in Northern Ireland, it was based on Fish's experiences of how his cousin was injured in a riot. "I realised no one really cared," he commented in the sleeve notes for the remaster. "News of his plight was difficult to extract from the Army, and the Irish situation had lowered in the agenda of the media." With its fierce reworking of the Lord's Prayer for the middle section, and Mark Kelly evoking church choirs during the coda, the song is almost a religious experience.

Fish summed up the album saying, "We would never sound so innocent again..."

The cover introduced us to the jester, standing in his dingy bedsit, with his records and litter strewn across the floor, trying to write the love song that will show him the way out of his dismal lifestyle. EMI were apparently so concerned about copyright infringement, they hired musicians to try and play the randomly placed notes!

Dramatic and moody, the gatefold cover with its "Mars Bar" logo courtesy of Jo Mirowski harked back to the original prog age. It gave prospective listeners an instant sense of the likely musical content and a strong visual identity that would carry them through the Fish-era, borne across many a T-shirt and poster. Marillion had done their time working the pubs and clubs, proving themselves as a great live bound. And now, in one bound, they established themselves as a great album band.

Zipping In

Second albums can be challenging, particularly if the first has been a success. In Marillion's case, EMI pressure to build on the reputation of *Script* and demonstrate that this band was no one-disc wonder was exacerbated by the fundamental absence of a band member; to cap it all, the players had used up most of their material on the debut album, singles and B-sides and now had to develop something new. Following a little time off at the end of the tour, the band locked themselves away at Mountain rehearsal studios in Monmouth, Wales. "It was more a hippie commune than a professional recording studio," laughs Mark. Agrees Rothers, "God knows how the record company found it. I remember there being a druidic stone circle on a hill behind the house that everyone used to go and sit around. The two women who ran the place were called Sunshine and Nutkin. That should tell you all you need to know!"

Despite the environment, initial attempts to generate new material were not proving successful. "I thought the game was up," Mark said later. "We only really had one song written." Fortunately, as Mark and the others were to discover, a creative hiatus would often be necessary before the ideas started to flow.

MORE DRUMMERS THAN SPINAL TAP

Meanwhile, the band had to find a new drummer. Mick's sacking was a break with tradition in that no replacement had been found before his departure. Following adverts and a number of dead-end trial runs, the first nominee for the vacated stool was ex-Camel drummer, Andy Ward. It was clear from the outset he was a good fit with the rest of the band, and as such was virtually given the job without interview. Said Steve, "Andy was one of my favourite drummers. When we bumped into him it was like manna from heaven." He joined in May 1983, meeting the others in Wales to help develop the ideas for the next album. His first visible contribution to Marillion history was on May 29, with the video for 'Garden Party' in which "band members dress up as 1950s schoolboys and play hilarious pranks on unsuspecting revellers." Released on June 6, the single reached No.16 and stayed in the Top 40 for four weeks. UK music journos did not want to be caught out again, delivering highly complimentary write-ups in a number of rags (*Sounds* referred to 'Garden Party' as "the classic single").

This time it was the TV stations' turn to tackle the paradox. Marillion were clearly popular, even if the band were totally out of synch with the diktats of fashion. Commented Fish, "We're supposed to be Genesis clones, yet we've had three hits, How come? People get annoyed..." As a result, Marillion's appearances were begrudged rather than welcomed. The band were introduced with a sneer on *The Old Grey Whistle Test*, and cold-shouldered by other 'pop' acts on *Top of the Pops*. "The thing is, we don't change our style or our image to accommodate those programmes," Fish remarked. "We look the same on *TOTP* as we do the next night at Bradford City Hall, or at Glastonbury." The band's performance was enough to entice new fans such as Judith Mitchell. "I was into the Police and ELO when I saw Marillion play 'Garden Party' on *TOTP*," recalls Judith. "They kept getting chart hits after that, so I started to follow them."

TV and radio appearances were not confined to the UK. Recalls fan Rod Taylor, "I can remember watching *The New Music*, at the time Canada's one-and-only music programme, and hearing, 'This is the first video from a new UK band called Marillion, and the song is called 'Garden Party'.' And the rest, as they say..." Dutch fan Jolijne Viergever remembers her first listen. "I heard some tracks - 'Market Square Heroes', 'Garden Party' and part of 'Script' - on a radio programme, and it just gave me the shivers!" she recalls. "They were introduced as a very promising band that had released a single last year."

All appeared well with the new drummer as Marillion departed on their maiden foray across the channel, with a series of festivals planned in Germany, Denmark and Holland and then back to the UK, including on June 17 1983, the CND festival at Glastonbury. "We were hip for an instant," joked Fish. Recalls fan Adrian Holmes, "Despite a far from perfect sound mix, the band soon started to win over the audience. Andy Ward was playing well and the 'new' track 'Assassing', with its long build-up and rocky main section, boded well for the second album. The highlight of the set had to be the closing 'Forgotten Sons', which, after Fish's introduction outlining the subject matter of the lyrics, went down a storm with the Glastonbury crowd. I think the band made quite a few new friends that day."

As the companions travelled together, however, it appeared that Andy liked his drink more than was appropriate. The issue was exacerbated by the demanding life on the road, but he was likeable, a good drummer and besides, who didn't like a drink? So he stayed.

Building on the festival successes, Marillion set off for the US and a flit down the East Coast starting at Youngstown, Ohio on July 14. It wasn't a great success. For most of the band, the US club circuit was a sobering experience; for Andy it was very stressful and anything but sobering. Andy was not a happy man, it turned out: the reason he had left Camel the year before was that his playing had been limited following an attempt to slash his wrists. He frequently argued with other members of the band and was clearly uncomfortable being associated with such upstarts. To quote Andy, "They had a ridiculous opinion of themselves!" Recalls Pete, "Some nights he was fine and some nights he wasn't so fine, which was a shame. I think he was going through a bit of a depressing patch." "Andy was a great drummer and a good friend," remarks Rothers. "It was very sad what happened with him." Sad indeed, and ironic given that his drink problem was no worse than what several others in the band would experience before the decade was out. "He was a man before his time," comments Mark.

The incidents started to pile up – other band members started to notice the can of Coke Andy would nurse and sip from all morning, for example. Explains Steve, "I'd brought a half bottle of whisky with me, he had nicked it and was topping up his cans." Or driving through Harlem throwing empty beer bottles out of the window, with the rest of the band saying, "Please, don't do that!" It became inevitable that the band would be looking for another drummer, a big disappointment, as Andy really had seemed to fit the bill. Things came to a head at the Holiday Inn in New York, the day before a performance at Pier 84 on March 9. The band and Paul Lewis were attempting to check in (the rooms weren't ready), when Andy went off to get some fags. "All of them came out of the machine at once!" remembers Mark. "He started giving them out, asking around who wanted some..." This didn't go down well with the hotel staff, who told the band they couldn't stay. It all proved too much for the hapless Andy. "We asked him, 'What do you want to do?" recalls Mark. "He wanted to go home, so we started planning to cancel the tour." Remembers Paul, "I booked Andy's flight ticket home that afternoon." Nobody plucked up the courage to tell him before the gig, however.

The night of the Pier 84 gig in support of Todd Rundgren's band Utopia was the last straw, if one had been needed. Tempers were fraying all round: it may have been inappropriate for Fish to have said, "We shouldn't be supporting this shit," but it was equally unfortunate that the singer received a rotten peach to the chest from an overzealous fan. "Fish turned on the person in the audience," remembers John Arnison, "and the audience turned on the band from that point." Andy expressed his disquiet to Fish in no uncertain terms, but it was too late: immediately after the gig Andy was informed that his flight had been booked, and Paul drove him to the airport for 6am the next morning. "I checked him in and waited until he went airside to try and be sure he got the flight," says Paul.

And then there were four again. As the remaining members followed Andy home a few days later, they were feeling pretty sanguine, explains Steve, "It was the most fun we'd had in the US. It was all so new to us!" Still, they were faced with the daunting task of another Reading festival. With under three weeks to go, John Arnison proposed session drummer John Marter (who had previously played with Mr Big - the UK version, who'd had a hit with 'Romeo') to fill the gap. "John was never really in the band, he was always just a stand-in," says Rothers. Following a hasty warm-up two days before, at the Royal Court Theatre in Liverpool, the drummer was up and running in time for the festival itself, on August 27. Marillion played second on the bill, before a recently-reformed Black Sabbath (with Ian Gillan on vocals). Recalls Mark, "We were on one stage and Black Sabbath were on the other stage following us. They had these enormous plastic stones, like Stonehenge. While we were playing, their stage caught fire." Black Sabbath were paranoid about being upstaged, as demonstrated by Reading Council's u-turn on permission for Marillion to use lasers in their show. Explains Mark, "We found out that the council had already agreed, but Don Arden [Sabbath's manager] knobbled the council people so they refused the application."

In the crowd on that day was fan Andy Rotherham, seeing Marillion for the first time as he attended in support of his then-favourite band, The Stranglers. Marillion opened with 'Grendel', and what an opening. Recalls Andy, who was next to a remotely placed speaker stack at the time, "They literally blew up the PA speakers. I spent the rest of the gig listening to the distorted sound of Marillion through the remnants of the stack. I just took it from there." Also present was Mark Wilkinson, who quickly revised his views of the band. "Everything was exponentially better than before. Fish had stopped arsing about with a rubber plant on stage, had taken to editing out his more florid prose and worked the audience like a seasoned pro. They were a different band," he says. "If not quite the road to Damascus for me, it was a revelatory experience. I spent the next few years trying to tell my other pals that 'actually, despite what you might think, Marillion are fucking great... forget what you read in Q magazine and listen to them.' They didn't of course. I dare say if I hadn't worked for them I would not have given them a cat's chance in hell either."

The encore saw Andy Ward replacing John on drums. Recalls Adrian Holmes, "We found out that although John Marter was now occupying the drum stool, Andy Ward had specifically asked to play this gig as he was really looking forward to it. As a result, we heard the only outing of the band with both a drummer and a percussionist." According to Pete, "He just turned up, bless him. We got him to play the gong and a bit of percussion towards the end of the show, just to say thank you." By the time Marillion left, the crowd was so exhausted it could only manage a lukewarm response to the main attraction.

It was in high spirits that the Marillos returned to the studio with Nick Tauber, to lay down new versions of 'Market Square Heroes' and 'Three Boats Down From The Candy' - ostensibly to give John Marter a proper try-out. In the end he was not to be - he was a fine drummer but he was not deemed up to the band's ever-increasing demands. Comments Pete, "He was solid, but not as musical as Andy or Ian." "Steady but not enormous flair," agrees Mark. John was also a little over-verbal for the incumbents. Laughs Mark, "He talked himself out of the gig!" Nothing was wasted from the studio sessions, as the tracks were later included on the 12-inch release of 'Punch And Judy'.

John also agreed to join the band for its second bash at West Atlantic shores, playing five nights at New York's illustrious Radio City Hall, in support of Canadian trio Rush. The idea sounded wonderful: "The stage was enormous - we had to take a lift to get to it," recalls Mark. However, if the last US tour attempt had been a crisis, this was an abject disaster. The band were restricted to ten-minute sound checks and limitless rules and regulations; to add insult to injury, before the gig there would invariably be a Peter Gabriel or a Genesis track playing. And when they actually walked out on the stage, the fans treated them like unwashed peasants. It was awful, terrible, humbling. "The audience hated us. I remember one guy standing on a seat in the front row with his trousers down," remembers Mark. "It was a nightmare!" By the end of the stint, the guys used to travel up in the lift saying, "It's Christians and lions time – off we go!" After the five days were up, the boys went home, despondent.

One good thing came out of the Big Apple so it seemed: a young, talented drummer called Jonathan Mover. Ironically Jonathan, who had picked up copies of *Script* and 'Grendel' when he was in the UK playing with Toyah Willcox, had not been taken with Marillion on his first listen. "I was so not into it, merely for the fact that too much was blatantly stolen from Genesis," he recalls. "I think I played it once or twice and shelved it for good." As happens in the music industry, Nick made a comment to Phil Spalding (Toyah's bassist), which was passed on to Jonathan. By the time the band came to New York the loop had been closed. "I got the call to meet them if I was interested in auditioning for the gig," recalls Jonathan. "Of course I said I was interested, figuring maybe the newer material would/could have some potential, or it would at least be a stepping stone to more." Unfortunately, his first live experience was to watch Marillion's ill-fated support act at Radio City Hall. "I felt terrible for Fish, all made up with his grease paint and believing in himself, but the audience just laughed and booed. Meeting the band though, I liked everyone very much and wanted to get back to London for musical reasons, so I accepted the offer to audition."

Two days of auditions took place the following fortnight, with Jonathan being one of the last to play. Despite this and with only a twenty-minute try-out, he got the gig and was even offered a place on Fish's floor. "We were inseparable," says Jonathan. In what was now a tradition, days later Jonathan was rushed to Baunatal in Germany, to play a gig that was broadcast live on the radio, before the fivesome headed back to the Old Mill House studio in Monmouth, Wales, to continue the writing sessions. Things started out fine, but before long Fish was having misgivings about the new drummer. "It was all very exciting to be doing things now on a 'professional' level, or so I thought," recalls Jonathan. "It didn't last very long... just enough time for me to co-write and record the demos for 'Punch And Judy', 'Incubus' and 'Jigsaw'." As the uncompromising Fish remarked later, "I didn't like him or his technical abilities, which I thought were out of line with our quintessentially British style."

The comments became increasingly barbed, until one night they reached a level that was beyond the pale. What started as an open discussion about whether *Fugazi* could be a concept album, ended with Fish saying some things he probably shouldn't have done. "That was the straw that broke my back - whether or not he is anti-Semitic or was just using that to get to me, his remarks were tasteless and completely uncalled for," says Jonathan, who gave as good as he got. "I firmly told Fish where to go and woke up the next morning to find out that he told the band it was him or me... obviously it wasn't going to be him." So that was that.

PICKING UP THE PIECES

By now the boys were getting distinctly worried. John suggested bringing in another session player on a temporary basis, so that recording could start – in his mind was Ian Mosley, who had been working with Steve Hackett and who had applied for the Marillion post after the band had already accepted Jonathan Mover. The band's initial reaction was that Ian Mosley was "too old!" but John rang him and suggested he join the band up in Monmouth. He arrived at about tea-time and joined Fish in the canteen. "As soon as I walked in, I saw the glint in his eye and I knew we would get on well," remarks Ian. "I asked Fish what had happened with Jonathan Mover, he said, 'He's American.' So I said, 'You'll get on well with my (American) wife then.' Fish just put his head in his hands..." The next thing Ian knew, the door to the canteen had been knocked off its hinges by the arrival of another band member. "That was Mark, he hasn't changed much!" laughs Ian.

Ian's experience and cool personality worked their collective magic over the days that followed. "My first reaction was that I was enjoying the playing, I wasn't thinking of the long term but I knew we were getting on well," says Ian. Smiles John, "They rang two days later and said he was the one!" All ended well for quick-thinking Jonathan, who went on to work for Steve Hackett on his supergroup project GTR. "Ian's name was on Marillion's audition list from a few months before, so when I heard that Ian got the call after I split, I called Steve Hackett to see if he was looking to fill that spot," explains Jonathan. "He had just finished auditioning quite a few drummers and had chosen one. I convinced him to hear one more..."

On November 14, a now-stabilised Marillion went to record the album at Richard Branson's then-famous Manor studios, at Shipton-on-Cherwell near Oxford: Mike Oldfield (with *Tubular Bells*) and The Sex Pistols had previously passed though the hallowed halls of the 15th century building. Nick Tauber was tapped for producer once again, with Simon Hanhart as sound engineer. It was not to be an easy ride, however. "We went into the studio unprepared, to say the least. We hadn't even finished the writing," remarks Pete. The challenges were compounded by dodgy equipment, such as two 24-track analogue decks that suffered continually from synchronisation problems, resulting in minutes of delay every time a playback was attempted. According to Pete, "It was just a nightmare!" Eventually the pressure (and certain habitual behaviours) got too much for Nick. "He had a bit of a domestic problem," explains Ian. "He wanted to work on Christmas Day - that's always a bit of a giveaway." The band started to take action as Nick's attention to detail went beyond the call of duty. Continues Ian, "He was making me change my drum heads every day. Once, he asked me to change them when they'd only been used for half an hour. I left them, went away for a bit, came back and said, "How's that?" Nick agreed it was much better!"

Eventually the band and John decided to relieve the pressure on Nick and co-produce with Simon instead. Recalls Pete, "We'd just managed to talk Nick out of finishing the project when a chap came down from EMI, who wasn't privy to all of this, and he persuaded Nick to carry on." So much for that... things got so fraught that John Arnison proposed a tour at the end of the year, simply to give everyone a breather and to allow the engineering works to catch up. "How about rehearsing?" asked Ian at the time. Nobody seemed that bothered - apart from Pete, who helped Ian learn the two albums' worth of material in two weeks flat. After all, Pete had been in the same position himself; his main concern was that Ian had raised the bar. "Ian was such a good drummer, I spent a couple of tours wondering if I was good enough," he recalls.

To Ian, the live dates were "magical". As he explains, "When we walked out on stage I felt something special, I can't put my finger on it, I can't pin it down." This was no starry-eyed remark from a young fan. "Before Marillion, I'd played with some top musicians - you can get four or five fantastic musicians together and they won't always get that same magic." The frivolity both on and off-stage helped cement the relationship, notably when the crew hired a girl in bondage gear to come on stage during the encores when Marillion had invited support act Pendragon back on stage. "We were on stage with Marillion jamming 'Margaret' for their last encore when she came after Fish and anyone else with a big whip," recalls Peter Gee. "Fish and Pete and Steve all had wireless systems and ran off, that left us Pendragon guys who were plugged in with leads. Fortunately we got off safely in the end." Half way through the tour Ian was offered what he later referred to as his "dream job" – a permanent post with Marillion. "John came up to me on the tour bus, he said, 'You're an official member of the band now, if you want to be.'" And he did, following a brief negotiation about pay. "I said, I can't live on seventy five quid a week. So we all got a wage rise to 150 quid. I was really popular after that!" This was still a pay cut for Ian, but that was of less concern than joining a band on the up, playing music he loved.

On the band mates' return there was an album to finish, and the time slot at the Manor had run out. Thus began a frantic chase around various London studios, still with Simon Hanhart as engineer. It didn't help Pete's situation that his Mum had a heart attack half way through the process, leaving the bassist rushing back and forth between the studio and Aylesbury in between sessions. The studios included Odyssey and Wessex, as well as Maison Rouge and Sarm, where the assistant engineer was a certain Dave Meegan, fresh from working with U2. "We asked if we could take him with us, 'cos he was so good," recalls Mark. As Marillion darted around London to complete the recording, Dave ended up working with the band at a number of studios. It became his job to ensure all the equipment was set up correctly each day, quite a challenge when a change of studio was involved. Recalls Dave, "We'd finish one night, I'd have to pack up and have it all set up in the new studio the next morning." This included the intricate job of lining up tape machines, which could take an hour by itself.

Deadlines continued to be missed, schedules were overrun, studio time became tighter. On one occasion, a man threatened to break into the studio wielding a machete. Fair play, he did have most of an orchestra waiting. Exhaustion was the order of the day. "I remember one occasion when I was falling asleep at the desk, and Simon Hanhart was falling asleep in the room behind," smiles Dave. Adds Simon, "We'd all roll up at lunchtime and then sit there staring at each other, we were so tired. Nobody thought of stopping and taking a week off to consolidate, then blitzing it." Eventually Tony Platt, producer of a number of albums for Iron Maiden, stepped in to help with the remixing at Abbey Road. According to Mark, "He mixed 'Incubus' and 'Fugazi' at the same time as the rest of the tracks were being mixed by Simon, to speed things up."

Finally the album was finished. While Dave also checked in for a few days' hospital leave at the end of the process, diagnosed with "extreme exhaustion" (says Dave, "It's stuck in my memory as enjoyable but painful,") the band could only hope that the birth would be less painful than the gestation.

UNLEASHED MELODY

Following the same approach as *Script*, EMI released 'Punch And Judy' as an appetite-whetter for the album, on January 30 1984. "The song suggested a single," recalled Fish. At least it did to him - he had informed EMI it would be the next single when only the lyrics had been written. It was a good critical choice - writing in *Sounds*, Jay Williams commented that, "The most common criticism levelled at Marillion is that they are irrelevant, but this is simply the direct result of preconceptions. When you come up against something so brilliantly sharp and at the same time so bittersweet as 'Punch and Judy', it's very hard to see why." All the same the single did not fare well, reaching only 29th position in the UK charts despite considerable publicity.

The collective Marillion headed out on tour a couple of weeks later, following a performance of 'Punch and Judy' on *Top of the Pops*. One fan to see the live act was Chris Brockwell: "I'd seen the band at the Zero-6 in Southend. In all honesty I don't recall it that well, but liked it enough to catch them again. The next time was at the Cliffs Pavilion. There was a very psychedelic light show, Fish burst through the stage backdrop, he took the piss big time by getting the idiots there to bleat like sheep. There was loads of heckling, Fish loved it, he slaughtered any wisecrack or jibe - the man was larger than life. I was caught hook, line and sinker." A regular Fish joke was: "How does an elephant tell you it's hungry? It says, 'Geezabun!'" which only works if said in a Scots accent while impersonating an elephant. According to fan Jeroen Schipper, "It became standard procedure at gigs and members of the audience would bombard the stage with buns at the appropriate moment."

The tour included a few nights at the Hammersmith Odeon with Pendragon as support, recalls Peter Gee, "It was also a dream come true for us - the Hammersmith Odeon was the venue we most wanted to play in the UK." Off-stage spirits were as high as ever, with nights being packed with the kinds of drinking and debauchery one would expect of any rock band. In June the band also managed to get across to the US and Canada again, one date of which was attended by Dave Meegan, who was staying with a friend in New York. "I called up John Arnison and asked if there was any chance I could come along," recalls Dave.

The album itself was released on March 12, a month after Marillion hit the road in its support. Though it sold less than its predecessor, *Fugazi* solidified Marillion's position as a mainstream band. Expectant listeners were a mix of both old-timer fans and new recruits who had joined up on hearing *Script*. "I remember queuing for hours at HMV in Middlesbrough to buy *Fugazi*," says Rich Dowson. "It was release day and the boys were there doing a signing session. For some reason I was too terrified to speak when I got to Fish. I was only 15 at the time." For Lee Clark, the album was a revelation - "I fell in love with *Fugazi* and have followed the band ever since." US fan Ray Achord was initially attracted to Marillion through their outward appearance: "Every other week I would grab a *Kerrang!* magazine from the counter of the record store at my local mall. One particular issue had a full page picture of Fish in make-up, the headline, "*Fugazi*... what a scorcher. The image was shocking and strange, and I had to find out what it was all about. The same store also got in the British Marillion imports, so I bought *Fugazi* and though it seemed extremely strange to me at first, I listened to it many times, and fell in love with it."

Not all fans liked *Fugazi*: while some found that the despair of the record matched their own angst, others saw it as overblown, the lyrics a little too complex, the melodies self-indulgent. Comments Geoff Boswell, "Fish swallowed a thesaurus," a sentiment Fish himself confirms: "The danger is that you can become so involved with words that it ends up like masturbation. *Fugazi* became too wordy from an ego point of view." For Fish, the album was very personal: it was his own anger that was being explored in public, a reason why vocalist Steve Hogarth has always resisted performing any of the songs on *Fugazi*.

In April, 'Assassing' was released as a single, achieving No.22 in the charts. With Fugazi having satisfied both label and fans, Marillion were guaranteed a living for a couple of years at least. It would be folly in the extreme to rock this comfortable, if imperfect status quo. As fan Michael Huang noted, "Both

Script and *Fugazi* were inaccessible to a certain degree and while Marillion enjoyed fairly widespread popularity throughout the UK, they felt they could do something different."

In addition, the old complaint continued to surface. Genesis. Bloody Genesis. Every interview, every review mentioned the G-word, even though many of the journos had little knowledge of what they were comparing Marillion to. It was starting to grate with the boys. "Christ, I only saw Genesis once!" remarked Fish. "One-and-a-half hours isn't enough to build a career on." "I was never even a Genesis fan," laughs Mark, but he wasn't laughing at the time - "We're actually throwing out ideas, good ideas at that, because we are scared people will think they sound too much like them," he had commented.

Meanwhile, external pressures continued to build. Not least that a number of people, including Peter Hammill and Peter Mensch, had taken Fish to one side and suggested he should go solo. They cut no ice, at least not at the time. "Fish wanted the band to succeed, not a solo career," recalls Mark. Agrees Fish, "I was totally against it, I was fighting for the unit. I've always been a unit player. Besides, I thought, *we've just fought for two years*, it would have been totally mercenary for me to do it." And with John Arnison ensuring that the next booking was always just around the corner, there was barely time to sit down, never mind plan a sabbatical.

Following the six-month tour it was time to go home for Christmas, fall back, regroup and do something radical.

FUGAZI

"Where *Script* was bedsit thoughts, *Fugazi* was hotel thoughts," said Fish. Furthermore, where Script was wistful and grief-stricken, *Fugazi* was barbed and cynical; "anger at its finest," as one fan wrote. The album took its name from a British Army slang term, meaning "Fucked Up, Got Ambushed, Zipped In". The term was popularized by US Servicemen during the Vietnam conflict, and Fish picked it up from a book called *Nam* by Mark Baker.

The album was heavier than the debut (maybe the source for Marillion's unjustified reputation as a heavy metal band) and, with Ian Mosley taking over on drums, noticeably tighter and more rhythmically interesting. According to fan Michael Huang, "The music represented a large leap forward from *Script*. Shedding many of their Genesis influences, they began to forge a sound of their own."

'Assassing' was originally written about Diz Minnitt, but expanded to include

Mick Pointer. "We basically sacked them, it's about how hard it is," Fish recalled. The Islamic flavour to the track was inspired by an album Fish had been loaned by Peter Hammill, formerly of Van Der Graaf Generator and a support act on the *Script* tour. The song shows considerable musical development from the *Script*-era, adding more contemporary sounds to the band's original palette.

'Punch And Judy' offers a cynical mediation on marriage. It concerns a husband who, according to Fish, "takes out his frustrations on his wife, using her as a punch bag for his inadequacies." The notion powering the lyric for this and the next two songs was how "couples in the '60s would go to hops, then maybe get married via the idea of perfection that the music gave them. Then of course they'd get divorced; the music would let them down." The odd 5/8 syncopated verse rhythm, inspired by temporary drummer Jonathan Mover, certainly makes it an odd choice for a single!

'Jigsaw' was described by Fish as "about the relationship that splits up and forever comes together again getting worse each time." Although he still feels the lyric makes sense, he has also described it as "particularly wordy!" The music on the first two verses seems almost nursery rhyme-like, the guitar and keyboards chiming like a child's xylophone, underlying the sense of conciliation in Fish's words. The chorus could not be more different, as Ian Mosley batters his skins into submission, and Pete Trewavas's bass thuds like punches. As it gives way to the solo, Steve Rothery creates one of those soaring, melancholic guitar lines for which he is justifiably lauded.

'Emerald Lies' concerns an accusation of infidelity; the sense of power before the accusation is made, and the realisation that, though proven false, the accusation has destroyed the relationship. Perhaps the most straightforward song on the album, it nevertheless showcases some superb percussion work by Mr Mosley - imagine Mick Pointer handling it! It would prove not to be a band favourite; by the *Misplaced* tour only the opening bars remained as an intro to 'Script'.

'She Chameleon' describes the groupie phenomenon, which the band had begun to experience on the *Script* tour. "Who was using who?" Fish asked. Perhaps the most obviously retro-sounding track, the song betrays its *Script*-era roots.

Another Islamic-influenced track, 'Incubus' is a slow-burning number about a porn director, whose former lover and lead actress has just opened as the lead in a legit West End play. Spying her spurned ex-boyfriend in the audience, she freezes, not knowing whether he'll reveal her secret to the press. Much of the track is built on a groove until, the hurt building to a dangerous level, the band take us into a waltz, the director's Machiavellian manoeuvres likened to a dance. Rothery unleashes wave upon wave of heart-rending passion from his spiralling guitar lines, then the bile's really unleashed! The actress, mute on the stage, writes her own reviews for the watching critics, and he's watching it all, a glint of pure evil in his eye...

The closing, title track details Fish in mid-panic attack on the Underground en route to the Marquee in Wardour Street. On a comedown from LSD, Fish said, "Viewing the other occupants of the carriage, it summed up the album and my views on life at the time. 'Fugazi' we were."

In much the same vein as 'Script', the song has several distinct sections. Initially a cynical observation of the other passengers, Mark Kelly's piano gives way to steadily more edgy synth lines. We then move outside the carriage to consider unhappy relationships, racial unrest, prostitution and the treatment of war veterans. Then, as the whole world dissolves into a fearful smear of guitar string scrapes, screams and doom-laden keyboards, Pete and Ian paint a quasi-militaristic regime of Cold War nuclear paranoia.

Finally, as Fish desperately asks to be shown inspiration for a way out of this terrible mess, the band become the pipers of the apocalypse and Fish is swept along with the crowd as it marches to its doom. We would have to wait until the next album for some optimism!

Mark Wilkinson described his cover brief as "illustrating the Faustian 'payback' after the trappings of success had kicked in."

The jester lies, sheathed within a halo of distortion, whilst around him, his material possessions litter his hotel room. Successful, but no more content than he was in his bedsit, the jester has merely exchanged one hell for another. Along with the returning chameleon - first spied on the *Script* cover - we see a lone magpie. One for sorrow, no less.

With one of the weirdest perspectives ever seen, Wilkinson has described the finished cover as "overworked", whereas Fish declared it "a clean acid trip".

5

Childhood's End

With two successful albums under their belts, as the end of the *Fugazi* tour approached, the entity known as 'Marillion' could rightly say it had made it to the big time. Three options exist for bands in this position. First, take the money and live off the celebrity until the cash runs out. Second, milk the cow, repeating the same musical formula ad infinitum. Third (and typical of the era), reinvent as a pop band, throwing principle onto the pyre of commerciality.

Marillion settled on option four. Build something from scratch, ignore the preconceptions of fans and the demands of the record company, of the pundits with their fingers on the supposed pulse, or indeed of the amassed legions of listeners new and old. It was time for the band to leave behind, once and for all, any criticisms about being throwbacks, irrelevant niche players or copycat artists, and create something that was uniquely their own. As the formulation began to take shape, each of the players reached the same conclusion about the paradox they were heading towards. The next album would be a concept piece, the very idea inextricably associated with the progressive rock label that had so constrained Marillion's popularity. And yet, it would be mainstream, accessible, catchy, even radio-friendly.

Success was in no way guaranteed: it would be folly to see Marillion's direction as anything other than a gamble, even if time would prove it right. The last laugh was going to be with Marillion, as they decided to play the fashion game by being resolutely unfashionable, and won. But in winning, the band would pay the price.

ANSWERS TO THE QUESTIONS

The relentlessness of time on the road had been physically and emotionally draining, by the end of the tour the primary goal was to return to Aylesbury for a well-earned rest. August and September 1984 were quiet months for Marillion, punctuated only by a live date back at Nostell Priory. It was a time for families and friends, for cutting the grass and sweeping the porch. Occasional musical and lyrical ideas were being developed in various homes, cross-fertilised with a phone call or a meeting down the pub. While most band members continued the beer-fuelled socialising of the tour, Rothers was tempering his behaviour to prepare for married life with then-fiancée, Jo. "Until *Fugazi*, we did all those things you do when you're young, free and single," he explains. As for Fish, he wasn't going to let losing a drinking partner get in the way of a good time - he reported an unexpected boost to lyrical progress following a "white knuckle ride, roller coaster" acid trip!

The writing process proper began in October: John Arnison arranged a six-week stint at Barwell Court near Chessington, a huge, old Victorian house hired out as a residential rehearsal studio. Immediately obvious to the band was how much easier writing was going to be compared to previous sessions. "There was none of the mayhem of *Fugazi*, when we were still working out the writing partnerships," noted Pete. "We'd got comfortable with the things we liked playing on, and which of each other's ideas would work together." Gone also was any pressure to be overtly mainstream: after the constraints imposed on the last recording, everyone felt truly let off the hook. Comments Mark, "We were fed up with the whole idea of chasing a hit single and were preparing to turn our backs on commercial success." All in all the band couldn't have asked for a better starting point.

The first track to be trialled was based on a new guitar riff which came about as Steve tried to demonstrate to his Jo how he came up with ideas. "I wonder if I would have written it if she'd asked me if there was anything good on the telly instead!" he laughs. "I remember thinking, *This is very catchy!*" says Pete: the riff neatly fitted with a poignant set of lyrics Fish had written about his ex-girlfriend Kay Atkinson, whose middle name happened to be Leigh. While all but Ian felt uncomfortable about the song being so personal to someone they knew well, the title 'Kayleigh' stuck.

The decision to make a concept album was not premeditated; rather, it crystallised as writing continued. "It's just the way things turned out," Mark remembers. "We were so useless at coming up with starts and finishes to songs." Despite the obvious comparisons drawn with the 'proggist' '70s, the band was unrepentant. "We just wanted to do what excited us." Outside the band, not everyone was comfortable with this approach. "There was a nervous but respectful air that questioned our decision to pursue such an obviously un-commercial venture," recalled Fish. A different spin was offered in interviews at the time, with Fish remarking the release would be "our most successful yet". Laughs Mark, "He said that about every album!" Whatever the outside pressures, the Marillos felt unassailable. As Fish commented later, "With this one we've gone in and said 'Fuck it; if you want us, you take us. If not, screw you!'"

The attitude paid off, creativity flowed, and the first side of the album was virtually written in the first two weeks of the band's residence. The music for the 'Misplaced Rendezvous' section of 'Bitter Suite' was also written by Steve for his wife-to-be. "Funny that it became part of our most successful album," he smiles. As the Barwell Court sessions came to an end, the band had pretty much completed what was to become *Misplaced Childhood*.

Recognising it was important to keep visible, John scheduled in a live album and mini-tour for the end of the year. *Real To Reel* was based on material recorded by Simon Hanhart on the *Fugazi* tour in Montreal, Ontario and New York. "I had ten days away, it was great!" says Simon, who mixed the album at Rick Parfitt's home studio in Surrey. This was Marillion's introduction to overdubs (where live tracks are replaced by re-recordings of instruments or vocals). "Practically everything was replaced apart from the drums," says Mark. Concurs Simon, "A lot was reworked. Mark's keyboards had been recorded as a stereo pair and not as the full sound, some of the guitar sounds weren't quite doing it either. Fish came down and cut the vocals again to give me the choice - they were a bit of a mix and match."

The budget-priced live album was released on Monday November 5 1984. Looking to maximise the impact of its release, John Arnison decided to forego touring the US and get the band out to a number of European countries where their following was growing the quickest. Budgets were tight: expensive hotels were avoided in place of sleeping on the tour bus, enabling the band to travel further and play to more people than they could have otherwise. The tour also offered an opportunity to trial material from Barwell Court, notably the entire first side of the planned album. While the songs were musically close to their final form, the lyrics were still embryonic, sometimes changing from night to night.

In mid-December, Marillion played three nights in a row at the 3,800-capacity Hammersmith Odeon. As concert halls grew to arena proportions, the band was already distancing itself from some of its earlier glories, even if this meant losing touch with some hard-core fans. Cries for old stalwarts like 'Grendel' (which Ian has never learned) continued louder than ever, but fell on deaf ears: it was time to move on.

SO VERY FAR AWAY

With the album nearly written, it fell to the band to find a producer. This was no mean feat in itself: when prospective producers got wind that *Misplaced Childhood* was going to be a concept album, few wanted to take what sounded like a regressive step. "A whole lot of producers said no because they thought they couldn't make money out of it," Fish observed at the time. As an even greater challenge, given how Fugazi had sold less than *Script*, EMI had considered dropping them altogether. The band were oblivious: "John Arnison didn't think it was a good idea to tell us," says Mark. *Real To Reel* and its associated tour had granted a stay of execution, as the band were starting to break in continental Europe. All the same, EMI didn't want to expend any more money on the next recording than necessary.

At the beginning of 1985, the band trooped off to Bray Film Studios for six weeks to make a demo. The studios were owned by *Thunderbirds* creator Gerry Anderson, recalls Pete, "Gerry came into the studio when we happened to be playing the *Thunderbirds* theme. I think he was tickled pink!" At Bray the boys were introduced to Chris Kimsey, a producer with a number of Rolling Stones albums under his belt, who had been recommended by David Munns at EMI. Chris listened to the demo and offered constructive criticism to band members, thankfully without resorting to questions about hit singles. "I loved the idea of a concept album. It hadn't been done for a while and Marillion were that kind of band," says Chris, who was quickly brought on board. All the same, Chris did spend an evening weaning Fish away from certain influences. Says Chris, "Fish was playing *The Lamb Lies Down* and I was deliberately pulling the songs to bits! I just wanted to get Genesis out of his mind, to get him away from any idea of emulation."

By March, the album had been written as a near-complete demo – "The only track that wasn't written was 'White Feather'," recalls Ian. At times, the thematic approach to the album was a source of inspiration, at others (according to Pete) it was "a bit tenuous". Understandable, then, that EMI was not convinced there was a single on first listen, but Chris came to the rescue. "He put his foot down. He said, 'I'm the producer, this is what works, let me work on it,'" recalls Pete. Chris had proposed Hansa Studios in Berlin for the actual recording for a number of reasons: not only did Chris need to get back abroad as a tax exile, but from EMI's perspective, it would cost much less than recording in the UK. Not everyone in the band was convinced about spending three months out of the country, but all agreed eventually.

On arrival at Hansa, situated right next to the Berlin Wall, Chris introduced the band to Thomas Stiehler, engineer and general madman. Thomas remembers their arrival well. "They looked a little like a school band, so young and untouched. Mark looked like a crazy guy," he says. The studios were functional enough, despite having a dysfunctional mixing desk due to Geordie (Kenneth Walker), the guitarist from Killing Joke, the last band to record there before Marillion, having let off a fire extinguisher in the control room. Explains Thomas, "Chris and I had a day off, but the band had come in to rehearse. For some reason, the assistant was persuaded to unlock the control room, and there was too much alcohol; Geordie's not normally like that."

Rehearsals started in the main hall of the studios: Chris remembers Ian worrying about how the playback was sounding. "I was recording everything in-your-face and dry," says Chris. "Ian said to me, it doesn't sound expensive enough!" Agrees Ian, "Chris went away, fiddled with the EQs and added some reverb and said, 'How's that then?'" It was fine. Before long, the group was working as a unit. Unlike Nick Tauber's divide-and-collate approach, Chris Kimsey concentrated more on how band members worked together, to capture the essence of the band in every song. "I wanted it as accessible as possible, both sonically and in terms of production - everything was recorded as it could be played live," says Chris. Recalls Thomas, "Chris took real care with each little detail." Supported by Chris, the band shuffled lyrics and music back and forth, until the whole thing worked. "We had a huge chart up on the wall to see how it all segued together," says Chris. Overseeing the whole process was newly promoted production manager Andy Field, who had started to get pains in his legs. "It was diagnosed as sciatica," says Mark. Nobody realised it was something more sinister.

In between takes, Thomas's sense of humour outdid even Mark's in audacity. Four years previous, in 1981 Thomas had escaped from the East by hiding under a truck. "People were thinking for you. It was like living in school or kindergarten, I thought, *I don't want to live in this fucking shoebox!*" says Thomas, who had even left his girlfriend behind. "We used to wave to her from the studio windows," says Ian, recalling how she was eventually allowed to enter West Berlin. Remembers Thomas, "Four years just on the telephone, it was crazy!" Crazy indeed, and there was nobody crazier than Thomas. "He had this megaphone," recalls Mark. "Once there was a solitary old lady walking across the wasteland below, he opened the window of the studio and shouted 'HALT!'" Thomas also owned a "fucked-up old Volvo" which was involved in a number of scrapes. He recalls, "We used to do car racing around the streets of Berlin. Once I hit a traffic sign and smashed up the front. Another time Mark and Fish jumped on the roof - I didn't care." The megaphone also came in handy, says Thomas, "I pulled the window down and said to the other cars, 'Turn right! Stop! Police!' And they did."

"Berlin was an exhilarating place, it had a great vibe," recalls Ian. While the most depressing feature of the stay was the Hervis Hotel ("The beds were like Ryvitas with a fig roll at the end,"), with Thomas acting as chaperone, the boys didn't spend much time there. Nights were filled with a variety of extra-curricular activities, with alcohol on tap, drugs a-plenty and women and song were always only a stone's throw away. But then, so were the landmines and the Stasi. "Fish used to take the U-Bahn [subway] and go to East Berlin. I wonder why he wasn't caught by the border police," says Thomas. On one occasion he took the Marillion posse to Exil, an old Austrian restaurant reputed to have been frequented by Hitler. He recalls, "We were sitting at a long table, talking, drinking and joking. I noticed Mark and Fish were making a bet about something. The next thing I noticed, Fish had nothing on but his belt. The whole thing ended with half of us leaving the restaurant naked! A day later, Chris and I decided to go out without the band for a quiet evening. We said we couldn't go back to Exil but nowhere else was open. We expected to be told to get out, but when we went in, the staff stood in a row and welcomed us. That was really nice. It was very funny for us."

All in all, the surreal situation coupled with its remoteness served to catalyse the creative juices still further. Inevitably, the intensity of the cocoon-like, sometimes claustrophobic environment of Hansa Studios led to frayed tempers, as one incident would illustrate. "Fish came into the control room with a whisky glass in his hand. He threw it into the wall, and acoustic material came flying off," says Thomas. "The argument was about money. I thought, *Why do they do it, they're making a really good sound, why argue about money?*" Later, the ground floor café was witness to a major falling out between Fish and Rothers. "Fish and I had been talking to Hugh Stanley-Clarke about solo projects," recalls Steve. "Fish had this idea about a ghost rider who commits suicide while listening to his music, and Fish would sing covers of the songs the rider held dear. I had the idea of doing something more rock-based and less keyboards. Hugh really liked my idea and didn't like Fish's… The next thing I know, Fish grabs me and holds me up against the wall, screaming that I'm holding back the best songs for my solo album! I thought, *That's marvellous*. I'd just written the majority of the music for the new album and here's a 6-foot-6 Scot hurling abuse at me! Any friendship that was left in me for Fish went away at that moment. It was like a switch flicked off."

The team took a few days off at Easter, then returned to the madness of Berlin as EMI continued to be nervous about the commercial nature of the album. "They wanted us to come back, reorganise and regroup," says Chris. "We were recording the album in sequence, so soon afterwards we sent them 'Kayleigh' and they were alright after that!" As the last recordings were done, Chris took cassette tapes back to his hotel and played them on a portable recorder to ensure the sound was accessible. The lyrical ending of the album was furnished at the last minute by Mark Wilkinson, who had loaned Fish a copy of *Demian* by Herman Hesse. Then it was all over bar the mastering - after three failed attempts in the UK, Chris took matters into his own hands. "The masters came back sounding nothing like the original mix, they were just awful!" Chris had the album mastered back in Berlin, at vinyl mastering specialists Teldec.

Before leaving Berlin the band prepared the first single, 'Kayleigh'; on the B-side was 'Lady Nina', a thrown-together track based around a drum loop of Ian's. The band had managed to keep 'Lady Nina' at arm's length from the album (despite US record company Capitol's desires). The video for 'Kayleigh' featured Fish's future wife, model Tamara Nowy, who he had met in an exclusive bar a fortnight before it was made. It had all come together in the end but the process had taken its toll. "I think we all aged at least three years during our time there," admits Steve.

At £74,000, which was 6K under budget and half as much as *Fugazi*, *Misplaced Childhood* was the cheapest album the band had made. Fish later wrote that *Misplaced Childhood* was "the turning point of all our lives." Little did anyone know at the time just how much of a turning point it would be.

THAT LOVE SONG

'Kayleigh' was released as a single on April 7 1985, with a cover featuring Mark Wilkinson's neighbour Robert Mead. "I had to stand and look serious in Mark's living room," he recalled. To everybody's surprise, the single was hugely successful. HUGELY successful. It spent 11 weeks in the UK charts, only beaten to the No.1 slot by a charity record supporting the victims of the Bradford City fire disaster. "I was ecstatic, chuffed to bits!" says Chris Kimsey, recalling the immediate success. "It was as much to do with timing as anything, a bit of a happy accident," tempers Pete, modestly. "EMI was right behind it, it was marketed well and distributed well." Ian remembers Rothers saying, "That's a doddle, writing that sort of stuff." Whether through luck or judgement, the single could not be stopped - even with a US airplay embargo caused by some dodgy dealings ("The Head of Capitol was photographed handing brown paper bags of cash to underworld bosses," recalls Pete), radio play quickly became global. Even the commercially-focused MTV found room for the video, introducing Marillion to a new cohort of US fans, not least Jeff Pelletier. "I remember liking its unique sound and nostalgic and introspective 'lost love' theme. Yet the song seemed to end somewhat abruptly?" As Jeff would find out, there was more to follow.

Marillion toured Germany, Switzerland and Spain across May and June, immediately prior to the album release. Initially only the first half of the album was in the set list, but even this squeezed older mainstays such as 'Forgotten Sons' and 'He Knows, You Know' out of the set. In parallel Fish decided that his face paint was no longer obligatory: the mask had become redundant. For the first few shows, Fish unmasked himself half-way through the gig, but before long he walked on stage with his face as nature intended.

With the tour accompanied by numerous press interviews, radio and TV appearances, and with 'Kayleigh' being played on rotation on radio stations around the globe, it seemed inevitable that the album would do well. The band had already been told there was a fair chance of *Misplaced Childhood* reaching the No.1 spot, based on the number of albums that had been pre-ordered. This didn't prevent the shock when, on its release on June 17, it raced to the top of the UK charts. "It was an incredible feeling, a dream I had when I was a kid," says Fish. It immediately drew in legions of new fans: "As a big fan of progressive music and concept albums, I was immediately blown away by this album and it became one of my favourites of all time. It still is," says Mike Portnoy, who had seen Marillion on their ill-fated first Rush support slot. His experience is echoed by fan Angie Cooper: "I really only got into Marillion with *Misplaced Childhood*. I was aware of them before, but I did not reckon much to them." Over in Mexico, Bruno Galli also saw the light: "It was *Misplaced Childhood* that made me a believer."

Inevitably, some of the band's more stalwart followers were quick to scorn both the arrivistes and the album. "Many felt the album was too commercial and uninspiring," notes fan Marc Roy. Anne Bond's sisters Jan and Sue felt the same. "They didn't like the commercial exposure and felt Marillion were selling out," says Anne. Any disillusion shrank quickly in proportion to album sales: despite continued issues with Capitol in the US ("We had this terrible period where the album was hugely successful over here and not over there," says Chris), *Misplaced Childhood* went on to sell 1.4 million copies in its first year, turning platinum several times over in the process. Thomas Stiehler remembers a gig he attended at the Deutschlandhalle in Berlin. "They gave me a platinum record and said, 'Hey, Thomas, just for you.'"

All the same, single and album brought Marillion well and truly into the mainstream – before long, new-born daughters were being named Kayleigh and it became acceptable to use the lyrical apology in relationship disputes – all in all, the band had moved a long way from its fringe-progressive roots. Recalls fan Georgina Wistow, "My older brother St John (he was 15) was quite into Marillion. On a family holiday he inevitably snogged one of the waitresses.

Having phoned his girlfriend back home every day until then, he stopped ringing her 'cos he felt guilty. The girlfriend smelled a rat and when we came home wouldn't speak to him. But 'Kayleigh' was in the charts and he was inspired – he bought and sent her a copy, saying he wanted to say he was sorry but he was 'too scared to pick up the phone'. Obviously a move that smooth was rewarded and he got his girlfriend back!"

A single version of 'Lavender' (with 'Freaks' on the reverse) was released in the UK on August 27 1985, reaching No.5 in the charts and hanging in there for seven weeks. From EMI's perspective, all was forgiven.

LORDS OF THE STAGE

For manager John Arnison, it was a watershed moment. Of the opinion that Marillion were first and foremost a live act, he decided to capitalise on the success of *Misplaced Childhood* by continuing touring, rather than rushing to the studios to produce a follow-up. "The band hardly got any air play until 'Kayleigh', so the only way forward was to play live," says John. "When 'Kayleigh' was a worldwide hit, it opened countries for the band to play that we had not been able to get into." The strategy paid off. "We went into hyperspace," says Fish.

On August 17 1985, the band played the Monsters Of Rock festival at Castle Donnington, prior to headliners ZZ Top. As with Black Sabbath at Reading, Marillion proved a hard act to follow - ZZ Top arrived on stage to an audience already sapped of its energies by the Marillos. "I thought they were really good," says fan Simon Clarke, who saw Marillion there for the first time. "They did some of *Misplaced Childhood*, not all of it and in kind of a weird order. It was a scorching hot day, a good first gig." He was one of the lucky ones, however. The *Misplaced Childhood* tour was planned to kick off on September 4 with two nights in Dublin, then Belfast, then the Marquee Club for a fan club show before four nights at the Hammersmith Odeon. All of these (and another eleven dates) were completely sold out.

A fortnight before, Fish went with John Arnison to Japan, spending ten days in an intensive round of interviews, promotional work and late nights at hotel bars. When the pair returned, it was straight into the tour and a continuing round of excess. "Fish never looked after himself while he was touring," remarks John, and on this occasion he did himself proud - according to Mark, Fish didn't go to bed for three days running! "I went out razzing, something had to give," said Fish. When disaster struck, it chose its target well: the one instrument that couldn't be replaced. Fish started to lose his voice halfway through the first night in Dublin, struggling bravely on until, by Belfast on the third night, it went completely. "We couldn't believe it. We all said, 'He's finally done it!'" says Mark.

Fish was to lose the use of his voice for a month, "paying for my sins". A fleet-footed Mr Arnison quickly rescheduled the remaining dates for the following year, but it was too late to move the 'Misplaced Marquee' fan club show on September 10. Ian proposed leading a drum clinic, Pete joined for a jam, Mark and Steve threw in their hats and Fish mucked in as 'Maître D'. Two days later, Fish mimed along to 'Lavender' on *Top of the Pops*, ripping lyric sheets off a pad as he went along so the audience could sing along.

By the end of September, Fish's voice had recovered sufficiently to hit the road again. His over-indulgence was quickly forgiven as the tour commenced: he wasn't the only band member to enjoy a drink, and the bonhomie that developed as the band criss-crossed Europe left little time to dwell on past events. "We were riding on the crest of a wave," noted Fish. In West Germany, where both the single and the album had seen major success, Marillion were named the biggest selling touring act of 1985. Fish had to hire a bodyguard as some of the German crowds proved a little too fanatical, even for a man of his stature. Even the wardrobe found it hard to keep up – on November 11 1985, Fish's trousers split in front of 12,000 people at the Hans-Martin-Schleyer-Halle in Stuttgart. He remarked, "I had to shout at Steve to extend his guitar solo whilst I 'crab-walked' off stage..."

Under record company pressure, 'Heart Of Lothian' was released as a third single on November 18, just as the band were finishing in Germany and heading to Japan. It reached a gentlemanly, but unimpressive No.29 in the UK chart, and was gone in a fortnight. After dates in Osaka, Nagoya and Tokyo, the band returned to the UK on December 10 to film for *The Old Grey Whistle Test* at the Marquee, during which *Misplaced Childhood* was played for the first time live in its entirety. While the tour went from strength to strength, little time was left for anything else - the band had to turn down the opportunity to write the sound track to the film *Highlander* as there was simply no room in the schedules. December 19 saw Marillion play their first headline at the NEC, to a crowd of 11,000. Following a two-week break at Christmas, on January 8 1986, Marillion kicked things off again with the first of three sold-out dates at the Hammersmith Odeon. A month later the band returned to the venue for a further four dates, culminating in a gala performance on February 6, the proceeds going to charity. The event was a roll-call of collaborators past and present - Peter Hammill, John Otway and Robin Boult were joined by Mike Oldfield, Roger Chapman and Mickey Simmons (Oldfield's keyboard player) before Steve Hackett was welcomed to the stage. The 'big band' played a triumphant 'I Know What I Like (In Your Wardrobe)', the same song Fish had sung at his audition five years, a month and four days before.

It was time, once again, to tackle the USA. It had taken the 25,000 US album sales of *Misplaced Childhood* to convince Capitol Records that a full US and Canada tour would be viable. 12 of the 23 dates were playing to stadium crowds in support of Rush's *Power Windows* tour - a brave move considering Marillion's previous attempts to support the band. This time however, the band had achieved success in their own right, were no strangers to 20,000-strong audiences, and had received Rush's assurances that all would be well. "They asked us back," recalls Mark. "When we arrived, they'd left a bottle of champagne in the dressing room." This time there was none of the cat-calling or jeering - the crowds were more receptive, and indeed, left a lasting legacy. "Our audiences have always been strongest in places where we toured with Rush," comments Mark. Remembers fan Miles Macmillan, "When Marillion came to Toronto, six of us piled into my friend's VW Rabbit (one guy had to sit in the hatch) and took the three-hour trip down there. That was one of the best times ever for all of us and we still talk about what a great show it was!"

Marillion spent two months state-side before returning to play a series of festivals across Europe, four of which were second on the bill to Queen. Unlike with Black Sabbath and ZZ Top however, with Queen the band had finally met their match. "Freddie was very sharp," comments John Arnison. "After Queen went on, their tour manager came round the back and said, 'Freddie wants Fish on stage with him.' Of course, when he went on stage, the crowds went absolutely wild!" Fish departed after sharing a song, leaving the throng firmly back in the palm of Freddie's hand.

A late highlight of the tour was the Garden Party at the Milton Keynes Bowl on June 28, to which Marillion invited Magnum, Mama's Boys, Gary Moore and Jethro Tull , along with some 35,000 fans. "We were just trying to find a bunch of compatible bands who would draw some people," explains Mark. Reports of the concert were unanimously positive. "Fish sang with an intensity you could feel came from the heart. "'Garden Party' had thousands singing along," enthused one reporter. "It was a buzz for us," recalls Pete. "Having a band like Jethro Tull support us was great!" Tour manager Paul Lewis found it particularly special: "The band have played other stadiums but that was a home gig." Adds Peter Gee, "A band has really arrived if they can play at the Milton Keynes Bowl. It was a great show, and another coming of age for the band. They really should have continued to grow in popularity and been a long term band at that kind of level."

The writing was already starting to appear on the wall, however. The months away, the fatigue of incessant live dates, the repetitive press interviews, the long distance phone calls with loved ones were all taking their toll. "It was understandable in 1982, 1983, 1984, but by the time it got to 1986, it was becoming a bit of a joke," says Fish. First signs of disgruntlement were expressed in terms of who benefited the most from the incessant touring. The spotlight turned on manager John Arnison, who was "living a lifestyle that was reliant on the band being out on tour," according to Fish. Comments Pete, "I don't think John set out to rip us off, but touring was a way for him to make money." What is true is that he had little incentive to stop the band touring. Says Steve, "John was very good with people, very good at going to EMI and doing a deal, but that put us in a situation where we were always slightly in debt." John was following the only path he knew: given Marillion's credentials as an anti-establishment band, touring appeared the best option. Whatever the motivation the result was the same: no respite to the seemingly endless time on the road. "We were so focused on the music, we handed John our complete and utter trust," says Steve.

Off-stage, it is understandable that constant partying became a way of life for both band and management. "I thought we were just having a good time," remember both Mark and Ian. But the drink, drugs and decadence were taking over. "Take any seven people, and put them into a situation like the one we were in and see what happens," says Fish. "We never had the time to grow up. The partying was a symptom of people crying out for help." Only Steve and Ian were relatively immune to the drink and the drugs. Ian had never been a heavy drinker, and Rothers earned the moniker "St Stephen of Whitby" for his ability to stay on the straight and narrow. Says Steve, "I like to have a drink or several, as much as most people, but my life didn't revolve around getting fucked up every night."

Becoming more frustrated, Fish started looking for other channels for his art. He had taken on a theatrical agent and, feeling lyrically stale, was considering writing a novel. "Fish had written some fantastic words, particularly in the early days," says Steve, "but he'd peaked with the early stuff." Despite his frustration, Fish didn't see a solo career as a viable option. A solo album was discussed, but there was never time to fit it into the schedules: "The band was continually forced out on this tour-album-tour-album cycle?" Even his acting plans were held back as he recounted, "I was offered a part in *Highlander*, but the timing was wrong." Fish's growing aggravation surfaced in various ways:

his hot temper has been widely documented, and he didn't baulk at taking it out on the others. "Paul Lewis was in the firing line quite a few times, as was John Arnison," says Mark. "John was prepared to put up with a lot - he shielded the rest of the band."

On Friday August 1, Steve married Jo in Aspull in Lancashire, with Pete as best man. The party afterwards, at nearby Haigh Hall, included a performance by Dave Lloyd's band, Sliced Bread, following which Steve and Jo headed off for their honeymoon in St Lucia. The rest of the band had planned to attend the European Hydroplane Championships in Nottingham the following day, as Robert 'Chops' Flury, the band's lighting designer, was competing in a hydroplane called The Marillion. Unfortunately, the hangovers made it impossible for anyone to attend... The day after, the band played at a 'private' Roland exhibition in London, with Robin Boult standing in on guitar. Of course, several hundred fans turned up. It was the last time the band would play together for five months.

For Marillion, the honeymoon was over. Nobody could say exactly when the line was crossed, but most would mark it at some time during the *Misplaced Childhood* tour.

MISPLACED CHILDHOOD

The concept for the new album had already been established as part of a trilogy that saw a lovelorn jester go from grief, to anger and, on *Misplaced*, to reflection, acceptance and hope. According to Fish, "This album is the analysis, trying to come out of the problems by saying, 'Yes, that is a limitation; yes, that is a negative aspect of personality.'"

While being part of a trilogy, *Misplaced Childhood* breaks the mould - it is more accessible than its predecessors, and less fixated on the past (both in musical style and influence). Noted fan Michael Huang, "It was a backlash against the brooding nature of previous albums, a self-rebellion." A suitably peculiar result for an album whose lyrical impetus came from a nightmare acid trip!

From the opening notes of 'Pseudo Silk Kimono', it is clear this is not going to be a selection of jingles. Short and none too sweet, it glides smoothly into the opening notes of a love song, a story of a girl, of many girls, of break-ups and a breakdown: the enormo-hit 'Kayleigh'.

Second single 'Lavender' follows on and introduces the child, the boy in the man. As Fish wrote, "The guy's looking back on childhood all the time. He looks on his childhood as being the ideal world, the simplicity of then. He can't figure out at what point he stopped being a kid and became an adult and he's wrong because you never stop being a kid while you're still prepared to learn."

With 'Bitter Suite', there is no more childhood. The band leads us through several sections, memory snapshots of loves lost, climaxing with the return to the haunting themes of 'Lavender' in 'Blue Angel'. This emotive sub-section of 'Bitter Suite' sees Fish seeking solace in the arms of a lady of the night, although he has since admitted, "[She] wasn't a prostitute. That was a compounding of events made under poetic licence."

'Misplaced Rendezvous' and 'Windswept Thumb' see the band drag us back into the present, Fish in the middle of writing his acid-fuelled memoirs before he drops us under the spotlight in centre stage, for the first part of 'Heart Of Lothian'. The gloriously overblown first section has the rock star in full flow, singing his heart out to his fans, whilst recalling his Scottish roots. The introspection of 'Curtain Call' reveals the star desperate to go and live up to his hedonistic image, but hamstrung by the business side of being a musician, the photo-calls and listening back to the show.

Escape he eventually does, in 'Waterhole (Expresso Bongo)'. The band evoke the rush and head-fuck of rock star excess. And Fish? He's out of it - the girls, the booze, the powders - while at the back of his head there's an incessant nagging that something isn't quite right.

'Lords Of The Backstage' offers up Fish looking back at his relationship with 'Kayleigh', and realising his desire for success outweighed his need for her. Steve Rothery string-bends to perfection as 'Vocal Under A Bloodlight' revisits the fragmentation of a relationship and Fish realises the emotions of the love song 'Kayleigh' are nothing but "twinkling lies" that "sparkle with the wet ink on the paper".

'Mylo' recalls the band's friend John Mylett, drummer with Rage, who was killed in a car crash in Greece in June 1984. "He was the first of our own," wrote Fish. Chris Lewington, long-time friend and near-roadie for Rage comments, "Mylo was one of the nicest blokes I'd ever met." The music and lyrics see Fish cracking up under the strain of maintaining both sides of his personality: Fish and Derek William Dick. In mourning and sick of his rootlessness, he endures another press interview: his only way of coping is retreating from real life even further. Immersed in a drug cocoon of Pete Trewavas's ominous bass rumbles and Ian Mosley's heartbeat drums, he has a sudden recollection of a time when life was less complicated, a time of innocence.

'Threshold' sees him dancing on the razor's edge of insanity, as the cruelty of modern life - loneliness, war, homelessness, emotionally damaged children -

93

assault him. How the hell is he supposed to deal with this horror?

Then the payoff! As the drug fades into comedown and the sun comes up, the singer sees a future unfold before him. The band creates a bubbling, optimistic ode, tinged with Mark Kelly's poignant keyboards of regret. Steve Rothery's guitar squeals out with a heart-rush of excitement. Fish can see past his worries and we segue into the hopeful resolution of this dark trip.

Recalling the "Where are the prophets, where are the visionaries?" coda to 'Fugazi', Fish puts his faith in humanity. Together, he says, we can make it through, and to back him up, the music fizzes with thrilling elation. As the last notes fade out, the nightmare ends.

The cover sees the Jester, the symbol of heartache and disillusionment, disappearing through a window. Taking pride of place is the spirit of childhood, in the form of Mark Wilkinson's next-door neighbour Robert Mead. Although there are storm clouds behind him, a rainbow gives us hope, and the magpie transforms into a dove, the bird of peace. Simpler and more powerful than the previous covers, the image offers the perfect metaphor for the music.

6

Clutching at Hopes

After the phenomenal success of *Misplaced Childhood* and 'Kayleigh', things were inevitably going to be difficult. The 'second album syndrome' Marillion faced with *Fugazi* was nothing compared to challenge of turning out a second globally successful album. "Riding the crest of the wave" was still a stamina game, for all its outward thrill and excitement; internally meanwhile, the strains within the band were becoming ever-more wearing. This was due not only to the incessant touring, but also to the skewed media attention – the press considered the band and Fish as one and the same, to the discomfort of everyone involved. Meanwhile the big man himself felt a growing discrepancy between his cut of the takings and his dual role as front man and lyricist.

Marillion had become like a snowball rolling downhill, growing in size, momentum and indeed fragility even as it threatened to escape from the clutches of those pushing it. It was clear that producing a fourth album would be a challenge, particularly one of similarly high quality and impact as its predecessor. There was little choice however but to keep things moving and hope for the best.

JUST FOR THE RECORD

The writing process for album number four kicked off in the summer of 1986, with several, reasonably productive sessions at Steve Rothery's house spawning what would become 'Hotel Hobbies' and 'Warm Wet Circles', their cathartic themes reflecting the long, lonely nights on tour. Then, thirteen months after the band had been inside a studio, Marillion returned to the familiar haunts of Barwell Court, Nomis and Gerry Anderson's studios at Bray before moving to Stanbridge Farm, a studio on the road to Brighton.

The sessions became increasingly strained as, after a promising start, recording ground to a halt. Half the problem was that, while everyone wanted to see a similar level of success as with the previous album, the consensus was that they were done with the idea of the concept album. When EMI's Hugh Stanley-Clarke heard the first demos of the new material he thought they all sounded too similar to *Misplaced Childhood*, at which point it was back to the drawing board. The lyrics were being called into question as well, recalls Mark, "Chris Kimsey heard the beginning of the album, with 'Warm Wet Circles' and 'At That Time Of The Night'. He made encouraging noises but then went back to John Arnison and told him that Fish was lyrically losing the plot." John recalls being called to the studio: "Chris asked me to listen to what had been produced. I did so and said, 'It's not that good, is it?' Everyone heaved a huge sigh of relief. It's what they all wanted me to say, but nobody would stand up to Fish."

Marillion were floundering - but it was Fish, in his single-mindedness, who risked becoming more isolated than the others. The creative strains were not the only cause of Fish's misgivings, as he became increasingly uncomfortable about whether he was being duly compensated for his lyrical efforts, a sentiment that fell on deaf ears. Recalls John Arnison, "He said he wanted a bigger cut. I told him he was being unreasonable." Irrelevant they may have seemed at the time, but side projects such as co-writing the single 'Shortcut To Somewhere' with Tony Banks may not have helped improve Fish's mood.

As the unhealthy environment did its work, as tempers continued to fray, as old resentments grew in stature, it was inevitable that something had to give. "This was the first time I seriously considered leaving the band," remarked Fish - a feeling which, once acknowledged, proved difficult to shrug off. He certainly no longer saw John Arnison as an ally, given that the manager appeared to be siding with the rest of the band. "I knew I was in the firing line," says John. "That pressure certainly led to me hitting the booze harder than usual." All the same he wasn't the only one to seek solace in the bottle - booze was becoming part and parcel of the studio routine.

Such tribulations were beyond the ken of the fans who were simply keen to know how Marillion would follow their platinum-selling album. At the end of 1986, Marillion conducted a five-date Web fan club tour, their first gigs for five months. The Web gigs provided a welcome opportunity to preview some of the new material, notably 'White Russian', 'Warm Wet Circles' and 'Incommunicado'. "Oh, let it be a single!" wrote fan Judith Mitchell of the latter. The opening night, on December 27 in Aylesbury, was a charity gig and Fish wore face paint for the first time in years, to the delight of many fans. "It was completely wrong! I decided to do it for a laugh. It was like trying to squeeze into your school uniform," says Fish. There was to be no solace in the mask he had once used so successfully to protect his inner self. Oblivious, fan Clive Aspinall remembers the Liverpool date as, "one of the best gigs I have ever seen."

The respite was all too brief. In early 1987, the team entered Westside Studios near White City to start recording proper, with Chris Kimsey at the production helm once again. "We were in London because there was more money available," he recalls, disappointedly. "After Berlin, working in London was a real downer. I said at the time it was a mistake." Chris was assisted by Westside's house engineer, Nick Davis. "It was one of my first big engineering gigs," says Nick, who was quickly initiated into the rock and roll lifestyle. It was one big but not always happy party. Ian recalls when David Munns, head of A&R at EMI, stopped by for an unexpected visit: "Everyone was completely out of it. We played him 'Delilah'. John Arnison was crashing around in the vocal booth. David drove back with me - he was so worried he filled his car up with diesel."

Making *Clutching At Straws* was like walking a precipitous ridge, with debauchery on one side and hostility on the other. Things very nearly came to a head on Mark's birthday, April 9 1987. "Chris arrived at the studio with a woman," Mark recalls. "Everyone filed out - next thing I knew she was naked..." Festivities turned nasty when an argument blew up between Steve and Fish, once again about Steve holding back material for solo projects. "This was nonsense. I'd written most of the music on the album," frowns Steve. Continues Mark, "The next thing I knew, Fish had Steve up against a wall and was threatening to punch his head in!" As soon as he could extricate himself, Steve stormed out and caught the train home. "I'd had enough of the egos and temper tantrums. The thing I'd wanted to do more than anything else in my life had become something I hated. As far as I was concerned, that was it - I'd left the band."

Once the dust had settled, Ian called Steve at home and talked him back round. "If there's a person who can sort things out in the band, it's Ian," continues Steve, who returned to the studio long enough to finish the recording. "Fish hadn't realised how much he'd upset me. I'd made the decision that he'd never get to me in that way again." Fortunately he never would, though the drinking and drug taking continued without respite. "I was doing a lot of the work as Chris and Fish were partying," recalls Nick. Finally it was done, and the team celebrated the fact with a meal at Julie's Restaurant. Nick remembers, "I tried to keep up with Fish drinking. I got incredibly ill and was sick in the restaurant, it was very embarrassing!"

The following day Chris and the band relocated to Advision Studios, on Gosfield Street just behind BBC Television Centre, for the remaining overdubs and mixing. They were met by assistant engineer Avril Mackintosh, whose first Marillion encounter had been on the Scottish tour six years before. "When I heard they were coming in I said, 'I have to work on that!'" To Avril's surprise, Fish, who had been indifferent in Inverness and when she met him again a few years later, was the first to come over: "He said, 'I know you, I met you in Inverness.'"

While the album was progressing well at Advision, the mood was shifting from bad to worse. By all accounts, lead engineer David Jacobs ("a funny little guy with a squint," says Chris Kimsey) didn't help. "He didn't fit in, which didn't make the situation any easier," says Avril. "He just didn't have the right vibe." Despite the continuing party atmosphere of evenings at nearby restaurant Braganza's, day times were a morose affair where the slightest complaint could quickly be blown out of proportion. Rothers' remark about David's mixes being "boring and sterile" compared to Nick's monitor mixes was taken as a personal slight by Chris Kimsey, who began to criticise Steve's guitar playing. "He said I wasn't playing as well as on the last album," says Steve, whose reaction was to re-record the 'Sugar Mice' solo there and then. Recalls Avril, "He played this blinding solo. That shut everyone up." When it was done, the gang fell back to Braganza's. "We had a really good night," says Avril, who didn't think that much of the incident. "In bands, tempers flare, but they're usually smoothed over."

At a band meeting held at Fish's house the next morning, the vocalist was thinking otherwise. News that Pete had driven home the worse for wear and crashed his Porsche didn't help. "Ian and I stared at each other over a coffee and a smoke, firmly believing that the band was over," Fish wrote. But it wasn't, not quite: there was just enough momentum to carry everyone forward to the album release, and the tour from hell.

BURN A LITTLE BRIGHTER

With a collective sigh of relief, the band realised they had created a great album. "There was so much conflict and friction, but no-one had their own way," says Fish. 'Incommunicado' was released on May 11 1987, with both the cover and the video involving members of The Web. "A lot of the fans were those that had been to see us since 1982," says Fish. The video shoot had taken place on April 14 - according to Avril Mackintosh, "The most boring, tedious afternoon you could ever have!"

The lucky fans who participated were pushed to disagree. "Being a student (in name only, most of the time I spent following the band) I was pretty hard up, so I had to dig deep to find the fare down to London," says fan Iain Watkins who was living in Scotland at the time. Despite a toothache-enhanced "journey from hell" on the overnight service, Iain's effort was more than rewarded. "My heart missed a beat or two when Fish picked me out from the crowd of about 20 and asked me to stand against one of the lampposts and look up towards the Marquee sign. How I prayed for that pose to be the final choice for the cover, but alas it wasn't to be. I was slightly disappointed with the final choice, as most of my body was blackened out to make it look like it was night-time. Still, at least there was no mistaking my face, what little there was of it, a massive thrill!"

As a welcome change from the syrupy soft rock of the time, 'Incommunicado' entered the charts at No.6 in its first week - it peaked at No.5. Fan Paul Hughes writes, "I first heard the song on Tommy Vance's show. There was something intriguing in its construction, its Who-inspired maniacal dash for the finish line, that convinced me to buy the album on the day it came out." Agrees Irish fan Linda Southern, "I turned on Radio 2 [2FM as it's now called, the Irish version of BBC Radio 1] and heard this thumping loud rock song called 'Incommunicado'. A month or so later we made a trip to Bournemouth, and I bought the album *Clutching At Straws*. I was hooked; it was three days before I changed the tape out of my Walkman!"

Clutching At Straws was released to an expectant audience on June 22 1987, quickly reaching No.2 in the UK album charts. It did not disappoint, recalls US fan Jeff Pelletier: "As soon as I heard the 'Warm Wet Circles' trilogy for the very first time I was captivated, enthralled, mesmerized and left in a state of bewildered awe. This was literally unlike anything I'd ever heard. Such poetic phrasings and visceral images woven into musically complex tapestries, in a way that was completely accessible to anyone with a sense of adventure and open enough to appreciate it." For Max Rael the album was an escape: "I got into Marillion in 1987 after the school bully 'persuaded' me to purchase a copy of *Clutching At Straws*, which he'd nicked from a record store. It was on a school trip to Weymouth and in the dark on the coach I put the tape into my Walkman. From the opening chords of 'Hotel Hobbies' I was transported away from my adolescent hell into a new world."

As Marillion reached way beyond their progressive roots, they attracted new fans such as Martin Thorpe. "I was into Big Country, Simple Minds and U2 at the time. Previously, Adam and The Ants were THE band for me and then I just went off music. With *Clutching At Straws*, Marillion were the band that re-ignited the flame." Some older fans were less convinced, recalls Paul Rael: "When *Clutching At Straws* came out I remember my hard-core fan friend thought it a bit of a let-down. I thought it was a bit ropey too although I loved 'Warm Wet Circles'."

'Sugar Mice' and (a remixed) 'Warm Wet Circles' followed as singles in July and October respectively, each reaching No.22 in the UK charts. To the outside world at least, the ship was holding steady.

THE LAST TOUR

Touring started for real in Poland, on June 22. After the claustrophobia of the recording process, the band hit the open road with some relief. From the outset however, it was clear this would be another high-living tour, with all the trimmings - and traps. Nobody's personalities had changed, and the same resentments lurked under the surface. Fish knew the end was in sight. "He came to see me at the beginning of the tour and said he was definitely leaving at the end of it," recalls John. "I kept quiet with the others but asked him not to leave. I said, 'It's been a roller coaster for five years, go and do a solo album.'" Asks Fish, "Solo project? When was that supposed to happen?" For many band members, John Arnison could have created the space, if he hadn't been so distracted by his own drink-fuelled demons. On one occasion, at a production rehearsal in Aberdeen, John surpassed himself by throwing up all over the brand new stage set. "John didn't do himself any favours," says Ian. "If he had been stronger at the time then Fish could have done his solo project."

In homage to Gerry Anderson's Bray Studio, *Thunderbirds* characters were used as tour passes and pseudonyms. Fish was Scott Tracy, Mark was Brains, Pete was Alan, Rothers was Virgil and Ian was Gordon; meanwhile, Paul Lewis was Parker. In addition the infamous Zelda Club was formed, its name based on the excesses that had to take place for someone to end up looking like an old hag... Even Ian's usually sober reputation took a battering the night after a festival gig at the Loreley amphitheatre in Germany. He was found, unconscious, in a hotel corridor with coins lying all around him, clutching a gold album to his chest. He claims it was the brandy in the chocolate milk...

Following Loreley, everyone (including John Arnison and his heavily pregnant wife Ginny) headed back to Haddington in Scotland for Fish's wedding to Tamara Nowy. Ian and Privet were Fish's 'best men', both of whom had maintained a bond with the big man despite everything that had been going on. "I'd always got on really well with Ian: he'd already done a lot of stuff and ticked it off, he was very grounded and very solid. He was a lot more mature than I was. I was drawn to him for that reason," says Fish. One invitee to the events of July 25 1987 was Avril Mackintosh. "What do you buy someone like that?" she laughs. "I got him a whole Scottish salmon; I thought he'd like that!"

For Fish, marriage was an opportunity to gain a similar level of normality to the other band members. "A lot had a family situation waiting for them. Mark would go back to Suzy and his kids, Steve to Jo, Ian to Wanda. I didn't have a relationship to go back to, it was strange," says Fish. Immediately he got his chance to be 'normal' however, it was whipped away from him. Fish and Tammi spent their 'honeymoon' in the US, having 'volunteered' to do promotional duties around the single release, prior to the planned tour. Rod Smallwood, Iron Maiden's (and later Marillion's) representation in the US, offered use of his house and car to make up for the lack of honeymoon. When the single didn't do as well as hoped however, the tour was postponed - but nobody told Fish, who was left to fester for a fortnight. "John Arnison never had the balls to tell me that the tour had been put back," he says. Counters John, whose attention was on the soon-to-give-birth Ginny, "As I'd gone into partnership with Rod, I felt Fish was in good hands and that Rod would keep him up to date."

Fish and Tammi returned home in August, then just a few weeks later Marillion left to tour the US and Canada for real, leaving John Arnison behind with Ginny, who gave birth shortly afterwards. "Four days after, I travelled to Denver to meet up with the band," he recalls. By the time John arrived in the US, Fish was livid; with unfortunate timing, it was also time for the manager's contract to be renewed. Fish's view, unsurprisingly, was that it should be annulled. However, the rest of the band had come to see John as a protective buffer between themselves and the singer. "They were terrified that I would bring someone else in and turn it into the Fish band," says Fish. "I just wanted strong management." Things were getting out of hand for John, who turned up at most venues drunk (or worse). "We knew John was out of order, he couldn't function," comments Mark, but Fish's suggested alternative, Andy Field, was not much better. "All three were out of order."

The fans were largely oblivious to the shenanigans within the band. Having seen the band at Loreley "as a paid-up member of "the 'Marquee Choral Society', as we were known," fan Dan Henderson then scrimped and saved so he could follow the band on the US leg of the tour. "Patsy Smith ('Angie' from the Web) gave me details of the itinerary so I could plan my jaunt. I only got to three shows and I know the band didn't really enjoy the tour, but for me they were great!"

Questions of money quickly became hot spots in the seething cauldron of contention, not least how John took his percentage from the gross income, rather than the monies left after any bills had been cleared. As a result, John would always get paid, even when there was no profit to be made. "If we toured for a year and didn't make any money, he did," remembers Mark. "But that's what he knew, he was a touring manager, he was good at organising tours. There were tours we did where he didn't take a commission or he took a reduced commission, but if we let him get away with it, he would." John remembers it slightly differently: "It was quite simple, if the band did not make money, neither did I," he says.

Compounding the issue was that the band had no idea where and how money was being spent. "We were a running joke at the air freight company - when we came back from Japan everything was air freighted, it would have cost less to buy it all new," says Fish. Oblivious of cost, the boys would choose to sleep in a hotel for the night, rather than on the tour bus. So would the crew! The band required two articulated trucks to carry all their equipment across the American continent. Laughs Mark, "When we arrived at The Coach House in San Juan Capistrano, the owner couldn't believe it, two huge trucks for his tiny club!" "We only unpacked one of them," says Pete.

Despite the grumblings, the majority of the band eventually decided to stick with the management status quo. "Steve Rothery was my saviour," says John. "He came to me and basically said, 'John, you're a great manager but your drinking is starting to worry us. You need to sort yourself out.' So at the end of the tour, with a nudge from Ginny I did." From Fish's perspective however, the replace-John-with-Andy campaign had been more stipulation than suggestion: when it wasn't to be, his isolation was complete. "I was alienated from the band by their decision and my cards were marked by the manager, who now knew of my intentions and realised it was him or me," Fish confirms. To minimise dissent, John ordered a "ruthless" shake-up in the crew, sacking anyone he perceived as mates with Fish: even Andy Field was nearly out.

Thus was the scene set for the most successful tour of Marillion's twenty-year career. Any remnants of team spirit were gone: according to Ian, "Fish used to disappear into his hotel room and not come out for several days." The big man's grim mood became darker still as the tour took its toll. "It was tough," he says. "We were playing shit gigs with shit PA's, we went through monitor engineers like jelly babies!" In Canada at the beginning of October, Fish lost his voice again. To the initial relief of the others, he agreed to confine himself to quarters. Says Rothers, "When we went to find him two days later, he was completely out of it."

Marillion returned for a second European leg of the tour on November 3, starting with three nights at a sold-out Wembley Arena. "That was big time," says Ian - but it was also the last time the five would walk those boards as an ensemble. "It all started to come apart," recalls Mark. "We were partying pretty hard, we went nuts in Berlin!" It was becoming increasingly clear that Marillion were no longer a unit. Continues Mark, "We started to avoid Fish, he just didn't know when to stop. We used to make Paul room with him as nobody else wanted to." Agrees Pete, "I hated the tour. I could see the end coming, the shows were too big, the audiences didn't care, the band didn't play as well as they could, there was rowing all the time, and we were kept in a bubble, we couldn't communicate with anyone."

Date after date, playing in front of the largest crowds ever only fed Fish's paranoia. "The realisation of the success he'd craved had left Fish feeling trapped and exploited," says Rothers. Fish concurs, "I knew I was isolated, I was suffering, I was gone. I needed a break, I had girlfriend problems, my whole relationship was falling apart." Says Ian, "That tour was our most successful, but our most unhappy. We could tell he was frustrated. I've never taken anything for granted. I remember walking out on stage in the sound checks, there were thousands of lights above my head, three articulated lorries in front of me, about 60 people all working for us. It was amazing, but Fish took it all for granted."

With Christmas approaching, hindsight suggests it would have been a good moment to can the tour and salvage the situation, but the damage was already done. After a couple of weeks off, the band went back on the road and an increasingly alienated Fish found solace in the bar. "He overindulged his naturally excessive tendencies and became harder and harder to work with," recalls Steve. "He seemed to be on a mission to self-destruct - something was going to give." On February 12 1988 Fish lost his voice again in Modena, Italy, resulting in cancelled dates and long periods of isolation as the seams finally unravelled. "It was obvious to all of us that things couldn't continue like that," remarks Ian, who was party to frequent crisis talks – everybody was, apart from Fish. "The hotel walls were really thin. I could hear the band talking about how they were going to replace me," says Fish. One such discussion was in earshot of the bus driver, who reported what he had heard. Remembers John, "The boys asked me if I thought they could carry on without Fish. I said 'Yes' - you can imagine what his reaction was..."

At the end of the tour that February, John Arnison checked into a clinic in Chelsea for six weeks, prompted by his wife's declaration that enough was enough. "Ginny kicked me out. She accused me of being an alcoholic, so I checked in to find out." Various band members went to see him during his stay. "I remember saying hello to Frank Bough on the way in," laughs Ian. While drink was largely the symptom, it transpired that extreme stress was the cause of John's condition. According to Mark, "John told the story of what we had been up to, the clinic recommended that he should get the band in as well!" To Fish, John's sojourn was further proof of his inability to manage Marillion. "The band told me we had to give him another chance," says Fish, who was having none of it. Dwayne Welch stepped in as interim manager, but with John in the clinic, the man who was best at keeping the band talking was out of action for just long enough for it to matter.

Gigs resumed 10 days later in Cornwall, for what would be the last leg of Marillion's Fish-fronted touring history. The tour ended in Bourges in France, on April 4; three weeks later the band played the Marquee Club, following which Fish and Tammi finally had their honeymoon, in the Caribbean, "It was the first break in a long, long time," says Fish. It was also too little, too late.

CLUTCHING AT STRAWS

Clutching At Straws is mostly about the excesses of classic addiction, whether to alcohol, sex or power. Following much time on the road, the album was written in bars, about the people who drink in them. Indeed, specific bars are credited on the sleeve as the birthplace of individual lyrics, from Milwaukee to North Berwick.

The album is notionally based around the character of Torch - "The pivotal figure, a guardian angel at the end of a bar," as Mark Wilkinson wrote, a drunken, coke-addled train wreck of a human being, attempting to conquer his demons, his blocks to creating a new work. The lyrics are a barely disguised trawl through the singer's growing sense of frustration with the constant album-tour-album way of life, and the viewpoint frequently appears autobiographical rather than character-led. Bubbling eddies of keyboards introduce us to 'Hotel Hobbies' and bring the curtain up on Torch, trapped by indecision, addiction and self-loathing, in his hotel room. As he sits at his desk, desperately writing and knowing it's worthless, the dawn, effortlessly conjured by the band, peeks through the cracks in the curtains, heralding another day.

The beautiful, emotive 'Warm Wet Circles' follows Torch, searching for inspiration and ending up in his old local. According to Fish, it's "about small, hometown stuff; the dangers of getting trapped in the 9-to-5 syndrome and then going down to the pub and talking about things you'll never really do. The local hero's the best darts player and you marry the girl you met in the pub at 16. Torch goes back to his old haunts and sees how he used to be and it scares him." As Torch recalls losing his virginity, Steve Rothery breaks into an aching solo, full of pathos and longing, and the band execute one of the most finely wrought moments of their career. Ian Mosley's snare cracks and we feel the first bullet smashing into John Lennon on the steps of the Dakota building.

The band return us to Torch, sitting alone at the end of the bar, drinking once more, terrified by the thought he's perilously close to being one of the hometown guys, wistfully tracing the circles of liquid on the bar. 'That Time Of The Night' leads into a glorious outro, and the band create the perfect sense of tension to underline how close to breaking point Torch really is. "[It] still reads like a resignation statement," Fish commented in the sleeve notes. Added Ian Mosley, "The album reflects genuine camaraderie, yet exposed the decaying tethers that held us together."

'Going Under', a lyric written on the spur of the moment over a Rothery guitar motif, sees Torch languishing in the depths of his depression, close to giving up and taking the final way out. It was, as Mark commented "very much a snapshot of what was going on at the time."

Just as it all gets too dark, 'Just For The Record's jaunty keyboard intro brings a note of hope to the album, albeit tinged with a note of self-deception. Recalling past tracks such as 'Market Square Heroes' and 'Garden Party', the keyboard-led track has Torch cheer himself up with the thought that he could give it all up any time he wanted, the traditional excuse of the addict. Fish considers this to be a "non-song", one without heart or substance. The dark thoughts are never far away - Torch convinces himself he is a better writer when he's out of it.

The off-kilter rhythms of 'White Russian' bring to mind wartime dance halls, but as ever on this album, there's a Kelly-painted black cloud about to come down, as Torch observes the rise of Neo-Nazism in Austria. Knowing he should make a stand and say something, Torch fails and runs away, geographically and mentally, searching for a dealer with something for the pain.

'Incommunicado', written as a jam, is a necessary mood-lifter after the tense and skull-crushingly dark 'White Russian', and reveals Torch imagining himself as a "winner in the fame game". The bouncy, up-tempo number was only included on the album at the behest of producer Chris Kimsey, most of the band thinking it too much of a Who sound-a-like.

'Torch Song', and its segue 'Slàinte Mhath', document Torch's growing realisation that he's killing himself, and the notion he doesn't care, because it takes him away from the misery of real life. In arguably one of his best lyrics, Fish contrasts the wasted lives of World War I in the trenches, with the Scottish shipbuilders seeing their livelihoods destroyed by Thatcherism, and the band pull out all the stops to conjure up Torch's helplessness. Pete Trewavas's bass lines scream poignancy.

'Sugar Mice', "born in a hotel room after a bad phone call home to a very upset girlfriend," sees Fish ruminate on the break-up of a relationship. Commercial, yet impassioned, Steve Rothery launches into one of the purest guitar solos ever committed to tape.

The final track, 'The Short Straw', brings us back to Torch in his room. Hard at work, keys clattering against the paper, he muses on what he has seen, creating his masterpiece on the human condition. It's too late and the damage is done, the band turn savage and atavistic, building to a desperate climax as Torch realises it's too late to change and his addictions have beaten him. For him, it's the only way to survive, even though he knows it's killing him. In case we're in any doubt, Fish's mocking laughter tells us there will be no happy ending.

Shot in Colchester's Bakers Arms, the brooding cover depicts "The Great Bar In The Sky", populated with various artists, writers and poets who had a reputation of liking a wee dram. Great theory, but "it looked crap," Fish commented, Mark Wilkinson's timescale being considerably reduced to coincide with a hastily-arranged tour. "Some extra summer festivals slotted into the tour itinerary, produced a tighter deadline than I had originally been given," he remembers. "It was torture, but somehow I did it."

GOING UNDER

To outsiders, all seemed well as Marillion headed to Glenshee in Scotland to start writing a new album. The fan base was still going from strength to strength: when the compilation *B'Sides Themselves* was released on CD only, EMI caved under pressure from fans to release the album on other formats. "Again, fan power has succeeded!" *The Web* fanzine exulted.

Within the inner circle however, cliché followed cliché from this point on. The end was in sight, starting with the gig too far, Fife Aid.

CASTLES IN THE SAND

The date was May 27 1988, and the venue, the Wellhead Inn in Wendover. Trevor Dorking, who would later become Mark's keyboard tech, had just got married to Mark's then-wife Suzy's sister, and the entire band was in attendance. "It was just a party," recalls Mark. "Some of us got up and played a few songs." It was a low-key affair, an opportunity to relax and just enjoy the music for a change. Few in the audience suspected it was the last time Marillion would play in the Aylesbury area with Fish at the helm.

Then it was festival season. Two weeks later Mark and Fish appeared as part of Midge Ure's All-Star band, at the Nelson Mandela concert at Wembley Stadium. They performed 'Kayleigh' with Midge on guitar and Phil Collins on drums.

According to the *Web* fanzine, "Steve was in the audience watching, he gave a nod of approval" to Midge's attempt at the guitar solo!

On June 18 Marillion played a festival gig at the Radrennbahn Weissensee in East Berlin - "With an audience of 95,000 people it was the largest headline the band had ever done," wrote Paul Lewis in *The Web*. "It was one and three quarter hours, three encores long and it was wonderful!" Behind the scenes, things were not so great. "It was an amazing atmosphere, just before the wall came down," remembers Ian. "We played a blinding gig, I couldn't help being on a high, but as we came off Fish said, 'I didn't really enjoy that.'" I thought, we're in trouble here!" Mark, Pete, Ian and Steve all went to bed early that night, leaving Fish to hit the town alone. "This was a common occurrence by then," says Mark, "We avoided Fish as much as possible; no one could keep up with his partying!"

The Fife Aid festival, at Craigtoun Country Park in St Andrews, Scotland, took place a month later. According to Mark, Fish had manoeuvred the others with typical aplomb: "He told John Arnison that we were into it, then told us that John was into it - we fell for it that time." There was still little external indication that the band were on their last legs, remembers fan Paul Hughes when he met the band after the show: "I picked up very little in the way of bad vibes concerning the band's future. Their professionalism did them credit." As the band returned South, Ian's long-time drum roadie, crew boss and true gent, Andy Field told the others that he had been diagnosed with Hodgkin's Disease, a form of cancer. Remembers Ian, "He went through all the chemo, and came back all clear."

The only direction was forwards, as writing sessions kicked off proper at Pete's farmhouse in Aylesbury. "The band used to rehearse in Nomis Studio in London, but it got very expensive," says Pete. Priv and Andy Field sound-proofed Pete's double garage with Rockwool and hardboard, providing a perfectly acceptable rehearsal room. As the sessions continued however, it was clear that Fish's attitude was hardening. "He was forcing an awful lot of himself on what we had all worked on, and in a way lessening our input. Our work was becoming a bit too much of a musical backdrop," remarks Pete, "It seemed that we would spend months working on stuff, then he'd come in with a lyric he'd just written down the pub and just sing that, so we thought, *Why do we bother?*"

Finally the fivesome managed to create enough material for a handful of demos , which were recorded at Tone Deaf studios in Wallingford. The plan from that point was simple enough: hire a producer; find a suitable location to write and record with minimal stress and disruption; and press ahead, with fingers crossed. Bob Ezrin (who had co-produced *The Wall* for Pink Floyd) had been pencilled in as a potential producer, but at first listen he suggested that the material was nowhere near ready. "I had huge respect for Bob Ezrin until I met him," says Pete. "He didn't really like what we had done, he said it was stuff we could knock out in our sleep. But when he sat at the piano and showed us what he might do, it was much too Andrew Lloyd Webber!" Ironically, Fish recalls a better Ezrin experience than the others. "We got on brilliantly," says Fish. "He asked me to produce a drinking song, I came back with 'The Company', he loved it."

As for location, Fish had proposed (through Robbie the Pict, a Scottish Nationalist friend) a Victorian folly at Dalnaglar in Scotland, a suitably remote location. So the band and Andy Field trudged to the Highlands, with the weight of the world on their shoulders. Some writing did take place at Dalnaglar Castle, notably the lyrics for 'Internal Exile', a song rejected by the rest of the band due to its content. Fish was not unaware of the difficulties caused by his growing nationalism. "I think I used it to drive a wedge between me and the band," he remarked later. Visitor Paul Lewis swiftly noticed things were abnormal: "I had gone up on my motorcycle and, after dinner, Fish and I went to the local pub for a beer but none of the rest of the band would come out, which I thought was a bit weird."

The tentative progress wasn't helped when Mark Wilkinson unwittingly sent the band a proposal for the cover of a book he was producing about album artwork. The album covers had already been a cause of conflict, says Pete: "Fish was trying to put his stamp on everything. Some ideas were his, but some weren't." When Mark's proposal came through, it was the first anyone else knew about the project. "We thought Fish was going behind our backs," says Pete. "Fish appeared to want the rest of the world to think that Marillion was him, and that was unacceptable to the rest of us."

AN EXPECTED DEPARTURE

In the end, the walls of Dalnaglar were not high enough to keep the world from washing in. With timing bordering on the tragic, as the band headed home, John Arnison was in the middle of negotiating a seven-figure publishing deal with Charisma which would have made each member very well off. "It was a five-album deal and they really believed in the band, they were prepared to pay a sizeable chunk up front," he says, but it was not to be. "We agreed as a band, including Fish, that we couldn't really sign the deal," says Ian. "It would have taken another three years to sort out the litigation!" A wise choice, given that communications were nearly at breaking point.

Once home, sporadic attempts at writing and rehearsing continued. "We set up two separate creative camps," commented Fish, who would visit neighbour Mickey Simmonds to give him someone to work with. "Fish would turn up very occasionally; he just wasn't interested," says Ian. Adds Mark, "He used to stay long enough to tell us the music we were working on was 'shite' and then leave. To be fair, we were as complimentary about the lyrics he showed us." Not least the lyrical beginnings of 'Vigil In The Wilderness Of Mirrors'. Remembers Fish, "I sang the whole start of 'Vigil', and at the end of it, they just said, 'Nah.'"

The final nail in Marillion's coffin was nothing to do with music, money or management but the back catalogue of album artwork, in storage at Mark Kelly's as John Arnison was moving office. "I said I'd take them home," recalls Mark. "Fish said he wanted them all so I suggested he picked the ones he wanted. He said he wanted them all." Incensed, Mark took the hugely valuable, carefully crafted originals of Marillion's album and single covers, and dumped them unceremoniously on Fish's doorstep. Matters came rapidly to a head. On Thursday September 15, Fish wrote a three-page letter saying he couldn't believe the vitriol Mark was showing and by the way, he wanted 50% of the publishing income. According to Ian, "We called each other up and everyone's response was the same – 'Well, he can just fuck off!'" Fish was returned a half-page note with words to that effect, signed by Mark, Pete, Ian and Steve.

A final meeting at Ian's house between John and the five band members failed to resolve matters, and the following day Fish announced to the world that he had resigned from Marillion. His official resignation letter said, "I've had a brilliant seven years with Marillion; however, recently the musical directions of the band have diversified to such an extent I realised the time had come to embark on a solo career." Meanwhile, the remaining Marillos' statement to the fan club said: "During the process of writing the new album it became apparent that differences, both musically and lyrically, between Fish and the rest of the band were irreconcilable." Unofficially, Fish's reaction was, "Fuck it, I'm off, there's no point in hanging around," and the response from his band-mates was, "Bye." Once Fish had decided to go, there was no changing his mind, nor did anyone particularly want to. "I felt, what a bloody shame!" remembers Steve.

As well as terminating the line-up of one of the most successful bands the 1980s had seen, Marillion's announced demise spelt the end of a bigger family. "It split up what was one of the greatest crews I have ever worked on," says Priv. "That for me was at least as great a hardship as the band breaking up." For management and crew, the immediate impact was that they would have to go and find other bands to work for. "I was pissed off," remarks Paul. "That year would have been a big earner for all the band, myself included."

What of the fans? Fish's departure was unbearable, particularly for those who had stuck with the band through thick and thin. "I just about cried when Fish left," says fan Lee Clark. Judith Mitchell concurs, "I was really depressed, I didn't talk to anyone for about two weeks!" Paul Hughes remembers, "I was the only fan at my school, and well known for it. Many took great pleasure in announcing the news to me like they'd just caught a messenger pigeon carrying the details." The single 'Freaks' was released as a goodbye and thank you to fans on November 21 1988; eight days later a live album, *La Gazza Ladra* was also sent to the shops. Overdubs had been recorded at Westside with Nick Davis, with the two parties carefully scheduled to re-record their parts on different days. "Fish insisted none of us were there," says Mark. The album took its name, from Rossini's opera - as well as reflecting the magpie motif used on several covers - the music from which was used to quite specific effect in *The Clockwork Orange*. "It accompanies every scene of violence or rape," explains Fish, pointedly.

As far back as 1984, Fish had remarked that his stay in the band might have a sell-by date. In hindsight, it is hard to see how things could have ended any differently. Comments Paul Lewis, "Fish was in one of the most successful bands of the day, drinking lots and not happy with his life - something had to change. Perhaps a year off might have helped them all recover, but the band were hot and that would have slowed down their career a great deal." Concurs Mark, "We needed six months off. If we'd had that, we probably wouldn't have broken up."

And, with that, it really was history.

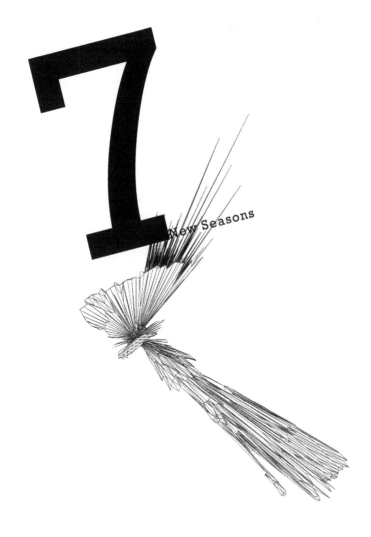

7

New Seasons

Fish's resignation lost Marillion a lyricist, a singer and a charismatic front man. While this spelled the end of Marillion to many, the remaining band members shared a different perspective. "We sort of expected it, so we weren't as devastated as people might have thought," said Mark, who felt like a weight had been lifted from his shoulders. Concurred Steve, "The biggest feeling I experienced was relief." All was not lost: *La Gazza Ladra* had bought a bit of breathing space; the contract with EMI was still in place, providing some guarantee of support; and Pete, Ian, Steve and Mark were as close as they had ever been, the unit underpinned by a re-invigorated and equally relieved manager.

Above all else was a feeling of confidence, if not bullishness from a musical perspective. There was no shortage of new material - the Dalnaglar sessions had yielded a number of tracks. "'King Of Sunset Town', 'Seasons End' and 'Berlin' were pretty much all finished," remembers Rothers. Parts of 'The Space' and 'Uninvited Guest' also had started to take shape. Music provided enough momentum to keep everything going, as Ian remarked later, "The music's powerful pull and unique sound is self-sustaining."

Nobody doubted the uphill struggle that lay ahead; in Ian's words, the transition was to be as dreaded as it was inevitable. As rehearsals continued in Pete's converted garage, the band reached a stark conclusion - Marillion were not seeking another Fish, if indeed that were a possibility. Remarks Pete, "We knew we were going to spend ages looking - we didn't want to be 'the best Marillion covers band around' - but we didn't really know what we did want."

The next few months would test Marillion's mettle and determination as they came to terms with their past and set about deciding their future. Quite early on it was agreed that quitting was not an option - each individual had invested too much, and there was too much opportunity, for anyone to throw in the towel. Rather than trying to find one person possessing all the facets of the now-solo performer, vocalist and lyricist, the fearless foursome set about filling the gaps, one by one.

WE WAKE UP WITHOUT YOU

While all commercial gigs were quickly cancelled, a couple of fan club shows were also booked in Utrecht and Liverpool, and these shows just had to go on. The first took place without a singer at all, explains fan Jeroen Schipper, who certainly chose his moment to get into the band: "I had just become a member of the fan club and went to my first meeting at the Tivoli Theatre in Utrecht. To my surprise the remaining four Marillion members were there and they played a few songs. The audience was responsible for the vocals (together with Pete), which was truly amazing!" At Liverpool's Royal Court Theatre, vocal duties were handed to Dave Lloyd of Rage, by then a good mate of the band. "Dave was a good choice, he could be front man and keep the troops going," comments Pete. Adds Mark, "It went down surprisingly well, especially considering that Dave didn't know any of the songs."

With hard-core fans satisfied, the next priority was to fill the lyrical void. "None of us really felt we could write a good lyric," says Pete. A number of songwriters were considered, including Viv Stanshall of the Bonzo Dog Doo-Dah Band. "He showed myself and Ian a bunch of lyrics that he'd already written but, although we thought they were good, we didn't think they had enough depth for Marillion," says Mark. Adds Rothers, "Charming chap though - and a complete nutter!" EMI had recommended John Helmer, who had been vocalist in Brighton-based post-punk band The Piranhas. John's only knowledge of Marillion had been the occasional TV experience and the tenuous connection of a past girlfriend having worked on a video with Fish; all the same, he was interested. "Marillion came at the right time for me," he comments. "I was making house records and doing some remixing, I'd just got married and I felt there were more things to do than being in a band." John was sent some sheets of Fish lyrics, which were immediately daunting: "They included lines like 'a hand held over a candle in angst-filled bravado'. Whatever followed had to be equally distinctive - I couldn't get away with 'Fish lite'!" Fortunately, John had his own experience of thinking man's rock. "I was into bands such as King Crimson as a teenager; to me it was like revisiting roots."

In early winter 1988, John met Rothers at a Hammersmith pub, just around the corner from the Odeon. First on the agenda was a piece of music inspired by the three months the band had spent in Berlin in 1985. "I'd never been to Berlin, so I referenced literary sources like Christopher Isherwood to see if anyone would notice," laughs John, who wrote a first cut of what would become 'Berlin', before heading up to Aylesbury to meet with the other members of the band. "John was the one lyricist who stood out to me," recalled Rothers. "It was so different to the stuff Fish was doing - good, strong, colourful imagery, but emotionally very direct."

The Marillos felt comfortable enough to get John going on some other ideas. To kick things off Mark and Steve ran through what they had in mind without playing him any music - not the easiest starting point but somehow John came up trumps. "My lyrics struck the right chord, something that really amazed me because they were borne out of a completely different style of music, but it worked," said John at the time. One brief concerned the environment - "before it got trendy!" remarked Rothers. "John went away over Christmas and wrote 'Seasons End' exactly as it is on the album."

The next, looming challenge was to find a singer. With Pete Trewavas filling in vocally during the writing sessions, that November an advert was placed in the back pages of popular music mags such as *Melody Maker*. Unsurprisingly the response was significant – there was no shortage of people who wanted to see whether they could fill Fish's shoes. Having worked through literally hundreds of tapes, the band auditioned a shortlist of potential singers at Westside and Nomis Studios, including Stuart Nicholson of Galahad and Nigel Voyle of Cyan. "We had some hilarious rehearsals," laughs Pete. "People would dance around - one guy even acted out 'Fugazi' word for word!" But nobody ever quite fitted the bill.

Six months after the fateful day in September the band had "an unexpected piece of good luck" - in the shape of a tape posted from the music publishing house, Rondor. Ironically, Rondor had been contacted as part of the search for lyricists, not singers. "I used to pick up bags of cassettes from the office and play them in the car on the way to Pete's," recalls Ian. "I put on the tape and straight away I thought, this fellow's got a great voice, it's going to be too much to ask." The rest of the band was bowled over as well. "I was very excited by what I heard," comments Pete. Even John Arnison, who usually kept out of the musical side of things, was impressed. "I listened to the tape and thought, that's the voice," he recalls.

The diminutive singer known as Steve Hogarth wasn't that interested, however. Following a significant number of pleas from interim manager Duane Welsh ("I kept fobbing him off!"), he eventually agreed to an audition at Pete's house the following Saturday. The start was inauspicious, to say the least – Steve arrived a day late because his car had been stolen, and had to meet the others on Pete's patio as he found himself "violently allergic" to the Trewavas household's two cats. Steve H remembers his none-to-complimentary first impressions – "They'd got all this gear set up in Pete's garage. It was just ridiculous, like all the gear in the world crammed into an outside toilet. Mark's set-up had walls of keyboards in those days. It was a bit like cramming into the back room of a music shop."

Despite the chilly March air and a somewhat brusque Mark Kelly (who was feeling a little miffed about Steve Hogarth's apparent lack of interest), the atmosphere quickly thawed when the singer asked what the musicians were looking for. "I expected them to say, 'We're this big progressive rock band and we sell this many copies. It's a good living, and do you think you can sing like this?' I would have gone, 'Well, no,', and 'Cheers,' and that would have been the end of it," he says. That wasn't the end of it, however: "They said, 'We've heard you singing, we've heard some songs you've written and we really like what you do. We just want you to do what you do and we'll do what we do and we'll see what that produces.'"

Clearly it was worth a try-out, so the fivesome spent the afternoon jamming in the makeshift studio, with Steve Hogarth singing over some of the musical ideas the band had already put together. Far from being put off, he took what he was given and adopted it as his own. As he tried adding John Helmer's 'King Of Sunset Town' lyrics to one piece of music, Rothers recalled later, "By 20 minutes of us playing together, it sort of existed as a song. It was evident immediately that we'd work together - creativity was effortless." Agrees Pete, "None of the people we had auditioned were quite real enough, but Steve was a real artist, his own kind of singer. All the things we saw were positive." Hogarth wasn't so sure at the time: "I thought I was out of tune and horrible!"

Whatever – he was in, if he wanted to be. "It was obvious to us all, right from the word go, that this was the guy for the job," remembered Rothers. "We felt that same magic that we'd had in the early days with Fish. Everything just clicked - the minute Steve started singing it was like our whole creativity became supercharged again." With first impressions fading fast, Hogarth's arrival proved an immediate catalyst, releasing the others from their post-Fish doldrums. Of least concern was his mainstream musical background - as with John Helmer that was seen as an advantage, an injection of new spirit and zest.

In February, following appropriate background checks (a.k.a. calling up mates - Pete telephoned Robin Boult, who knew Steve through John Otway, while Ian checked with old band-mate Darryl Way, who happened to be a drinking buddy of Steve's) - Marillion proposed taking Steve on for a trial period. What was more, the band wanted to bring him in on the same financial terms as themselves. "The band didn't want a salaried player any more than they wanted a dictator," remarks John Arnison. Laughed Steve H at the time, "It all seemed very, very fair, especially considering that they were already famous selling bucket loads of records and I wasn't."

True to form, the man to be known as H didn't rush the decision but asked for a week to think it over. Recalls Steve Rothery, "He didn't immediately say yes, he upped and went and thought about it, which we found very surprising." It wasn't his only offer, however, as H recalls, "I was lined up to tour with Matt Johnson (of The The) in the summer. Matt was about the hippest artist in England and Marillion were about the least hip artists." Tough choice. Meanwhile, the band were calling up everyone they knew who knew him, particularly the aforementioned Darryl Way. Says Mark Kelly, "We said, 'Listen, bend his ear a bit, 'cos we really want him to join.'" Darryl was only too pleased to help. "I thought that this was just the right thing for him to do at this stage in his career, especially as he had a young family to support," he recalls. "Also, the drummer in Marillion was my old Wolf drummer, Ian, and I was able to vouchsafe that Steve would not find a nicer guy to work with!"

THIS PLACE WILL NEVER BE THE SAME

The grinding down process worked. To Steve Hogarth's initial surprise he accepted the post, joining the others at The Music Farm rehearsal studio, a former mushroom farm near Brighton, for a fortnight to see how things went: very well indeed, it turned out. The fit between Steve and the other band members was uncannily close - for example, H and Pete's voices complemented each other perfectly. But there was more in the newcomer's armoury than a good pair of lungs - he possessed keyboard skills, lyrical capabilities and more. "That was such a creative time. The adrenalin was really going, it was incredible," remembers Rothers. Agrees Mark, "Everything was going well and we were all very excited." Remarks Steve Hogarth in the sleeve notes to *Seasons End*, "Joining Marillion was like coming in out of the cold. It was all new, decadent, a bit surreal and, for me, incredible fun!"

Steve Hogarth arrived at the studio with a red bucket full of cassette tapes, music and lyrical snippets that had never quite made it in previous projects. "If we ran out of ideas the boys would say, 'Have you got anything in the bucket?' I'd take out a cassette and say, 'What do you think?'" he says. One significant 'bucket moment' was when H played 'Easter' to the other members of the band. He had written the Skyboat-and-Yeats-inspired song a year before, based on his experiences of visiting Belfast for a gig, but it had never been recorded. As Steve sang and the band added their own interpretation of the music (including a now-trademark solo by Rothers), the relationship between singer and band was cemented. Says Priv, "You got the immediate impression that he wasn't joining them, they were joining each other."

Present from the outset was Nick Davis, engineer from *Clutching At Straws*, who was acting as co-producer and sound engineer. "There were enough factors changing what our sound was going to be, so we wanted to keep control," says Pete. "Nick was ideal: he'd worked with us before, we liked his sound, it was the right combination." To set a precedent that would last over two decades, jamming became the order of the day, the loose-knit approach proving ideal to discover what the artists could accomplish as an ensemble. The nascent band laid down, revised or adapted some song structures from previous material, while other songs, such as 'Hooks In You', were written and recorded from scratch on Steve Rothery's Akai 12-track. "It was a monster Portastudio thing, it used these big cassette tapes like Betamax," he says. In the timeouts and evenings the boys did as boys do - drinking, going out, playing pool and developing the rapport still further.

John Helmer was also invited to the love-in. Explains Mark Kelly, "Their styles not only complemented each other, but where they had to, they merged nicely too." In the end Steve Hogarth composed all the vocal melodies, not to mention a substantial portion of the lyrics including 'Easter' and 'Holloway Girl'. Only 'Seasons End' and 'Uninvited Guest' escaped his touch. "The whole thing with Steve and John worked out extremely well," noted Mark, with palpable relief. "It was almost too easy!" There was only one area where styles differed between H and the band: 'old' Marillion were accustomed to spending months in the studio "noodling" (his word) with the latest opus, which felt too indulgent for the pop-steady Hogarth. Laughs Mark, "When H joined the band he said, 'I can't believe how vague you are, what's going on?'" But nobody was going to let a little long-windedness spoil the general feeling of goodwill.

On April 28 the band went to Outside Studios at Hook End Manor, Stoke Row in Oxfordshire ("A lovely place, a very old country manor house that used to belong to Dave Gilmour," according to Pete) to record the album for real. The studios at Hook End Manor were residential, with each room being decorated in its own, distinctive style. H chose the oriental room and christened it The Opium Den. "It was just like being on holiday," says Ian, "We just played tennis every day and built hot-air balloons." The latter became more and more complex as the days progressed, remembers Nick Davis. "We started with a single laundry bag and a strip of balsa and we ended with ten to fifteen survival bags attached to a Calor gas burner." The ensemble would drive around the Oxfordshire countryside following the balloon until the Calor ran out, continues Nick, "Apart from one occasion when one went so high that we lost it completely. We later saw a headline that there had been a fire at a stately home?"

Progress was smooth and painless, despite the distraction of an ongoing legal dispute. Representing Marillion was John Ireland at Lee & Thompson, who had represented Roger Waters following his departure from Pink Floyd; working on behalf of Fish was Howard Jones at Sheridans, who had worked for Dave Gilmour and Co. "Ireland was still smarting from having lost to Gilmour and

Co. so he was spoiling for a fight," says Mark. The court case only held up recording on occasion, such as when a policeman turned up at the studio with a lawyer to serve an injunction from Fish. Explains Mark, "It was to impound our equipment because technically, Fish still owned one fifth of it." As both camps were intent on releasing an album before the other, the band stopped recording for a little while before getting back to business.

Both sides of the divide agree the only people to make money out of the split were the lawyers: eventually a QC advised Marillion to settle, while Fish was advised similarly. "Fish was right, we should have all been more mature then," remarks Ian, who used to take a chess clock along to meetings to keep the cost down.

With a weight off their shoulders, the boys could get on and complete what was to be Steve H's first album with Marillion. He later compared the recording to "getting in bed with someone for the first time, some really special moments but there was some awkwardness for me." On May 14 H celebrated his birthday at Hook End Manor, putting paid to his reputation as a lightweight: "I spent most of it upside down. I was doing handstands on the table because I was so drunk."

Mixing and completion of the album took place at London's Westside studios in early summer. The collective members of Marillion were justly proud, particularly bearing in mind the ashes from which they rose. Rothers commented to journalist and fan Rich Wilson, "Considering some people had written us off following Fish leaving, it was a very strong statement that the band still had a lot going for it. What we found was something equally exciting and original as we had found with Fish." The final word goes to new boy Steve Hogarth, speaking to journalist Mick Wall at the time, "I don't know about the rest of the guys but this is definitely the best piece of work I've ever had a hand in."

EVERYBODY'S GOT TO KNOW

All that remained was to package and release the silver disc. Marillion had been assigned to product manager Steve Davis at EMI, though not through his own choice. "I wasn't the biggest fan at the time," he says. Steve's first job was to identify a new cover artist, bringing to a close Marillion's six-year relationship with Mark Wilkinson. The band's hand was only slightly forced by Mark's decision to design the cover for Fish's solo album, *Vigil In A Wilderness of Mirrors*. "Mark tried to persuade us that he could continue to work with both Fish and Marillion without problems, but we decided we didn't want to work with him," says Mark Kelly. Agrees Pete, "We all felt it was a good time to change. Besides, graphic artists are so much quicker than proper artists!"

The band was introduced to Bill Smith Studios, famed for working with the likes of The Jam, Kate Bush and Mike Oldfield. "I met most of the band and showed them my portfolio," recalls Bill. "We all got on pretty well, I really liked Steve Hogarth. We agreed not to alienate the existing fan base, to go for a photographic approach but bring in idents from the previous, illustrated covers." Against this remit, graphic artist Carl Glover developed a photomontage for *Seasons End*, keeping the key symbols alive (though barely) from Mark Wilkinson's original designs. Along with the logo, it was the last time these images featured on a Marillion cover. The decision to use photography rather than airbrushing was also deliberate - recalls Carl, "Fish had Mark, so we needed to define another identity."

Not everyone thought the new approach was such a good idea: complains Jo Mirowski, who had designed the original logo, "They were successfully following the oldest formula in the book - the logo, the jester character, the artwork. From a graphic point of view they lost an identity." A touch of sour grapes perhaps, but Jo's words reflect the opinion of some fans who were already starting to feel alienated from the band they thought they knew. "There was a picture in *Sounds* of the band and the new singer - he had this foppish, Phil Oakey-style haircut," says fan Simon Clarke, "I thought, *You're fucking joking, how can he replace Fish? He's a New Romantic!*"

There was one, final complication. As Steve H pulled tapes out of his red bucket, he hadn't always checked their provenance – such as the end section of 'The Space', purloined from a Europeans song called 'Wrap Me In The Flag'. Recalls Steve H, "I forgot to make sure that the credits were included, so when we put the record out there was no mention of the Europeans. When we pressed the second run there's about seventeen names on there." Tricky, this provenance thing - if only that had been the end of the matter. Unfortunately, Steve's old cohort Colin Woore (who was still upset at losing his partner) took umbrage about another part of the song, derived from a co-written demo called 'So Far Away'. "I put my words and melody onto some chords that Mark had already written, but Colin said the chords were his chords, and they were too precious to him to be released," says Steve. "I'd done my damnedest to make that project work, but it hadn't so those songs were never going to see the light of day." While it was small potatoes compared to the legal harvest playing out between his new band mates and their previous singer, the end result (an out-of-court settlement) was the same.

A RAGGED MAN CAME SHUFFLING THROUGH

It was show time, after a fashion. The first live performance of the new line-up was to be a "nice low-profile gig" on June 8 1989, at The Crooked Billet, Stoke Row, under the alias of the Low Fat Yoghurts, a name coined by Nick Davis over breakfast. "It was a tiny little pub we used to frequent while we were recording *Seasons End*," recalls Pete. "We were talked into it by a charming Australian barmaid, and good sense didn't prevail." Everyone in the band and entourage remembers the Australian girl, particularly as she used to sunbathe topless by the pool outside the studio windows.

When the big day came, Steve H was bricking it. "I really had no idea what to expect," says H, who had been having sleepless nights about performing. The venue did nothing to assuage his fears - "I was dismayed to find there was no stage, that the equipment took up half the room, and there was absolutely nothing between me and the fans. If someone was to take a dislike to me, there would be nothing to stop them just reaching out. Given my size, it was going to be more nose-to-nipple than nose to nose." The planned set list mixed some new material with five songs from the back catalogue – he just hoped it would do the job.

Fans started arriving by late afternoon, and it quickly became obvious that the audience would be larger than the pub could take. "Coach-loads of people turned up - it was amazing!" laughs Nick Davis. As it happened, the enthusiastic fans lapped it up. "It was an amazing vote of confidence to have that sort of buzz," says Rothers. Agrees Pete, "It turned out to be quite a legendary experience, a nice way of introducing Steve Hogarth to the mad Marillion fans." Leaving the stage was a bit of an issue, as Paul Lewis remembers. "After the show the band was unable to get through the crowd so they climbed out of the very small window at the back of the room." And that was without the encores, continues Mark, "Climbing back in was a problem 'cos it was three feet high on the inside and about six feet high on the outside." Nonetheless, Steve H's reaction following the gig was sheer relief: "Having come through that, it was all downhill from there."

A second outing took place seven weeks later at the Brixton Academy, on the occasion of the video shoot for the planned single 'Hooks In You'. 600 fans paid six quid each to attend a mocked-up gig, no less traumatic for Steve H for being staged. "I was up in the gods, looking at the kids coming into the hall," says Steve. "I thought, *I wonder what they're gonna make of me?* I knew that if I dwelt on it, it would get worse..." He needn't have worried. "They really took to him.

I think they are quite a sensitive bunch, but they didn't tear us apart," said Mark at the time. Continues Steve, "As the shoot went on I realised there was the potential to have fun with the crowd. My grin was genuine, I did have a good time." It was going to be all right, decided Paul Lewis who was watching from the side lines. "He was a cracker, mental but a cracker!"

GOOD SEASON

The intentionally bold 'Hooks In You', was released on August 25. Exactly a month later, the album *Seasons End* reached its hungry audience and a raft of expectant reviewers. One review considered the album to be: "A very solid effort with no sub-par songs." *Kerrang!* loved the album as well, declaring it: "A legacy of some of the best and most beautiful music that can't be rubbed out with bad blood." In the same issue, Mick Wall wrote, "Musically, it's pretty much business as usual." As for the new boy, Mick noted, "Hogarth's certainly got a voice, smooth as glass and emotive as hell. When you listen to it on tracks like 'Easter', 'Seasons End' or 'After Me', you can almost forget the band ever had another singer." Agrees Steve Davis, "I was very pleasantly surprised!"

Not all reviews were quite so effusive. Underground magazine *Spiral Scratch* wrote of "obvious reservations about the ability of the new outfit to justify the name Marillion. Add this to the fact that the new material sounds a little tired and lack-lustre, and you are left with a fairly monumental hill to climb." No punches pulled there. A valid comment was the perceived move towards the mainstream, as Steve Hogarth was delighted to confirm later, "I smashed the progressive approach apart." But H had not been alone in wielding the sledgehammer - others in the band had also taken a swing, driven not by a desire to ignore the past, but to get on with the future.

A good proportion of fans were relieved and delighted by the new album. Geoff Boswell, who had gone off the band after *Fugazi*, happened to catch a German interview on cable TV. "I turned up the volume, gasped at the new songs and became a born-again Marillion fan," he laughs. Anne Bond, whose sisters had been such staunch followers in the early days, was discovering Marillion for herself. "I was interested to find out what they were like with their new singer," recalls Anne. "I loved it so much, especially Steve's voice, that I still really rate *Seasons End* as one of my favourite albums." As for still-dubious Simon Clarke, the first single put him right. "I bought 'Hooks In You' as a CD single. I thought it was quite a good tune... then I heard the B-side 'After Me' and I thought, *We're all right now*." Some fans, like Angie Coope, were slow to pick up the new disc, but were quickly won over. "When Fish left Marillion I thought that the band was finished. At first I never gave H a chance and it was three months before I bought *Seasons End*. How wrong I was!" says Angie.

Overall the band saw their fan base cut considerably however, particularly in terms of album sales. While Fish had only been one member of a five-strong band, many fans saw his crowd-pulling charisma and defining vocals as synonymous with the name 'Marillion'. His absence proved unacceptable to many, not least John Chudy: "I followed them avidly until the day I bought *Seasons End* and heard the new singer. My fan-hood lapsed then and there." Marc Roy notes, "I can attest that I, along with at least five friends, had a very unpleasant reaction to the 'Hooks in You' single. Then *Seasons End* was released and we all were won over except for one fella who decided to call it quits. Simply that. Bye-bye, and thanks for the music." Paul Rael took a similar path - "I remember watching the video for 'Hooks In You' and thinking, *Jesus, what have they done? These guys used to be good.*" Ironically, it was the places where the Marillion had been biggest, that they took the greatest hit. "We lost the heavy metal side of the fans," remarks John Arnison. "We never really got as big again in the UK or Germany."

Some older fans saw the new vocalist having an undue influence on the band's direction. "Naturally they blamed him, he seemed to be subverting Marillion's progressive edge," writes fan Michael Huang. There was no going back however. Having decided to pick up the mantle, Steve H planned to carry it with pride. He explained to interviewer Mick Wall, "When I joined I wrote a letter in the fan club magazine announcing myself and telling everybody that I wasn't here to impersonate Fish, I was here to be myself. I also said I would be giving 100 per cent to help make this version of Marillion happen for them." It was never going to be plain sailing: in a later diary entry, he recalled carrying Ian's cymbals through an airport terminal when a man asked him who the band was. "He naturally assumed I was the drummer and when I said Marillion, he asked me what I thought of the new singer. I said, 'He is not as good as the old one.' 'No, I don't think so either,' he said. No pressure."

On the upside Steve Hogarth was clearly nothing like Fish, as vocalist or front man. "I was so completely different in every sense, nationally, physically, where my head was at," he remarked. H's arrival offered a fresh start, an opportunity to relaunch the whole band. The promotional campaign included a number of prime TV appearances, including *Rock Steady*, *TV AM* and *Top Of The Pops*, the latter viewed by fan-to-be Vicki Harding: "I thought, bloody hell, he's a vast improvement on Fish." You can't displease everyone!

Such events were a mere preamble to the real tour, which started properly on October 5, in front of a 10,000-strong crowd at the Palais des Sports, Besançon in France. While all agreed the new line-up would only cover songs that the vocalist "could feel" H remembers how the band felt obliged to play some older songs. This proved to be quite a few: while 'Kayleigh', 'Lavender', 'Incommunicado', 'Warm Wet Circles' and 'That Time Of The Night' were relatively straightforward, others, such as 'Script For A Jester's Tear', were more testing. 'Heart Of Lothian' was also an option, but as Steve suggested to Mick Wall, "Maybe we should ask the Scottish fans what they think. I am Scottish on my grandfather's side though." Some songs were out of bounds, not least the deeply personal 'Fugazi' ("Only Fish can sing that one properly and make it work. One or two of them they'll have to see Fish for.").

Each night would start the same: first the four older members of the band took their positions, then the new singer arrived from the back of the stage in time to deliver the first line of opening number, "A ragged man came shuffling through…" Explained H, "That was deliberate to let the band say hello, to be welcomed back by their audience before I showed up." It was only when he walked out at Besançon that he fully appreciated the nature of what he had taken on. "Nothing really prepared me for singing with Marillion," he recalled at the time. "Steve wasn't aware of the sort of audience we had," agreed Mark Kelly. "He had never seen the band, he had only heard the albums." As the song built, so did Steve's confidence: when he thanked the fans half way through the gig, the roar of the crowd convinced all concerned that he was the man for the job.

Four days later, when the band played the Rolling Stone in Milan, it was H's unexpected pleasure to bump into old chum Dave Gregory from XTC. Dave was working with an Italian singer-songwriter named Alice (as had been ex-Japan keyboard player and sound-smith, Richard Barbieri). Recalls Dave, "I'd just checked into my hotel room when there was a knock on the door - who should be standing there with a grin from ear to ear but the esteemed Mr H, now a fully-fledged member of Marillion!" The evening was memorable to Dave for all the wrong reasons – "I'd agreed to meet Steve and the Marillos for an after-hours bevvy in the bar, and in a rare and rash moment of generosity, I stood the whole band a round of drinks, only to find that I didn't have enough spondulicks to pay for the round. The bar staff refused to charge it to my room, and it became obvious they were on the take. I mean, thirty quid for six drinks, in 1989! I emptied my pockets, and the band made up the rest; I was so ashamed." Fortunately, the incident did little to tarnish his reputation!

127

The tour rolled on like a wave, with Steve winning fans over as he went. "Every night was the same," said H. "I'd wander out onto the stage to luke-warm applause and by about the fourth or fifth song you'd feel this kind of wave of relief going through the crowd. I was conscious that they didn't want me to ruin their favourite band, but I never had to face an ugly or malevolent crowd, ever." Riding an adrenalin high, he climbed speaker stacks and balanced precariously on top, and could do karate kicks with the best of 'em. "I did that stuff to generate a vibe," chuckles Steve. "The tour managers used to get cross - it always used to look more precarious than it was. Having said that, looking back I don't know how I didn't fall off." Recalls Paul Lewis, "It was fraught – off stage there was Steve, a nice polite chap, and on stage he was an absolute maniac with no regard for personal safety."

So, what did the fans think? Lucy Jordache, who attended the London Astoria gig on November 5 , remembers the palpable tension. "I stood on the balcony watching, with my arms crossed, thinking *Come on, then...* the notes started for 'Script For A Jester's Tear', and by half-way through the whole audience was on his side. For me it was two for the price of one - I was still following Fish, and I had Marillion with H as well." The gig at the Barrowlands in Glasgow was attended by old-timer Paul Hughes: "From the moment H came on stage the crowd was behind him, and there was a real magical feeling of rebirth in the room. I went home with my confidence renewed." H even had the confidence to "perform a snippet of 'Margaret' during 'Market Square Heroes'," noted Shaun Ryan. "The Scottish contingent went crazy. In between songs the crowd chanted 'Geezabun!' and 'Stevie, Stevie!' It was one big party." The Barrowlands gig was nearly attended by ol' Geezabun himself. "I was interested to see the new band playing the old numbers, and watching Marillion from the audience perspective," Fish wrote. Fish arranged with the crew to sneak in "after the lights went down" at the show, but Paul Lewis got wind of events and called Fish to suggest his non-attendance. Comments Paul, "This was not because of the bad feeling between the band and Fish but the fact that his presence would have disrupted the performance, don't forget he is 6ft, 6ins and cannot stand to one side and not be noticed." Despite feeling a little peeved, Fish decided not to turn up after all.

'Uninvited Guest' was released as a single on November 27. The initial plan was to ask John Cooper Clarke to narrate the lyrics on the 12-inch version, but there wasn't enough time. 'Uninvited Guest' included a none-too-subtle reference to the previous singer. "It was originally eighteen-stone first footer," says Mark, "but Steve Rothery said he thought it was a bit much." Ironically, the one song that looked clearly to be written about someone was a complete accident. "'Berlin' looks like it's written about Fish's wife Tammi, but John Helmer wrote those lyrics, it's a total coincidence," says Mark. Clearly, the sensitivity dials were turned high, however well the tour was going.

The tour jalopy traversed continental Europe before heading for a lightning visit to the USA: two dates, one on each coast. The reception was equally good across the pond. "Upon hearing *Seasons End*, I was devastated and actually didn't listen to it for weeks. When I reluctantly went to the concert at Park West on that tour, I was astounded at the new songs and wondered what I was missing," says US fan Dan Sherman. "I was impressed that Steve had the guts to tackle old songs, especially 'Script'. I thought people would throw stuff at him but he sang it with such love and admiration that I believe he earned great respect." Many new fans were picked up along the way, including Karin Breiter. "I had broken up with my boyfriend; he was in a band that covered a few Marillion songs. I wanted him back so I bought us tickets," explains Karin. "He ended up not going, but I dragged along a friend who had never heard of them. I met the band after the show and thought they were a great bunch of guys so I went to see them the following weekend. Two weeks later I drove to Canada to see them again." For new fans of course, Fish's departure was irrelevant. "I didn't have anything to compare H's stage performance to - I thought he was very energetic and fun."

One moment captures all that was right about Steve Hogarth joining Marillion. For the band's December dates back in the UK, he suggested performing the Christmas carol 'O Come, Emmanuel', singing a capella. One onlooker, at the December 13 performance at the Royal Court Theatre in Liverpool, was fan Alan Hewitt: "Steve came to the front of the stage and proceeded to sing the carol totally unaccompanied until the now familiar strains of 'Season's End' began. The hairs stood up on my neck and I was absolutely awestruck. The rest of the gig passed in a blur for me but one thing was for sure: my membership of the Marillion family was guaranteed. It was one of those magical moments that sadly don't happen often at gigs these days." H wasn't a Fish clone, he wasn't even 'just another singer'. Here was a man who could hold an audience in the palm of his hand, in his own way.

RIO TEARS FOR SALE

Marillion broke for Christmas at the Hammersmith Odeon on December 18, the band's twenty-first time at the venue (for which each band member received a plaque) and Steve H's first (he was given a plaque as well!). After a short break Marillion headed back across the Atlantic - this time aiming south: on January 27 they played to an 80,000 crowd at the Hollywood Rock Festival at the Sambadromo stadium, Rio de Janeiro. It was H's biggest ever performance. "They weren't just there for us, we headlined with Bon Jovi, but it was still quite something," he commented. Indeed - Steve joined the crowds at the Sambadromo the night before to watch Tears For Fears, but didn't expect to be recognised. "There was a flash of light and someone was pointing a microphone at me asking, 'What do you think of Brazil?' And I said, 'Well, it's great!' And they asked, 'What do you think of the women?' And I said, 'Well, they're gorgeous. To die for.' The following day I was on the six o'clock news, dancing around and telling this guy how beautiful the women are. They made me incredibly famous in three days flat." Steve made the front pages of the papers, including a half-page, full colour cover shot in national daily, *O Globo* - arms stretched out Christ-like with Copacabana beach behind him. No wallflower, our Steve.

With appropriate timing, 'Easter' was released as a single in March 1990, its accompanying video recorded at The Giant's Causeway on the coast of Northern Ireland, which had been an inspiration for the song. It featured band members balancing precariously on the rocks - recalls Paul Lewis, "Several times a large wave would be seen bearing down and the entire crew would run for cover." More live dates ensued, on both sides of the Atlantic again: indeed, Marillion spent the best part of a year touring. Recalls Mark, "We played 110 shows around the world, and not once did we get a bad reception from anybody." Support in the UK was from the aptly named Cry No More, an irreverent duo that served as much as a warm-up show as a support act. "We were fed up of having dodgy progressive rock bands and dodgy pub bands," says Pete, "They were totally different." Supporting the band in Europe was Sylvain Gouvernaire's band, Arrakeen. "It was very exciting for us. Marillion was one of our main influences at the time," says Sylvain. "In Lille, Steve Rothery came on stage for one of our songs 'Folle Marie', and played the final guitar solo with me. That was a great moment!"

Travelling the world as a new line-up was a very different experience than previously. Comments Pendragon's Peter Gee, who played one date in support, "The appearance of the band on stage changed from being Fish up front with a band behind him, to being five equal guys on stage, all working on presentation together." Management was impacted as well. "I had to change my whole style of management," comments John Arnison. "While Pete and Ian stepped back, Mark, Steve and H all played a part." The touring tales were told as a video, entitled *From Stoke Row to Ipanema*: it wasn't the best produced *(Kerrang!* called it "worthy but stodgy"), nor was it of the highest quality, but it quickly sold out.

On one of the last nights of the tour, on December 20 1990 at the Junction Ten in Walsall, an overzealous fan handed Steve Hogarth his wife's brassiere. "I didn't quite know what to do with that," said Steve, but there could be no doubt that he had been accepted into the fold. Steve was no longer the new boy. From now on Marillion were a complete band again.

SEASONS END

Marillion's first album with the new singer had to work. Although press interviews at the time gave the impression the band weren't worried about finding someone to replace Fish, there must nevertheless have been considerable tension as the album was released. So, how does Hogarth compare?

The honest truth is that Hogarth doesn't compare; he contrasts. Where Fish could be bitter and twisted, Hogarth is more wistfully optimistic as illustrated by the two eras' comments on the Irish Troubles: Fish with the barbed anguish of 'Forgotten Sons', Hogarth with the plaintive lament, 'Easter'. In general terms, Fish is Lennon using horizontal tones - dissonant and harmonic, keeping close to the cadences of speech - to Hogarth's McCartney with vertical tones - consonant and melodic, the latter's musical mind always creating ways for his words to swoop and soar.

Lyrically, the album covers a broad palette of issues - climate change, wrongful imprisonment, the Irish Troubles and the Iron Curtain - but "it's more of a humanitarian thing, than a political thing," argued Pete to the *Melody Maker*. It's interesting how much of this album is now anachronistic. The Wall has fallen, it has snowed again (though the essential concern was well-placed) and Ireland is at peace. Upbeat rocker 'Hooks in You' still splits the fans, though.

The album's opener, 'The King Of Sunset Town' begins with a whisper of bubbling keyboards, punctuated by smoky clouds of atmosphere. Pete's bass offers glimpses of something approaching through the mist before Ian starts to raise the tension with some nifty cymbal work. Just as it gets all too much, Steve Rothery cuts loose with an exuberant, uplifting solo, and Ian beats his drums to shiny pieces, before coming back to Earth for the entrance of Steve Hogarth. After a soulful verse, Hogarth launches into his first chorus and by God, the man reaches the outer stratosphere!

As a dissection of the Tiananmen Square massacre, the song's obliqueness reveals its dual lyrical authorship - outside writer John Helmer provided the original lyric, inspired by G.K. Chesterton. Musically not a million miles from traditional Marillion territory, the listener is under no illusions as to the power of the newcomer's talents, and there's a palpable sense that we can rest easy as it draws to a close. It's done its work - it's still the band we loved, and the new boy sure can cut it!

'Easter' starts out like a distant relative of the 'Skye Boat Song', folky and melancholy. Steve Hogarth paints vignettes of fortitude, lyrical images of the Irish people who carried on in the face of the violence that, while unwanted by most, pervaded their society. The chorus is a plaintive, though perhaps simplistic, plea for peace. Steve Rothery delivers a heartbreakingly beautiful solo, before the song changes direction and provides the beginnings of an answer. Based on W. B. Yeats' *Easter 1916*, Hogarth argues passionately against the violence, telling us it only harms one's own, and it's time to find a different way.

After such a song, 'The Uninvited Guest', both musically and lyrically seems like light relief, being a cod-gothic tale of the consequences of selfish behaviour. In fact, Helmer's lyric, far from being Hammer Horror, is a cautionary tale about living with the HIV virus, not that you might guess without being told. Musically it was designed as a sing-along rocker for the audience, and as such works perfectly.

The title track tells of the destruction of the ozone layer, reflecting on the implications of our arrogance as we poison our planet. The lyrics were inspired when John Helmer's wife mentioned the morning's headlines, "It will never snow again in England. Never Ever." The line gave Helmer the link he needed between writing a lyric about the ozone layer and making it relevant: "I thought about the year before, when I went for a sleigh ride with some mates, and I thought that will never be repeated." The band play with a restraint that almost seems to plead for common sense, as Hogarth imagines looking out over a barren planet and apologising to his children. The song slows for a moment and then we hear signs of something stirring and building. Is it the emergence of a common conscience?

'Holloway Girl' shines a light on the treatment of mentally ill people caught in the prison system. Specifically, it addresses the case of Judith Ward, imprisoned as an IRA bomber, despite overwhelming evidence of her innocence, largely to placate a hysterical public. While in no way blind to the reality of the situation, the song is nevertheless one of optimism that such injustices will be righted.

In contrast to its predecessor, 'Berlin' sees the band at their most atavistic as they watch a man machine-gunned to death in the no man's land between East and West, at the Berlin Wall. In his hand, the man clutches a picture of a girl

- a symbol of his desire to reach the West. As the blank-faced soldiers swing their guns around to cut him down, the players whip up a maelstrom of vicious anger. Unable to fathom how the death can be worth anything, Rothery's guitar rips nastily against the military brutality of Mosley's pounding drums and Trewavas's unstoppable, throbbing bass. In the coda, we learn that the girl who made a man risk and lose his life is a prostitute, living a life of deprivation of her own. No lessons here, no answers, just senseless brutality.

'After Me' is a simple paean to love, Steve Hogarth's dedication to a wife who understands his urgent, impatient and insatiable need to do his music. In it, he tells us that anything he manages to create is a reflection of the love she has given him in the first place. The exhilaration of the play-out seems to be in direct recognition of this fact.

The album's first single, 'Hooks In You,' is an atypical rocker, musically and narratively simple. It split the fans upon its release, but the fact that it is so different is perhaps what made it so enticing to release in the first place - 'You're not getting Fish; we're different.' Lyrically, the song is about a girl who captivates and emotionally ensnares men, and the effect that has upon them.

The closing track, 'The Space', is dominated by Mark Kelly's Nyman-esque keyboard lines. Beginning with a montage of images from Hogarth's life, we see how people alternate between aggressor and victim. The image of the tram crashing into the car was one that Hogarth had seen for real in Amsterdam, and he mused: "I have occasionally been the tram. And I have often been the car." In a heartfelt plea, the end section reminds us that all of us feel the same urges and desires and that we're all so very fragile.

The album artwork presents a bridge between past and future. Although Wilkinson's expressive airbrushing no longer graces the covers, there are elements of his work - a feather, a chameleon, the belled cap and the clown from *Fugazi*. All have been re-contextualised in panels featuring the Aristotelian elements - Fire, Earth, Water and Wind. The 'Mars bar' logo remains as well. A grey sea rages in the background, and icons depict the movement of celestial bodies and snowflakes, further reinforcing the idea of nature. Finally, the apostrophe-free title reminds us that seasons do indeed come to an end. Perhaps we're left to work out for ourselves that each is followed by another one..?

8

The Eden Project

Thrilled by their success, the Marillos started planning the next album as soon as the *Seasons End* tour was over. They eagerly returned to Brighton, which had been the backdrop for so much inspiration - this time to Stanbridge Farm, another residential rehearsal studio. Once there, however, the band came down to earth with a bump. The honeymoon period was long since over, and the fivesome had to start working together from scratch, something they had never done before. This time the band was starting as a unit, and all involved were to discover that success would not always be as smooth as the previous album had suggested. "*Seasons End* was easy, as we had a huge stockpile of material," says Rothers. Not so for this album, but it didn't lessen EMI's barely disguised commercial demands. "We were under a lot of pressure for singles," remembers Ian.

Meanwhile John Arnison had been getting his own act together, signing up with Tony Smith's management company, Hit And Run. "I had to persuade the band," he remarks, recalling his optimistic aspirations for the group. Tony came to Stanbridge Farm in his Aston Martin to assist, hinting he would get Marillion's next album onto the Atlantic label if they joined the firm, as well as dangling the carrot of touring with Hit And Run's flagship, Genesis. Neither happened: the only real consequence was that John could no longer give the band all of his attention. Recalls H: "No longer were our destinies intertwined, we kind of lost him as a manager from then - he was given other things to manage."

This was going to be no holiday, Eden or otherwise.

DOWN ON THE FARM

While the Stanbridge Farm sessions were never going to be easy, nobody expected quite how much effort was still required for the band to operate as a unit. "It was a bit like *Fugazi* all over again, we had to work out how to work together," says Pete. "Although we didn't want Fish, we would have been quite happy to write the same kind of music and we didn't really want Steve H to mess with it. We'd got into the habit of working as a four-piece, so he probably felt some of the same frustrations that Fish had felt." Mark puts it more bluntly, "We'd gone from being, 'Oh no - we'll do it your way,' to being, 'Oh fucking hell - can't we do it my way?'"

What was more, the old-timers had their suspicions confirmed - that Marillion's preferred approach to writing did not sit well with the new singer. Whereas most of the band were happy to jam and capture the occasional idea, the goal-driven three-minute boy grew bored with the long sessions. Eventually the stress became too much for the hapless singer. "I got ill with it," he explains, "I went to bed for a week." In fact Steve took two weeks out, leaving the band to stew. "I thought, there's a bit of a problem here," says Pete, "I just hoped we could work it out. He was frustrated at the speed we worked, but he was right to be." In an ironic turnaround, when Steve H emerged, it was with the completed lyrics, piano and voice melodies for the highly un-poppy 'The Party'. "I kind of had it during the writing of *Seasons End*, but I didn't have the confidence to give it to them," says H. Meanwhile, the rest of the band had written the deeply mainstream 'Holidays In Eden' title track.

The sessions weren't all dark and gloomy – various high-jinks earned Mark the nickname 'Mad Jack' based on two attributes - his reputation (of "being absolutely off his head") and the *Blackadder* quote "He's madder than Mad Jack MacMad, winner of last year's Mr Mad contest." As the Stanbridge writing sessions came to a close, a rebalanced Marillion realised they had formulated a more inclusive writing approach. Explained Steve Hogarth, "There are elements of me doing what I do and them doing what they do on the new album. It took us the whole of the time recording the album to come to that conclusion." John Helmer also contributed, but not as much as on *Seasons End*. "I wasn't available at the time the band could have used some help," he recalled. In total, the writing process for *Holidays In Eden* had taken eight months. "The sun was shining when we got there and when we left it was snowing," says Steve H.

By January 1991 the quintet emerged, united once more and clutching what they felt was a good 30 hours of song material. From a business perspective, Marillion recognised that their album sales had taken a battering with the departure of Fish. As a couple of songs had the feel of potential singles, the boys looked to Chris Kimsey, producer of both *Misplaced Childhood* and *Clutching At Straws* to help them record a potential hit. While Chris was in favour, the timings were not. First the album wasn't sufficiently ready for Chris in his window of opportunity in January. "I said to them, you haven't got enough songs," says Chris, suggesting another slot following the production of the live Rolling Stones album *Flash Point*. Then, by the time the band were ready for recording, Chris was not. "He said he'd be a couple of weeks," commented Mark in an interview with Mick Wall.

Following a number of delays, Steve H suggested, "'Ring him up and tell him to either shit or get off the pot.' So I phoned him up and came back to the rest of them and said, 'Well he got off the pot!'" He did indeed: shortly after, he went to Scotland to help Fish with his second solo album! Wanting to increase the chart-friendliness of Marillion's sound, Nick Gatfield, head of A&R

for EMI, proposed producer Chris Neil, who had achieved chart success for characters such as Mike Rutherford (with Mike and The Mechanics) and Sheena Easton. "EMI brought me in to ensure a single and to help Marillion produce more contemporary sounds," says Chris, who had first experienced Marillion in Paris back in 1983. "I was in Paris with Sheena to record a load of B-sides," says Chris, "We went out one evening to this weird club. Fish came up and pointed at me, he said, 'I know you!'" Chris had already been suggested for *Seasons End*, but the band had decided against him at the time. Commented Steve Hogarth to Mick Wall, "What with me just joining the band, wheeling someone like Chris in at that stage might be too much." With everybody hungry for a hit and time getting shorter, such qualms were put to one side this time around.

Following rehearsals at Nomis Studios, the band returned to Hook End Manor to record the new album. The studios were not nearly as much fun as before, recalls Steve Rothery, "There was a different studio manager, funnily enough the guy who recorded the demos for *Clutching At Straws* at Bray Studios. The studio was a bit like Stalag 17, a shame really." Agrees Ian, "There was a different vibe then - but it was snowing!" Chris was under no illusion of why he had been selected, but was also conscious of the sensitivities of the band - and their fans. "Chris promised not to lighten up the sound and turn us into Mike and The Mechanics," recalls H. Mark concurs, "When we first met him he said, 'I know your music better than you lot do. I wouldn't mess it up because my son [who was a Marillion fan] would hate me!'"

In 1990 Marillion recorded 'Sailing', a charity record with Steve Hackett, a cover of the Sutherland Brothers' song made famous by Rod Stewart. The song appeared on Rock Against Repatriation, and it's the only time that Steve Hogarth and Fish have sung on the same recording - although neither knew the other was there!

As soon as Chris arrived he set about introducing the band to some alien concepts, such as how to write a song. Says Steve H, "Chris Neil was good at generating a light-hearted atmosphere and he's got a pop instinct that homes in on the hooks like a laser beam. He's got a great talent for knowing what will move the masses." Agrees Pete, "We learned lots about song construction from Chris. In the past we'd spend a lot of time overdubbing but he didn't. He'd say, 'I want to hear the vocal, and let's have a hook - that guitar.'" Chris also introduced more technology into the picture. "I brought electronics in tentatively. I didn't want things to go too synthetic," says Chris. It was the early days of sequencing, which Mark put to good effect on 'Splintering Heart'; Ian also became acquainted with the joys of electronic drum pads.

Things went as well as could be expected: the band's occasional fears (such as the speed of recording - it took an unprecedented ten weeks from Chris's arrival to get to mixing) were countered by the prospect of commercial success. The remainder of the process was unnervingly smooth, marred only by the unexpected appearance of Janice Long, Michaela Strachan and Keith Chegwin at Westside Studios, who were recording an edition of TV show *Go Getters*, in which the presenters have to perform three tasks in a 24-hour period, one being to perform in a recording session.

The resulting album was unabashedly commercial, with only a couple of songs reaching past the six-minute mark. Even the cover suggested shrugging off any vestiges of the past - no jesters or magpies were to be seen. "I wanted to go back to illustration," says Bill Smith. "I can't remember why but we went for cave-like drawings, with simplistic shapes and colours." Even the logo was not immune, as the band worked with Carl Glover on new designs. "We had loads of ideas," recalls Carl.

WAITING TO HAPPEN

Having decided to go commercial, the band were keen to see the rewards, hoping for as many as six potential singles: 'Cover My Eyes', 'No One Can', 'Dry Land', 'Waiting To Happen' and 'Holidays In Eden'. Laughed Steve H to Mick Wall, "It's like *Thriller* or something." After some debate, 'Cover My Eyes' was planned as the first, released on May 28 and reaching No. 34 during its fortnight stay in the UK charts.

When the album was released on June 24 1991, there was no dispute about what it was trying to achieve. "Unashamedly commercial, it is still better than anything you'll hear on the radio," said one review. Not everybody was so polite: more conservative sections of the fan community found their suspicions confirmed. Writes fan Michael Huang, "Some prog fans assumed that Marillion had gone the way of Phil Collins-led Genesis and sold out to pop." A fan letter from W. Cox to *The Web* fanzine summed up the feelings of many, "You got big by writing those early songs, now you're forgetting those who made you famous. What about a full Marillion album next time?" Comments fan Jeff Pelletier, "The US version opened with two quite poppy songs in 'Cover My Eyes' and 'No One Can'. My initial negative reaction to these songs kept me from appreciating a majestic track like 'Splintering Heart' until years later." Max Rael adds, "I attended quite a few dates on the tour, but after the tour was over I found I didn't ever play the album, so that was that."

Some fans were more upbeat however, as illustrated by another letter to *The Web*. "It is now my considered belief that you are writing the finest music of your careers. Keep up the good work!" wrote Stuart Wright. Another fan, Matthew Hammond responded in the next issue, "*Holidays In Eden* is a 100% Marillion album - 101% even!" So it wasn't all bad. Neither was it the commercial success that had been hoped for, however. 'No One Can' was released on July 22, and like its predecessor slipped into the top forty for a few weeks before dropping off the radar. Unfortunately for Marillion, the band's label had decided to promote Vanilla Ice (with 'Rollin' In My 5.0', which didn't fare much better) instead. "We were losing the confidence of EMI," remarks Steve R.

As confidence waned, so did the chances of success. 'Dry Land' was released on September 23, reaching a similar position. Unfortunately, though EMI may have cracked the commercial whip, *Thriller* this album was not. As chart success refused to materialise, the band members took an unspoken vow about their artistic integrity. Chris Neil's involvement was in part due to external pressure from EMI to create a more commercial album. As the next album would prove, no record label would ever again exert such a hold over the band, artistic or otherwise.

On July 13, Marillion headlined at the Cumbria Rock Festival as a precursor to the 'real' tour - this did not start until September, as the band had kept August free for Ian. "His wife, Wanda, was having a baby and we didn't want to travel too far afield," recalls Mark. As the tour kicked off, some dates bore the brunt of fans' disappointment. Recalls the *Dutch Progressive Rock Page*, "During a concert in Ahoy in Holland a substantial part of the audience booed when Steve Hogarth announced they would be playing quite a lot from the new album." There were high points - such as the hilarity caused by H's sometimes-unsuccessful stage antics. On October 11, Marillion played The Saga in Copenhagen, which has a castellated stage. Half way through the show, H fell headfirst into a hole. "I climbed back up, then launched myself straight off the other side to make it look on purpose," he grins. Also worthy of mention are events following a gig ten days later in Brussels, the last night before a two-week break. The lead guitar in support band The Violet Hour was a bit the worse for wear at the after-show party, recalls Steve H, "They gaffer-taped him to a chair, then they carried him to a lift and down twelve floors, out of the hotel and over to the middle of a dual carriageway."

September 22 1991 at the Edinburgh Playhouse finally provided Fish with an opportunity to see the new line-up. Fish (and his minder, he'd had one since the *Clutching* tour) met Steve in the dressing room after the gig, just as the latter was coming out of the shower. H recounts, "I turned around and there was just me and him and his minder. I was severely outnumbered physically, and I was half-naked. You never feel at your most confident when you're not dressed. But it was alright and we had a chat."

Despite nearly deciding not to cross the pond, the band eventually consented and conducted an extensive tour of the US, starting on March 16 at Allentown, Philadelphia. It was here that the band were first introduced to a 'guitar tech' known as John Wesley. "US immigration was being tricky about bringing crew, so we started to use local people," says Mark. One evening, Wes and the band went for a meal at a place where live music was playing. After a few beers, he got up on stage (as you do) for a jam, and launched into a Led Zep-style solo. When he returned, the boys said to him, "You're not really a guitar tech are you?" Just three days into the tour, the band agreed with the production manager that it was worth giving Wes a shot at the support slot. "And that was it for seven tours!" laughs Wes. Explains Mark Kelly, "He was someone we liked, the changeover was convenient and he was guitar tech as well." He was also a good sport, finding himself quite regularly the butt of practical jokes, including regular 'heckle checks' rather than sound checks. Wes was pelted with grapes by the stage hands throughout his last performance in Copenhagen. Thinking it was over, he was then covered in custard!

Despite vehement denials at the time, the band admit to ending up with a poppier sound than they were comfortable with. Comments Rothers, "I don't particularly like *Holidays In Eden*. Chris took all the rough edges off the album - that would be OK for a single but it blanded it out too much for my liking." Agrees Mark, "Though not in any way bad, the end result was that for certain songs, Chris maybe wasn't the best choice." In particular, it is unlikely that 'Cover My Eyes', 'Dry Land' and 'Waiting To Happen' would have made it onto the release. "I think we were his acid test," says Steve H. "It was a test that cost a lot of money and, insomuch as we never had a hit, it failed." Chris agrees that it was perhaps a mistake to give Marillion the pop edge that had worked so well for Genesis. "In hindsight, Marillion was not a pop band. Mike's writing and Phil Collins's voice helped Genesis make the transition, but Marillion did not have the same pop sensibilities."

Holidays In Eden might not have been an artistic success, but it satisfied the bean counters, reaching number 7 in the album charts and staying in the top 40 for 7 weeks. Unfortunately, the band had expected much more, and the commercial compromises had been thrown back in their faces. "They had been convinced that it was going to be huge and that the old guard would flock back in droves, but it didn't work," comments the ever-sanguine John Arnison. "But just think - if they'd had a hit with 'Holidays In Eden', they wouldn't have made *Brave*." Indeed.

HOLIDAYS IN EDEN

Whereas *Seasons End* was a bridge between old and new, *Holidays In Eden*, with more straightforward songs than we were used to, suggested a departure from the band's established style. Unhappy that *Holidays* might be the start of a journey into poppier waters, one part of the fan base bemoaned the lack of prog and left (shame they didn't stick around!). That said, Steve Hogarth's comment, "If 'Splintering Heart' and 'The Party' are pop songs, I'll eat my pink telecaster," is more than fair.

A throbbing, mechanised rhythm opens 'Splintering Heart', before a rejuvenated Hogarth starts weaving his magic. A girl struggles to cope with her emotional pain, the unfamiliar sensations causing her all sorts of anguish and distress. The singer knows how she feels all too well but it's 'not as much as this..!' As a snare cracks, your spine snaps straight, your head flying back as your heart explodes through your ribcage as the band pour every ounce of pain into a tormented scream, every little hurt you've ever suffered comes back to haunt you and the only way to cope is to harden up, and bury your emotions so deep nothing can touch them.

The lead single from *Holidays*, 'Cover My Eyes (Pain And Heaven)' ruminates on 'that woman'. The one that every man has seen, the one who blows you away so absolutely utterly, she could crush you with a mere glance. Dangerous isn't the half of it. Steve Hogarth commented that the various images were stolen "from movies, art, literature and pop videos. See if you can spot David Niven." An anthemic, crowd-pleasing singalong par excellence.

'The Party' is an affecting tale of innocence lost, the band conjuring a sense of trepidation and expectation as a young girl goes nervously to her first party. Beguiled by the new things she sees and experiences - drink, drugs and the coupling up - she allows herself to be seduced in a seemingly magical garden. Steve Rothery's unusually phrased solo evokes the sense of wonder and strangeness as her first toke on a joint takes hold. These scenes were written after H's first magic mushroom experience, as he watched the moonlight 'dripping in the trees like the juice of some unearthly tropical fruit.' And in the morning, the comedown; was losing her virginity love? No... It was just a party.

'No One Can' sees the band at their most commercial, with Steve H narrating a tale about the difficulties of being separated from the people you love, commenting that the distance doesn't matter, 'It's okay, you're here with me.' The band always considered it a travesty that it wasn't a hit. Much of the fan base considered it a travesty that it was on the album in the first place!

The title track starts with bird song, followed by the roar of a jet overhead as the band whisk us off to foreign shores. While we reinvent ourselves, John Helmer's lyric reflects on the fact that one day we'll have to return, and our new personas won't impress our old friends. In the sleeve notes to the remaster, Steve Hogarth comments, "We could have made it a lot wilder musically, to reflect the primitive connotations in the lyric."

'Dry Land' first appeared on an album by How We Live, Steve Hogarth's pre-Marillion band. Producer Chris Neil suggested the band try it out, and against their instincts they did. It's a song about trying to get past someone's defences and finding they've built them too high. While the song is basically the same as the How We Live version, this is more dynamic, and most fans agree that Steve Rothery's solo is superior to the original.

'Waiting To Happen' seems to start in a similarly reflective mood to 'Dry Land', but all this is just a prelude, building tension through the middle eight to the bursting exuberance of the chorus. A paean to the magic found in love that transcends the greyness of ordinary life, the song contains one of Hogarth's most enduring and touching images; that of memorising your partner's face, and it becoming, 'a jigsaw of an angel I can do when I feel low.'

'This Town' is the first instalment in a cinematic suite, describing the corruption of a young couple moving to the big city to chase their dreams, losing not only each other but their very humanity in the process. Steve Rothery's chugging guitar conjures the confusion and excitement of someone caught in the crowds and lights of the city. Like the girl in the title track, half of the partnership embraces the new surroundings. The other, however, shrinks.

'The Rake's Progress' is a bridging piece which asks, 'What do you do when your roots have dissolved and broken down?' The song provides the answers with a tension-filled passage of tom rolls, bass pulses and shimmering, dreamlike, echoing keyboards. It charts the transition of the man as he becomes cynical and manipulative. Terrifyingly, as he emerges, as if from a cocoon, the music lifts... and we realise he's finding this experience liberating...

In the final section, '100 Nights', our anti-hero walks out as master of his world, able to bend anyone or anything to his will. We realise that his satisfaction is gained through manipulation and destruction of anything of beauty or value - he delights in destroying a marriage. The coda, a reprise of the chorus from

'This Town' was conceived by Steve Hogarth as a Greek chorus, "All the people on the escalators at Waterloo Station, mumbling the mantra together."

Sarah Ball's cover art portrays Eden as a study in blue. The animals, seen flocking to the Tree of Knowledge, are reminiscent of the cave art found in Lascaux in France. With its highly impressionistic feel, the cover represents the H-era band's first album cover wholly divorced from the work of Mark Wilkinson, as well as being the last to be developed without the aid of computers.

9

Brave, Brave World

In early 1992, to appease the fans and celebrate the band's tenth anniversary with EMI, the compilation album *A Singles Collection* was released. It included six tracks from the Fish era and six from the Hogarth era (hence its UK title *Six Of One, Half A Dozen Of The Other* - according to Mark, "The US company said people wouldn't get it."), and it also included two bonus tracks - a cover of 'Sympathy' and a new track called 'I Will Walk On Water'. The disc achieved an entry in *Kerrang!'s* 20 best albums of 1992 - not bad for a compilation! 'Sympathy' was released as a single following a sold-out concert on September 5 at Wembley Arena, celebrating Marillion's decade with EMI. "I wanted to make an event of it," explains John Arnison. "It was also trying to get the old fans back. We sold 7,200 tickets - the maximum capacity is eleven thousand, but it can be arranged to hold 6,000 or 7,500." The gig was memorable, particularly for Steve H who continued his theme of falling off the stage. "I had to go round security to get back on, still singing," laughs Steve.

'Sympathy', fared reasonably well, reaching No.17 - the first time the band had been inside the top 20 since 'Incommunicado'. Still, it was not the great relaunch: almost as a litmus test, 'No One Can' was reissued as a follow-up single in July. At No.26, it fared better than the first time around but it was no giant-killer. On the upside, the band's firm foundation of fans was as strong as ever. Friday May 1 1992 was the tenth anniversary of The Web, celebrated with a 'party' at The Borderline Club in London attended by The Low Fat Yoghurts. Mark played host to an auction of Marillion memorabilia, including guitars from Steve R and Pete, Fish's trousers and a number of items of clothing from other band members, raising a total of £1,560 for Andy Field's family. "The auctioneer and MC was of 'humorous but sarcastic banter'," wrote a fan. "Did he start out as a stand-up comedian by any chance?"

Meanwhile, there was an album to make. Whatever the concerns inside the band, commercialism rocked as far as EMI was concerned. The record label took delight in seeing the next album as "A rough and ready, garage-y album, fresh-sounding and edgy." Meanwhile, however, many fans were wringing their hands in despair at their icons, seemingly forsaking their art for mammon. Two years would pass before the release of *Brave*, an album that turned these opinions on their heads.

STARING OUT OVER THE BRIDGE

It was time for a fresh start, in a fresh location. For convenience as well as cost, the band rented a couple of units on an industrial park close to Aylesbury and kitted the place out as a rehearsal and recording studio – which quickly became known for numerous, nefarious reasons as The Racket Club. Ironically, just as they got a place of their own, Ian moved to Florida due to his wife's asthma. "I was commuting," he explains. "It was only an eight-hour flight to Orlando, the boys seemed to think I could come over and work in blocks." The writing sessions began in November, with Ian coming over for a few weeks at a time and staying at his flat in Aylesbury (he nicknamed it "cell-block" because it was so small) - at least, that was the plan.

Some music and arrangements (such as a riff from Steve Rothery, which would make up part of 'Hard As Love') already existed and John Helmer had proposed some lyrical ideas about a girl in crisis. A few weeks into the writing, Steve Hogarth suggested that these ideas be married to a police announcement he had heard a few years previously, on GWR Radio in Bristol. "The police had picked up a young woman wandering on the Severn Bridge who refused - or was unable - to speak to them," he recalled. H's suggestion that the album be linked "to a series of snapshots about her life" was welcomed by the rest of the band. Notes Rothers, "It seemed to lend a meaning to the half-finished ideas we had." The downside was that the band were once again considering a concept album. Nearly ten years had elapsed since *Misplaced Childhood*, and the idea was more unfashionable than ever. Given the fashion-conscious (and subsequently disappointing) *Holidays In Eden*, this counter-intuitive factor captured the mood of the band. "Suited us just fine," laughs H. Concurs Rothers, "We felt we could do anything we liked!"

In January of 1993, EMI's A&R man Nick Mander suggested Dave Meegan as producer, a familiar face due to his involvement in *Fugazi*. "My wife was working for EMI at the time so she knew Nick," remarks Dave. "He wasn't aware that I'd worked on *Fugazi* but was pleased, - it made it easier to convince the band." Nick's suggestion was willingly accepted. "We loved the vitality in Dave's work and felt he could bring a different dimension to the band," recalled Rothers. For his part, Dave initially felt he was a strange choice for the project. "Up to then my productions were almost exclusively indie style," says Dave. In fact, that was exactly what EMI had in mind, taking the band further from its progressive roots. Dave received strict instructions from Nick to record the album in as a short a time as possible.

Marillion played Dave what they had done so far and he found that it was good. As Dave recalls, "I listened to a series of early, early sketches, roughly patched together lyrically. The band was trying to tie it together so they could record it and play it live." The lyrical work demonstrated how closely aligned

Helmer and Hogarth had become. "The right hand really knew what the left hand was doing," remarked John.

The next challenge was to find a studio, a problem quickly solved when Miles Copeland offered the use of his French pad - Château Marouatte, in the Dordogne. The opportunity had come during the US leg of the *Holidays In Eden* tour, when a chap from IRS Records (which Copeland founded) mentioned the place to Rothers."I mentioned it to John Arnison, who gave Miles a call," he explains. Dave Meegan was delighted - "I love working on location." And what a location it was - an imposing structure on the top of a hill, with house and grounds jammed full of "gothic statues, pillars and other artefacts," according to Rothers."After a few weeks I started to feel like I was in a Stephen King novel!"

The band arrived at the château with a truck full of hardware - perhaps a little too much - "I didn't quite realise how much gear we had," H's diary commented. Dave and Privet set about installing microphones wherever they could, ostensibly to tape atmospheric sounds. It took two days: mics were installed in empty staircases ('to pick up any passing ghosts') and a water-filled cave, used for the splash that completes 'Paper Lies'. "There were even a couple of mics in the fireplace to pick up the crackle of the fire," laughed H. The main banqueting room was set up as the studio, with the mixing desk and other paraphernalia installed in the master bedroom. Amps were situated in various rooms including the wine cellar, the study and the chapel, all linked together with wires running up and down stairwells and according to Pete, "draped like washing lines between neighbouring wings."

As the cabling and equipment transformed the château, the band moved inside their artistic cocoon. The environment provided a creative hotbed to complete the writing sessions and start recording overdubs - the sounds and rhythms that provide the backdrop for the music. Steve Hogarth spent the first few days at the château locked in a room "with a keyboard full of drone sounds" - eventually coming up with the first few bars of 'Brave'. But not before disconcerted glances at such strange behaviour were shared outside the room. It was downhill from there - "It just seemed to fall into place so easily," remarked Dave. The combination of the château and its technology performed their collective magic, as Steve H discovered while he listened to Pete recording the bass for 'Living With The Big Lie'. "From where I'm sitting it sounds like God's own bass sound," Steve remarked.

Steve H spent happy hours with a "Rickenbacker 12-string Tom Petty limited edition beautiful sunburst" guitar, which he had bought in San Jose on the previous tour. "I had to learn to play the guitar really," says H. "Rothers showed me a few basic chord shapes and I spent my spare time at Marouatte fiddling around with it." Meanwhile, there was nothing else to do but relax. "We used to go into town a bit, or we'd drive around and look at the scenery," says Pete. Not quite the same as Berlin in 1985! Meals were cooked in what used to be the servants quarters, ironically by an English couple. Rest assured, the wine did flow!

Time was short - the band had the château for two months, by which time the bulk of the recording was expected to be complete. Such a goal lay outside the reach of the collective - unsurprising, as every take was being recorded, logged and carefully sifted in the evenings by Dave as a potential source of material. As H remarked, "Dave was dedicated to capturing our most inspired moments." While the writing was done and bass section recorded, only one third of the overdubs had been committed to tape by the time the French castle had to be vacated. Unfortunately for Ian, this meant time slowed to a standstill. "I spent four months at home in Florida, waiting for things to finish," he explains. "After a month, I was starting to think there's only so much of sitting by the swimming pool and driving speed boats that I could take, so I gave the lads a call and asked how it was going. They said they hadn't even finished the bass - I was going potty!" Indeed, he got so bored he bought another house and did it up, just for something to do.

At the end of the two months and with some relief (it was a lonely experience, as H commented, "That's the trouble with a castle in the sky,"), the guys headed back to Blighty. Following a "week off" during which the band, Dave and Privet spent time recording sounds such as London tubes and coins being thrown onto pavements, on April 19 the seven made their way to Parr Street studios in Liverpool, managed by old mate Paul Lewis. A sequence of events (kicked off by Wes's arrival as guitar tech which freed Tim Bricusse to take over from Paul as tour manager) led to Paul breaking away from the touring circuit and accepting the role of running Parr Street, also owned by Hit And Run. "We got good rates there," laughs Dave. Assistant engineer was local lad, Mike Hunter. "*Brave* was such a logistical thing, my main job was to make sure all the gear was in the right places," says Mike. "I don't know if we did seven days per week, but Dave can be a bit of a monster worker when he gets going."

Despite everyone's best efforts, Rothers recalls how, after eight weeks in Liverpool with nothing to show, "Nick Mander was starting to have a fit. The band and Dave had decided however that we were in the middle of making a very special album and that it would be ready when it was ready. Fortunately

Nick had little choice but to let events run their course." Nobody was having an easy ride - working evenings and weekends became the norm. "Technology was not on our side," remarks Dave. "This was hard editing with razor blades and sticky tape." One of the obstacles was making the material flow - not only did it have to be in the right order, but key and tempo changes needed to be smooth, often requiring additional pieces of music to tie different song elements together. Band and producer had to always consider the complete album, "A bit like playing a game of chess," remarked Dave at the time. Everything was up for grabs: new sounds were added all the time, including the voice of Cathy, the Japanese receptionist at Parr. H 'found' an Uilleann pipes player called Tony Halligan busking in a doorway in Liverpool, so he went on as well.

One early listener to the near-final album was fan Judith Mitchell. "At the time I was writing for the *Flaming Shroud* fanzine so my brother Andrew and I, plus editor Alex, managed to arrange an interview," she says. "I was very nervous despite meeting the band several times before, but not really in this context. Mark took us to the actual recording booth and we were asked to sit behind the mixing desk, he showed us how the controls worked and put in a tape. He said, 'Listen to this, then we'll do the interview.' We listened, sat in the console chairs with the album blasting out over the PA system. Mind-blowing! Imagine trying to take in all of *Brave* in one listen! Mark returned with a big grin - we were a bit short of words."

Nobody doubted that something entirely new and very special had been produced, but something that was most definitely Marillion. As Dave recalled, "I deliberately tried pointing backwards in the direction of *Fugazi*, and it worked." But did it? The label, the fans and the wider world had yet to discover and, more importantly, to judge the new work.

THE GREAT ESCAPE

By May 1993 the suspense was killing many fans, particularly as the album had originally been touted as having a September release date. It was not to be - September became the completion date, pushing the release back to January the following year. "The labels have peaks during several months of the year for releasing an album. If they miss one they pick another one and that's usually several months later," explained Rothers in a *Web* interview, promising the album would be worth the wait. "It's all enormously exciting and it sounds sensational, I can promise you. It's the most sparkling thing we've ever made!" Paul Craddick and Doug Ott of US band Enchant, who were recording at Parr

Street at the time, had the opportunity to preview the album and the band's own reaction to it. "Being long-time Marillion fans we've seen them, well, almost 'depressed' but it's great to see them so pleased with this one!" Keith Andrews, who was mixing Enchant at the time, was able to sneak a preview. "I was absolutely knocked out by the sheer power, the detail, the expression and the absolute glory of the sound. It's fantastic!"

Things were looking good. August saw final touches added to *Brave* at Sarm West studios, before it was moved to Abbey Road studios for assembly. Finally, at the end of a hugely draining, yet productive thirteen months and at a total cost of £375,000, the album was complete. As far as the band was concerned, the result justified the time and money spent, and Dave's creative involvement and hard work had been of primary importance. "He did a really great job," recalls Mark. Dave was equally complimentary: "It was such a pleasure to sit back and listen to the band create something from nothing, developing purely using that special gift they had of 'inter-band telepathy'."

Despite the pride, the players were just a little nervous about having produced a concept album. Noted Steve Rothery at the time, "The idea is something of a cringe. But we wanted to make something like The Who's *Quadrophenia* - a story set to music." He was later to laugh off the criticism that the band wrote one long song because they couldn't think of 10 short ones. "It's the most natural, extensive and complete album we have ever made," he remarked. Progressive the album might have been, in that it pushed against musical boundaries, but everyone felt its sonic structure and style were a far cry from the fantasy landscapes of '70s prog. "What I call progressive is not anything I've ever worked on," frowns Dave Meegan.

There was one, final complication. With their masterpiece complete, the band had to go before EMI and explain why they hadn't produced a pop album. Writes Steve Hogarth, "I'm very proud of the fact that it was quite a dangerous commercial decision we took to make *Brave*. I wonder if it damaged our career; I think it damaged our relationship with EMI." Despite their concern, the label did accept a number of additional features, including Mark Kelly's idea of specially-cut fourth side of the vinyl album - two grooves, each with a different ending. This solved the issue that the single version of 'The Great Escape' ended differently to the intended album version. "I stole the idea," grins Mark. "There was a Monty Python album called *Matching Tie And Handkerchief*. I thought, *That's good*. Side Four of *Brave* was only twelve minutes long so it fitted quite nicely." For the listener it was random chance that determined whether the girl jumped from the bridge or was 'Made Again'.

There was also a cover to produce: fortunately Bill Smith Studios found the album material painted its own picture. "*Brave* is in the top ten album covers I have ever produced," says Bill Smith. "Out of all the Marillion covers, it was the one that came closest to fulfilling the idea of words, music and images as a complete entity." Concurs Carl Glover, "It was like developing a book cover." The initial idea was of a female form taking the shape of a cross: explains Bill, "EMI and the band were worried, so we looked for a facial representation." Despite being produced on a computer for the first time, an obvious boon, the artwork was stored as nine separate images as the whole picture could not fit on a single hard disk.

Finally, a no-logo decision had to be made. "We wanted to put the name about without it getting in the way of the artwork," comments Carl. The handwriting on the cover was, in fact, a fragment of Anne Frank's original diary, written about July 15 1944. "I didn't want it to be obvious what it was saying, but I liked its form," explains Bill. This was initially unknown to the band, and following its discovery the link was played down for fear of a misleadingly direct association between the experiences of the album's heroine and Anne Frank herself.

Before the album hit the shops, the band went their separate ways to fall back and regroup. "Everyone needed a bit of a release," remarks Pete. Rothers returned to Parr Studios to produce Enchant's album; meanwhile Mark produced the album *Under The Red And White Sky* for John Wesley, in Florida. "I'd already told Wes I'd like to produce him, we'd stayed in touch, Ian was living in Florida at the time so I went out for a month," explains Mark. A complication was that Wes had also told the studio owner's brother, Jim Morris, that he would produce the album: "Wes then persuaded Jim to co-produce - the first few days were a bit of a battle." Mark eased his way into the situation, gently demonstrating that his production ideas did actually work. Unsurprisingly, he also ended up playing most of the keyboards.

On January 5 1994, all bar Ian went to the Netherlands to record acoustic versions of a number of tracks from the album , for a live broadcast. Then the familiar release cycle began. 'The Great Escape' was released on January 10 1994 as a taster single, followed by *Brave* a month later. The album received an immediate, overwhelmingly positive thumbs-up by the press. One magazine reported that "*Brave* is the first great concept album of the decade." *Brave* was awarded a 5-star review by *Kerrang!*, and is also listed in the *Rough Guide to Rock* as the best ever prog rock album - that's ever, folks! Paul Elliott wrote in *Q* magazine, "*Brave* is a tale of ordinary madness set to clever, spliff-assisted rock, and when it peaks on 'Fallin' From The Moon', it's beautiful."

Fan Simon Clarke remembers the very day of the release. "I went out and bought it in all three formats, I had to go to three different record stores," he recalls. "That night we did what it said on the cover, we listened to it loud with the lights off." As they did, they were caught in the same wave of passion that crashed onto the heads of many. A letter from Ellie Purtill to *The Web* commented, "What can you say about *Brave* that wouldn't be hopelessly inadequate? I've questioned my whole existence since I heard that album. It's a drug." "It is difficult to assess *Brave* and be objective," says Alan Hewitt, a view echoed by Wayne Kensett, at the time running the Web UK. "How do you remain objective when confronted by 70 minutes of something that must surely rank as one of the most complete pieces of music ever written?" Paul Hughes comments, "With *Brave*, Marillion moved up from a band I liked a lot, to by far my favourite band in the world. To this day, this piece of music utterly stuns me." US fan Mike Osborn was on vacation in Las Vegas when he bought his copy. "I will always remember that moment in time, racing through the lights of the Vegas strip, music surrounding me, tears wetting my cheeks as I felt the moment of epiphany when the melody, the arrangement, the lyrics all met in a swirl," remembers Mike. "In the words of Lenny Bruce [describing an injection of an opiate], it was like kissing God." Well, really.

As Dave Meegan comments, "*Brave* re-affirmed Marillion's relationship with its fans. People who were into it, or who were in that situation took it surprisingly seriously; it took a lot of people a long time otherwise." Dave remembers the letters from fans: "Many talked about turning points. I like it when it upsets a bit."

'The Hollow Man' was released as the second single on March 14, reaching a disappointing No.30 in the UK charts. The band members had been encouraging each other to write solo material, out of which came Rothers' 'Winter Trees' B-side for 'The Hollow Man' ("It looks like I was the only one actually doing it," laughs Steve). In the end, B-sides for subsequent singles came from live tracks. "The whole process of making the album took up so much time, it seemed the easiest thing to do," recalled Dave in a *Web* interview. Finally, 'Alone Again' was released on April 25.

While EMI had allocated £100,000 for promo videos, Marillion proposed to follow in the footsteps of opuses such as *Quadrophenia* and *Tommy* and use the lot on a full-length movie. "We collectively felt it was pointless to make three pop videos for this album (EMI's normal expectation at the time) and thought it might be better spending all the money at once on a very low budget film," explains Steve H. Adds John Arnison, "The promo videos weren't being shown that much anyway." The band commissioned Richard Stanley, director of art-house films as well as music videos, as producer. Says cult movie fan Rothers (who had seen *Hardware* and parts of *Dust Devil*, both by Stanley), "We auditioned scripts and it was Richard's that really caught our eye. He seemed to concentrate on the darker side of the story."

The band were involved in two days of filming, according to Steve H. "We had very little to do with the ideas contained in it, apart from having inspired them in Richard," he says. "Our only involvement in the film was as actors/ performers." "Missing out 'Mad', 'Paper Lies' and 'Made Again' for budgetary reasons, the film was first shown on German TV/satellite channel RTL+, then edited to get past the UK censors for the video release. It failed the first time round - to quote Mark, "Richard Stanley wasn't really known for making children's TV." Some scenes were deemed "likely to have far too powerful and dangerous an impact on depressed, potentially suicidal young people."

A few months after the release of *Brave*, H was in the offices of EMI International chatting to a staffer called Carol Baxter who remarked, "Those Radiohead boys were in here yesterday, and they all took a copy of your *Brave* album away." Praise indeed, yet despite its critical success the album didn't do so well commercially, clipping the top ten before staying in the UK charts for four weeks; a final single, 'Alone Again In The Lap Of Luxury' reached a paltry 53rd position. "It was a difficult album to listen to for a lot of people," Rothers noted at the time. While it still stands for many fans as the pinnacle of everything Marillion stand for, it posed a clear problem for the labels. At least in the UK there were people at EMI who understood the album, whereas US label IRS couldn't get a handle on it at all. Explained Steve H to Jon Epstein, "They had a lot of trouble doing anything with it, especially on radio."

Whether EMI 'got' the album or not, ultimately the bean counters held sway. Disappointed with the return on their investment, the label became increasingly difficult to work with from this point on.

HEADING FOR THE RAVE

Following a whole year without touring, the band were hungry to get back on the road, not least to give *Brave* the attention it deserved. Says Mark, "We agreed to a longer tour, to see if we could increase sales." The initial plan was to play smaller venues, explained Steve in a *Web* interview, "We want something really special - they enable better interaction between the band and the crowd. There is a chance we may play *Brave* in its entirety." And they did. The whole-album-in-its-entirety thing was not a guaranteed success, as Rothers admitted, "It will be a bit of a learning process, to put it mildly. But everyone we've played the album to has been really enthusiastic." Agrees John, "It was a bit of a crazy thing to do."

Following fan club warm-up gigs in Germany, Italy and Liverpool, the first official gig of the tour was in Cardiff on February 22. John Wesley was back in an acoustic support slot. Then the ambient 'River' music played through the PA, mixed by Mike Hunter at Parr Street using samples and off-cuts from the two previous Marillion albums; overhead, screens showed images to accompany the *Brave* story. "It was Steve Hogarth's idea," says Mike, "*Brave* starts very quietly so he didn't want the usual live thing where the sound engineer is playing AC/DC beforehand. He asked me if I fancied doing it and I said, 'Yeah!'" Rather than hunting through the miles of discarded tape on the studio floor, Mike raided Mark Kelly's bank of pre-loaded samples. "I messed them about, reversed them, twisted them up and layered them onto tape. Any extra instruments, like drums, I played myself." It was also the first time Mike would act as crew for anyone other than a pub band, as he was dropped in at the deep end as Mark's keyboard tech. "Mark's a boffin, he didn't really need anyone to set his keyboards up but the first couple of months were blind panic."

Brave was the pièce de résistance of course, seventy-four minutes of music with only a brief pause before 'Hollow Man' for H to say hello to the crowd. The show provided an opportunity for H to really perform, with bunches of tulips, black eyeliner and orange lipstick, pigtails, men in balaclavas dragging him off stage, candles in candelabras, incense and a variety of costumes. The *Brave* gigs also saw H's first live use of a guitar. "Before the tour it was decided (not by me) that it would be handy if I played a few power chords during the live show," he says. He needed a six-string for the power chords, so Tim Bricusse sold him a red Fender Stratocaster. Explains Tim, "I'd bought it for Duran Duran's Andy Taylor, but he told me it was the wrong colour red so he let me keep it..."

The audience was held spellbound, night after night after night. After the triumphant finale came an entire Marillion set including songs from both eras, though with two albums now to draw on there were only a couple of pre-1988 songs. For many disgruntled old timers the *Brave* tour was a one-way ticket back to fandom. Mike Palmer recalls, "A work colleague of mine saw them on the previous tour and said that I must go and see the new guy. I went on the *Brave* tour and that's where it started again." Newly re-ignited Paul Rael also saw the band perform *Brave* live. "I caught a gig at Cambridge and it was just phenomenal, I was staggered at how good Hogarth was and how brilliant his vocals were on stage. Steve Rothery's solos were heavenly. When they encored with six or seven tracks from the two albums I'd ignored, I instantly realised how much I'd missed out." Liverpool-based Alan Hewitt remarks, "Having missed Genesis's *Lamb Lies Down* tour, I think seeing *Brave* performed was probably the closest I will ever get to that. Seeing it for the first time and in my own hometown and on my birthday is something I will never forget." Wes himself rarely missed the opportunity to be with the audience. "*Brave* was one of the most intense shows I have ever seen," says Wes. "It was a consistently moving experience - I went out every night and watched; I must have seen it sixty times!"

The show brought in new fans as well – such as Rob Crossland and his wife Alexis, who saw an ad in *Q* magazine. I only spotted it the day of the Cambridge gig, so off Alexis and I went to see what these guys were like. *Brave* was completely unknown to us. It was as much a play as a rock gig, and I was mesmerised not only by Steve Rothery's guitar playing (I love a guitar virtuoso) but also by Steve Hogarth's presence, his fabulous voice and the total passion of all the boys. We were fresh to the band, let alone the plot, and it was hair-raising. A real shock and a surprise. We were hooked. I really felt part of it straight away and as a visual communications person it started me thinking creatively about the slide show and lighting they used to such great effect... We fell in love with Marillion that night... in fact, I don't think Alexis and I between us missed a single UK gig from that day until 2001."

Another attendee was Simon Clarke, who at the time was evangelising his new girlfriend, Vicki Harding. "With *Brave*, Marillion became the best band on the planet," says Simon, who had booked tickets on the understanding that this chap was nothing like Fish. "Vicki asked me whether he dressed up or wore greasepaint, I said, 'Nah!'" Vicki was one of many in the audience who stood, incredulous, when H reached for the lipstick. Nonetheless, both Simon and Vicki knew they had to see the show again, at the Royal Concert Hall in Nottingham. The pair stood a bit closer to the front than was healthy - but became firm followers from that point on. Says Simon, "The intensity of the performance was amazing We could feel the heat of the lights. H was just fucking scary! The bug sort of bit."

With such a long set, it is unsurprising that H followed his forebear and lost his voice, on Tuesday March 22 1994 in Hamburg. Monitor engineer Geoff Hooper came to the rescue, advising H to eat "fresh pineapple soaked in honey," according to H's diary. After a brief sojourn in New York for Steve, during which he discovered that the music industry was child's play compared to the theatre, as we shall see, the *Brave* tour came to an official end on September 2 at the 12,000-capacity Auditorio Nacional, Mexico City. "It's a fantastic venue, made for rock gigs," says Mark. John Wesley remembers the gig as "magical - just the number of people!" Amongst the thousands was fan Bruno Galli, who recalls, "When they finished playing *Brave* I thought I had been in Heaven, but ha, I was just standing at Heaven's gates. The encore was around 12 songs. What a treat! I have been to a lot of shows, including Marillion and Fish, but none has had the same impact as that one."

Brave didn't rock everybody's boat. "It is very easy to say that it was all brilliant for everyone, but that wasn't true - I can remember people walking out of gigs, complaining that they just didn't get it," recalls fan Andy Rotherham. Simon Hoban concurs, "I'm convinced the release of *Brave* started a downward spiral which the band have never recovered from. I know it's much lauded by fans and band alike, but it can't be denied that among the general populace *Brave* went down like a lead balloon." EMI didn't think it was worth creating a video of the tour; neither would they give permission to other labels (for example UK label Castle, which was keen to film the Rotterdam show); also the few TV recordings (in Poland and Argentina, as well as the recording of the Mexico City show by MVS, a copy of which was blagged by a certain fan in Mexico) were not considered to be of sufficient quality to make 'proper' releases. What a waste of eyes.

BRAVE

Inspired by the true story of a girl found wandering near the notorious suicide spot of the Severn Road Bridge, the band confound the expectations they built with *Holidays In Eden* and conjure up an altogether different experience. Laced with depression and melancholy, the music takes us into a young woman's psyche. Deeper and deeper we go, sharing her most private memories.

Brave has an intimacy that is almost claustrophobic, making us feel uncomfortable at being party to such things. Built around the smoke and mirrors that camouflage the truth of the girl's tormented mental state, this album is largely one of atmospheres. The entire band contribute to the cinematic feel: Mark painting water-coloured low hanging skies; Pete building expectations with an increasingly resonant bass line; Steve Rothery searing nerve endings, his tortured solos drenched in aching poignancy; Ian punctuating proceedings with deliberate, foreboding tom rolls; and Steve H's voice never more emotive. Simply, it is one of the most moving albums ever created.

From the opening, mournful foghorn guitar, to Mark Kelly's haunting keyboard entry to 'Bridge', it's clear that *Brave* isn't taking the easy route. The intro gives way to a plaintive Steve Hogarth setting the scene of the girl, stopped in the act of throwing herself to her doom, before revealing her first tentative recollections of what has brought her to this point. It's all here: family, love, drugs, homelessness, the chaos of modern life... All the themes that build to the album's inevitable conclusion over the next seventy-one minutes - linked by the ironic refrain of 'I got used to it!'

'Runaway' takes us onto the uncaring streets of London. The girl is found, scared and alone, and taken home once more. But her family believe that a bit of sympathy is all that's needed to make it okay again, too fearful to investigate the terrible, hinted-at truth of what might have made her decide to jump. And so the pain festers...

'Goodbye To All That' showcases Pete Trewavas's incredible bass skills as it takes us back to the bridge, preparing to let go and embrace the dark comfort of the waters... When we hear the maelstrom of what's coming next, is it any wonder she feels the way she does? We are flung, like a bottle caught in a rip-tide, through the pressure to conform, being institutionalised and accepting the welcome oblivion of drug abuse and the false friendships that accompany it - always using, always taking, always false but still better than what waits back in the real world. When pain runs this deep, any semblance of concern earns nothing but contempt.

'Hard As Love' is the first respite, musically at least, from the descent into ever-darker waters. Packed with Purple-esque keyboard flourishes from Mark Kelly, and with Steve Rothery delivering a slew of cuttingly heavy riffs, the track exposes the difficulty of opening up to love without being left vulnerable to emotional destitution. The story seems to say that the girl is being implored to let someone through her defences, to help her. Though she wants to (needs to?) it's too little, too late... During the song's middle eight, Steve Hogarth spills out the dangers of allowing someone to love you. Ian Mosley's toms thunder down as Hogarth sums it up: 'Nothing's ever been as hard.'

'The Hollow Man' shows the other side of emotional lock-down. This restrained ballad is inspired by T.S. Eliot's *The Hollow Men*, and the spacious, tasteful track captures the feelings of emptiness caused by denying oneself love. 'We're tin hard and we rattle when we're shaken.' Indeed.

'Alone Again In The Lap Of Luxury' takes us back in time once again, entering a middle-class family house that shows all the signs of being entirely conventional. We scratch the patina of respectability to discover the far more distressing reality: a father who commits the ultimate transgression of his responsibilities while his wife buries her head in the sand, praying that the evidence before her doesn't really add up to what it seems. Does the girl have the strength to run away?

'Paper Lies' is the track that least obviously fits the story, and indeed most obviously betrays John Helmer's influence on the lyrics. On the surface it is a wry, witty dissection of the British press and their ways of bending the truth to their own ends. Although the song does not appear in it, Richard Stanley's *Brave* film illustrates this theme: when the papers get hold of the story of the mad girl who attempts suicide, they twist, corrupt and pervert it until the victim barely recognises her own tale.

For the title track, the band conjure up a smoky, Celtic spirit, reminiscent of the traditional song 'She Moved Through The Fair'. The song is presented from the perspective of a man who tried to throw the girl a life line. He reflects on the remarkable strength of character shown in coping with her many tragedies (despite the fact that despair won out in the end), carrying her memory inside himself, 'She's inside you, and she's crying.' The 'age section' follows in which each voice is older than the last, starting with the chattering of an infant - Steve Rothery's daughter Jenny, who also provides the crying at the start of the album - and finishing with an old woman saying, 'What a brave, brave girl.'

'The Great Escape' sees us heading for the bridge, the inevitable beckoning. Rather than seeing suicide as a terrible thing, the lyrics suggest that in this act the girl gains her redemption: 'heading for the dignified walk away.' The music, as ever on this album, is in perfect harmony with the words: just listen to Mark Kelly's music-hall piano flourish after the phrase, 'Quiet applause will do'. The music builds until Steve Hogarth's agonizing cry, 'You're holding on': both meanings are completely obvious.

With 'The Last Of You' we are returned to the girl's father once more; perhaps his memory becomes flesh as she stands above the water on the wrong side of the stanchions. For the first time, rather than running away, hiding from what is going on, she is at last able to accuse her tormentor, 'Why did you hurt the very one, that you should have protected?' Musically, the 'Last Of You' reprises the 'alone in the city' section of 'Big Lie', bringing the whole thing full circle; the same music with a very different feel.

Anger gives way once more as we segue into the gorgeous, emotive 'Fallin' From The Moon'. Alongside the deep melancholy, we feel the weight of the pain, neglect and abuse lifting as they cease to matter anymore. With a sense of wonder pervading the music, it's as though we are witnessing a birth, rather

161

than a death. As the girl ruminates, "a mountain isn't far to fall, when you've fallen from the moon," Steve Rothery launches into one of his finest solos, each note pure and evocative. With the girl's body sinking into the water, her last thoughts slipping away, we're left with the sound of gentle waves lapping on the shore.

'Made Again' was something of an afterthought to the album, and it shows. While a beautiful and affecting number, its optimism is nonetheless at odds with the preceding 65 minutes of music. The opening bars were written by Steve Rothery for the birth of his daughter, which goes some way to explaining its sense of hope. The track is perhaps a necessary addition, changing perspective from musing on someone for whom death is a merciful release, to a sense of glowing optimism. I like to think it is for the real girl who inspired such a powerful album - the band saying, "I hope you're doing okay."

Bill Smith Studios' cover artwork for *Brave* is the simplest, yet possibly most effective of all the H-era covers. Featuring a heavily-shadowed girl's face taken from a photographer's card of a model, her eyes seem to stare out at us, and we immediately make a connection to her. There's something guarded about her. Pretty though she is, it is hard to shake the sense of much going on under the surface. The band's name and album title are small, as if to say, "It's the music you should be paying attention to."

10

Looking for
the Perfect Microwave

After *Brave*, the artists known as Marillion returned to the real world emotionally and artistically exhausted. At the same time, EMI were feeling more than slightly duped, and hungry for the album that Marillion had promised *Brave* would be. "There was a major question mark over whether EMI would carry on with Marillion," comments John Arnison. "Fortunately for us, when Jean-François Cécillon (who now headed EMI) was a junior product manager, *Misplaced Childhood* was his first gold album so he agreed to give it one more shot." Sentimentality aside, the company would not let the band get away with another eight months in the studio. "We had a fairly strict deadline," says Rothers.

It wasn't a problem – nobody particularly wanted to make another *Brave*, even if that were possible. "Every album we make is a reaction to the one before it," commented H. All the same the next disc still managed to tell a story. Helmer and Hogarth managed to put yet more emotion into the lyrics, and to many fans it contains some of the best music the band have ever made.

KNOCKING IT OUT

Before the writing sessions kicked off, the Racket Club was moved to a bigger location, another business park in the depths of rural Buckinghamshire. This time it was lyricist John Helmer's turn to kick things off - he'd just finished writing his book *Mother Tongue* and was in a storytelling mood. His lyrics, together with a number of musical ideas left over from the previous two albums, provided the bedrock upon which *Afraid Of Sunlight* would develop.

Dave Meegan's sixth-member status was confirmed when he was brought in very early in the writing. "I was quite surprised - I thought they'd never want to see me again," he laughs. The Irishman's presence ensured continuity, taking the pressure off by ensuring production decisions could be made with less risk of offence. "He doesn't have the baggage that comes with being in the band," says Steve Rothery, who also welcomed his capacity to drive the players beyond their respective creative envelopes. Dave had a particular impact on the guitar section, pushing Rothers towards new sounds and shapes. "You perceive yourself with certain strengths - doing something outside of that, you need external reassurance," says Steve. "I'd always try and do something over the top, to freak Dave out." Rothers wasn't only looking for the complex. "I was going to see Crowded House a lot at the time," he explains, which spurred an interest in more acoustic playing. "It's a different mindset. Acoustic is more dependent on the rest of the band for the arrangements, it can easily sound samey so it's harder to make acoustic songs sound different."

Rothers came up with a number of musical ideas that the band tied into the lyrical outputs of the two H's. 'Afraid Of Sunlight' and 'Afraid Of Sunrise' both started with Helmer and were developed by Hogarth. Following the *Brave* tour, Steve Hogarth in particular had a lot to get off his chest. "I'd reached critical mass on tour," he explains. "After a while I was starting to lose myself, I was taking on a new self. It became hard to reconcile the person I'd become with the person I was at home." Steve started to put more of himself into the lyrics, rather than the thinly veiled drawings from his life that had made it on to *Brave*. "The pain in *Brave* was partly fictional - I was projecting myself into somebody else, who I made up, but the pain in *Afraid Of Sunlight* was one hundred per cent personal. I'm a feeling person, sensitive to the feelings of others to the point that I'd given more than I should."

After a gentle start, the gang got into their stride and started producing some fresh material. "The boys were so full of ideas that once they started writing new bits there was enough to choose from," recalls Dave. With Mike Hunter at his side, Dave once again logged everything he captured. Dave's involvement was not without its problems, in hindsight. "I think we made the mistake of asking him to get involved too early," considers Mark. "He was there in the writing process and we started relying on him to make decisions that we should be making - which tunes to work on, which ideas. He did a really good job as a producer; I just think we put too much work his way that we should have been sorting out for ourselves." It probably didn't help that Mark was living with Dave (and Mike Hunter) at the time, having just split up with his wife, Suzy.

Returning the band to a song-based format, *Afraid Of Sunlight* took about five months to write and a further three to record. In March 1995 the team headed back to Parr Street Studios, for Dave Meegan to mix everything apart from 'Beautiful' and 'Cannibal Surf Babe', which were destined to be singles. 'Cannibal Surf Babe' was passed to Nick Davis. As he recalls, "It was such fun to mix. I mixed it differently to how it was sent. I thought they'll love this or hate it. Fortunately, they all liked it."

Meanwhile the band asked EMI to identify a suitable producer for 'Beautiful'. "It took weeks simply to get a list of possibilities out of A&R," recounts H. "We made a decision and asked Michael Brauer to mix it. I was ringing up Nick Mander at EMI and he was saying, 'We haven't heard from him, he doesn't like it.' I'd lie in bed at night thinking, *Shit, we can't even give people money to work with us Are we that awful?* Suicidally, I decided to call the guy myself 'cos I had to know. So I rang his manager in New York and he told me EMI had never sent

SEPARATED OUT ... REDUX

a tape. They just couldn't be bothered, 'Let's just tell them he hates it. What's for lunch?' " Suffice to say, Michael Brauer was very happy to remix the track. Above all else, the incident served to show just how much EMI valued having Marillion on their roster.

The cover art proved equally controversial. H had been working with Bill Smith Studios to agree a concept, which was finally unveiled to EMI and the rest of the band at Parr Street. "I thought it was wonderful," says H. Bad start - nobody else did. For some reason, the dayglo picture of the Rio statue of Jesus Christ was seen to have religious connotations. "Steve H and I were pushing for it, but the band and EMI said no," says Bill Smith. As safety valves started to pop, Bill came to the rescue. "I had a quick idea, 'Why don't we keep the religious theme but use a figure of an angel on the cover, an Icarus-type, innocent figure?'" Continues Carl, "Everyone liked that one so the front became the back." Following a hastily arranged photo session the cover was completed, but the damage was done - Bill Smith Studios were virtually dropped by EMI. "It broke Bill and Carl's heart," says H. "I felt ashamed - they had something inspired, a committee had thrown it out and the best reason given was that people might think we were a Christian band."

'Beautiful' was released as a single on May 29 1995, with backing vocals by Hannah Stobart. It reached No.29 in the UK charts; it also topped the charts in Brazil, mainly because it was used as the theme tune in a Brazilian soap series. As the first sign of a developing, Internet-based fan movement, Mark Kelly found out how the song was being used through the fans' online forum 'Freaks'. "I phoned our manager, he contacted the label and 'Beautiful' was put out as a single over there." The video for 'Beautiful' was made by Russell Young and was, according to Steve Rothery, "Six hours of hanging around for five minutes of work." Hogarth adds, "I had to climb a ladder to get on top of this building at eight o'clock in the morning. I was half naked and it was freezing cold. At two o'clock the following morning I was still climbing ladders. The things we do for fame!"

The single release was the last time for a decade that Marillion would see chart success: despite 'Cannibal Surf Babe' being readied as a single, it was never laid to CD. "EMI had lost faith," comments fan Simon Clarke. It was ironic in the extreme that *Afraid Of Sunlight* was released on June 24 to genuine critical acclaim. Even the oft-cynical *Q* magazine included it in its fifty best albums of 1995. "Sad to say that if *Afraid Of Sunlight* had been by a new, no-baggage of the past combo, it would be greeted with open arms, hailed as virtual genius," noted the music mag's Dave Henderson. "I heard the press hated us, so when that happened we went on medication!" remarked Steve Hogarth. "I almost got the feeling that it was a grudging nod, in the direction of well, we don't like them yet, but we'd better soften the ground for maybe we'll like them in a couple of years' time." But for EMI it was a case of too little, too late.

Many fans thought *Afraid Of Sunlight* was the best thing the band had ever done. Some, like Paul Rael, were still on a high from *Brave*, and *Afraid Of Sunlight* cemented the relationship. "The music, lyrics and vocals blew me away, I was hooked now and 'Beautiful' just did it for me. I caught several gigs on the tour and on each occasion I was more and more impressed." Paul Hughes concurs: "*Afraid Of Sunlight*, is possibly even better than its predecessor!" For lapsed fan John Chudy, *Afraid Of Sunlight* would be his welcome back home. "I found a copy of *Afraid Of Sunlight* and thought, these guys are still around? I'd better listen! *Afraid Of Sunlight* blew me away and I became a fan again!" Others, like Alan Hewitt, were less convinced. "At the time, *Afraid Of Sunlight* did not much feel like a complete album; merely a collection of demos, rushed together to get away from EMI." Yet such views were in a minority.

If *Brave* was a return to the band's progressive roots, *Afraid Of Sunlight* offered a more digestible counterpoint – still deeply considered music and words that touched the soul. From the perspective of the majority of the hard core, Marillion could do no wrong – and those who saw the tour could be forgiven for thinking that the band were back on the up. Pete and Lynne Wells, who joined the infamous 'Horny Rhino Tour' coach trip to catch a few live dates on the continent, saw only wild crowds and a band doing what it was best at. "When Marillion hit the stage the place went mad!" recall the pair of a gig in Germany. "The following night, the highlight was H deciding to climb up the speaker stacks during 'Garden Party', about forty feet above the stage - the rest of the band just shook their heads." From balconies and pits across the continent, it looked like it was business as usual.

So it might have been, if Marillion had been in the driving seat and not the record label. As events would show, it was EMI in a rush to wash their hands, not Marillion.

AFRAID OF SUNLIGHT

Featuring the legend "This album was knocked out," the album muses on the destructiveness of fame. Despite this, there is a lightness of touch to much of the music, considered missing from the previous album. One track, 'Cannibal Surf Babe' is dripping with musical in-jokes. Although not truly conceptual, it would be fair to describe the record as thematic, given its musings on the effects of fame and the many fallen idols that crop up over the course of the album.

An American boxing MC introduces Jake La Motta's championship heavyweight bout, John Lennon describes what appears to be a drug trip and a voice says something about a house being surrounded by helicopters. Starting with a jaunty rhythm, the lyrics to 'Gazpacho' are somewhat at odds with the music, discussing a boxer who breaks down under the pressures of fame, most noticeably in his violent abuse of his wife. As she mops up the blood from her face, his main concern is convincing the press he's still in control. As the song comes to an end, we hear a radio report of the OJ Simpson car chase and we realise whose house was surrounded.

'Cannibal Surf Babe' comes in with a Beach Boys harmony then kicks in with a gonzoid bass line that reminds us of surf guitarist Dick Dale. Steve H leads the band along a supremely silly and fun romp through a tale of a sex-crazed surfer chick, replete with a brilliantly-observed Kelly-led Beach Boys chorus. Unfairly derided by many for not being 'typical' Marillion, the song deserves kudos for precisely that reason.

A reading of a passage from 'Cannibal' in French segues into 'Beautiful', a ballad that speaks up for those among us who are made to feel worthless because they dare to believe in beauty. It implores us not to let the sniggering and the name calling cause us to give up those beliefs. In short, it's an anti-cynicism song. The song perhaps suffers from a slightly glossy production, making it seem a little saccharine sweet, something the rawer live versions overcome with ease. It remains a favourite for many fans.

'Afraid Of Sunrise' is the first part of a diptych of songs, again centred on the cost of fame. 'Sunrise' is the introspective side of the coin. Its gentle rhythms and melodies are evocative of a car journey through the American deserts. Special mention must be made of Pete Trewavas's fluid and supple basswork here. A widescreen slow-burner, the song's power is derived from its very simplicity. There's no Rothery solo as such, just simple and tasteful lines. Ian Mosley sticks mostly to brushwork on the drums, and you can hear the white lines passing incessantly under the wheels of the car. Lovely.

'Out Of This World' concerns the British speed king, Donald Campbell, and his attempt to break the water speed record. We start at the end, the band conjuring up a waterscape full of hidden tensions, as Campbell starts his run across the waters of Lake Coniston. Listen as we reach that heart-stopping moment where H sings 'at such speeds, things fly...' and Rothery's guitar becomes the nosecone of the boat, lifting... lifting... too high... until physics takes over, and the machine flips under its own momentum. For anyone who has seen the black and white footage of the disaster, it's an impossibly evocative moment. The remainder of the song is a dissection of the motivations that made Campbell take that fateful ride, a force so overpowering that even love couldn't overcome it.

'Afraid Of Sunlight', with its impassioned chorus sees us back in the car, driving through the night desert. This time, though, the calm has been replaced with the knowledge that, come morning, the newspapers will be full of career-destroying stories: 'I'm already dead, it's a matter of time.' The build-up of desperation, brought on by the encroaching fear of exposure, starting 'all your spirit rack abuses' and ending in Kelly and Rothery's searing solos is enough to make the tears prick behind your eyes.

'Beyond You' is a song that apes the famous "Wall Of Sound" production of the legendary Phil Spector. The lyric is immediately recognisable to anyone who has been left by someone they love, replete with the hopelessness of knowing their own actions are to blame. Ian's tampered-with drum sound, replaced with timpani and tubular bells, gives the song a timeless quality, as effective now as it was the first time you heard it.

Although on tour it has been dedicated to the Spice Girls and Bill Clinton (amongst others), 'King' directly concerns the spiral of inevitability that led to the suicide of Nirvana front man Kurt Cobain. Musically, the band have only reached such savagery once before, in the middle section of *Seasons End's* 'Berlin'. Here, as H describes the effects of sudden fame as "the ensuing, all-consuming mess," the band change pace and summon up the whipping, whirling confusion in Cobain's head to great effect. Brought back to earth once more, H brings to life the constant in-your-face pressure of being on the fast track to fame; the faces, the praise, the outpouring of emotion, the blunt trauma of the road, the lies, the bullshit... and now it's gone too far, there's no turning back as the band thrash out the frenzied, fear-filled 'Kingasm' and the sudden realisation that the silence at the end of the song is because the pressure you just heard building and building, getting just too intense, ended in a shotgun blast... It's all too much.

Bill Smith Studios' cover for *Afraid Of Sunlight* features a grubby child (who happens to be Bill Smith's son) with angel's wings, surrounded by a halo of fire. It remains the least pleasing cover of the Hogarth era, something that is especially galling given that the other images produced for the CD booklet are extremely evocative and effective photomontages of elements from the lyrics - Elvis's suit, La Motta, the tail fin of a classic US Ford Thunderbird, the poppy (symbolising heroin) and the dayglo-ized Brazilian statue of Christ.

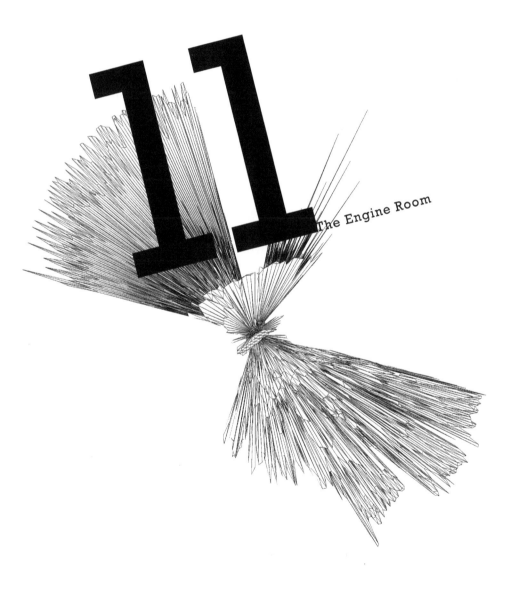

11

The Engine Room

The year was 1995, the month October. An extensive tour was coming to an end and with it, an entire chapter in the history of the band. Over the next four years Marillion would turn their back on the majors and re-enter the fray on an independent label. They would cast themselves adrift from their management team and launch into cyberspace, gambling the future on their creative abilities and their self-belief.

Cynics might have said that Marillion had reached a point where the future was predetermined, that the inevitable termination of their contract with EMI would signify the beginning of the end. From here, warbled the Greek chorus, record sales would shrink tenfold, venues would contract from halls to clubs, hard-won reality would be replaced with alcohol-tinged nostalgia and thus the cycle of rock and roll would be complete. Time would show that things don't always turn out as expected, as the Marillion fan base was to prove itself more resilient, resourceful, and downright proactive than the band could have imagined.

At the end of this period in the independent wilderness, the band felt confident enough to trust their fan base completely, the results of which would take the music world by storm. First, however, there were bills to pay and hungry listeners to satisfy. Following the last dates of the *Afraid Of Sunlight* tour, the five players returned from the manic, chaotic life on the road to the more mundane, regular pace of autumnal Buckinghamshire where they could catch a breath, collate a few thoughts and plan the direction of the next album. While spirits remained upbeat, nobody was in any doubt as to the rocky times ahead.

LEAVING THE NEST

The *Afraid Of Sunlight* tour proved as successful as its predecessor in the end, though initially slow ticket sales left an uneasy feeling that was hard to shake off. Like its predecessor *Brave*, promotion of *Afraid Of Sunlight* had been less than adequate; there was little airplay for 'Beautiful' on either Radio 1 or Virgin, at the time the main target stations in the UK, though local radio stations were playing the single quite regularly. To cap it all, underlying album sales had been diminishing ever since Fish had left. Mark recalls, "I drew a graph of sales, to explain it to the rest of the band." It showed 1.4 million sales for *Misplaced Childhood*, then 900,000 for *Clutching*, 600,000 for *Seasons End*, 450,000 for *Holidays In Eden* and 300,000 for *Brave*. Over the same period, the band had continued to take advances from EMI rather than negotiating better royalty deals. "We were always in debt - it was obvious that we were heading towards a crash."

The Marillion collective didn't see EMI as the only weak link. The summer of 1995 witnessed one of the few times that H fell out with John Arnison, with the culmination of a chain of events that had kicked off a couple of years earlier leaving the band with time on their hands. Back on the *Brave* tour, H had been in discussions with German promoter Peter Rieger, who was planning on acquiring the rights to the stage musical *Tommy*. "He was going to buy a theatre, deck it out, put on the show and make some money," says H. Peter flew Steve to New York to see the Broadway production, but his impressions were diluted by the raw emotion he had been injecting into *Brave*: "There was no feeling of restrained power there. I thought the lead wasn't 'it' and I could be 'it' but I didn't know if I wanted to do it." Informing Steve that the role was his for the taking, Peter went ahead and bought the rights, flying Steve back to New York from Mexico to meet with the show's producer. "I liked it a lot more, but" - and this is a big but - "but when I went out for dinner with the producer, he didn't have a clue who I was. It was a bit embarrassing."

Unfortunately for Peter, the small print of his contract gave him absolutely no artistic control over the show. And John Arnison, who should have been handling the affair on H's behalf, was flying back and forth to Japan with one of his other clients, reggae band Aswad. Remembers John, "Steve complained, he thought I should have been back with him rather than out there with them." As John apportioned his time between his multiple acts, Marillion were shifting, noticeably, down his priority list. *Tommy* was eventually staged in Germany in 1995, with the lead from the Broadway production; Steve's discomfort at being dropped from a role he'd never accepted was nothing compared to Peter's suffering. Relates Steve, "The next time I saw him, he'd had a heart attack and a nervous breakdown. He lost his shirt on that one."

As John had blocked a six-month gap to allow for H and his stagecraft, when it failed to materialise the band were left at a loose end. "We were thinking of other ways to fill our days," remarks Pete. A couple of public outings ensued: first a charity gig with Rothers and Pete at Buckingham Town Hall, organised by ex-Whitesnake guitarist (and "really nice guy") Bernie Marsden. As Rothers noted in *The Web*: "We murdered 'Kayleigh' and Pete sang 'Sugar Mice', so it was... interesting. We did a good version of 'I Saw Her Standing There' though."

On December 12 the Marillos were largely reunited at the Classic Rock Society awards, held at the Herringthorpe Leisure Centre in Rotherham. The event proved a little incestuous - Pete had already been asked to present the awards, but one went to (absent) Steve Hogarth as Best Male Vocalist and another to Marillion for Best Gig of the Year. With Arena headlining, the awards ceremony was also "Mick Pointer's comeback gig," according to Martin Hudson, CRS Editorial Manager. Rothers joined Mick for a rendition of 'Crying For Help IV', a track from *Songs From The Lion's Cage*, on which Steve had participated. The ensemble also played 'He Knows, You Know' and part of 'Grendel', which hadn't been played since Mick left the band 12 years before. "All came back to my house for a party afterwards and I can remember one person saying that he had his favourite three drummers in my kitchen, Ian Mosley, Mick Pointer and Fudge Smith," recollects Martin.

It was during the solo months that John and the boys decided to bow to the inevitable, and throw in the towel with EMI. Everyone was frustrated by the diminishing support and increasing meddling by the label. "We felt frustrated, we thought things could only get better," comments Steve R. Breaking off the relationship was no idle whim - the band still owed EMI several hundred thousand pounds due to the costs of *Brave*. "The record company put a fixed amount of money up front for the recording so when we went over it started coming out of our own pockets," explains John. Everyone had hoped the sum would be recouped with *Afraid Of Sunlight* but it wasn't... on the other side of the scales, the lack of publicity for *Brave*, the pressured production of *Afraid Of Sunlight* and the tightening corporate manacles on artistic freedom, all added up. Ultimately, agreed the collective, it was better to be free and a bit less well off. Equally, better to jump than be pushed.

A four-month gap in the schedules after Christmas offered the players time to fall back and regroup creatively. As well as a welcome respite from the album-tour-album cycle, it also offered an opportunity to clear a backlog of artistic ideas that had not been seen as suitable for Marillion as a whole - Steve Rothery had his The Wishing Tree project, Steve Hogarth was recording *Ice Cream Genius* and Ian was collaborating with Sylvain Gouvernaire on *Crossing The Desert*, leaving the others to their own devices. Said Steve Hogarth later, "Doing a solo project is a safety valve – all those things you wanted to do, you can get them out, it's also an opportunity to explore a completely different area of music." "It felt weird - it was the longest time the band had been apart since the earliest days," recalls Mark.

In parallel Marillion hunted for another deal with a major label, but it was not to be. "We hadn't been able to sustain the sort of interest with the record labels to get the message across," commented Steve Hogarth. Eventually the band confirmed its independent status with a signing to UK-based Castle Records, an established name that included rockers such as Black Sabbath and Uriah Heep. Remembers Steve H, "A guy named Douggie Dudgeon was very knowledgeable about music - he was into the band and wanted to sign us." Castle's traditional model was as a catalogue label - it would buy copyrights then release "Best Of" albums at budget prices - but now it was trying to broaden its portfolio with more current acts. "They wanted to become more credible," remarks Pete. Perhaps the band should have reconsidered their options when owner Terry Shand sold his interests to a US company... the band pressed on with a three-album deal regardless, almost immediately finding promises of freedom of control turning to dust as the US company sold its interests on to Red Ant, which cared diddly-squat about the verbal principles behind previous deals. Says Rothers in hindsight, "Little did we know that a huge label like EMI, even when doing badly, would still do better than a small independent label like Castle."

The final disc to be released in the transition from EMI was live double CD *Made Again*, which not only released Marillion from its obligations (as the fifth album in a five-album deal), but also paid off past debts without creating new ones. Funnily enough, its release displayed a certain symmetry with the first seven years of the band. "Our first four studio albums were followed by a double live album that signalled the end of that chapter. Now, after another four studio albums, followed by a live album, we move from EMI," explained Mark. Featuring *Brave* in its entirety, the two-disc *Made Again* was released on March 25 by EMI in the UK, with Castle handling the release in Europe and the US to give the band the best possible start with the new label.

The live album release was followed by a brief tour at the end of April 1994, ostensibly to promote the live album but also giving the band an opportunity to gel before a return to the studios. The band played four dates in the traditional strongholds of the Netherlands, Germany, France and England. For fans Simon Clarke and Vicki Harding, the best night of the four was the first, at the Muziekcentrum Vredenburg in Utrecht on April 22 1996. "It was amazing!" says Simon. "The best venue in Europe, the best crowd in Europe, it was just awesome!" Whatever the band did from this point on, they knew they had the fans behind them.

THE ACCIDENTAL PRODUCERS

Without their own solo projects, Mark and Pete had started sifting through previously unused material. This included near-complete songs such as 'Accidental Man'; other elements were still in a very raw form, such as the music that would become the first section of the title track. Following a couple

177

of months' none-too-productive effort between Ian, Mark and Pete (according to Ian, "It was hard work, out of the months of work we did, we used about a minute,"), the band reunited at The Racket Club in May 1996. The break had done everyone a lot of good; furthermore, the influences that had been picked up in the solo months were to prove just as liberating. As Steve Rothery commented, "The solo projects revitalised the band. When we got together not only did we appreciate the chemistry, but our enthusiasm had increased and we had new ideas. We had a flood of inspiration." Adds Pete, "What was nice about it was coming back to Marillion. It felt very right."

While the separation with EMI freed the Marillos from any artistic shackles (real or imagined), there was no longer direct access to producers, designers, promoters and distributors. Each decision had to be cost-justified by both John Arnison and the band against an all-too-tangible bottom line, which meant losing a major creative catalyst - Dave Meegan as a producer, even if he had been available (he was making Phil Campbell's *Fresh New Life* at the time). Instead, the band opted to produce themselves, involving Dave only at the mixing stages. The decision was also expedient, given the feeling that Dave had come in too early in the previous album. "We wanted to have more control musically - this way we could record what we wanted," says Pete. But oh, did they miss him! "It's like going into town without your Mum - you know what to do but..." remarked Pete at the time. Sound engineer Stewart Every also picked up the producer's baton on occasion. "I made suggestions, of which about 80% were ignored and 20% were laughed at," he laughs. A spirit of collaboration arose in the absence of a 'real' producer - as Steve H wrote, "I took 'Memory Of Water' away and then arranged it, and then Mark took it away, and then he rearranged it, and then he gave it back to me, and I rearranged it again, so we just kept passing it back and forth, so it was a fifty-fifty thing."

The band's first solo venture enabled the band members to practise what they had always preached: to work outside the musical box. Tracks drew on influences from Salsa to Slavic Folk, using trumpets and (synthesised) hunting horns, dulcimers and string samples. The album emerged with a lighter feel, thanks largely to Steve Rothery's recent solo experiences. "With the Wishing Tree album, I was playing the acoustic guitar more often," recalls Steve, yielding the sonic background to songs such as 'Eighty Days' and 'Man Of A Thousand Faces'. And with the title track , Steve Hogarth put the last nails in the coffin of his rock-steady reputation by rubber-stamping one of the most proggy tracks the band had done for many years. "Oddly enough, I was the one who started it," he conceded. "I'm now at the stage where I think it's nice to do something retro-progressive." The words came to him at about 4 o'clock in the morning, during a sleepless night in the summer of 1995. In the end he had no choice but to get up and write down what would be his life story, from birth to being stung by a cloud of wasps and riding pillion on his father's motorbike. "It all came flooding out - it was over the space of about 20 minutes," he recalled.

This Strange Engine was completed within six months in November 1996, which was pretty fast for a Marillion album. In an ironic twist, this time it was H who slowed the production process down, leaving the rest of the band frustrated. "Steve likes to spend a lot of time on the mixing and I haven't got the patience," says Pete. "It was a difficult birth," remarked H, "but we came through it without even a minor fist fight." Touché! Steve Rothery felt the result was both forward- and backward-looking. "There are some moments that take me right back to the beginning, particularly the synthesizer solo in the third section of 'This Strange Engine', when it goes back to the tom-toms it takes me back to 'Market Square Heroes' and all of that…"

Dave Meegan took care of the mixing at Parr Studios in Liverpool, picking up where he left off with *Afraid Of Sunlight*. "When I came to mix the title track I knew the mood from the start," explains Dave. "I knew that a lot of the two albums came from the same mother, so they were like Side 1 and Side 2 for me." Another Christmas passed, following which the disc gained its "classy" (according to Rothers) packaging. The band had parted company with Bill after the 'design by committee' controversies around the *Afraid Of Sunlight* sleeve and furthermore, Castle had its own art department headed by designer Hugh Gilmour, who had put together the *Made Again* sleeve. He went on to design and assemble the *TSE* cover, using a copper steam engine built by his neighbour, Andrew Gent. "The engine is made of 'every-day-items' such as a drain pipe, stop-cock and plastic pipe, but no sign of any sticky-back plastic," says James Fishwick of the Web UK team, who was later tasked with restoring the 'engine'.

For the band's major label swan song, in February 1997 EMI released *Best Of Both Worlds*, a double CD containing tracks from both Fish and H eras of Marillion. Much of the effort had been co-ordinated by an EMI employee Lucy Jordache, who was working in the catalogue marketing department. "I saw on the call sheet for the year that there was to be a Marillion best-of," explains Lucy. "I called up, said I was a huge fan and asked if I could help." Yes she could, but not as her day job - "I was taking stuff home in the evenings!" Having put herself in the driving seat, Lucy was tasked with gaining agreement from all parties – a sensitive role to say the least. "I'd met Marillion but not Fish, and I had to fly up to Edinburgh to meet him," explains Lucy. "By the time I arrived

I was a blithering wreck." Everything went as well as could be hoped - "We got on really well - Fish called me Henry Kissinger!"

With project co-ordinator Nigel Reeve, Lucy planned two separate discs, one for each era. "We wanted two covers, with Mark Wilkinson designing the Fish-era cover and Carl Glover designing the H-era." Not only did the album bring the two sides together in an unprecedented fashion, it also closed the gap between record label and fans. "Mark Kelly sent an email to the Freaks list, saying that fans should email me at EMI to say what they wanted to see on the album," says Lucy. "Suddenly I was receiving all these emails out of the blue!" Lucy took the plunge and joined the Freaks list herself. It was a revelation. "There were all these fans out there, talking on the Internet," she says. Whatever was happening out there in cyberspace, it was clearly worth tapping into.

This Strange Engine found its way to the shops on April 21 1997, nearly two years after the release of *Afraid Of Sunlight*. Stated the press release, "Although it is often soaring and majestic, the band never give way to musical excess or over-indulgence." Well, not too often anyway. *Kerrang!* awarded the album 4 K's out of 5. "The commercial realities of running their own affairs have given Marillion a right old boot up the arse creatively," said reviewer Liam Sheils. *Q* magazine's Rob Beattie also applauded the album, saying, "If occasionally they're still vulnerable to the charge of overindulgence, the deft pop melodies and substantial musicianship demonstrate that everyone recognises where the edge is these days. Mind you, anything that can survive all the sleeve note guff about 'Jungian collective thought' has to be a good record." Across the Atlantic, reviewer Joe del Tufo wrote in New York's *Good Times* magazine, "*This Strange Engine* is a magnificent collection of eight tracks that balances the band's strengths with their propensity to seek new directions."

Some fans were won over immediately to the new direction of their favourite band. "My first impressions of *This Strange Engine* were: what a fantastic album!" remarks Mark Donald. "I hadn't been to see Marillion live for four years, but when I heard this I thought I'd been out of the picture too long." Despite its length, there was general agreement among the fans that the title track, some 17 minutes long, was one of the strongest songs on the album. "It was just brilliant!" remarks Paul Rael. "It is now one of my top three Marillion tracks - an absolute masterpiece!" Adds Paul Hughes, "Three words: acoustic, well-produced (that'll have to count as one) and emotional." US fan Mike Richichi wrote, "This album doesn't disappoint, the feel of the music just carries you in and the songs are snippets of life."

The effects of the production process were not lost on the fans. "The aim of the album was to project a strong feeling of optimism; of hope for the future," notes fan Robin Lauren. "*This Strange Engine* was definitely a turning point," adds Alan Hewitt. "The band branched out into areas which they had barely (if ever) touched on before. As an album it was definitely a challenge to the perceptions of both the fans and the critics... a challenge which some people are still coming to terms with."

One song in particular captured the imagination and touched the hearts of many fans – 'Estonia', written in homage to the victims of the sinking of the Baltic sea ferry The Estonia in 1994. 852 lives were lost, and a chance meeting between Steve Hogarth and film-maker Paul Barney, the only British survivor, provided the lyrical impetus for the song. "No one leaves you when they live in your heart and mind," went the lyrics, words of comfort for fans such as Angie Coope whose mother had been diagnosed with cancer. Recalls Angie, "That night, my best friend (and Marillion fan) Gina Andree rang from Michigan, USA. I told her about the day's events, the highs and lows. I did not know, but Gina e-mailed the Marillion office in the hope that H might read it. The following day I received an e-mail from H, who suggested that if the worst should happen then I might gain some comfort by listening to 'Estonia'. Sadly my Mum died a few days later. It hit me really hard. Up until this happened, 'Estonia' was just another great Marillion song. I listened to the lyrics and I saw what H was trying to say: 'No one dies, they just move to the other side.' It is comforting to know my Mum is still watching over me. 'Estonia' says to me: 'Don't be sad at my passing. I will be with you always.'"

The resulting album didn't work for everyone, particularly in its lighter feel: 'Memory Of Water' was considered to be "tricky"; other tracks were judged "lacklustre". Steve Rothery's folksy-bluesy guitar left some listeners concerned that they had heard the last of his trademark soaring solos. Fan Rick Collins writes: "I was really keen to love this album, but I can safely say it's my least favourite with H." Canadian fan Marc Roy concurs: "I felt there was a little something missing to most songs to take them right up there." Max Rael is more blunt: "I hated *This Strange Engine*, and to this day I don't like it much. I keep waiting for the moment when it all clicks into place, but so far, it ain't happened!" You can't please everybody.

The Strange Engine tour started on April 30 1997, at the Garage in Glasgow. One of the best nights was, according to fan Paul Rael, May 2 at the Cambridge Corn Exchange. "It was magical and Steve's voice was like being hosed down by cool champagne after a month in the desert. 'This Strange Engine' was almost a religious experience, there was a moment when the music stopped dead for a few seconds and the whole place was silent... you really could have heard a pin drop." The first single was released two weeks later - 'Man Of A Thousand Faces' on May 16, with a computer graphics-based video directed by (the charmingly named) Golden Shower. The video didn't quite live up to the hype, however. "Not enough money was spent on it to make it look good enough," comments Pete.

Then, following a two-week breather at the beginning of June, it was off to South America for a fortnight, playing Brazil, Argentina and Chile. A couple of festivals followed, notably Rock In Madrid on July 5 and, on July 27, the Kingdom Festival at Bellinzona, Switzerland. On October 4 it was back to Germany, France, Luxembourg and Holland for the final dates of the tour, which terminated on October 27 at the Paradiso in Amsterdam. The tour's success was tempered by the truth in fan Martin Thorpe's observation – "It would be smaller venues (and shorter tours) from here on in." At least, for a while!

The release of *This Strange Engine* constituted a watershed. No longer signed to a major label, the album marked the end of an era and a whole new start. On the upside, Marillion were moving with more confidence into new musical areas, despite the risk to their fan-based life support system; meanwhile however, mainstream support outside the core fan base was diminishing further. By June 1998 *This Strange Engine* had sold sufficient copies to pay the bills, but it did not amount to a lottery win. There was little interest from Castle to promote the band with any gusto, as it reverted to an unapologetically catalogue-based label that valued quantity over quality. "It was like a treadmill," comments Mark. "They just wanted to milk the fan base."

Over the months that followed, Marillion were to discover just how strong that fan base was.

THIS STRANGE ENGINE

Goodbye to EMI (for a while) and in with Castle. Marillion's first album with a new label was, like its predecessor, thematic. According to the press release, the album was about, "human memory. Personal as well as biological [memory] is explored and a strong feeling of optimism and hope for the future permeates the music." The other key factor at work was Steve Rothery's use of acoustic guitars. Inspired by his work on his solo Wishing Tree album, there is an acoustic feel to much of the album, making it feel rootsy and organic - very appropriate for an album about memory. *TSE* sees the band continuing to develop the scope of their influences, with Crowded House, Russian and Caribbean folk influences nuzzling in amongst more traditional Marillion territory.

This Strange Engine opens with a simple but effective acoustic guitar motif from Steve Rothery. H begins to weave a tale inspired by folklorist Joseph Campbell's *The Hero of a Thousand Faces*, a book which postulates that one can trace common archetypes throughout history and different cultures. According to Steve Hogarth, "The song links Freud and his thoughts and Jung and his philosophies with tribalism and rites of passage. It takes in the Masons, secret societies, all the way from the Holy Grail and the Knights Templar to some of the conspiracy theories that still go around in the modern age." Mark Kelly shifts into an almost honky tonk piano break as we are taken from Adam and Eve to humanity's first forays into space; via ancient Greece, to the age of the machine, the dawn of the media age and rock and roll. Just as the song seems to be coming to an end, H begins to reiterate the themes over a pedal-toned outro that builds and builds, until you can almost hear the entire world singing the same song. It's a tribute to this astonishing band that a children's choir, rather than sounding trite or saccharine, sounds inspiring and emotive, and just listen to Pete and Ian punctuating and directing the end into something truly powerful!

As the end of 'Thousand Faces' fades away, Steve Rothery breaks into a bluesy intro that gives way to a reflective chiming guitar line. 'One Fine Day' is a John Helmer lyric that deals with passivity, specifically the idea that it's all too easy to wish your life away waiting for that magical moment, rather than building towards it, and making it happen for yourself. It's a good enough song in its own right, but frankly, when you're talking Marillion, you need to be so much better than merely good, and it's one that perhaps doesn't do full justice to their powers. 'Eighty Days' is a song H wrote for the fans, written before his first Marillion gig at the London Astoria as he watched the fans file into the venue from a window above. It is a tribute to you and me, the people who pay our money to stand outside in the rain and cold because of our devotion to the unique beast that is Marillion. It's also a song about being on the road and the drudgery that can accompany those off-stage moments. It marries these two notions in the idea that it's on stage where it all becomes worthwhile, where the fans' love of the music wipes out the tedium of hours spent travelling in tour buses. Laughs H, "I really did lie in that bunk in the tunnel under the Alps all the way from Zurich to Milan, thinking of Iceland and Japan."

H has said he would like 'Estonia' played at his funeral. The song was written after he found himself sitting on an aeroplane with film-maker Paul Barney, the only British survivor of the Estonia Ferry disaster, in which over 800 people lost their lives. Coupled with the fact that a friend of his had recently lost his father, H attempts to find some solace, if not reason, in such loss. Listening to the interplay between Rothery's guitar, chiming out almost like a sonar call, and Mark Kelly's echo-drenched keys, you can imagine the sight of the ferry disappearing under the waves with its terrible cargo. And then the chorus - so much choked emotion... 'No one leaves you when they live in your heart and mind.' With guest musician Tim Perkins on balalaika, it's close to overwhelming. 'Memory Of Water' is a sparsely orchestrated dirge (and I mean that in the dictionary sense, rather than it being dreary) about memory, and indeed life itself having come from water. Almost funereal, the music carries a measure of solemnity which we're somewhat unused to with the band. But, then again, as the recent live versions have proved, you should always expect the unexpected with this band. The Big Beat version of the song is an exercise in contrariness - frenetically lively and exuberant!

'An Accidental Man' sees Rothery unleash a deceptively simple groove, over which Pete Trewavas pops wonderful bass harmonics. Cue Ian, four to the floor and Mark on Hammond organ and... we're in. Concerned with how breeding - social and racial culture - imprints itself upon us, the song specifically addresses a tale of a man who realises that his whole identity has been formed by forces outside of his control, and realises, to his regret, he doesn't know how to break this programming.

'Hope For The Future' opens with a taut-strummed guitar full of tension that we just know has to break. It's just that... well... we weren't expecting this! 'Hope' is a gorgeous, lilting pop romp through the hidden mysteries down the ages, and is laced with a liberal dose of Caribbean rum! Rosicrucians, Egyptian astronauts, the limbic brain (the part which links emotions to specific memories)... If it confused some of the fan base then perhaps it's no surprise, but this is the sound of a band cutting loose and having some unrestrained fun.

The glorious title track is a tribute by H to his father, who gave up his seafaring life for a job in a coalmine so that he could be close to his family. From its opening scene of the young H feeding swans, to Hogarth senior on the deck of his ship seeing the mysteries of the world, 'This Strange Engine' is one of the most expansive songs the band have ever attempted, mood after mood, scene after scene brought vividly to life. Just listen to the confusion of adolescence in the 'I never felt that I belonged' section. Or the evocation of the childhood thrill of riding on your dad's motorbike. You don't have to have done it to recognise the truth in these lyrics. As H's dad watches the sun dip beneath the water-kissed horizon, Steve Rothery slips into one of his best solos, full of regret, longing and most of all, the sense that this is a sight he'll remember all his life. We move into the final section with H realising the magnitude of what his father has given up - something he himself is unable to do, even for his own family - and the understanding of the love involved in tearing himself away from his privileged existence to a life in a dreary northern town. There's simply too much great music here to comment on in detail, but a couple of standout moments come to mind. Listen to the loose, jazzy swing of the bees section; doesn't that just conjure the confusion of the air as they whirl above the young H's head perfectly? Or listen, in the final section, as H sings 'this love' and the purest guitar note rises and drops back again. Haven't you felt your heart do that when you're on the point of becoming overwhelmed with emotion? Sheer genius. No wonder the band look shattered when they play it live!

The cover design for this album was again a break from tradition, with the Bill Smith Studio making way for Castle's in-house design team. *This Strange Engine* features a copper steam engine, in which a heart fuels the flames that burn. Strange that an album concerned with memory should feature a heart. Or maybe it's completely right. Maybe we're back at the old limbic brain again, with emotions being intertwined with memories.

12

The Tour Fund

As the year transitioned into 1997, it was becoming clear that something new was afoot in the world. While technologies such as the Internet, email and web sites were all still in their infancy, they were becoming increasingly in vogue, particularly with more technology-savvy segments of the Marillion fan base – a factor Racket headquarters was keen to exploit. The sleeve notes for *This Strange Engine* included the band's first 'official' email address – the (now-defunct) dorianmusic@dorianmusic.co.uk - but evidently, more could be done. The band's most tech-literate member, Mark Kelly was no stranger to the Internet. "I check out what people are saying about us... and to see what's being said about the band in countries we're not visiting soon," he remarked at the time.

Spotting the opportunity to build a fan database, the keyboardist wrote an email to the Freaks fan list offering a number of pre-release CDs to UK fans. Explains Mark, "We wanted their names and addresses!" Racket Records was swamped by requests - as well as complaints by disgruntled fans from overseas. It got worse: the exercise quickly became a cruel lesson in open-ness, as the CDs were never issued. "Castle said they would send out the CDs," says Mark. "I compiled a list and sent it over but they never were sent out. We got a lot of grief for that." While the Internet offered great promise, it clearly needed to be used with care.

Occasionally, Mark felt moved to join in with some of the ongoing debates on the Freaks list. As one innocuous email opened the flood gates, the Marillos were about to discover just how powerful the conduit could be.

AN IDEA IS BORN

It had always been Marillion's intention to play the US again. The only model that made sense was to tour the club circuit, as Pete explains, "Even bigger bands do it, but it's a strange thing for European bands to come to terms with." But economics were not stacked in the band's favour - the overheads of crossing the Atlantic, paying for visas, transporting equipment and employing local staff left little chance for profitability. "We'd just left EMI and we reckoned we'd lose quite a lot of money," said Mark at the time. The previous US tour had lost £30,000 and, in addition, it only included dates on the East Coast and in the Mid-West, leaving West Coast fans out in the cold.

This wasn't good enough for many US fans - on the lists, criticism of the band by US fans was running high. Finally, on January 27 1997 Mark Kelly wrote:

Hello to all the best Freaks....

188

We love touring. It is just too expensive to tour some places! I'm not saying it's impossible to tour everywhere, but it is expensive to put on a Marillion tour... we are not prepared to put on half a show with second rate equipment and a crap sound system, just so we can get to the west coast and not lose our shirts!

Mark's post generated a flurry of responses, including an off-the-wall suggestion from fan Jeff Pelletier. "There had to be something that could be done," he says. "Marillion charged less than $20 a ticket on the *Afraid Of Sunlight* tour - of course they lost money. The club was packed, but that's still not a lot of income when you take out the middlemen and the expenses of an international tour. I had just paid $160 for a pair of Eagles tickets - surely Marillion could charge more than $40 a pair, couldn't they? Every North American on the Freaks list would be willing to pay more if that was the only way to make a tour happen. That's why they call us Freaks." With 1,500 people on the Freaks mailing list, Jeff realised there might be another way. "If 500 of them could put $50 into a hat, that would make $25,000. Why not do that and give it directly to the band in exchange for a tour?" he thought, before tapping out his now-infamous post:

What if all the US freaks donated to a "Marillion Tour The USA" fund. I'd gladly throw $50 in the hat if that guaranteed a chance to see them in several US locations? What do you think? There's several hundred US Marillion fanatics on this list alone, right? I know it wouldn't cover all the costs but it might help?

Jeff's post generated a storm of responses. This response, from Kevin La Rue, was typical: "Count me in for much more than $50, and a whole lot of time." Another Jeff, this time a Mr Woods, thought it was a fabulous idea. His email, aimed directly at Mr Kelly, asked: "Shall we talk, or is this idea just another sugar mouse?" Mark was quick to reply, "I think you're all crazy! It would make a great story if it came off." Jeff Woods' response was to act, not talk. He recalls, "Given a large number of Freaks knew who I was, due to my proposal to Michelle the year before , it was one of those 'hell, why not?' moments!" Setting up a shell company and a trust fund, Jeff posted to Freaks, "All I need is a go from a Marillo... and I'll kick the fund off with $200." Before long the 'go' was received, and the fund became a reality. "We'd met Jeff before, and he seemed like an upstanding guy," says Mark.

Having fired off his initial message, Jeff Pelletier remained largely oblivious to what his post had kicked off. "I was busy at work and hadn't had a chance to read the posts waiting in my Inbox. Julie called me up and said, "You're a genius!" I said, "Huh? What are you talking about?" "You haven't read Freaks yet? Read it! Everyone responded to your Tour Fund idea and Mark Kelly said they'd do it!" Pledges had poured in, dozens and dozens of them, and not just from North America. This wonderful little community wanted this idea to succeed so much that people were pledging from all around the world. People that wouldn't even get to see the tour were promising their money. I couldn't believe it... but then again, actually I could."

The band put its seal of approval on the initiative by proposing a one-off CD to be given to contributors. The CD proved quite an incentive for fans on both sides of the pond, according to UK fan Tony Wood: "If I'm honest it was the 'We'll give a CD free to anyone that gives more than $x' - can't remember the figure. I admit it - I can be a mercenary b***ard!"

Nothing else was offered to the fans who contributed. No free tickets, no venue decisions, no special concessions. Donations came from all over the world - not just the USA, but from other countries including the UK, Germany, Netherlands, France, New Zealand, Thailand and Mexico. Even Mark Kelly donated - he was the fourteenth person on the list, "to give the whole project a certain legitimacy," according to Jeff Woods. "The further it went, the more I was in awe of people's generosity!" Most donations were between $25 and $50, with a UK fan in the Bath area proffering $1,500! Says Mark, "Once it got past the $25,000 mark, we started making plans for the tour."

GETTING THE TOUR MOVING

By April, the Freaks' pockets were all but empty. Dan Sherman of the Web North America provided a thousand mail addresses, with respondents almost doubling the subscriptions to $40,000, but still more was needed. MC Jeff Woods wrote: "We are short $13,281 as of Monday evening and we are running out of time. We've pretty much got a deadline of this week to meet the Tour Fund Goal - some basic decisions regarding a US Tour are likely to be made THIS WEEK." Behind the scenes, John Arnison was meeting with the band's record label in the US, Red Ant, and needed to make an impact. "We wanted a big dollar amount there," noted Jeff. Once again the fans came up trumps. John was amazed. "I'd put a tour budget together and said it needed 50K. They raised it. It was incredible!"

Jeff Woods visited London on May 12, meeting with Mark and John to make arrangements, based on Mark's plan to keep Red Ant-fronted shows separate from Tour Fund shows. Jeff was sent back to the US with the objective to identify places away from those already planned by the promoters, but near enough to big cities to ensure attendance. "We'd raised so much money, we could stretch it out a bit," says Jeff. "Mark had sent a schedule; there was a huge gap after California so I suggested a convention at Rochester. The band were quite happy with that." Jeff's involvement included everything from bookings, selling tickets and provisioning the rider at three dates: Pittsburgh, Poughkeepsie and Rochester itself.

It was not all plain sailing: more complications came from both record company and management. Tensions had already surfaced in May with Red Ant, who did not want to accept the money at all, "They thought it made Red Ant look bad," said Jeff. "Mark feared something like this might happen from the outset." By June tempers were fraying, and matters came to a head with Wally Version at Hit And Run USA who appeared to be anti-fund. Matters were quickly resolved, as a post by Jeff confirmed:

The tour will happen. It will be extensive.
The CDs will happen, exactly 1000 of them.
The fund has succeeded and will continue to succeed.
The fund is in good hands with Hit And Run.

Jeff's optimism nearly proved misplaced in July, as calamity struck: Red Ant's mother company, Alliance Entertainment, filed for bankruptcy. Suddenly it was all hands to the pumps again, to raise another $15,000 to replace money the record company had planned to put in. Meanwhile, the band turned to their old colleagues from Castle UK, in particular ex-CEO Terry Shand and ex-MD John Knowles who had formed a new company, Eagle Rock, itself allied with US label Velvel. Are you following this? Well, nor could anyone else! According to Steve Hogarth at the time, "We've had the kind of year where I no longer believe anything that they tell me - management or record label."

As it turned out, Velvel were looking more proactive than Red Ant had been, both concerning the tour and the release of *This Strange Engine* in the US. "They seem really committed to the band and they're having a lot of ideas. So we're more optimistic about the future than we otherwise would have been at the moment," continued H, sanguine despite the fact that the album release was being delayed until the end of the tour. "The timing wasn't nearly as useful as it could have been, but we had already committed to this tour and we weren't going to try to move it."

With all the ducks finally lined up, the band crossed the pond and toured the USA, Canada and Mexico, squeezing in 25 dates before it wrapped up on September 27. Jeff's baby, the fan club show in Pittsburgh, was on August 30, at the Graffiti Showcase. There was an unexpected treat for fans that arrived during the afternoon, as nobody was on security to prevent them from entering the sound check. Early arrivals witnessed Steve Hogarth grappling with the lyrics to a couple of Fish-era songs - 'White Russian' and 'Warm Wet Circles'. "It is harder to remember what you're supposed to be doing when there's a few hundred people in front of you all cheering," recalled Steve at the time. "In the end, I gave the microphone to one of the kids in the crowd and he sang 'White Russian' while the band played."

The following day, all bar Steve Rothery played an acoustic set, including 'Made Again' with Pete on guitar, at the House of Guitars in Rochester, New York State. Meanwhile Jeff was discovering the kinds of things that can go wrong on a tour. "There were no towels at the venue," he recalls. "I had to find 20 towels for the band to wipe off the sweat during the show. Eventually I had to run back to the hotel and beg the desk clerk to borrow the towels, then race back." That evening's gig (in fan John Stevens' opinion "the best I've ever seen the boys play") was recorded and mixed by Stewart Every, for release as a limited edition CD for tour fund contributors. The band headed north, playing three dates in Canada before playing a dozen more in the US. The show went on – and on: even Pete getting mugged and beaten up in Toronto wasn't enough to slow the players down. Despite the fact he went to hospital with concussion and horrendous bruising he still got up and played the next evening. "I was a mess but I felt I owed it to the fans."

Determined to make the most of the tour was fan Jodi Tack, who attended the first two shows, August 24 at old haunt The Coach House in San Juan Capistrano, then the next night in Hollywood before heading for the Massachusetts leg, before a final gig (for Jodi) at La Spectrum in Montreal. "Yes, I am completely insane and I did travel thousands of miles and spend hundreds of dollars just to see a band," she laughs. The Montreal show was made particularly special by an extra encore, played by H in memory of Diana, Princess of Wales, who had been killed in a Parisian road tunnel a week before. "H came out and sat in front of the keyboard. He started playing an old song about great political figures who'd been assassinated ['Abraham, Martin and John', a 1968 hit for Dion]. In place of the last verse, H sang, 'Have you seen my friend Diana...' On the last line his voice cracked with emotion, he turned sideways on the bench, put his head down in his lap and I could see him wiping his eyes. I lost it. I just started weeping. As the crowd clapped and cheered respectfully, H approached the front of the stage. His eyes were a little red and you could still see the tears threatening to spill over yet again. It was the most moving, emotional experience I have ever had at a concert."

Jeff Woods' efforts didn't end with the tour – there remained the matter of distributing the tour fund CD to 1,400 eager benefactors. Jeff, his wife Michelle and willing assistant Karin Breiter set to assembling jewel cases, inserting numbered liner notes and CDs, all the while avoiding paper cuts. The first two hours were the worst, says Michelle Woods – "It took us about 2 hours to do 200 with 3 people, but we did hone the process down to an efficient assembly line." Calamity struck when the trio realised the CDs were misnumbered – a printing error on the original CDs ("Marillion" was spelt wrong) meant the CDs had to be re-pressed, but the serial number counter wasn't reset so numbering started at 1,354. "At this point Jeff had a minor (okay it was a MAJOR) meltdown," says Michelle. "Most of it came from his feeling like he was letting down the Freaks, a group that he cared a lot about. Finally we realised there was nothing we could do to rectify the situation, and we continued getting the CDs ready for shipment to the best of our ability (all the while drinking heavily!). It was a very good feeling when we finished and stuffed the last Jiffy mailer."

LOOK BACK IN SURPRISE

This Strange Engine was finally released in the US on 7 October 1997. The preceding months had been revelatory - with the tour fund they had created a first, not just for Marillion but for the whole world of contemporary music. Since it happened, other fan-rich bands, from Dream Theater to Alphaville and the Foo Fighters, have considered using a tour fund to get to otherwise off-limits places but none has succeeded to the same extent. It was no easy ride - there were several points along the way where the fund could have been canned, the money misdirected, the fan support withdrawn. Yet, somehow, despite the record company shenanigans and other complications, it had come together in the end.

So - why did the fans do it? Says Steve Rothery, "I don't know many groups that have such a supportive and passionate fan base, to the extent that they would be willing to invest so much time and money." Of course, the fund could not have happened without the Internet. "What a leveller the Internet is turning out to be," remarked H at the time. "It gives ordinary people the freedom to talk to each other, to publicise something and to bring together small international communities of enthusiasts for whatever it happens to be." Perhaps most importantly, in the band's first year on an independent label, the fans gave Marillion something they needed more than tour money - the assurance that whatever the band did, there would be a solid, loyal fan base to support them. "The tour fund gave us much more flexibility and freedom," recalls Rothery. "There's a refreshing honesty in that."

As the transatlantic fun came to an end, the band returned to complete the last dates on its European leg of the tour and fans such as Jeff Woods could return to their normal, more mundane lives. "In hindsight I didn't know what I had got myself into - booking three shows, selling tickets and so on. I have nothing but respect for the tour managers - Paul Lewis and Tim Bricusse." Jeff's final words on Freaks were: "The only people that made any money on this strange tour of America were the crew. Marillion themselves did not take pay cheques from the shows. They paid the bills for travel, paid the crew, paid the expenses, but didn't get paid themselves. How many of YOU would work for six weeks, travelling nearly every day, without pay, just because someone 'called you a genius'?"

The tour fund saga ended as it had started, right in the hands of Marillion's devoted audience. "I'm not sure that Marillion really took us seriously at first," Jeff Woods later said. "They gave us tacit approval to at least try, but in the beginning I don't think they expected us to pull it off." Indeed. "This was a one-off event, a combination of luck, bright ideas, circumstances, goodwill and hard work that consummated once and for all Marillion's relationship with its fans. For all these reasons as well, it could never happen again," says Steve Hogarth. "It would be like getting a present, and then coming back and saying, 'That was nice, can we have that again?'" So, there would be no more tour funds. But this wouldn't be the final demonstration of fan power, nor the greatest.

13

Born To Run

This Strange Engine offered Marillion the first opportunity to stand on its own two feet without a major record label acting as either prop or shackle. All the same however, Castle offered no respite – while the band wasn't under particular pressure to produce a new album, financially it had no choice but to keep turning the handle. "As a business we were struggling a bit," says Mark, understatedly. Following the completion of the impressively extensive 1997 tour (including Marillion's 1,000th gig, on October 27 at the Amsterdam Paradiso), the band took a few weeks off to recharge creatively before returning to The Racket Club and getting on with the job.

While the previous album had largely been an acoustic effort, as the jamming sessions began a strong desire emerged to increase the tempo and bring in some more mainstream influences. Alongside the continued development of their musical style, the Marillos felt the time was right to get in control of their own destiny. Between January and March 1998 changes were planned to both organisation and approach, strengthening Marillion's independence still further.

SOMETHING COMPLETELY DIFFERENT

On January 22 and with some aplomb, the band launched its first Web presence. "Marillion's Racket Club Online is now officially live!" proclaimed the email as albums on the band's home-grown Racket Records label, as well as commercial releases, were made available for online purchase for the first time. Marillion's first eWeb newsletter came a month later, emailed to fan club subscribers and others who had registered on the web site. The missive announced the launch of a new-look, "tremendously improved" UK fan club, "with whom we're maintaining a cosy relationship to ensure we minimise the distance between you lot and us lot."

According to the eWeb it was not just the fan club that was changing - the boys had also reached a collective decision to part company with John Arnison. John had been managing the band for 16 years, but "things change and our vision and his were no longer one-and-the-same," went the official line. John had been finding it increasingly difficult to devote the time Marillion needed, proposing Tim Bricusse for day-to-day management tasks. The band had also been seeking more visibility on the accounts. Says Steve Rothery, "John seemed to adopt a policy of 'deliberate vagueness'." Things came to a head when John and the boys met in a pub and he made some stark suggestions. "I said that, the way the finances were looking, Marillion could take up six months of their time and they should find something else to do for the other six," recalls John, whose pointed statements provided a wake-up call. "We don't want a manager who says that sort of thing," was Mark's response. Says Mark, "He said, 'What do you want me to do?' We all shrugged - he got the message!"

As John drove away from Marillion after a decade and a half, he felt like he had been through a divorce. "I'm not sure they did need me any more," John comments, ever the pragmatist. "Besides, it gave them a kick up the backside - it's probably what they needed!" Management tasks were passed to Iron Maiden's manager, Rod Smallwood. "He heard we were without a manager so he approached us," says Mark. The relationship only lasted about a year before it was clear that Rod, too, was unable to allocate sufficient time for the band. Says H, "Rod struck me as a very moral and straight man (rare in artist management) but he was too busy managing Iron Maiden to focus on us. I remember him telling me he reserved one afternoon a week specifically for Marillion. It was supposed to impress us! I never managed to find out which afternoon it was."

A live release was in the plans to sate the hunger of the fans, based on a number of shows from the *Strange Engine* tour, notably The Vooruit in Gent, Belgium, Paris's Bataclan and the Hanehof at Geleen in the Netherlands. In an eWeb Mark Kelly asked for suggestions for a name - "this live engine" or "these strange gents in Gent" or "whatever suggestions you can come up with that are better!" Eventually, *Piston Broke* was released June 1 1998, with a cover by Bill Smith Studios, which had been welcomed back into the fold – a beneficiary of the band's new-found status. Robert Lewis of AMZ wrote, "Buy it, because it's a great taste of what I believe to be the best live band ever!" No bias there, then.

Work on the new album was proceeding smoothly, with a number of strong arrangements already developed in sessions known as "Trawling for Olives". The list of songs included 'Answering Machine', 'Now She'll Never Know', 'These Chains', 'Tumble Down The Years', 'Under The Sun', 'Deserve', 'Or You Could Love', 'This House Aches', 'Upside Down' and 'Swing Doors'. Said Mark in an eWeb, "These songs may or may not appear on the album, and those that do may sound completely different than where we are now!" Eventually, the band divided the tracks into an A-list of compatible songs and a B-list that needed more work. Once again the album was self-produced, with in-house engineer Stewart Every receiving co-producer credits for the first time – said Mark Kelly, "More like having a sounding board than somebody steering the ship." Steve Hogarth agreed: "Using Stewart as a producer was a natural step. We've all got a lot of respect for his ears and his ability to mix."

As the album progressed, the band members' desire to break new ground increased, recalls Steve Rothery, "I disagreed at first but went along with the challenge to do something different." Mark Kelly made extensive use of a new JP8000 keyboard, avoiding the generic strings sounds. "They are a fall-back position when you can't think of anything else to do," he said. Pete Trewavas reverted to his old Rickenbacker bass guitar, and Steve Hogarth used a recording Walkman in places, to distort the vocals. Eventually Rothers was persuaded to borrow a few guitars from Dave Gregory. "I think Steve H was anxious to tempt Rothers into experimenting with more retro, organic sounds. There was a Gretsch Country Club, a Gibson SG Junior (that actually sounds like a Gretsch), and I think my Charvel Surfcaster," he says.

The approach worked. 'This House Aches', or 'House' as it would be known, came together in a moment of rhythm-fuelled inspiration for Pete: "We must have been jamming for a couple of hours, I think, and everyone was getting laid back, probably not even thinking about what was going on. At times like that my mind usually wanders and I start to think that nothing else is really going to happen today. Then that drum rhythm starts up and I find myself just knowing what I should play. It's as if someone has planted it in my mind. At times like those it is great being in Marillion. Those are the moments we look for and nurture — doesn't matter what style it is, if it has real meaning and soul that is what counts." Steve Hogarth took the original jam, added a drum beat and an arrangement. "We worked on his version and incorporated that in with the original. Not everyone was convinced at first but it became one of those songs that really comes to life while recording."

'A Few Words For The Dead' evolved into a multi-layered opus of which even Dave Meegan would have been proud. A total of 96 tracks were in the mix, including a crew jacket from the *Brave* tour (played with fingernails). "We had a whole load of things going," says Mark. "It was almost written in the studio. It could never have been written unless we recorded it." The track also includes the happy accident of a live chorus of 'Easter' - the band were re-using an old tape for the mix, previously used to record a gig at Middlesbrough. "They sounded great where they were, so we left them in." The result was worth it - adds H, "It has that tension that holds and breaks like a wire, if anyone else had done it, people would think it was amazing."

For the first time since Steve Hogarth joined the band, there was no writing credit for John Helmer. The "decision" was more by chance, as Helmer-penned lyrics to 'Interior Lulu' and 'Tumble Down The Years' had already been recorded: trouble was, the band didn't feel comfortable with the state of either. Explained H, "At the last minute we decided not to master them due to musical reasons, nothing to do with the words and they may well reappear on the next album." And so they would, but it still led to a bit of discomfort. H noted, "I'm a total coward and I haven't yet had the guts to tell him... If he believes me when I tell him it wasn't deliberate, I'm sure he'll understand. I always got on very well with John."

Racket Records staffer Erik Nielsen also picked up a production credit for 'The Answering Machine'. Originally acoustic, the band were nervous that it was "a bit Jethro Tull" according to H. Explains Erik, "I said it was a bit Hey Nonny Nonny, you should speed it up a bit and give it a bit more guts." So that's what they did - the album track was recorded in a single take.

RADIATING OUT

In June 1998 the Marillos returned to Phil Beaumont's Forge Studio at Oswestry to mix the new album. Says Ian, "The World Cup was on, Nick Davis was there, it was great fun." Following Steve Hogarth's successful one-nighter at The Walls restaurant the year before (with the first incarnation of the H-band), he suggested holding a low-key, light-hearted event, with an acoustic set and a minimum of publicity - a "candlelit dinner with Marillion". Once he had the go-ahead from the rest of the band, Steve approached restaurant manager Geoff Hughes with a proposal: the band would be fed for two weeks, in exchange for a one-night performance on Friday June 26. Geoff readily agreed and printed up a hundred tickets.

Low-key? Pah. The Walls mailed out its regulars, a couple of whom happened to be Marillion aficionados. Within days, the beacons on the worldwide network of Freaks were lit and air, hotel and restaurant bookings were being made from as far away as Mexico, Australia and Japan. A second night was fixed to accommodate the demand, and also, said H, "We decided a couple of verses of 'Easter' simply wouldn't do... we rehearsed for a week!" On the night, fans arrived to see a discreet set-up with a couple of extra touches. Sitting on top of the restaurant's own grand piano, was Andrew Gent's Strange Engine.

The set included certain songs that were destined to be acoustic, such as 'Runaway' and 'Now She'll Never Know', as well as "some surprises" including 'Beyond You' and 'The Answering Machine' (in its original, "Tull" version), a reggae take on 'The Lap Of Luxury' and a bluesy 'Hooks In You'. A number of covers followed, including 'Fake Plastic Trees', a "conscious tip of the hat" to Radiohead, Marillion's stable mates during their EMI years. This made it to the B-side of the 'These Chains' single, says H as a deliberate "throwing down of a gauntlet and going, 'Well there, what do you make of that then?'" to the press and sceptics.

The Walls gigs were an inspiration to fans and band alike, as an indication of how popular the band remained and how solid was the globally dispersed foundation that supported them. One lucky fan was Dave Rogers, who had stumbled across the event when he called the Web UK hotline. "My timing had been (unintentionally) perfect," he says. "The whole experience was utterly magical, and the first time I really got to mix and meet up with folks that had the same music running in their veins. Yes, any gig has fans, but this gig was full of the most devoted, beautiful people. Everyone had time for everyone else, and it was so relaxed you could be forgiven for thinking it was a family celebration; it just happened that a few relatives could throw a tune together! The stripped-down performances were absolutely sublime." Agrees fan Krys Boswell, "What a place to hear them live for the first time. I was overwhelmed." Also in the audience was Simon Hanhart, who had engineered and mixed both *Script For A Jester's Tear* and *Fugazi*. "It was possibly the best gig I have ever been to," says Simon. "A wall of texture just washed over me."

The band didn't feel that the quality of the Oswestry recordings warranted a CD release – not least the difficulties miking the restaurant's piano. "It was a standard piano, miked up so all the noise of the room was spilling into the piano mikes," explains Mark. "In particular, it was right next to the drums." The initial intention was to take the acoustic arrangements back to the Racket Club and make a studio-grade acoustic album, but in the end Mark re-recorded the piano parts, and the band released the June 28 performance in its entirety as the *Unplugged At The Walls* double CD. It remains one of Racket Records' best selling CDs. "If anyone ever needs proof as to the skill of the band, that album is the evidence," continues fan Dave Rogers. One audience participation moment that couldn't be erased from the disc was a certain fan's repeated announcements of where he was from: "Bishop's Castle, Steven!" The perpetrator finally turned up on the Opium Den mailing list in November 2001, and has since apologised!

Following a final mix by Stewart Every in Oswestry before its assembly at Abbey Road, *Radiat10n* was released on September 21 1998. Illustration duties were returned to Bill Smith Studios, "coming back in through the side door," says Bill in reference to some work Carl had been doing on Marillion's own Racket Records releases. The front and back covers were graced by Carl's partner Christine Bone, with images taken from an afternoon session on Hayle Beach, near St Ives in Cornwall. "There were lots of holidaymakers staring at us as I was also in the sea covered in camera gear," says Carl. No, her head doesn't normally look like that.

Prior to the European release date, Mark Kelly emailed his fellow Freaks, requesting that fans planning on buying the album did so in the week of its release - resulting in chart positions for the album across Europe. Despite a feeling among members that *Radiat10n* was maybe a bit of a mistake, the reviews were as positive as any. On AMZ, Robert Lewis wrote: "*Radiat10n* is definitely something you don't want to miss. As a whole, this album steers Marillion in a whole different direction from which they were pointed with the last album." ITVNet remarked, "It demonstrates an impressive level of musical intervention while maintaining a playfully humanistic energy." Dale Jensen wrote in *All Music Guide*, "'Answering Machine', 'These Chains' and 'Under The Sun' are appealing tracks, while 'Three Minute Boy', yet another Marillion examination of the impact of fame, contains some of Steve Rothery's best guitar work in years." Oh, the irony!

Many fans were quite happy with the new sound. "Believe it or not, *Radiat10n* is my favourite album," writes fan Chris Brockwell, "I return to it time and time again because of its raw edge and deeper-than-deep meanings!" Mark Donald writes, "'Cathedral Wall' is up there in my top five, whilst 'A Few Words For The Dead' gets better with every listen, and it's had many I can assure you!" Mike Richichi wrote how, "*Radiat10n* is, quite simply, amazing. It's probably the most stylistically varied Marillion album, going from near-metal to quiet, haunting ballads." However, for some fans, the concern this time was the album's modern influences rather than their lack of them - in particular an accusation of sounding like Radiohead, which was met with raised eyebrows by the band. As for the deliberate attempt to ditch the 'prog rock' image, Steve Hogarth noted, "The whole progressive label is yours, not ours, in the first place!"

Criticism of the production values met with differing opinions from the band members. "The choice of sounds and arrangement of parts was deliberate and radical," says Pete, but Rothers is more dubious: "It was a half-baked attempt to sound younger than our years." "I haven't got a problem with that, I don't agree," says H. "I didn't enjoy that album," says Ian. "We tried to step outside ourselves. It sounds like a second rate version of who we were trying to copy. It backfired. I found it too harsh, not musical enough." All players agree that the sonic quality could have been better, even for the US version which was mastered again by Simon Heyworth at Chop 'Em Out Studios (owned by Sanctuary), before its release. "If we were going to remaster one album of recent years, it would be *Radiat10n*," says Pete. Agrees Rothers, "It's more edgy than it needs to be. Steven Wilson thought it was a good album but really wanted to remix it." Concurs Steven, "I think it's an album with good material, poorly mixed. Sonically, it's a bit flat."

Money, or lack of it, was a deciding factor when the band came to decide the tour itinerary – if the band couldn't guarantee an audience, they wouldn't play a venue, explained Mark Kelly, "On the *Afraid Of Sunlight* tour we didn't get that many people when we played Glasgow so on the following tour we weren't going to play there. We were hounded by people so eventually we put a warm-up date in Glasgow and of course we didn't get that many people, which was exactly what the promoter predicted..." The tour started on September 14, following warm-up fan club shows in Oxford, Utrecht and Cologne. The continental fan show dates were significant for their transport arrangements - both the Tivoli Theatre, Utrecht on September 5 1998, and Alter Wartesaal, Cologne on September 12 were performed with a cut-down rig that could be put through the check-in desk rather than going on as cargo. "We did get hammered a couple of times for the extra gear," laughs Mark.

As with the album, after the more acoustic nature of *This Strange* tour, the new tour featured a more dynamic set list. "The last tour seemed like a slower paced set, I suppose we were compensating for that in a way as well," says Mark Kelly. Ian Mosley agreed: "There's 'Gazpacho' and 'Cannibal Surf Babe' which we really get off on. That's why we do them." For the first time ever on tour, there were no Fish-era songs. Again, pragmatism was claimed as the key - "We're playing our most recent material really which is six albums' worth," claimed Mark at the time. Added H, "When you've got a two-hour show it's natural to spend 40 minutes on the new album which leaves you 1 hour 20 minutes to cover the previous nine. So it's unlikely that the first two or three albums are going to get much of a look-in." The end of an era, then, even if there had been a couple of stumbles into the new one.

Fan Paul Rael was at the Oxford Zodiac fan club gig: "It was during one of the blackest periods of my life, a severe low point. The music hit home like a lightning bolt that night and 'King' in particular was like the band were talking directly to me. This wasn't a gig, it was a revelation - it was time to change my life! The music just got into my soul that night." Whatever was happening musically, the band's fine romance with their fans was developing as strongly as ever.

RADIAT1ON

The second album with unsupportive Castle doesn't prevent the band from turning in a collection of songs that show them well into their third era, (Fish being the first, and *Seasons End* to *Afraid Of Sunlight* being the second) ushering in the song-writing and sound experimentation that culminated in 2001's *Anoraknophobia*. *Radiat10n* doesn't have a clear theme or concept, but is no less coherent for that. One thing that does emerge from the writing is the suggestion that all was not well chez Hogarth. To whatever extent this was borne out in reality, several songs appear to be about the disintegration of a relationship.

This album is particularly notable for Steve Rothery's changed guitar sounds: one moment funky wah-wah, the next Brit-poppy, then a Beatles pastiche and then a sheer blues tone, all the while conjuring magic in such a way that only the remarkable Rothery could have done. Again produced by the band, there's something a little muddy in some of the production. A crying shame, since it took live versions of the material to really showcase how strong it was.

Well, if you wanted a seriously different way to open an album, here it is! The whole album compressed into a forty second slap in the face, followed by a Noel Coward-esque music hall number, 'Costa del Slough'. This sarky little nugget is the anti-*Seasons End*! We then segue via a Hammond swirl into the scratchy funk of 'Under The Sun', which continues the faux-naïve idea that global warming is a benefit to us, and that only a fool could think otherwise... Steve Rothery's guitar wah-wahs away over Pete's grooving bass and Ian's thumping drums, whilst Mark lays down slabs of Lesley-speakered Hammond organ that lift under us like a rolling wave against the shore.

'The Answering Machine' is another rocker, first previewed at the Walls restaurant show the year before. In that incarnation, it was an acoustic number with more than a hint of Jethro Tull about it. Now, it's a rollicking great juggernaut of a tune, powered by Ian's strangely off-kilter rhythms and Mark's arpeggiating keys. It's the first hint of the relationship theme which pokes its head up throughout the album, and whilst the music is fun, the lyric is anything but, Steve's metallicised voice phoned in from a distant continent trying to save his relationship, but being confronted with the eponymous answering machine.

'Three Minute Boy' is Marillion rising to a challenge. Okay, Oasis, you reckon you have a monopoly on the Beatles? Well, stitch this! H said the song is "Rock and Roll anthropology really. It's a cocktail of all my earliest memories of seeing John and Yoko in the registry office and Paul and Linda and Mick and Marianne Faithfull, all those kinds of early bits of films I used to watch." And if that isn't Liam Gallagher and Patsy Kensit in the third verse, I'll eat my hat! Steve Rothery is in great form on the extended outro, with a two-minute solo, during which the Beatles influence is acknowledged with a low rendition of the harmony from

'Hey Jude' thrown in.

After three big-sounding songs, we settle into the impassioned 'Now She'll Never Know'. There's an intimacy here which makes it almost uncomfortable to listen to, a sense of 'Wooah! Hang on! I'm just a fan - this is too personal; you're not supposed to share this much with us!' With Pete playing acoustic, and faint keyboards from Mark, it's as though we're in the vocal booth with H as he sings, and the regret and introspection in his voice as he tries to make amends is almost that bit too much. Can you have too much heart?

'These Chains' finds H at his lowest ebb, desolate, alone and broken, with nowhere to go. Desperate for something, anything to break his black mood, he takes the car and drives out into the countryside, where he sees the first breaks of colour in the night, and as dawn breaks, he takes inspiration from the sight. If he can just forget about what is expected of him, if he can ignore the strictures of convention and society, maybe he can find the hope and the strength to get over it. Another Beatles influence kicks in over the chorus, a first cousin to 'All You Need Is Love', with riffing strings, a '60s-sounding production, and a lovely solo by Rothery over the outro.

The bluesy 'Born To Run' concerns the people of the North of England, where H grew up. In many respects, it's a song about folk who put their heads down, and get on with life, regardless of the challenges they might face. Having run with his dreams, H reflects on the fact that while he may live elsewhere with the trappings of success and a life that is so different from those he grew up amongst, he is still a product of that upbringing. Kudos goes to Steve Rothery, displaying yet another side to his mastery of the guitar, as he turns in a breath-taking performance of control and expression.

The band have described 'Cathedral Wall' as a James Bond villain's theme, and there's certainly something of John Barry's influence in the powerful string intro to the verses. The song sees an insomniac H finding solace from what we again presume are troubles at home by lying against the imposing stones of the cathedral. Dark and terrifying, Mark Kelly's vast chords tower above us like the walls of the darkened church and H's double-tracked vocal certainly lends a creepy feel to the whole thing. As we reach the end, there is a reprise of 'These Chains', but with H alone on a piano.

A song about hope reprising at the end of a song about despair, which brings us nicely into closing track 'A Few Words For The Dead', Marillion at their unconventional best. Beginning with the intoning voice of a Native American mystic saying that his music comes from the heart, and must be treated with respect, the song feeds into a mysterious mist of sound, through which we are vaguely aware of other sounds moving past. Hypnotic rhythms and motifs build and change against which H spins a tale of machismo and blood feuds. Hate-filled and nihilistic, we're just at the point of wondering what has happened to the humane Marillion we know and love, when the song suddenly changes tack, and suggests, 'Or you could love...' And it unfurls into an exquisite alternate universe of possibility and redemption that shimmers and sparkles its way into the distance, tempting us to join it.

Bill Smith Studios were back on board for this album, the cover of which features a flame-spurting girl with a clutch of wildflowers in her hands standing on a beach, possibly that of the Costa del Slough. The flames that belch from the headless body resemble nothing so much as the terrible oil fires seen during the Gulf war in the early 1990s. Behind her, the beach is a lurid red, perhaps as a result of all that radiation. The album cover was distinctive and eye-catching. And as for the girl? Well, the tide's coming in...

14

You Get What You Deserve

Christmas 1998 saw Marillion's first fan club CD, the brainchild of Simon Clarke and the first fruit of the brainstorming sessions between the new Web team and the band. "We thought it would make a nice change, instead of giving you a newsletter or a dodgy piece of A4 parading as such, to put out a CD this Christmas," announced H, against a background of laughter and heckling from the rest of the band. "Please spare a thought for those less fortunate - people in the media, bankers, politicians?"

The CD featured a selection of cuts from the new album, plus several karaoke tracks. "We've put down a few of the masters without my dulcet tones," explained Steve, "So make a tape, sing on the karaoke and send it to us." The prize was a visit to the Racket Club to record the winning version professionally - "You'll be able to take a CD away with you to impress your chums - we'll also be providing a CD for the very worst." A staggering 132 entries were received, and the band painstakingly set to listening to the tapes to find the best - and worst - among them. On May 1 three winners were announced - Anne Bond and her primary school class (singing 'Beautiful'), Michelle De Luca ('These Chains') and Bob van Ingen ('Beautiful' again).

School teacher and fan Anne Bond recalls having the "crazy" idea of entering the children in her class: "It wasn't easy teaching them the song, it was not really in their range and I did not think the end result was brilliant so I left it at home for a few weeks thinking that I was being stupid to enter it. But a friend told me I had to send it off." Little did she know that it would be the winning entry, and that she would be taking her class to the Racket Club the following October. "It was a brilliant, special day. I remember being really nervous, especially when I had to sing a line of 'Beautiful' in front of Steve Hogarth. Everyone was lovely and Stewart Every was very patient with the children. H played them all the instruments and they all crowded around him and asked questions. Some of the girls were totally smitten and asked him for a kiss. I asked Steve Hogarth about it later and he said it had been a lovely, special day for him too and it had meant a lot to him to hear the words he had written sung by children."

What was the future to hold? Under the terms of the deal, this was to be the third and final album distributed by Castle, a label which had delivered little on its promise. The band might have achieved musical independence, but at the cost of poor promotion and a still dwindling broader fan base, even while its core community appeared as strong as ever. The circle needed to be squared, and as Marillion took stock of experiences such as the Tour Fund a new strategy started to emerge, the crux of which involved getting the band away from labels completely and into... something else. What it was, nobody knew.

CAUGHT IN THE NET

The Castle treadmill continued to turn. Writing sessions for a new album kicked off almost immediately after the final scream of the *Radiat10n* tour, at the end of November 1998: time was money, and the band did not have the luxury of either. A couple of John Helmer-penned tracks were already in the bank - 'Interior Lulu' and 'Tumble Down The Years' - but both needed better arrangements. Other, postponed *Radiat10n* ideas were lining up, including 'Enlightened' and 'Go!', and additional Helmer lyrics were available, notably what would become 'A Legacy' and 'Built-In Bastard Radar'. "John had delivered a few juicy lyrics right at the end of the *Radiat10n* sessions," remarked H. "It was too late to do anything with them." Technically there was one variation on the now-traditional process - recordings were made to Minidisc rather than DAT. Otherwise, it was business as usual.

Events took a near-calamitous turn on January 11 of the new year, when Pete Trewavas was hit by a car as he cycled home from The Racket Club. He suffered multiple injuries, spending time in intensive care and ending up with a metal pin in his leg. Pete's progress was encouraged by "incredible support" from his colleagues, but there was no respite. "I felt obliged to get back to writing and being part of the band as soon as possible," he says. "It was a huge struggle at times before I got sufficiently fit. I remember being in quite a lot of pain just from the exertion of getting around." Pete recovered quickly enough to make not just a Marillion album but also, six months later, an album with his prog supergroup, Transatlantic. What a trouper.

The show had to go on. Rothers had been working at home on a completely new arrangement for 'Interior Lulu'; at the same time H was developing the ideas for 'House' and 'A Legacy'. By January, the songs were arranged in more comfortable ways, with any harsh edges smoothed off. Explains Pete, "We'd learned with *Radiat10n*, so we tried to choose warmer, nicer, more encouraging sounds." The other lesson the band had been forced to learn was how to write songs without layering instruments on top of the bass section. Mark was particularly pleased with 'Go!' - "We wrote that for *Radiat10n*, but just couldn't get it to happen. It was a nice surprise how it turned out."

Recording started in earnest at the beginning of April, and by June 1999 the band headed to The Forge at Oswestry, where Nick Davis mixed the more commercially oriented tracks, 'Deserve', 'Rich' and 'Tumble Down The Years'. "I spent a long weekend up there and bashed out the three tracks, two of them were very good," says Nick, intriguingly. Stewart Every remained at the Racket

Club to work on the "marathon" 'Interior Lulu'. Unfortunately, on the band's return they weren't keen on the result. "Unfairly to Stewart, we'd bought this brand new digital desk, and expected Stewart to just get on with it," explains Mark. "Stewart didn't like the sound he was making, but didn't know why or how to make it better." The band didn't like it either, so with much relief it was agreed to can the desk and bring in Trevor Vallis (who had worked with The Europeans) to mix the remaining tracks at the Racket Club on the old analogue desk. When they heard the results, however, the band didn't like what he was producing either. "He had this little box you plug everything into - it was supposed to make everything sound more dynamic," says Mark. "It was the sort of thing everyone used in the Eighties, until somebody said it was rubbish!"

There were moments of respite, not least another example of fan power one Friday morning on July 23 1999, when BBC Radio 1 DJ Simon Mayo prompted the inevitable by asking the question, "Where are Marillion now? And who cares anyway?" in the "dead or alive" segment of his show. Over the weekend that followed, Simon received 1600 emails from Marillion fans all over the world; these continued during the week. A month later, after Simon had taken a well-earned (though surely unrelated) break, his first guest was Mark Kelly. Who cares indeed!

Back at the Racket Club the feeling of impending doom was building fast: the band had already booked the cut of the album and the mix had to be completed by August 15 for a 1999 release. "The press needs a three-month deadline, so for an interview to appear in the press in time, you have to do it three months up front," explained H. A couple of fan club shows had been planned at the Zodiac, back to back with the shooting of the video for 'Deserve', so in July it was time to come out from under the rock. On camera duty were the Boom Boom Boys, South Africans Paul Rowlston and Jeremy "Jayce" Briers ("Pretty much the luckiest 'vidiots' in the whole world," says Paul), who had contacted the band on-spec for the privilege. "With the benefit of hindsight it's easy to see how our timing, for once, was just perfect," says Paul, who had been looking for videos on the marillion.com site with Jayce. "We found what everyone found when they came in search of content for their cathode - nothing! We stewed on this for a short time and then - being uniquely positioned to actually do something - we chose to do something!" So the pair sent a proposal and a storyboard off into the ether and waited. "When Erik wandered into the Racket Club clutching our unsolicited proposal, it could not have been at a better time," says Paul. "They sent us a show reel, it looked like they could hold a camera and edit," says Mark. "Plus they said they'd do it for nothing - that clinched the deal! We were a bit nervous as we knew we'd be stuck with them for a week, but as soon as we met them we knew it would be alright."

Another attendee at the Zodiac gigs was Porcupine Tree front man and long-time Marillion fan Steven Wilson. "Steve Rothery mentioned they were having a few problems with the mixing of the new album," explains Steven. "I said I would be happy to have a crack at it and so they sent me over the tapes to 'Interior Lulu' as an "audition". It took me a couple of days (well it's 15 minutes long!) and I took a few liberties with it, editing and moving things around, but the 'audition' mix is the one that's on the album." Says Mark, "He's a talented guy; we liked what he did. We had to persuade him to use a bit less of the megaphone voice though - he said, that's my trademark." With tangible relief, Marillion let Steven loose on the other tracks. "Steve Wilson was a saviour!" says Pete. Agrees Mark, "We kept saying, 'Could you just mix one more?' He mixed five tracks in a week!"

Only 'House' remains from Trevor's ill-fated sessions with the analogue desk. "His best one," says Mark. The final mix was completed on August 16 and the master completed the next day. All in all, the band members were feeling decidedly up-to-date, with 'House' considered by Steve Rothery as "the most contemporary sounding track we've done in a long time." Even Country and Western influences were acknowledged in 'Deserve'. "We've finally written a song you can line dance to!" laughed H. Incidentally, the lyrics for 'Rich' were based on a number of quotations from female writers. Explains Mark, "A PR agency had produced a proposal for us, it used these quotes so Steve H took them away and made a song out of them."

Following the completion of the album the band went their separate ways, working on projects of their own (such as Ben Castle's 'Postmankind' for Ian) or taking some well-earned time off. Four Marillos reunited at the International Managers Forum awards at the Hyde Park Hilton in London on September 22 1999, with ex-Kula Shaker drummer Paul Winter-Hart standing in for Ian, who was on holiday in Maui. "My wife had bought a house there, so I felt I should go," smiles Ian. It's a good job he did - the gig is reputed to have been one of the worst in Marillion's career, kicked off by Mark reciting the lyrics to 'Manager's Song' (originally by Chas and Roy) which went down like a lead balloon. "The boys rang me up and told me I'd done the right thing," says Ian.

VIRTUAL LIGHT

Little about the cover art of *Marillion.com* was by accident, explains Bill Smith

Studios' Carl Glover, who was looking to capture the impact the Internet was having on everyday lives. Says Bill, " I'd just bought a medium-format camera that could take sixteen-second exposures. We wanted a layered feel going further and further into the void - from the girl holding the laptop, through the passport pictures and finally into the screenshots. The combination held the whole thing together." After spending a couple of hours in a London pub waiting for dusk, ("The nights were long at that time of the year," he grins,) Carl and photographee Justine Leyland headed out to look for appropriate locations. The cover image was taken at the end of Long Acre, and the album centrepiece was outside the Palace Theatre on Charing Cross Road, the slow shutter capturing a montage of light trails. "They symbolise the Internet and our relationship with it," recalls Carl. "Buses kept stopping which was a bit of a problem."

As for the passport pictures on the inner sleeve, "We wanted to make the sleeve relevant to the website itself, which is obviously visited by fans," explains Bill Smith. "I suggested asking fans to send passport pictures, some 700-800 did so and we used them all." As easy as falling out of a pub, Bill had captured everything that was right about Marillion. "It was a beautiful thing, and a statement," said H. "It was saying, "It's not us and you anymore, it's all of us." Fan Martin Thorpe comments, "It was good to get on the cover... just a shame that the pic I sent made me look like a Lebanese pimp." A final element of the album packaging was a mail-in card for a supplementary CD. Seemingly innocuous, in fact this was the central plank of Marillion's emerging strategy to develop a relationship with the fans. Explains Pete, "We thought, to safeguard our futures, the best thing was to build up our database. It was win-win-win, whether we resigned from Castle or not." The question was, would Castle include the form? At one time it was missed from a draft of the artwork, a cause for near-panic. Comments Mark, "It was really hairy for a time that they'd fuck it up!" But fuck it up they didn't - the album went out with the mail-off card intact.

With the release of *Marillion.com* on October 18 1999, the band confirmed their new style, not in terms of their influences but the approach of trying new ideas, of never standing still. Many hailed the album as a return to form, following the less than enthusiastic response for *This Strange Engine* and the tacit approval for *Radiat10n*. Q magazine's Rob Beattie wrote, "After 'A Legacy' (typically and wilfully unpredictable) this settles swiftly down with some of their most memorable and direct songs since *Afraid Of Sunlight* - melodically sound with refreshingly unfussy arrangements. The 15-minute 'Interior Lulu' is a troubling but somehow inevitable stumble back into extravagance, but 'Tumble Down

The Years', 'Deserve' and 'Go!' offer considerable compensations."

A good sign from the fans was that in the (frequently cynical) online forums, the album was talked about more in terms of the few tracks people didn't like, than the few tracks they did. Echoing the views of many, Mike Richichi wrote, "This is an astounding album synthesizing the best of their sound, '90s British pop and psychedelia, with some '70s prog rock widdly-widdly thrown in for good measure. It will both grab you at first listen, and grow its way into your head, riffs, sounds, and details working your way in, Steve Hogarth and John Helmer's lyrics suddenly resonating like they hadn't before." For "old faithful" fans, still hoping for a return to the more traditional Marillion, *Dot Com* was still not there, nor would it ever be. The band was finding a new groove, and the majority were saying that it was good - which was all that mattered.

Things were looking good. In the HMV Music poll of December 1999, Marillion were voted 82nd best band of the millennium, one above historical stable-mates Iron Maiden. The band was also voted best band, best live act and best album by *Classic Rock* magazine. And, more importantly still, by the end of the year many thousands of applications had been sent in for the CD, swelling the band's eWeb mailing list from 2,000 to 16,000 subscribers.

Marillion.com was their last album on the Castle label, freeing the band from any contractual obligations. It was with a sense of calm and realism that the band reviewed offers from various parties – including Rod Smallwood of Sanctuary, which by this time had bought Castle. Said Ian: "Rod had us in his office, he wanted us to re-sign." This led to a bit of a conflict of interest, as he was still managing the band: negotiations were between Rod (representing Marillion) and Rod (representing Sanctuary). Things came to a head pretty quickly. "Rod put his hands up and said, 'We can't manage you,' so we parted company with both label and management," remembers Pete. "We felt a bit let down; maybe we'd been expecting more than they could give us."

Fan John Deveraux recalls bumping into Steve Hogarth the day of the negotiations, on a bus transfer due to a cancelled train. "I was vaguely aware of a guy next to me. I looked down at his open-toed sandals and checked trousers, and realised that I recognised his voice. It was one of those 'Don't look now, but...' moments..." he says. "While I was trying to formulate that all-important opening line, Steve leaned across and spoke to me. He was only asking me how long the journey would take, but it sparked off a conversation that lasted for the whole hour or more before we disembarked. The band had spent the day in London at meetings with various management companies, including Rod Smallwood. We parted with a handshake and a heartfelt, 'Pleased to have met you', and I ran home like I did when I was told I was in the junior school football team and couldn't wait to tell my mum!"

As incidents like this illustrated, key was the very strength of Marillion's relationship with their fans. The main service missing from Castle was promotion, yet as the size of the band's mailing list grew, it became clear that the band would be in a position to do as good a job as any label. Indeed, explains Steve H, "Our fan base gave the labels a disincentive to market the product. Our experience was that they would be queuing up to sign us, then come the time of the record release, we would be lucky to get a quarter-page advert in a magazine." The decision was tough, but inevitable: against a background of more label interest than the band had experienced for years, the increasingly business-savvy members were unlikely to accept any offers.

The *Dot Com* tour started for real on October 13 1999, at the MCM Café in Paris, and ended on December 5. Then it was time for something completely different again.

MARILLION.COM

By the late '90s Marillion were one of the foremost innovators when it came to the Internet to keep in touch with their fans. *Marillion.com* was named in recognition of this factor. It also finds the band expanding their musical palette once more, although it should be noted that 'Tumble Down The Years' and 'Interior Lulu' were originally produced during the sessions for the *Radiat10n* album - 'Deserve', 'Rich', 'Go!', 'Enlightened' and 'Built-In Bastard Radar' came from ideas originating at the same time. Again produced by the band, the disc benefits from having the touch of Porcupine Tree main man Steven Wilson on five of the nine tracks, but even the self-produced tracks sound much better production-wise than *Radiat10n*.

'A Legacy' is a song of many parts - according to H, "Film-noir through funk, grunge and The Beatles, with an accidental Beach Boys moment." With lyrics written by long-term collaborator John Helmer, the song dissects a marriage on the edge of destruction and the notion that ending the relationship doesn't necessarily mean all slates are wiped clean, or that everything turns out for the best. Its dominant musical motif, courtesy of Mark Kelly has been likened to a Bond theme - the flip side to the previous album's Bond Baddie theme 'Cathedral Wall'. The heroic sound however, is very much at odds with the almost callous lyrical content. If there's a fault with the song it's perhaps that it's a tad busy in the earlier stages, and perhaps it seems somewhat out of step with the rest of the album. The upbeat 'Deserve', featuring saxophone by Ben Castle concerns thinking about making positive changes to your life - because you might actually succeed! More specifically, as H wrote on the band's website, "You create your own joy and your own misery. Unhappiness isn't really related to anything other than state of mind." The song ends with a stomping Motown-sounding groove, and is guaranteed to get the feet tapping. It's great fun.

Coming down the gears, 'Go!' starts with a bass pulse, and processed feedback, before Steve Rothery comes in with a delicate picked verse. Its serene gentleness is evidenced by the amount of space in the music itself - listen to Ian's cymbals shimmer like lazy sunlight across a Caribbean sea... Wistful and dreamy, the song is lyrically not dissimilar to 'These Chains' but without the barbs of that track. Steve Rothery delivers a smooth solo that caresses gently over Pete's cool bass groove. The song plays out with a coda that sees H, Pete and Mark building a delightful theme over Mark's enticing keyboards. Lovely.

'Rich' threatens to giggle as H leads us in a do-wop, sing-a-long intro! This is a song that is happy without being twee, joyous without being at anyone's expense. All through, the listener is struck by its gently quirky rhythms and the melodies which lead us to a chorus that demands to be sung out loud, "No fears, no lies, no pain, no doubt, no darkness, no confusion, no loneliness, despair no more, no way, no how, it's all illusion" and its positive belief that thinking happy thoughts, and facing life head-on can be its own reward. It includes an idea taken from the French writer Anaïs Nin, "We don't see things as they are, we see things as we are." If you're not smiling during this song, you have a heart of stone, and that, my friends, is a fact!

'Enlightened' is almost a sister song to 'Go!'; again a very gentle track. The lyric was conceived in a Sao Paolo café called 'Viva Vida' (literally 'Live Life'). It concerns a feeling of gentle euphoria which, H says, can occur in moments of extreme tiredness, and is bound up with feelings of love and lovemaking with that special person. The song has a languid feel to it, reflecting the many references to tiredness and sleep. Steve Rothery's guitar is almost scratchy on the early part of the solo, yet, as it glides into a smooth outro, there's no sense that the serenity has been breached. A perfect song for when you're relaxing with your head against the one you love. Beautiful.

'Built-In Bastard Radar' sees John Helmer kick sand in the faces of men who once stole women from under his nose. Kicking in with a heavy guitar riff, almost reminiscent of heavier Queen, and with a Deep Purple riff on the Mellotron, it quickly gives way to a gentler verse. The lyric details the way that some women seem attracted to blokes without an ounce of decency in their

217

souls. After a Garbage-y fuzz bass solo from Pete, the song implies that the writer (and by extension, H as singer) is now outdoing them all, using his fame as a lure for those self-same women. A case of 'Once I was but the learner, now I am the master...' H has commented that he doesn't know whether Helmer was taking the piss by making him sing such words. 'Tumble Down The Years' calls to mind Crowded House, as H and Helmer look back across a couple's relationship and muse about how they managed to end up where they are. John Lennon once famously said 'Life is what happens to you while you're busy making other plans' and that seems to be the key to one of the most melodic songs on the album. It's a bright summery song with a great lyric, married to what is, although good, one of the less distinctive tracks on the album.

'Interior Lulu' is a sprawling epic of a song. Opinions amongst the fans are equally divided as to whether this song or 'This Strange Engine' is the best long song by the Hogarth-era band. The intro sees Pete lope a meandering bass over Ian's almost reggae percussion, while H sings about a girl who has transformed herself on the Internet into a bohemian, whilst being rather drab in real life. Mark then launches into a Keith Emerson-esque extravaganza/mess (delete as applicable) of a Moog solo, which becomes a tour de force of pent-up pain with Ian and Steve Rothery straining at the leash to emote. We then see her trying to catch her essence in emails, attempting to write her pain into ASCII characters, before shifting focus to find H is able to understand exactly what is going on. Over an acoustic chord vamp, H reveals she's not telling him anything he doesn't already know; in one of his best lyrics, he describes how "by writing from personal experience, you empower your work only to cheapen the memory or the emotion which inspired it." He describes the process in a subtextually ironic passage that rates as highly as anything he's ever written:

If you can carry it out, you can take it away,
If you can buy it, it can be bought,
If you can buy it, it can be stolen,
If you can break it, it's already broken...

The coda finds H standing on top of London's Primrose Hill, staring down at the city below him, musing on how the Internet can connect us, but we never touch. As the thought hits home, the band explode into a squall of biting, nihilistic fury; bass and drums going crazy, Steve Rothery pouring sweat and tears into every finely wrung note, Mark's keyboards writhing like a nightmare-tortured sleeper.... Genius! The thought always occurs: 'What must H think of people like me who pour over the lyric sheets trying to wring out every last nuance of meaning?' I don't think I want to know.

'House' is a real change for the band, being a laid-back, dub/trip-hop-type vibe, partly inspired by Massive Attack. This one split the fans right down the middle - there doesn't seem to be much middle ground here - but if anything, 'House' was the track which pointed to the direction the band would take with *Anoraknophobia*. The song is a study in bluesy, smoky jazz of the near-disintegration of H's marriage - something that had informed the *Radiat10n* album to quite a large extent. H said, "The house seemed to somehow ooze the pain we were in, even when nobody was there. There wasn't a level to which I could turn up the hi-fi that drowned out the silence that was still there." With Ian and Pete laying down a soulful rhythm, Mark, Steve H and guest trumpeter Neil Yates conjure a moving picture of a dark house full of longing and loneliness. A sublime, calming antidote to the aggression released at the end of 'Lulu'.

The cover features a young, alternative-looking girl standing on a cold London street corner holding a glowing computer monitor - possibly Lulu. Around her, what at first glance seem like time-lapsed tail lights slash across the scene. On closer inspection, they appear to be too well defined. I imagine them as kind of electronic ley-lines, signifying the interconnectivity of the Internet. Inside, there are 784 passport photos. Who are they? They're some of the band's fans, contacted via the Internet. *Marillion.com*? They really are connected...

15

A Better Way of Life

Business was good. It might have taken five years' learning but the Marillion collective now knew how to manage themselves, produce and sell records, organise tours and otherwise satisfy both the appetites of fans and the finances of the business. It had been no easy jaunt – said H, "It's been hairy, a bit of a roller coaster ride. Fortunately, the car never left the rails, but we have had to negotiate some tight corners." Nonetheless the band had – through sheer necessity – gained both experience and a truly independent mindset.

Marillion's most important metric remained album sales, which was stalled firmly in the "could do better" category. Sales had continued to fall since the band first adopted 'indie' status three years before: while they had stabilised at about 70-80 thousand per release – a level that covered Marillion's operational costs – a remark by H illustrates the dilemma: "If a band's new album consistently fails to outsell the album before then you reach a point where you either have to call it a day, or change drastically the way the band's operating."

The overwhelming support for both the tour fund and the CD mail-in offered signposts in the sand, surface indicators of a rich vein that lay untapped. With the relationship still strong with its core fan base, Marillion knew it had a key to riches it could not yet fathom. Nobody was seriously considering throwing in the towel – says Ian, "What else am I supposed to do? Be a plumber?" – but neither was it an option to carry on regardless. Which left the band two other choices. To look for a new label and hope that it would live up to its promises, or to do something so bizarre that even Monty Python would be proud.

Once again, they went for option four.

BETWEEN YOU AND ME

With a weary sigh, attention turned back to writing in January 2000. "We weren't in a hurry to come back," said Mark. *This Strange Engine, Radiat10n* and *Marillion.com* had each kicked off with material left over from the album before – but this time the band members were starting with a clean slate. As Mark commented, "That usually makes it interesting," – "And long!" added Pete.

Early on, self-confessed gadget fanatic Steve Rothery turned up with some gizmos that set the scene for the whole album. "I brought most of my studio equipment so I had the capability to play loops and sequences to jam over. It made for an interesting change in the writing process," he recalls. Says Ian, "These were not standard drum loops, they were great to play along with." The immediate effect was a more groovy sonic foundation with emphasis on the bass, a theme Pete quickly picked up on. Before long the boys settled into the familiar routine of jamming and planning the next album, capturing and logging the happy accidents like so many albums before.

Finding a record deal was not proving so simple, however. Ironically the very existence of the Marillion fan base, in all its directly accessible, responsive and indeed hungry glory, left the band wondering what value record companies such as Castle/Sanctuary and Eagle Rock could bring. "We were able to create as much press coverage as the record labels, without them creaming what they could off our percentage," recalls Pete. "They even wanted to deduct packaging costs for mp3 downloads!" The labels were keen to have Marillion on the roster, who wouldn't be? But the prospective deals offered little more than a continuation of a treadmill existence. "When we got the contracts we decided that to sign them would consign ourselves to being fairly helpless about our career," said H.

Something had to give. The first conclusion was, if the band was running with its own communications ideas, why not employ someone to manage the process rather than paying a record label? As a preliminary step the band approached EMI staffer and long-time ally Lucy Jordache – who was quick to accept the offer of employment, joining the Racket Records staff at the end of March.

A few weeks later, the most Internet-active band member proposed a novel alternative to a record deal. "I know," suggested Mark as he stood in the kitchen in the Racket Club, "why don't we ask the fans to buy an album a year in advance, raising enough money to pay for the album's production?" The maths stacked up – up to £200,000 was required, so at 15 quid a shot the band needed to sell about 14,000 pre-orders. H recalls the response of the rest of the band - "Good idea, let's ask the fans if they'd go for it."

So it was that Marillion sent an eWeb that would change music history. The email didn't ask for money, not yet; merely, whether fans thought the idea of a pre-order was sound. The majority of the feedback was highly positive – as noted a later press release, "Some even said they would buy two copies." By the time responses were added up a staggering £80,000 had, in principle, been pledged. It wasn't enough, but it was sufficient to convince the band that they were doing the right thing.

On June 16 2000 Marillion decided to kick off the campaign for real. Fans were asked for £16 to pay for a special, two-disc edition of the album with exclusive packaging, including the names of those who pre-ordered before a certain date. In the two weeks that followed, the rate of pre-orders had already crashed two servers! By the end of the campaign some eight months later, the band had received 12,674 advance orders, raising the massive sum of £180,000 to fund the album. "We feel completely flattered and privileged to have the trust of our fans to send us their money before we have even written a note," remarked Ian. "It enables us to spend as long as we think we need to, to make the best album we think we can."

The band's delight was compounded by the almost-immediate publicity generated by the pre-order. Publications as diverse as USA *Today*, the *Financial Times* and the BBC called the Racket Club to find out what had happened, not to mention a number of bands including The Levellers and (the more famous) Toad The Wet Sprocket. Commented Steve H, "We get emails from people saying 'I'd like to pre-order a copy of your album - and here's two hundred quid. I only want one copy, but I want to be part of this thing.' That doesn't happen to Duran Duran!"

Not only was it clear that Marillion had found the keys to a new kingdom; equally, the campaign provided the last nail in the coffin of working with a record company. Announced the next newsletter, "We have decided to take the ultimate leap of faith in our fans. We're going to kick out as many of the cynics and the businessmen as we can, and replace them with our own team of accomplished professionals who are driven by as much faith as we are." Fewer middlemen meant more control – and more income. "Because we didn't have to sign any record agreements, we regained the rights to our recordings," said Pete.

The band did not get everything their own way. In May 2000, the Freaks list got wind of an Internet poll where fans could vote a band onto the Glastonbury shortlist. True to form, a carefully orchestrated plan to vote for Marillion followed. "It was quite subtle hype and that was great," commented Mark. Marillion reached the top three on the site, but despite the show of hands the application was rejected. "The management said they couldn't take us, or the poll, seriously. They were completely ignoring the results," said Mark.

Can't win them all, but the runes were looking good.

PLAY ME A SONG

Back in the studio, it was jamming, jamming, jamming. "We jammed forever!" says Ian. With several songs coming together and the money rolling in, the boys realised they could afford to pay a producer – "Of course we picked Dave Meegan," said Pete. Dave's attention to detail (and determination to get the best sound possible) required time, which meant money - but he had also helped deliver what remained two of the band's most popular albums. "We'd been thinking about Dave ever since we hadn't used him," continues Pete. "We wanted to make an album that people believed in. Bringing Dave in at a relatively early stage gave us a sense of belief, and the fans as well."

Dave arrived to find a relaxed atmosphere, with the band allowing time for each others' side projects even as they pulled together the music for the album: three tracks were arranged with Pete out of the country with Transatlantic, for example. Meanwhile, Rothers was drawing inspiration from his new gadgetry. "Different guitar sounds are like different colours for an artist," he remarked. "If you have all of these new textures you can call upon, it gives you more freedom." Nobody was more pleased than H. "He had such a distinctive sound, but it was a sound of its era. He had the choice of sticking with that and impressing the same people over and over, or moving forward. I really admire the fact he had the guts to take it somewhere else."

Once recording started, it proceeded at a brisk pace over the summer. "*Anorak* was one of those moments in time where we felt we had something to prove; we were very excited," remarks Pete. Some songs came together more quickly than others: the lyrics for one in particular weren't working, recalls Steve Hogarth. "I'd rewritten it about five times, every time I took it to Dave he'd say, 'Oh yeah, you know...' and I'd go away and write it again." In October he spent a week away in Bath, "To hole up there and get poetic for a bit," he said, but still the track was struggling to emerge. When at Christmas it still hadn't come together, Steve contacted old mate, Nick Van Eede of Cutting Crew, who invited Steve to his pad in Barbados; it would have been rude not to accept! H recalled later how Nick had written the words 'Map Of The World' on a sheet of paper. "I suggested we try it as a chorus. On the fly he came up with the melody, and I moved it to coincide with a different part of the music. This, at last, unlocked the song for me."

Barbados all too nearly turned tragic when, walking along the beach, H took a bite from a small green apple he saw lying in the sand. He became a little perturbed as locals ran towards him saying, "That's a Manchineel apple! Did you eat some of that? You gonna die, boy!" Steve took the advice to drink "seawater, a bottle of PeptoBismol and a can of condensed milk" while the island doctor asked questions over the radio. Fortunately, Steve was advised that the small bite wouldn't be fatal. "I felt dodgy for the next three weeks, but that could have been down to drinking seawater, condensed milk and too much rum punch!" he says. Where was that last one in the instructions?

By January 2001 the album had picked up its name: *Anoraknophobia*. "What we are saying with the title," noted Rothers, "is that we have no fear of being known as a band with a devoted following." As H wrote on the fans-only, pre-order special edition cover, "We're anoraks too!" Dave Meegan took the role of chief fan. "On *Anorak* there was an obligation to represent the fans," he says. "It makes a huge difference knowing that people really do care about the result. They spot the subtleties." Echoing past successes like 'Out Of This World' on *Afraid Of Sunlight*, he used news clips in various tracks – reports on conflicts in Vietnam and the Middle East, and references to Sarah Payne, Damilola Taylor and Mohammed Jamal, children killed through acts of violence. "If you have a tool like a song, you should take the opportunity to say something," he said.

The pre-order deadline was extended from December 31 2000 to early February 2001, by which time mastering was complete. True to form, Dave was mentally frazzled by the end. "It's unavoidable when you're making records that have emotions in them," he said, but the result justified the effort. "It's probably the happiest I've ever been about anything I've worked on, 100%!" "Dave's done a fantastic job, it's the band grooving, I mean *really* grooving for the first time ever. The man is a God," laughed H. "It's like having your own priest, engineering genius, philosopher, arbiter of taste, diplomat and best mate rolled into one." Nobody benefited from the grooviness more than Pete, who had made the most of every opportunity to shine. "I guess it was my album," he smiled.

WORTH PAYING TO SEE?

It was time to rock and roll, and communications manager Lucy Jordache seized the PR initiative whenever it presented itself. "I was booking tickets to Holland for the fan club tour and said I would be using cheap flights. When asked why, I said it's 450 quid, but that's for 10 people." On the EasyJet website there was a question - "If you are flying with us in the near future and have an interesting reason for your trip, why not let us know?" – so Lucy made the call, landing a high profile TV appearance on ITV's *Airline* documentary series. The boys ended up playing an acoustic 'Eighty Days' to an impromptu audience in the middle of the arrival lounge, with a number of people (including Ian) throwing coins at them.

As summer turned to autumn, a BBC researcher contacted the Racket Club about another documentary – *The Future Just Happened* – about how the Internet was changing people's lives. When presenter Michael Lewis visited in December, he was sufficiently impressed to pre-order the album himself. Such appearances reinforced the ensemble's nascent reputation as a tech-savvy band making its own way in the modern world.

Marillion's emergence back into the lights started with a handful of one-off gigs in November 2000. First stop was the Bass Museum in Burton-on-Trent: bar manager Sam Hill had contacted the band to propose a couple of dates; the venue was unusual and there was a gap in the schedules, so why not? "It was the novelty factor," says Mark. Unfortunately, like Oswestry before it, Bass was not equipped to cope with the international onslaught of fans. 'The Bass Museum telephone hotline' – in fact a two-port switchboard – was jammed within minutes of lines opening, and tickets sold out within a few hours.

Matt Urban and his team from Möbius Media flew over from the US to record the Bass gigs for a Webcast. "We love these guys," says Matt. "It's just an excuse to cover the things we enjoy." The band aren't likely to return to Bass however, in part due to a *Blues Brothers*-esque incident on the second night. Explains Mark, "We were offered free beer for a year if we performed. Trouble was, the first night we practically drank the bar dry, so they went back on their offer."

Christmas saw a whirlwind fan club tour with dates around Europe, then early in 2001 the band decided to "go back to its roots" and play to a new generation. Explains H, "We'd got into an impasse with our agent, we were a standing joke with the *NME*, we were not being played on the radio, we thought if students could see the band it would cut through the prejudices. The agent said, 'There isn't a university circuit any more,' but what he really meant was that he wouldn't make any money. So Lucy got on the blower." Smiles Lucy, "People didn't believe it was Marillion when I was phoning up. They wanted to know why we wanted to play in such small places. I said students had no preconceptions and would love the music if they got a chance to hear it."

To go with the tour, the band had 1,000 'Crash Course' sampler CDs made, "to be sold at the 'Student Loan' price of £1," says band archivist Andy Rotherham. The discs were quickly recognised for their collector value, however. "Each evening we were inundated. It became apparent from the stampede that we would have to limit the number of copies sold at each gig. Also, they were held until the end, to allow students a fair chance..." In hindsight, the University tour wasn't an out-and-out success – while it didn't turn a profit, at least a new audience was made aware of the band.

In February, Steve Rothery played at the Royal Albert Hall with The Eddie Jordan All Stars for the Professor Sid Watkins Brain and Spine Foundation. Rothers managed to entice Tony Hadley and Nick Mason along, as well as bringing Ian and Pete for musical and moral support. The following month Steve, H and Pete headed up to Oswestry for a 'Stranger By The Minute' performance, the line-up including Phil Beaumont on drums, Paul Sturman on vocals and guitarist Matt Prior – as well as Darren Wharton, keyboard player from Thin Lizzy and Dare. "He was a very late addition," said Pete, for whom a highlight was to sing 'White Room' by Cream and Tom Petty's 'Freefalling'. "This was the first time I'd done any lead vocals since I was in my teens," he says.

MAKING HISTORY

Few incidents would demonstrate just how profoundly Marillion's music touched their fans more vividly than those of March 2001, when Newcastle-based entrepreneur and established diver Bill Smith headed to Lake Coniston to look for Donald Campbell's Bluebird. "I was testing some kit when I first heard 'Out Of This World'," says Bill, who had been drawn in by the footage Dave Meegan included in the middle section. "Donald Campbell was saying, 'Alpha to Base, Alpha to Base,' then I couldn't work out the next bit so I went and bought a video of the crash to see if I could figure it out." As Bill deciphered Donald's words he knew he had to go and look for the ill-fated craft. "I was hooked on how it went from grace to violence in a split second... I thought, a couple of months up at Coniston, make a nice break?"

After four years of weekends searching (and working through nearly an entire team of divers), on January 17 2001 Bill found the remains of the craft. With assistants Graham Woodfield manning the surface vessel and sonar operative Al Douglas, Bill had dived with only one torch working. He was about to return when his flipper snagged on a piece of aluminium. "My blood turned to ice water as I realised what it was," said Bill, who wiped away the grime to reveal a painted Union Jack on a tail fin that had lain in the cold waters for 34 years. As a final test of patience, Bill had to spend several minutes decompressing just yards from the surface, before he could tell his co-conspirators. "I was buzzing!" he laughs. In the following days, as well as informing Donald Campbell's daughter Gina and the BBC, Bill obtained Steve Hogarth and Steve Rothery's phone numbers from old pal Fish and called to tell them what had happened. "I asked, 'Do you want to come to the lifting?'" he says. Not only that, he requested Rothers' services as his official photographer.

On March 7 Steve and Steve headed north, checking into The Black Bull in Coniston for the night. They arrived at Lake Coniston the following day to be met by wet-suited Bill Smith, sporting a crocodile-tail hat - his 'searching hat' over ten years of diving. Bill marched them past the lines of police and "bemused officials" and out on to the jetty, where Steve Rothery readied his cameras. Given that Bill had deliberately kept the massed ranks of media behind a barrier on the shore, journalists were visibly spitting when they saw the pair out on the jetty. "I was asked, 'What about him with the cameras?'" remembers Bill. "I said, 'He's a rock guitarist, name's Steve Rothery, you can ask him yourself if you like.'"

Eventually, at 10.45, the Bluebird reached the surface. Remembers H, "I stood right next to the Bluebird as the tail fin broke the water. I was thinking, *My God, I've brought this about and nobody knows*." Rothers was similarly honoured. "To have reported something in history, and for that to be a catalyst for more history being made, it was amazing," he says. It was a sombre, drab occasion for onlookers and crew alike. Following a quiet pause for Tonia Bern-Campbell (Donald's third wife) to contemplate the still-rising craft, Bluebird was carefully manoeuvred onto a trailer, towed up to the jetty and into a boathouse. Steve H was photographed by Reuters man Jon Super, looking down the shore as he held the nose-cone. "To be handed the nose-cone, which was the first thing that hit the water..." But his most moving moment came in the boathouse, when he spied a fragment of seat belt, still attached to a bent bolt.

That evening, the boys joined Bill and the divers for dinner at the Black Bull before heading to the nearby Sun Inn. Realising they might be locked out of their accommodation, H went looking for a pay phone and, unexpectedly, found himself in the presence of Tonia Bern-Campbell. "Excuse me - aren't you the chap who wrote the song?" she asked. Following a conversation about how she had not initially wanted the boat to be raised, H promised to send a copy of the song that made it all possible. At 11.30, the two Steves went back to the Bull, somehow managing to negotiate the key code and get to bed.

No doubt upset at being ostracised, the world's press were in no mood for celebration – accusing Bill Smith and his team of jubilant behaviour, both during and following the raising of the Bluebird. Bill's case wasn't helped by his penchant for silly hats, not to mention his irreverent thumbs-up sign from the back of the hull when it emerged from the water. The final straw was, apparently, the behaviour exhibited in the Sun Inn that evening. How very undignified to share a few jars at the end of a four-year journey to find a heroic craft, inspired by a song.

SEPARATING OUT

On the back of the pre-order, the band found itself in an unexpected negotiating position with the major labels – this time, for worldwide distribution rights. "It costs money to put records in shops," says Pete. "Big record companies do have the bargaining power." The labels also had man-power and an international presence. Ever the pragmatists, Marillion chose to woo the majors with the promise of greater sales to come. "We told them we had already sold 12,000 albums, the projected sales were at least 100,000, the record was made and all they had to do was get it in the shops," says Lucy. H remembers the meeting with EMI in particular. "We came into the building and presented to them and at the end of the meeting they practically broke into applause. Basically, we were offering them free money – all we wanted was a decent royalty rate and a reasonable marketing campaign."

In the end, the album was released on the EMI label in the UK and Europe, Sanctuary in the US and Canada, and EMI Liberty everywhere else. "We're very excited at the prospect of returning to EMI Group and all the benefits that being signed to a major label will bring," said the band. What with *The Future Just Happened* being broadcast in August 2001, spirits were high and The Racket Club was buzzing with ideas and initiatives. While not everything would happen as expected, nobody could have predicted the reasons why.

ANORAK AND ROLL

In once-traditional style, Marillion planned a single prior to the album launch... but this was to be no traditional single. 'This Is The 21st Century ' was released as download-only, achieving No.1 in the alternative charts and No.2 across the MP3.com site. Before the album went on general release, a special edition was delivered to the pre-ordering fans, listing the first six thousand contributors. "This is your album," said H in the sleeve notes. And didn't the Racket team know it – as Colin, Erik, Lucy and anyone else that could be mustered spent many happy hours packaging CDs!

The official launch was accompanied by what was more plea than press release, written in part by fan and music journalist Rich Wilson, the rest dictated by the band. "You're all wrong about Marillion, just listen to it!" it implored, perhaps a little too strongly. "That was a bit of an over-reaction," said Mark later. "It's very frustrating when you've been in a band this amount of time - most people have heard of us but many don't have any idea what we do." As it was, the effort backfired - journalists were in no mood to be dictated terms. "I see rockers Marillion are as pretentious as ever," mocked the *Sun* newspaper's daily *Bizarre* column. Of course, it wasn't long before fan emails started to fly. According to Lucy, "The *Sun* was overwhelmed, they said they had never seen a response like it."

But what of the album itself? Robert Adams of *Rock Sound* certainly thought it was a winner, "I haven't listened to Marillion since I was a kid in the mid '80s. After listening to *Anoraknophobia* I had to check the sleeve to make sure that this was the same band I remember from my spotty youth. The biggest thing holding Marillion back is the name and all the baggage it carries. I am on the floor having been felled by an enormous feather. A phoenix-like rebirth." *Classic Rock's* Phil Wilding awarded 4 out of five stars, saying, "A progressive piece of work then, but not in the way you might at first think" – reflecting the theme. Even *Kerrang!* – long oriented towards younger bands – gave it credit. "It comes as a shock that this album is actually pretty damn good. Marillion have never given a flying fuck what anyone in the world thinks of them. Still, this conjures up a pretty contemporary feel with its classy mix of blues, country, and even trip-hop stylings. Who says you can't teach an old dog new tricks?"

Not all press attention was welcome – Marillion had become more popular, and therefore more susceptible. *Classic Rock's* Dave Ling pulled no punches when he probed Steve Hogarth about the press release and raked the embers of events over a decade old – "If Steve Hogarth really loves Marillion as much as he claims, why doesn't he leave and let them bring Fish back?" went the question. Retorted H, "They wouldn't have him. But I don't love the Marillion that that guy's talking about. I'm in love with the Marillion that exists now. Fish has no place in that, I dare him to try." Commented Fish in a follow-up interview (again with Dave Ling), "That was unnecessary and I put it down to the fact that perhaps the interviewer was winding him up! What does Hogarth think I'm gonna do? Turn up with a bunch of SAS stormtroopers and take over Racket Records?" H put the matter to rest with a direct public message: "Good luck, mate, and don't let the press convince you that I've got it in for you. Those buggers'll do anything for a bit of scandal…"

Another bit of controversy was generated by Pete's remark following the success of the Transatlantic side project – that he might even consider quitting Marillion. "It definitely puts out the wrong signals," remarked H. "But then I don't think Pete much cares what signals it puts out. Pete's such a pure musician that everything excites him." Pete himself soon set the record straight. "Transatlantic wasn't really thought of as a long-term thing, so we didn't have to be too serious about it," he said. Indeed, the way that Marillion were going, it would take all of his time – and passion. As he was later to say, "I personally would like to have a couple of years just really concentrating on Marillion as this is very important to me. We feel that there is a buzz we're creating here, and we should keep it alive."

Despite such incidents, the heart-shaped ball was well and truly rolling. By

May it was time to head back on the road, with (according to *The Web*), "The most intensive bout of European touring in recent years." The first date was in Dublin, where H finally had the chance to sing 'Easter' on its native island. "I have waited 14 years," he said. "It was a massive moment for me, also knowing that Dave Meegan had taken the trouble to come over." The Manchester Academy gig four days later was attended by the Bluebird team including Bill Smith, who was chuffed to hear the "fantastic" reception for 'Out Of This World'. UK support was from White Buffalo, a band Dave Meegan had taken under his wing. Remembers bassist Rex Horan, "I was stoked, it was our first time as a group to play outside the UK." The rapport between the two bands grew until, says Rex, "Our relationships had spilled over into our music and Steve R asked to perform 'Stormtrooper' with us. He played with us at the Polish shows. He was communicative and considerate in his playing. The punters loved it." Remarks H, "It was a privilege to have them there, just for the vibe."

"It's scary what can happen when you watch Marillion's 'Shot In The Dark' video, well, in the dark. All kinds of crazy thoughts can suddenly seem reasonable. Like how England isn't really that far away from Los Angeles..." remarked US fan Andy Saks, who travelled over to see the band. Andy took in dates at Hemel Hempstead, Manchester, Wolverhampton and London – where it was, reputedly, Barry's 21st birthday. "As he was born on May 22, 1980, everyone suspected the band would do something special for the occasion. We soon discovered how we'd celebrate: between 'Rich' and 'Man Of A Thousand Faces', Lucy brought a giant cake onstage, in the shape of Barry himself! We sang a sloppy version of 'Happy Birthday' and Lucy retreated backstage, promising to come back later and hand out the pieces. Sure enough, between encores, Mark came onstage with a box full of Barry cake, and started throwing pieces into the audience. He tossed one right to me, and I'm ashamed to say I dropped it. The "five second rule" was in effect, and I managed to quickly pick it up, and hand out a few scraps to the folks around me, who eagerly took their bites. As it turns out, Barry tastes a lot like cornbread!"

With a set list largely decided by fan poll, the tour crossed the UK, France, Holland and Germany before finishing at Bydgoszcz in Poland. Sadly, a US tour remained out of the band's reach. "We had been offered a 40-festival tour in September 2001, but the people organising it dropped off the radar," commented Steve Rothery. As the route unfurled, it became clear that something was afoot – the fan base were reacting with increasing levels of vigour and affection. While H wasn't happy with all of his performances ("After a while the performance can become mechanical and I start to feel like a performing dog," he said), after the gig finished in Amsterdam he found himself carried by a greater force. "I really never have been mobbed in quite the same way in my life. I must have kissed and been kissed by over 100 men and women in ten minutes."

Such incidents ensured that confidence was running high as the first leg of the tour came to an end in early summer. On September 9 2001, the band decided to release a CD-based single of 'Map Of The World', the first since 'These Chains' almost 3 years before. There was a twist: fans buying the single from Marillion's website could benefit from a two-for-one offer, the plan being that the second copy could be sent to radio stations, music mags, friends and family. Which, of course, the fans did. Two days later, Steve Hogarth was down to sing at Donald Campbell's funeral, a poignant event which, as a welcome aside, was almost inevitably going to reach the newspapers.

Then, tragedy struck in a way nobody could have predicted, and on a global scale. With the events of September 11, all plans, thoughts and aspirations went out of the window. Recalls fan Joe del Tufo, "We were listening to 'This Is The 21st Century' on the morning the World Trade Center was destroyed. It was hauntingly appropriate." Steve's most personal of shows, at Donald Campbell's funeral, had to go on: he had the honour of casting a handful of earth onto Donald's coffin, once it had been lowered into the ground. "I said goodbye and wished him well as I did so. All this to a man I never knew," commented Steve in his diary. "And so, for me, a strange cycle was complete."

The show had to go on for the rest of the band as well, despite the fact the world was still reeling in shock. "We didn't contemplate cancelling the tour. Hard as it sounds, life had to go on or the terrorists would have won," remarks Lucy. The 15-date second leg of the tour was planned to start at the Palazzo Ducale in Lucca, Italy on September 15. H confided in Lucy that this gig was the hardest he had ever done, because nothing seemed important any more. One line from 'Separated Out' - "There's a man up in a mirrored building, and he just bought the world" - nearly brought everything to a halt as H could barely make it through the rest of the song. Continues Lucy, "Emotionally, logistically, everything was difficult."

One date that lifted the mood was in the Azores archipelago, odd not only because of the scale of the audience –10,000 people. "Our promoters got excited when they saw us play live in Portugal, and they asked if we'd play the Azores as well," recalls Pete. Adds then-guitar-tech Colin Price, "It was the biggest gig the island had ever witnessed!" Unlike the kinds of gigs the band had grown accustomed to, the audience were largely unfamiliar with Marillion. Said Steve Rothery, "We could have been anybody as far as they were concerned. Playing to that many people who don't know you from Adam, it's very hard work." The band's final date in Bydgoszcz, October 26, was the first time Marillion had visited Poland since 1994, but not too far for a posse of UK fans, recalls Paul Walmsley. "Nine of us headed off to a tiny town three hours from anywhere. They played a tiny sports hall and the atmosphere was the most electrifying of any gig I've ever attended. Just amazing."

Back at the Racket Club, Lucy Jordache was determined to keep the singles campaign on course despite world events. Aided by long-time fan (and New Yorker) Christine Cooper, Lucy focused on the uphill struggle to gain the band some radio airplay. Comments Christine, "The politicians told us to try and live our lives as normal, so we felt the best thing to do was press ahead." Fans worldwide emailed where they had sent singles, and before long, confirmations of radio stations that had played it. While the bulk may have been from well-established bases in the UK, France, Germany and the USA, emails arrived from further afield – Australia, New Zealand, Mexico, Chile, Venezuela, the Czech Republic, Poland and even Brunei!

The fans were in their element – one manned the telephone lines of a charity telethon ("so he could slip it on to the airwaves") while another hired someone to dress up as a banana, march into the studio of his local radio station and hand a copy of the single directly to the DJ. Remarks Christine, "These are by no means unusual examples." In the UK the single was playlisted on a number of BBC local radio stations as a result, and was picked up by 'Whispering' Bob Harris on BBC Radio 2. Over 10,000 copies of the single were sold overall, easily sufficient for UK chart status had the mail-order channel been seen as valid.

As well as a planned live album (mixed by Dave Meegan) and a short tour for the H-band, the last of many initiatives was the Front Row Club (FRC). Inspired by a similar project by King Crimson, Steve Hogarth proposed the idea to release live material "warts and all" from Marillion's extensive archives. "If you look at the description of the King Crimson Collectors' Club, it's word-for-word the same as the Front Row Club," says Erik Nielsen. "We decided we'd be happy as long as we hit 500 members, the number we'd need to break even." The FRC was announced shortly before Christmas 2001 – in the event, subscriptions more than tripled expectations.

LOOKING ON THE BRIGHT SIDE

As winter turned to spring, the Racket Club was a still-simmering cauldron of ideas. To add to the pot, Lucy Jordache ran brainstorming sessions with fans across the UK. On her return and with brain still buzzing, she started to think about how fans meet up around gigs for a meal and a drink. What if fans came together for an entire weekend of music and socialising? "Here was a chance to get two thousand people to meet up with each other, in a setting where it was acceptable to be a Marillion fan," says Lucy, who had worked with The Stranglers' manager Sil Wilcox while at EMI. "I saw The Stranglers were having a convention, so I called up Sil and it turned out he was setting up a company to manage such events."

The band members were unsure at first. "It made us sound like a holiday camp act," said Pete. Agreed H, "A bit 'cabaret' rather than rock n' roll!" Lucy was quick to put their minds to rest – "I said, 'Don't worry, it'll make a lot of money and the fans will love it.'" Continues H, "Sil Wilcox had done it, it had been a success spiritually and financially, and it sounded like a laugh." With the boys on board, Lucy followed the tried and trusted formula of asking the fans by email – "If we run a convention at Pontins holiday camp at Brean Sands, would you come?" As soon as sufficient 'Yes' votes had arrived in Marillion's inbox, the decision to make it happen became easy.

Almost immediately, however, the scale of the challenge became clear: there were bands to invite, side events to organise, set lists to decide. "It was quite a scary prospect at first, as there are a lot of hours for us to fill," said Pete at the time. "But we have come up with some great ideas along with some guests and old friends to help..." As icing on the cake, the band decided to play *Brave* in its entirety for the first time since 1994, with all the trimmings including Michael Hunter's 'River' music, slide shows, men in balaclavas and even Steve H's red Stratocaster. The rehearsals were less fraught than expected. "We all did a bit of homework," commented Ian, "It's burnt into the old memory banks somewhere because, when we actually start playing, I'll start doing fills and whatnot and it'll just happen." The drummer suggested performing *Brave* on the Friday night so the band could relax for the rest of the weekend. He recalled, "The whole weekend should be a party, but it's a bit difficult with *Brave* in the way, to have a laugh."

As information started leaking out, fan excitement became palpable. "Wild horses couldn't have kept me away from hearing *Brave* live at last," says fan Krys Boswell. Adds fan John Boye, "Ironic indeed, considering the mixed reaction that *Brave* had received the first time around, that it would be the mainstay of the weekend seven years later." Before the weekend proper, the band organised a *Brave* warm-up gig at Jumpin Jaks club in Cardiff, which was operated by an old friend of H, Billy Manning. "He asked, would we fancy doing it?" recalls

SEPARATED OUT ... REDUX

H, but the band was worried about spoiling the one-off nature of the gig. In the end, pragmatism trumped such fears. After all, commented Ian, "Every show in the West End has a dress rehearsal."

The convention took place that April, with fans from all over the world braving holiday camp hardships to spend a weekend with their favourite band. Filming the entire event was Joe del Tufo and his team at Studio M, together with Paul and Jayce from the Boom Boom Boys (who took charge of the *Brave* filming, with a nine-camera shoot). Joe remembers his first sighting of Pontins. "A surreal, Stephen King-like carnival atmosphere rose over the horizon. I remember someone mouthing, 'I hope this isn't it.' But it was." Only Pete stayed on site – the rest moved back and forth from a holiday cottage about 8 miles away. "We thought we might be disturbed by fans when we were trying to sleep - we should have known better," says H.

Despite the peeling paint and plastic mattresses, the event did well. Recalls Joe del Tufo, "It was worth the trip just to finally get to experience *Brave*. I saw a lot of tears in the crowd during 'Falling From The Moon'. As I stood on top of the riser with the camera, I saw a kid on his dad's shoulders, and a woman who must be pushing seventy, all singing along." Another highlight was Swap The Band, which offered fans the opportunity to take the place of their favourite band member. "It was much cooler than I had imagined," says Joe. "This was really the heart and soul of the weekend, and it was appropriate that it anchored the event. Could there be a better story than a guy who sells his drum kit to fly from Australia to the event to play drums with his favourite band? If you thought that guy nailed the solo in 'Easter' you should have heard it during soundcheck. I was standing next to Rothers sidestage, he raised his eyebrow and grinned."

Some of Marillion's favourite support acts attended, including Robin Boult, Aziz Ibrahim, White Buffalo and Cry No More. There was an outing of Steve Rothery's Wishing Tree project, with Hannah Stobart, Paul Craddick and Steve's wife Jo, and a memorabilia museum run by Andy Rotherham showed off Mark's original Mellotron (which had been gathering dust in his parents' garage) and a newly restored Strange Engine. "It was a task slightly bigger than I anticipated," remarked James Fishwick of the Web UK, who undertook the restoration. "Most of the parts I made had to be hand-finished from either wood or metal to look like the photo."

The band were on hand for most of the weekend, milling around, chatting and signing autographs with aplomb. During the official signing session, the queue grew so long that after several hours of diligent attention to their fans, the band members had to call it a day. After all, they had a gig to play! Even then, the boys organised another session the next day to deal with those who had gone away empty-handed.

To cap it all, a team of journalists from *Q* attended the event, giving the band its first column inches in the music mag for years. When the weekend was over, as the fans departed with their T-shirts, photos and happy memories, the band, crew and staff were left to clear up, tie up loose ends and make their own way back home with smiles on their faces. "Pontins isn't most people's idea of a good place to visit, but despite the shabby accommodation and dodgy food, it was brilliant," said Mark. Concurred Ian, "One of the most enjoyable experiences of my career."

As the shutters went down at Brean Sands, so closed a chapter. Wrote Steve Hogarth, "We've all become caught up in something that transcends any relationship a band has had with its fans in the past." Agreed Joe del Tufo, "I don't think I'd really gotten the Marillion community until this weekend. Not just obsessed, not just emotionally invested, but also related. It's cool to be part of." Furthermore, the sentiment that the band had worked so hard to develop was starting to pay back – in spades. "The dynamic has started to shift," said Steve Hogarth a few months later. "There's something going on… and it's as rare as it is precious."

ANORAKNOPHOBIA

As *Anoraknophobia* was funded entirely by the fans, the band were conscious of the additional pressure to pull something special out of the bag. As they would write in the fan-only edition of the album, "This is the 21st Century and everything is about hype - but not this. This is about passion." A key difference was the ability to bring in Dave Meegan, previously responsible for *Brave* and *Afraid Of Sunlight*. The University Tour enabled a preview of material, which hadn't taken place for a while: those lucky enough to see 'Between You And Me', 'Quartz' and 'Map Of The World' receive an airing knew they had something special waiting.

Anoraknophobia, then; a uniquely-funded, history-making, foot-tapping, gut-wrenching, heart-breaking, soul-shaking, brain-engaging, soaring, grooving, gloriously funk-tastic beastie of an album.

From the opening notes of 'Between You And Me', the music is biting deeper, harder and more quickly than the last couple of studio recordings. There's a freshness and an exuberance not heard for a while, and while 'BYAM' isn't seeking to be anything other than an anthemic rocker, it does this so well! Concerned with the magic that powers special relationships, it is somewhat lightweight lyrically, save for the middle eight with its quiet, insightful musing. If only someone would play this on the radio...

'Quartz' is one of the most radical songs on the album. It's based around a monstrous walking bass line from Pete, and Steve Rothery's gonzo-funkoid wah-wah. The song details two people who are just that little bit too different to get along. The later part of the song uses a metaphor of two watches to contrast the two people – the clockwork watch always half-an-hour late, easily wound up and susceptible to the elements, the digital one immune to outside influence and always right. If there is a possible complaint to be made about the song, it is that (although it would mean losing a wonderful Rothery solo) it really should finish with the line, "One of these days... you're just gonna stop!"

Were 'Map Of The World' to come in contact with the song 'Holidays In Eden', they would probably explode! Where 'Holidays' was barbed and cynical about the idea of travelling, 'Map' is joyous, looking at the journey as an escape from grey drudgery. There is something of Bruce Springsteen's 'Tunnel Of Love' to the main riff, and much of the spirit of Crowded House about the whole song (without rendering it a pastiche). It is a song that revels in strong and simple songwriting.

The lush and expansive 'When I Meet God' certainly caused something of a stir when it came out. Powered by Mark Kelly's warmly textured keyboards, the song was described by H as saying, "Come down from that cloud and help us, you uncaring, callous bitch!" While he was clearly being facetious, it gets to the core of the argument. His frustration came from his belief that such a beautiful galaxy seemed to betray the hand of a guiding conscience... but how could such an entity not have the necessary compassion to help humanity rise above its failings? The sublime end section suspends the listener in the vastness of space. "It's full of stars!" indeed...

'The Fruit of the Wild Rose' opens with a jazzy riff from Steve Rothery, then, with a clatter of snare from Ian, Pete adds an insistent bass line. As H begins to sing, Mark comes in with a counterpoint melody. A love song from the perspective of someone on tour missing his lover back in autumnal England, the lyric somehow calls to mind a 19th century sailor on the high seas. A sudden burst of Nyman-esque keyboard picks up the tempo, while, almost buried in the background, Steve Rothery lays down a fuzzed solo. As the traveller heads for home, the song becomes full of glorious, pent-up eroticism, in anticipation of the two lovers reuniting. H spins a wonderful image of the woman's subconscious writhing in her sleep - the pun "stir your hips" also referring to the red fruit that dot English hedgerows in the autumn.

'Separated Out' concerns feelings of unworthiness – "Am I enough of a freak to be worth paying to see?" Interestingly, the use of the samples from Todd Browning's 1932 movie *Freaks* was not a knowing wink to the Fish-era track 'Freaks', but a happy coincidence at the hands of Mr Meegan. The thumping track also resembles Julius Fucik's 'Entry Of The Gladiators' (the clichéd music used for clowns).

The centrepiece of the album in many ways, 'This Is The 21st Century' sees Marillion layer a moody classic over a drum loop. The lyric has two main strands: a discussion of science's debunking of life's mysteries, and a couple finding their own magic in sensuality and love. H commented, "I refuse to accept that magic doesn't exist, I think the day you accept that, you might as well throw yourself off a high building." As the song moves into an extended coda, the music becomes fierce, with Ian's drums smashing along with the beat, Pete's bass prowling malevolently, Mark's keyboards mechanised, with brutal bass chords throbbing underneath and Steve Rothery's guitar howling like a beast. Bizarrely, this section manages to be the most modern-sounding the band have been up until this point, yet also recalls some of the more atmospheric parts of *Misplaced Childhood*. Sheer bloody genius!

'If My Heart Were A Ball, It Would Roll Uphill' is a strange hybrid of quasi-metal and film soundtrack stylings. H has said the lyric concerns "having a mad heart, really. That simple. Having a heart that doesn't behave and can't and defies the laws of physics." Once more Pete's bass playing is superb, thrumming excitedly on the choruses and skulking along like the darkest funk you'll ever hear in the verses. Ian is having a ball too, battering his kit like a mad thing. Both 'Separated Out' and 'If My Heart Were A Ball' recall the feel of heavier *Brave*-era tracks such as 'Hard As Love', but where those weren't entirely convincing, these fare better. The playfulness on show makes them more believable than if they had been played straight. An echo of the past appears in the middle eight, with a sample of the debut album's 'Chelsea Monday'. This gives way to an 'Interior Lulu'-esque outro, with instruments gradually building and pushing the song home, while H overlays a collage of lyrics taken from all the songs on the album, until it gradually subsides into silence.

It may be a little difficult, four albums later, to see why *Anoraknophobia* caused such a fuss when it was first released. Some fans have niggles about the production slightly smothering the songs, while others feel they go on longer than necessary. It feels like the very best of the band distilled into 63 astonishing minutes – a huge amount of ground covered, leaving the listener with one certainty – the magic in the music certainly isn't dead.

The cover was a total departure from what had gone before. Featuring the iconic cartoon anorak Barry , the artwork was brighter, simpler and fresher than anything in recent years, although it's fair to say that Barry had as many enemies as friends amongst the fan base. Notable was the extensive use of Carl Glover's evocative photomontages to illustrate the music, particularly in the special edition made available to pre-ordering fans.

242

16

The World's Gone Mad

The vein had been tapped; the door had been opened. Like a mid-life company worker who leaves a steady job and sets off to follow a dream, Marillion chose to break with convention and trust their instincts. The result, *Anoraknophobia* had been a great success, both commercially and creatively, and the relationship between the band and audience had never been stronger. On April 22 2002, twenty-five years after the partnership between Mick Pointer and Doug Irvine was first cemented, Marillion released the live album *Anorak In The UK*. "It sounds like a band I'd wish I was in... if I wasn't already in it," remarked Steve H. Agrees Pete, "There was a sense of us having a new beginning after a few difficult years. It was a very uplifting time." The band was riding the crest of a wave and, while there was no immediate financial pressure to record a follow-up album, the fivesome were ready to get to it.

The real question was, if the last studio album was an experiment, just how far could Marillion take things if they really pulled out all the stops? "How could the band exceed the enormity of *Anoraknophobia*?" asked fan David Brown, pointedly. The model they had discovered seemed amazingly simple, with the margins of self-management far outweighing anything the band had seen when they had been signed to a label. Said H, "It's ludicrous – you'd have to be selling 20 million albums to commit to two years for five guys, a producer and staff!"

Of course, the Marillos needed to find out whether the pre-order model had succeeded only as a one-off, or whether it offered a genuine alternative to being signed. The only thing to do was to try it again – in a repeat experiment that would turn into the most ambitious project the band had attempted for years

LETTING THE GENIE OUT OF THE BOX

After the final couple of gigs in Bonn and Geleen in May 2002, the band headed back to the studio. Upbeat the Marillos may have been, but writing was no less a challenge, commented Mark, "Starting from scratch on a new album always means a lot of groping around in the dark to begin with, hoping something will take shape soon. It can be quite frustrating at this stage because there is little we can do to hurry the process." Agreed Ian, "We're all sitting in a room going, 'Right, how did we do the last one?' and then there's that kind of [looks at watch...], 'Oh, got to go,' that stuff. That's probably the most nervous time."

In the knowledge that the next album would likely be a pre-order, Dave Meegan was invited back from the outset and set to work with the rest of the boys. "He has had the most input he has ever had on a project, right from the idea and arrangement stage," said Rothers. This was a double-edged sword, however, as it threatened to blunt his objectivity. Continued Rothers, "Sometimes the most difficult part is agreeing what's good. We all have different tastes in music and it can be hard work sometimes to try and find the common ground – ideas that all the band and Dave Meegan enjoy."

As the weeks turned into months with nothing but the occasional gig to break the monotony, tempers started to fray. "We did bicker," said Pete – it didn't help that the band's new-found commercial freedom had turned them all into managers. "We felt like we were becoming businessmen and not musicians, we needed to get away so we could just concentrate on making music." To resolve this (and while the Racket Club was reorganised and recarpeted), the six fellows headed to a rented farmhouse near Bath for a fortnight before Christmas. "Great atmosphere, great restaurants, a great pub," says Ian.

The experiment worked – just about – with four songs emerging from the Bath sessions. Ideas started to flow more smoothly as the band returned to Oxfordshire, aided by the use of recording tools such as Logic, which meant people could work from home on occasion – notably when others were being recorded. "It's all computers with these boys, these days," laughed H. Rothers had grown his gadget collection to include a chord machine linked to his guitar, and a new AdrenaLinn effects pedal, "a synth-like sound filter". One song to benefit was 'Invisible Man', the intro to which came about when Rothers was playing with a program called 'Live' and Mark was playing the bass notes against it. "We thought, that's an interesting direction, so it made the beginning of the song," says the guitarist. "You've still got to have a decent idea, but technology can be a catalyst."

With a few songs in the bag, band and entourage headed for a well-earned break – but not before launching what was set out as the mother of all pre-order campaigns. Following the still-apparent weaknesses in EMI's marketing (though the distribution had been sound for *Anoraknophobia*), the plan this time was to focus on marketing and promotion. "This email is intended for the believers," went the eWeb. "For every copy of *Marbles* pre-ordered, profits from that sale will go into our Campaign Fund. Using this money, we will take out adverts in magazines, advertise on radio stations - in short, try to reach all the people who don't necessarily visit our website or receive our eWeb, and potentially reach NEW fans too!"

At the time, a 'campaign' CD was envisaged as an album, plus a second disc of additional songs. The plan didn't meet with universal approval – not least because of the more-than-you'd-normally-spend-on-an-album price tag of thirty pounds. Some fans even questioned the band members' own finances,

SEPARATED OUT ... REDUX

leading to the band issuing a follow-up email. "Unfortunately, as some helpful soul suggested in an email to us, we haven't all got £100,000 each lying about that we can put into the marketing budget..."

All the same, there had been sufficient positive response for the band to continue with the project as planned – even if it was becoming clear that there would be more than enough songs for a single CD. "We came up with too much material; Dave told us to stop," laughed Pete. H concurred – "Quite suddenly I'm beginning to realise that we're sitting on a wealth of good ideas. Inspiration has finally struck!" The main issue was becoming how to decide what to leave off the final album, which was still intended as a single disc – "We were told that the shops wouldn't like a double album," explained Rothers. Said Mark, "I see the problems starting when we have to decide which to leave out and which to take on to completion. There could be bloodshed."

All too soon it was time to down tools in the studio and prepare for convention time again – but categorically not at Pontins. "Two main responses have been prevalent," said July's *Web* mag. "Why don't we do it again?" and "Can we have better facilities than Pontins?" The fans had spoken, and without further ado, Butlins in Minehead had been booked. Continued the mag, "Yes Butlins, don't laugh... it's a LOT nicer AND bigger, trust us!" Indeed – the booking could accommodate 2,000 people.

The weekend offered the opportunity to 'out' a few songs from the album – the rocker-with-a-message 'Don't Hurt Yourself', as well as the track then-called 'Pacific Rower' and demos of 'Angelina' and 'Neverland'. The lyrics to 'Don't Hurt Yourself' started as a self-catharsis for H and quickly became an anthem. "In some people's eyes I'm seen as a sort of spiritual doctor myself, someone who has got the answers... which of course I haven't. But I do attempt to write songs which might shed a positive light on people's lives," he said. The original inspiration for 'Pacific Rower' came from the quiet heroics of long-distance rower Tony Bullimore, who survived in an air pocket for 3 days after his boat, the Exide Challenger, capsized between Australia and Antarctica. Of the performance, said Mark, "We hadn't finished it at that point: there were lots more lyrics that Steve had written but there was no music to go with them. So we did a bit of a hatchet job to finish it and make it playable."

Swap The Band included an outing of *Fugazi* with Martin Jakubski of Marillion tribute band 'Forgotten Sons'. "I had absolutely no problem with it and Martin did a fabulous job," said Rothers. Said Ian, "It's so weird playing it, it feels like last year that we used to play all that stuff. What is strange is that we don't even have to rehearse, all these old tracks are still in my head. The audience seemed to love it."

The 2003 convention also boasted a record-breaking achievement – 63 hours between recording the *Afraid Of Sunlight* performance and it appearing in a retail outlet, "The fastest DVD filming and production in history," said the press release. On cameras once again were Paul and Jayce of the Boom Boom Boys. "Erik had arranged a John Le Carré-style meeting at the DVD duplication facility for seven that morning – we left at five," says Paul, who accompanied Erik on the journey to Wales and back. "I think I was up for 28 hours straight that night/day, but it all became a bit of a blur - as you can imagine," says Erik. "I clearly remember listening to Smashing Pumpkins VERY LOUDLY on the way, to try and stay awake!" Less than 48 hours after the cameras started rolling, Erik was heading back to the site with several boxes of DVDs. Continues Erik, "I remember finding a DVD player to test it out... I had The Fear about putting it on sale and none of them working because of some fluke error. But when it played, someone bought me a pint of Guinness, which I walked onstage with to interrupt the band's Q&A session to tell them it had arrived. It was at that point my body went into exhaustive shutdown." It wasn't over yet – to qualify, the DVD had to be available for sale from a real shop – this was to be The Record House in Aylesbury. 15 hours later and after "a frantic dash" the record was secured. "It was an amazing achievement, to have that co-ordination," said Pete.

"I really didn't think we could top the Pontins convention... Oh me of little faith," said Ian. Mark's highlight was being asked to sign a baby – on its T-shirt. Agreed Pete, "I think we outdid ourselves. We all got ill for two weeks afterwards." Nonetheless, particularly having received such a positive response to the new songs, it was a buoyed-up band that headed and back to the studio.

Following some final jams, arrangements and tweaks, the band started recording properly at the end of May. "We have arranged two or three quite long songs in a *Strange Engine* thematic kind of way," said Pete, intriguingly. These included 'Invisible Man' – a song so strong that its "world's gone mad" opening line became a mission statement for the whole album. Said H, "I did start to feel that nothing made sense to me anymore. It's about being able to feel injustice and not being able to do anything about it." This theme of frustration quickly extended as other songs – 'You're Gone', 'Angelina', 'Neverland', 'Fantastic Place' – all presented opportunities for release, for leaving the past behind. Continued H, "The process of escape, the desire to escape, the possibility of escape, the value of having the idea that you can escape, is so crucial; even if you never leave the cage, it's good to know that the door is open." 'Pacific Rower' was renamed 'Ocean Cloud' to celebrate oarsman Don Allum – explained H,

"The only guy to row across the Atlantic in both directions. The fact that he remains unknown is an outrage!"

By August 2003, the album had a name – *Marbles*. Given the sheer wealth of material, the band decided that a supplementary disc wouldn't work and *Marbles* would be a full-blown double album, the first in the band's history. "The decision came about on its own as we had gathered far more material, while trying to write the perfect album, than we could possibly fit on a single disc. Once we had decided that a double album was the way forward, then it all started to slot into place," explains Pete. There was a conscious decision to organise tracks into darker and lighter discs, said Mark. "The second disc should be a lot easier to cope with on first listen." This included "eccentric piece of psychedelia" 'The Damage', based on a rising and diminishing string piece from Mark, as well as the whimsical wordplay of 'Drilling Holes', based on the memory of a new hot water tank being fitted in the Racket Club many years before. Recalls H, "Stewart Every said to me, 'A man came to drill holes in the afternoon.' And I said, 'I suppose by the evening, most of the afternoon was gone, then...?' That started it!" H recorded the vocals in his kitchen. "I was screaming my head off when everybody was out. Any passers-by in the village would have wondered what the hell was going on in there..."

The plan was for Dave Meegan to edit the tracks together, before the band started overdubs in September. Not all of his production choices met with universal approval – some songs almost had to be forced through by the quiet-spoken Irishman. "He's quite a dictator," remarked H. "He explores the things he's excited about, and he'll gently guide you away from the things that he doesn't really think are happening." Notably with 'Fantastic Place', which Rothers in particular struggled with: "Parts of the writing I've found extremely stressful (which is very unusual for me) as I didn't always agree with Dave's choice of which ideas we should make into songs," he said. It wasn't just Rothers, says H, "Dave forced us to finish that song, we thought it was all a bit too soft and airy fairy. He used every bit of cunning and guile to get it through. I'm glad he did."

But still, the album was nearly there – and what was emerging more than justified the effort. While the process was dragging on, all knew they were on to a winner. The "shout my name in public places" section of 'Invisible Man' gave the band shivers as it came together. "I remember thinking that's going to wipe people out, 'cos it's wiped me out doing it," said H.

FINDING NEVERLAND

Despite initial apprehension, more than 18,000 fans stumped up the cash for the pre-order, creating a substantial promotion and advertising war chest. "We'll be spending more money than was spent on marketing us in a decade," H commented. Having spent several years agency-side working for companies like Saatchi and Saatchi, Lucy's background in marketing and advertising was invaluable. She put together a plan that covered online and print ads, poster campaigns, retail store racking... you name it. "Straightforward stuff, but with Marillion in charge," said Pete. "The ideas could be amazing if done well, but it could screw up, so we have to be careful."

Christine Cooper was on board as well, kicking off a series of street team and e-team initiatives and co-ordinating activities such as the London cab-inspired 'car wrapping', in which fans volunteered their vehicles to be decorated in the *Marbles* cover art. Says Lucy, "The brief was simple: *"Just Drive! (Oh, and keep to the speed limit!)"* " Through fortuitous timing, in parallel Mark Wilkinson was working on some new artwork for a Front Row Club early years box set, to be known as *Curtain Call*. Lucy co-ordinated with Fish and other early band members to decide which recordings should be used, and to confirm the sales model – the six-disc set would be available from both Marillion and Fish websites.

Otherwise, there was little time for anything else other than getting the album done, and working out the plan. Pete managed to squeeze in a contribution to a Kevin Gilbert tribute album, and in October H took his H-band on tour for a handful of nights, the first time since the convention that any of the Marillos had gone out on the road. For a spot of light relief, December 22 saw a special outing of 'supergroup' Stranger by the Minute, back at The Walls in Oswestry. The Wishing Tree kicked off events and Paul Sturman once again led the vocals on the main set. "A wonderfully fun and musically entertaining evening," wrote fan Judith Mitchell.

Finally, by January 2004 sound clips were up on the website. As time was running short, both Mike Hunter and Steven Wilson were brought in to do some of the mixing – indeed, said Mark, "It was a case of, 'It's just never going to get finished if it is all left for Dave to do...' " Mike set about 'The Only Unforgivable Thing' and 'Neverland' plus everything beginning with 'M' or 'D', while Steven tackled 'Angelina', which had remained largely untouched since its original demo. "Steve's guitar was so perfect that Dave wouldn't let him change it," said H.

Two more months passed before the album was finished, but the mood remained upbeat, given the quality of the result. "These albums don't take three years for nothing," said Pete. Concurred Mark, "It's almost as if it's another band." Indeed, while Dave might have worked at a sometimes near-glacial pace, it was to the overall benefit of the music. "I think he's got quicker," laughed Ian, who remained in awe of Dave's ability to catalogue the band's outputs in infinitesimal detail – largely in his head. "He's perfected his art," said Pete. Nobody was happier than Dave himself, as he recalls, "It was the album I always wanted and was trying to make with the band. I finally felt I had achieved what I set out to do."

With an album as good as this, all at Racket knew it was essential to keep up the momentum with both fans and media. Mark, H and Ian went on a whistle-stop circuit of Europe for a number of listening parties (with H undeterred by food poisoning in Spain – "It was the oysters that got him," said Ian), while Pete and Rothers headed to New York (undeterred by blizzards) and LA. In parallel, the band members got stuck into interviews with local and national media – according to H, 96 interviews in 3 weeks. "Everyone has a great feeling for this record, and the journalists present seemed to respond very positively also," he remarked. Aided and abetted by the fans, the band were receiving more press coverage than they had in years. Said Pete, "You should all pat yourselves on the back. It's great to know that real fans can make more of a difference than record company hype."

But would it make a difference? Crunch time came on April 19, with the release of 'You're Gone' as a single. Incredibly it raced up the UK charts, reaching a top 7 position in its first week of release – the first time the band had reached the top ten since 'Incommunicado', seventeen years before. Says Ian, "I remember turning on either BBC or Sky News and them saying, 'Marillion are back!' I thought, *Bloody hell!* The whole band was on a high." "We laughed and laughed," said H. "I was amazed at all the fuss it caused and how people on the radio suddenly wanted to talk to us. I sometimes make the mistake of thinking that the media responds to the quality of an artist's music – it doesn't. It responds to statistics and trends and nothing else." Marillion had played the game – and won.

There was no time to lose as the band had a promise to keep – to deliver "the biggest tour in ten years". Rehearsals kicked off back at the Racket Club, with all the usual issues of turning recordings into live arrangements. One challenge was for H to learn the guitar intro to 'Don't Hurt Yourself'. "Not sure I'm cut out for it, but I'll stick with it," said H. Recalled guitar tech Colin Price, "The band wanted me to play it as H was having a nightmare with the chords. He mastered it in time though… and I think he became a much better guitar player on that tour."

The album was released just as the tour was kicking off, generating another round of interviews. "Things are more positive now than they've ever been. We have control, we have our own studio, we make the albums we want to make," said Steve Rothery, reflecting the band's new-found confidence. As did the album's press release: "A creative milestone – you'll either 'get it' or you won't. The choice is yours," it went.

Suffice to say that the critics "got it", with strong reviews across the board. "There's a lot to like," wrote Betty Clarke in *The Guardian*; agreed Sarah Donaldson in *The Daily Telegraph*, "Displaying a knack for knob-twiddly production effects, the band run the gamut of AOR, from laboured prog-rock to toe-tapping country-lite via Simple Minds stadium-rousers." The music press were similarly effusive – "One of their best albums to date. Strong lyrics and superb performances all round," said Roger Newell in *Guitarist*. And in *Classic Rock*, it was Jon Hotten's turn to implore a better rap for the band. "With *Marbles*, Marillion have cut one of their very best records. That genre thing has been a bugbear of Marillion's, but it no longer seems relevant. What are Radiohead if not a progressive band? And what are Pink Floyd, for that matter? Fans of either of those two bands would find much to enjoy in *Marbles*. Ultimately, though, it's not a derivative record, and Marillion are no longer a derivative band. They are making strong, singular music with the courage of their convictions, and we should treasure them more than we do."

If the reviewers liked it, the fans were bowled over. According to fan Peter Tornberg, "*Marbles* came at the right point in time. The fans and the world were ready for the BIG Marillion album. With *Marbles* it all came together… with the singles-campaign, the extensive artwork and the collection of fantastic, accessible songs, in some ways the sum was bigger than the pieces." "A landmark album, unbeatable in its completeness," says Sascha Glück; agrees Anthony Craig, "I have to accept that they may never top this but hope they come close. I wouldn't change a thing even if I could."

Following a couple of warm-up shows, the tour proper started in early May, supported by Kid Galahad and Gazpacho. "After the first couple of shows we knew we were on to a winner," said Rothers. One song that became a surprising hit in the live setting was 'Fantastic Place' – "It seems to fly itself," H remarked. "The tour felt like the *Seasons End* tour all over again to me. I really enjoyed playing *Marbles* live and it was a thrill (and a relief) to watch the audience reacting

so positively to our latest 'baby'. I'll never forget the ovation in Montpellier."
The European leg of the tour was not without its complications – H snapped a
tendon in his finger in Turin, and a tour bus broke down in France – "We woke
up in a scrapyard," recalled H. "We later borrowed buses from Simply Red and
Rufus Wainwright."

Remarked Ashleigh Wallace of the *Belfast Telegraph* of his local gig, "The ghost
of Marillion past was well and truly exorcised last night. It was an encore that
proved the high point of the evening. A clearly emotional Hogarth told the
chanting crowd, who had been waiting for the climax, that it has been 17 years
since Marillion had played 'Easter' – written about Northern Ireland – to the
people of Belfast. 'If this doesn't make me cry, then I'm a harder man than I
thought,' he pronounced, before launching into the song which had fans old
and new alike singing with one voice."

At the Manchester gig was long-time fan Mike Ainscoe. "I knocked at the back
door of Manchester Academy and chanced upon Lucy who let my wife and I sit
quietly through the sound check," he recalls. "Afterwards, H meandered over to
the merch where we were perusing what was on offer. He was after something
warm to wear – I offered him my long sleeved Web UK shirt, which he offered
to swap me for a *Marbles* shirt. I chose one off the stand, stripped my own shirt
off and handed it to H in a football-style swap!"

'Don't Hurt Yourself' was released as a follow-up single on July 12. While it
didn't do so well (reaching Number 16 in the UK charts), it kept the flywheel
of publicity spinning, as did digital-only download 'The Damage' on October
11 – continuing the band's "love affair with the internet", according to the press
release. A week later saw the release of the *Marbles* on the Road live DVD –
incredibly, the band's first live video release available in the shops since *From
Stoke Row...* in 1990.

In parallel, the band had fifteen dates booked across the Atlantic – but not, this
time, at a loss. "We've played fewer venues and the ticket prices are a lot higher –
people are prepared to pay it," said Steve R. The jaunt was nearly wrong-footed
as the band found themselves on the same plane from Heathrow to Mexico
City as Yusuf Islam, better known by his stage name Cat Stevens. Following a
seven-hour stopover in Bangor, Maine when the pacifist singer-songwriter was
pulled off the plane , the band spent the night in the terminal at Washington DC
before finally getting a connecting flight via Chicago. The attention garnered
when H broke the story of Mr Islam's unfortunate detainment to the UK press
quickly paled compared to 36 hours without sleep. As he noted in his diary, "The
problem is, I have to sing live tonight at the Mexico Auditorium, in front of 9,000

people – tonight, Wednesday. It's being broadcast live on national television – and I haven't slept since Monday. No pressure…"

Fan Rick Armstrong recalls the Swap The Band audition he organised for his niece, Kali, at Bogart's in Cincinnati that October. "Having participated in the inaugural Swap The Band at the 2002 convention, I thought it would be great for Kali to do, as she is a really talented singer… but the band were not sure that a 14-year-old girl could handle it," he recalls. "I suggested that Kali auditioned at the sound check, and fortunately the band agreed to give it a go. Kali was on crutches due to some reconstructive knee surgery, but she was definitely up for it. Family and friends came out to watch. Fortunately my Dad was in town and came out as well - I think he enjoyed meeting everyone and seeing the performance even though rock music was never really his thing." Rick's father was, for the record, space pioneer and global hero Neil Armstrong - who would eventually see Marillion play on more than one occasion. This included in the UK, leading to what H called his most rock and roll moment as he drove Armstrong father and son between Heathrow and Gatwick airports. "I was driving quite fast because I know they are late," he recalled. "I suddenly thought, oh… I just said, 'Is this alright for you? I'm not driving too fast, am I?' And Neil just said from the back seat, 'No, that's fine.' I thought, *I've just asked Neil Armstrong, who was sat on a skyscraper full of liquid oxygen, if he's worried about me driving him too fast round the M25…* I don't suppose he would be, really…"

Despite the travel hiccups, the North America leg of the tour was a successful end to a successful year. Reported H, "4 'Top 15' singles, including a shocking No7 in the UK chart and a stellar No2 in the download chart. Of course, they're only numbers… but such beautiful numbers…" Following a Los Trios outing to Barcelona in November, it was time for a well-earned break. And then, it seemed, the world really did go mad. It was time to push up, and out.

MARBLES

Marillion's 13th album was the second with a pre-order. The retail version of the album was a single disc affair, but the definitive version was that sent to the pre-ordering fans, two discs containing an hour and forty minutes of some of the finest music the band had ever recorded. The reaction from the fanbase was adulatory: the album quickly attained classic status, and many consider it a career high to this day. Adding to the excitement was 'You're Gone' reaching No7 in the UK singles chart. As for the outside world, well, there was certainly more press than there'd been for a while, but it's probably fair to say that most gave a collective shrug. Little did they know what they were missing.

'The Invisible Man' commences with what seems like someone randomly switching between effects pedals. The listener is quickly drawn into a 13-minute noir tale about how H has become a confidant of the fans, who write to him with their most intimate and awful secrets, and the impotence and guilt he feels in being unable to do anything to help – "When you stumble / You will stumble through me". Musically, the piece moves through a number of sections and time signatures, the tension and unease building up until the singer can take it no longer and screams into the ether... Powerful stuff.

Although the four 'Marbles' pieces are musically distinct, they began life as a single lyric of reminiscences from Steve Hogarth's childhood. Producer Dave Meegan suggested that breaking them apart and giving each its own musical identity would stop the words from being perceived as too saccharine. The first part is based in the present day, with H on a tour bus wondering if he's gone a bit mad. The music feels appropriately hesitant and we are not quite sure how it's going to resolve.

The heavily Trewavas-influenced 'Genie' is an apparently true story about a woman who approached H on tour and revealed that, in a former life, he was a French fisherman and they were lovers, and that he needed to spend some time with her to discover who he really was. The main thrust of the lyric is H's reluctance to actually follow through and discover whether the woman was really onto something or just a bit deluded, for fear of what he might find. 'Genie' seems to be something of an overlooked song, yet it is a singular gem on an outstanding album, starting gently and building through some wonderful chord sequences and vocal harmonies to the "house in your mind" section, followed by Rothers' lovely solo.

It seems difficult to imagine now, but when the band were recording 'Fantastic Place', it was not universally liked. The song is regularly cited by fans as one of the standouts from the album, with its uplifting lyric about withdrawing from the ordinary world to somewhere better (whether the fantastic place actually represents a real place is not entirely clear).

'The Only Unforgivable Thing' also seems much overlooked, yet like 'Genie', it too offers a sublime Marillion journey. This one is about guilt: it is not difficult to read between the lines and imagine what the root cause of this might be. The song is full of evocative lyrics and phrases; the chicken bones sticking in the throat is especially noteworthy. Just when the song seems stuck in its own, melancholic vibe, the mood changes. H reveals he has given up sky and the stars to keep the earth, and we suddenly understand why he is bothering to look for a way through his guilt. The final lyric suggests that he might not be the only one to have transgressed.

'Marbles II' is a hazy recollection of youth, of collecting and trading marbles with friends as though they were jewels. The bittersweet lyric has the sense that they were right, that the marbles really did merit such importance, with the unspoken corollary that the failure to properly value things now is tragic. Live, Steve Rothery cuts loose with the most marvellous solo, and it is something of a shame that it does not appear on the recorded version. Producer Dave Meegan has since commented that he deliberately reined in the guitarist in order to bring out the best in Hogarth.

Another long track, 'Ocean Cloud', concludes the first disc of the set. A widescreen epic, it's a song about aging and ambition represented by solo transatlantic rower Donald Allum. Excerpts from Allum's powerfully moving log of the journey (from the website of the Ocean Rowing Society) further enliven the song; the segment that moves from the boat being becalmed to being hit by the towering wave is particularly harrowing. For many, 'Ocean Cloud' remains the finest long song the band have ever recorded.

Disc Two begins with 'Marbles III', reminiscing on a young H using a tennis racquet to bash his marbles into the sky, with inevitable consequences. The cheery, naïve music changes into a tension-filled minor chord as the enraged neighbours knock at his parents' door...

The band have been quite candid about the fact that a quirky song like 'The Damage' could only have been written in the spirit of freeness that a double album allows, which some might say evidences the fact that the band are not always the best judge of their own material. With something of *The Bends*-era Radiohead, lyrically, it's another slant on the ideas in 'Genie', hence the re-use of 'I let the genie out of the box'.

Second single 'Don't Hurt Yourself' is a catchy number based on a simple acoustic riff. Almost a self-help mantra, the song is essentially saying that very little matters so much it's worth getting hurt over. It's notable for Mr Rothery's rather nice bottleneck playing.

The hit single 'You're Gone' harks back to Marillion rockers like 'Incommunicado' or 'Cover My Eyes'. Very much a Rothery showcase, the song is strongly dependent on the guitarist's e-bowed and delayed guitar lines. Some fans were upset with the prominent use of drum loops, but Ian is present – he just plays so sympathetically that the dual percussion tracks sound like one. Hogarth's words are about dealing with the loss of someone of great value to you, all the while managing to celebrate the time you'd had together.

'Angelina' was inspired by a roadside advert for the radio station Capital FM that said, "Marguerita takes requests", which made H laugh because it sounded rather too much like a telephone sex line. Built on a bed of languorous Kelly soundscapes with some tasteful blues from Rothers, the song tries to walk the line between the different notions of what Angelina is offering. It features Carrie Tree on backing vocals in a chorus that recalls Soft Cell's 'Say Hello, Wave Goodbye'. Whether Capital DJ Marguerita Taylor has an opinion on the song is not known.

If 'The Damage' would never have made it onto a single disc, 'Drilling Holes' would have been out of contention still earlier. Steve Hogarth admits that the words came from a desire not always to have to tear himself to bits to come up with a lyric. It is, nevertheless, constructed from real memories. The man with the plastic shoes is his H-band guitarist Aziz Ibrahim. This very English, psychedelic piece was created by Dave Meegan, who insisted that each time the band jammed with Steve Hogarth's demo, they had to come up with something completely new.

'Marbles IV' is a final lament for H's sanity, over a quietly dignified, yet slightly fraying backing track.

And then, finally, 'Neverland'. From its first outing, prior to the release of the album at the 2003 Marillion Weekend, it was clear this was one seriously good piece of music. The album version didn't disappoint. The first half of the song is about how having someone's love over a long period of time can inspire one to better things, particularly in times of hardship. It's also about trying to overcome shame and guilt over some transgression, to become "someone someone would want to be". Punctuated by Steve Rothery's powerful, cutting guitar motif, the song builds over wonderfully moving bass lines from Pete and euphoric chords from Mark Kelly until the acoustic breakdown.

The second half of the song uses images from *Peter Pan* – Wendy, the tick tock of the crocodile, Hook and, of course, Neverland itself to discuss the idea of escape. With some wonderful moments from all the musicians, the plaudits must go to Mr Hogarth's clever mock-echoed delivery with its twists and turns, and to Steve Rothery for some quite magnificent soloing. The song brings itself full circle by acknowledging that it is only with the love of that special person that escape from guilt and shame is possible. It's a real tear-jerker and a strong contender for Marillion's best song ever.

The double album features some of the finest artwork of the H-era. Designer Carl Glover merged the faces of his niece and nephew holding marbles in front of their eyes to create the wonderful front cover image, as well as creating an iconic marble design that could be used across the album and its related releases. The interior booklet features some beautiful and creative photography. Special kudos goes to the pictures accompanying 'The Only Unforgivable Thing', which mimic the way guilt insidiously takes over every aspect of your life.

17 Moving Somewhere Else

"What a disastrous Christmas" read Marillion's first newsletter of 2005, reflecting on the tsunami that devastated communities across South Asia. To help with the global fund-raising effort, the band donated all profits from a show at the Aylesbury Civic, as well as offering several prizes to *The Sun's* fundraising auction, including a drum lesson and a VIP package for the next Marillion Weekend. As events continued to unfold, it was a sober, thoughtful band that made their way back into the studio.

Sober, perhaps, but not downbeat. With two pre-ordered albums in the bag and a still-growing profile, the Marillos were better placed than they had been for years. Not least financially: the *Marbles* pre-order, coupled with the success of the FRC releases and the *Marbles On The Road* live album, had put sufficient money in the bank to make another record. Whatever trials might exist, global or domestic, there would be no restrictions on their freedom to make music.

A VOICE FROM THE PRESENT

When the band first started going through leftovers from the *Marbles* sessions, the aim was to release an EP. There was sufficient material overall; indeed some songs, like 'Faith', were just about ready to go. By common consent, Mike Hunter was nominated as co-producer – he had helped out towards the end of the last album, and had also mixed *Marbles On The Road*.

Mike was a very different beast to Dave Meegan; not least, he was more of a musician. Explained Pete, "He wanted us to learn the songs and then record them, kind of opposite to what we'd normally do. It was like stepping back to the first time we were in a studio." Mike knew how to handle the band, said H, "Mike's similar to Dave in that he knows what he wants and he knows how to get it out of you without pissing you off!" (Said Mike, "I always get my own way in the end!") The boys collated some samples and sent them up to Liverpool for Mike to play with. "I whittled these down to about 6 or 7 ideas that I edited into rough arrangements at home," he says. Following a few more to's and fro's, he headed off to join the band.

Dave and the boys had started to exploit multi-track recording during the *Marbles* sessions, which meant that each instrument and vocal could be captured individually, even if part of a jam. This approach fitted neatly with Mike's production style. When the band did jam, Mike would look at using the material directly, rather than simply turning it into demos. The result was a cleaner, less cluttered sound, requiring fewer overdubs. "We sound more like a live band performing in a room," said Steve Rothery – which made sense, as that was exactly what was happening.

The approach worked, particularly for Rothers as it suited his more instinctive style – playing along to vocals, rhythm and keys multiple times and seeing what resulted. "Most of the time, I don't even want to know the chords I'm playing. It's good to look upon things from an instinctive point of view, because if you know exactly what the music will be doing at a certain moment, you tend to think in straight lines." The player had started composing on keyboards, making his playing more textural than ever. "This time the music just needed *so much* guitar. It's good, because there's more balance now between the instruments," he said.

The jamming approach was a revelation to Mike. "He was constantly amazed by the fact that we don't know exactly what each other is about to do but it sounds like we have already decided," said Mark. "I suppose we have just been doing it for so long together that we just anticipate what each other is going to do next, without it sounding contrived." As the strands of music evolved, so did Mike's approach: too much good stuff was going on to expect songs to emerge directly. Mike started to develop arrangements himself, pulling elements out of jams. "He'd take ideas away and put a completely different spin on them," said Pete. On occasion, the urge to add a bit of music proved too hard to resist. Explained Mark, "He'll go away and record something, and say, 'I'm not trying to join the band, but have a listen to this.' We will say, 'That sounds really nice, did we do that?' and he always says, 'Well, I didn't do much…'"

The lyrical content for the album was proving just as personal as its predecessor – albeit more direct in its language – based on both world events and Steve Hogarth's own circumstances. The singer had been particularly moved by the 'Make Poverty History' campaign that was launched on New Year's Day. "Five years ago, I had no idea 30,000 people were dying of poverty," he said. "Simply the fact that this obscene statistic became known to me just lit a fire underneath me." To H, such knowledge could not go unmentioned in his lyrics or indeed messages to fans. Responding to accusations of him 'carping' at gigs, H said, "I'm not talking about politics, I'm talking about a lot of people dying every day. When I open my mouth, maybe eighty or a hundred thousand people on the planet will hear what I'm saying. It's probably something that comes with age; I don't want to croak my last breath and think I didn't do or say something I could have."

In parallel, H's personal life was there in black and white. "The breakdown of my marriage and, later on, the blossoming of a new relationship with my girlfriend played a major part," said H. "Both of those things are reflected – both the pain and the feeling that anything is possible looking down the road." The other band members gave H lyrical free rein – "We share so much in terms of what we think is great, both musically and lyrically, that it's almost never been a problem," said Rothers. All the same, some of the lyrics made uncomfortable reading. Added Mark, "I don't envy him at all. I find it very odd putting your life story into words for everybody to have a look at. If I was writing lyrics I would steer well clear of personal stuff." H, however, found he had little choice but to bare his soul. "I could write fiction, but I've backed myself into a corner where I've got to write about true things. That's why I hate writing, there's so much pressure to dig another piece of flesh out of myself."

Before long, it was convention season again. While there had been no Marillion Weekend the previous year, the band more than made up for it with a three-day event at Butlins in Minehead. The 2,700-strong audience was treated to a full outing of *Marbles*, followed by "up-tempo" Saturday night and "atmospheric" Sunday night performances. Immediately following, Pete headed off to Germany to perform a date or two with his side project, Kino, before the quintet headed back to the Racket Club.

By May, Marillion had completed the main part of two more songs started during the *Marbles* sessions, codenamed 'Circular Ride' and 'Say the Word' - the latter being "a bit of an experiment" according to Mark. Said H, "We had abandoned 'Circular Ride' because we couldn't get the verse and chorus to work; 'State of Mind' "was as good as rewritten." Says Pete, "There is always a sense of suspicion about songs left over from projects – if they weren't good enough for one album, would they be good enough for the next? It isn't really the case but you can't help having that feeling in the back of your mind. We decided to write a couple more songs to go with them and carried on." By the end of the month, five songs were underway including 'Real Tears For Sale' and 'Throw Me Out'.

Los Trios Marillos had another outing planned for June – this time to the US, as a consolation prize for cancelling a summer tour that had been scheduled alongside a number of festival dates. "One by one the festivals fell through, and we made the decision to pull the rest of the planned shows. Grr..." went the apology. Following a couple of warm-up gigs, Pete, Rothers and H headed to New York, Chicago, Philadelphia, Boston, Montreal, Toronto and Washington DC. Said H, "The acoustic format made for a more relaxed and spontaneous atmosphere. We could change things in the moment, adding or removing songs and responding to the two-way conversation with the crowd." It wasn't all plain sailing, particularly for Pete: "I was more of a fish out of water because I was playing a lot of guitar. The first couple of shows were a bit nerve-wracking."

All such discomforts were laid to rest at La Tulipe in Montreal. "The 700-capacity crowd went completely wild as one," said H of his arrival on stage. "It wasn't hysteria, it was raw affection. In that three minutes of pure joy, I felt that every hardship and petty frustration I have endured over the years of making music was of no significance whatsoever." To the singer, the ovation eclipsed even the one at Le Zenith in Paris, on the *Seasons End* tour. One participant in the group hug and resulting, clamorous gig was fan Joe Serge. "There's a very religious feel to a Montreal show. I know it's a cop-out to say, 'You have to be there.' But I do not have the talent to describe in words what it is." He adds: "The songs were so beautifully arranged that, honestly, I forgot Ian and Mark were missing…"

Wallflowers Ian and Mark hadn't forgotten they were missing, however. Said Mark, "It was down to finances… I was a bit jealous, actually; I thought it would be nice to go as they are playing places we haven't played before." He was kept busy thanks to a surprise phone call from Adam Wakeman, touring keyboard player with Travis who had been asked to headline the Isle of Wight Festival at rather short notice. Adam couldn't go as he was on the road with Black Sabbath, so he asked Mark to step in. "I wasn't sure – there was a lot of stuff to learn and only two days of rehearsals," recalls Mark – but 15 minutes later, he decided to go for it. "I listened to the songs I thought they'd probably play and it's all very straightforward stuff, just a case of making lots of notes." In the end, Mark played twice more – at Live8 and T in the Park, both in Scotland. "That was fun - a nice change."

As Los Trios returned, a reunited Marillion headed for a couple of festivals of their own: Bospop in the Netherlands, and Guildford's Guilfest. Fan Rich Harding was at Bospop. "There seemed to be a fairly sizeable contingent of fans in the audience, but many more Marillion virgins. 'The Damage' rocked a fat one – best I've seen it played – and 'Between You And Me' and 'Cover My Eyes' brought yet more converts on board, judging by the facial expressions and outbreaks of foot-tapping and mild swaying all around me. An excellent festival outing and a great advert for the band."

And then, on the morning of Thursday July 7, it all went mad again, as four co-ordinated terrorist attacks took place on London's public transport system, killing 52 people. Marillion sent a message: "Whoever bombs buses or tube trains is prepared to kill and hurt ordinary people irrespective of their race, nationality or religion." Just four days later, the band was able to reflect on some better news, which each of the million tiny voices loaned to the 'Make Poverty History' campaign helped make possible. "No G8 summit has ever done as much for the world's poor. Thank you. You were great," read the eWeb, its tone reflecting the mood pervading the music and lyrics of the planned EP.

By August the band were well into recording, with Mark in catch-up following a stint in jury service. Five tracks were being prepped: 'Real Tears For Sale', another reference to the supposed 'glamour' of being a pop star; 'She Threw Me Out'; 'Circular Ride'; 'Say The Word'; and the long-suffering 'Faith'. Reported Colin Price, "It's early days but everything sounds amazing. There are some mad ideas – we had Rothers playing [XTC] Dave Gregory's Fender Bass 6 guitar (think Beach Boys / Glen Campbell). Pure 'Wichita Lineman'!" The atmosphere was further lightened by the arrival of a rough cut of the Boom Boom Boys' documentary *Colours and Sound*, recorded during the *Marbles* tour. Said Colin, "We were crying with laughter. It's the best 'on the road' film I've ever seen and it's STILL not finished!"

Los Trios headed off to the US again for a handful of dates at the beginning of September. The moment the plane landed back in the UK, H headed straight to the studio to record some vocals, while he was still in the performance zone. "Live gigs will have made his voice different; if he leaves it, his voice will have moved off again," explained Mark. All was nearly done for the EP, with an anticipated finish date of mid-October – continued Mark, "It's quite fast, mixing with Mike."

Trouble was, of the five tracks none was particularly radio-friendly. No single meant it wasn't really worth releasing an EP so the whole idea was canned, instead planning a full album and moving the deadline to March 2006. Deflated, the band returned to jamming, under Mike's guiding hand. Said Mark, "There was a feeling that we should start again, we had all these songs finished but they felt quite old because they had been sitting around for a year." Creatively speaking, the prospect of a full album was as daunting as ever – particularly with *Marbles* having been so successful, "Whatever we do next has got to be a big statement," said Pete. "We've got to be totally convinced that what we are doing is right and that the music is good enough."

The *Not Quite Christmas* tour gave the band a welcome outing, including a trip to Luxembourg for the first time in 8 years. Youthful attendees at the Manchester Academy gig on November 20 included Stuart and Richard Sharples, aged 12 and 15 respectively. "I love Marillion – they are great musicians, play wonderful songs and appeal to all ages," said Stuart. Agreed Richard, "There is something about their music that makes us feel good, being at a gig makes us feel like we're part of a huge family. We've been to a lot of great gigs this year - Green Day, Rob Thomas, Arena and Alterbridge to name a few – but none compares with this!"

After the tour, Pete headed back out for another two weeks with Kino, while the remaining four band members went back to Oxfordshire. For some, the fires of home were burning brighter than for others. While Steve Hogarth had been keeping up appearances on the live circuit, as December approached so did the conclusion of a situation that had been building for a decade, obliquely documented across so many songs of love, attrition and, finally, escape. "I was shown the door," says H. "It wasn't her fault, it was entirely mine. I was an unfaithful, selfish and lost soul." Spending the holiday season by himself, on Christmas night the lyricist penned the self-berating words, "Mr Taurus ate a thesaurus, made the girls cry and skipped straight to the chorus... Mr Taurus had a great fall, all the King's horses were no good at all..." And then, just as telling, "Everyone I love lives somewhere else... " "These were the thoughts that came to me on Christmas night," he said. "I felt very lonely and isolated, very out of it."

In parallel with Steve's developing woes had come another world disaster – hurricane Rita, which caused havoc across the Gulf of Mexico that autumn. "Another body blow to our friends in the USA," went a missive, announcing more fundraising auctions. All in all, 2005 had been an Annus Horribilis both for the world and for Marillion's lyricist. For each, the New Year couldn't come soon enough.

RECORDING THE OTHER HALF

Progress was slow going into January, but the band were nearing the point they yearned for – when creativity started to flow. Said Pete, "It felt like we were getting absolutely nowhere. Then, all of a sudden, half a dozen tracks appeared. Then Mike came back down and gave us a bit of direction and a few ideas, and suddenly we had another few things coming out of the woodwork." As the evenings grew longer, it became clear that there would be no shortage of material. More stripped-down arrangements were emerging, both from the jams and Mike's simpler recording approach. "It's us all right, but a slightly different side of us," said H. Agreed Mark, "We felt that we were moving somewhere else musically." Equally, however, the end-March date was quickly written off – the album would take as long as it needed.

For a diversion (and, ostensibly, to pay the taxman) H set off to play a series of stages by himself: one man, one piano and a selection of songs. "If the vibe's happening, we'll just carry on till either I get bored or you do," he joked with his prospective audiences. Behind the jolly rhetoric was a jittery reality – would the still-raw, stripped-down Steve Hogarth be accepted without a band to back him up? Would he have enough to give, and what would be the response? Polish fan Mariusz Krause, who traversed Europe to attend the H-natural gig in Dublin on April 29, was left in no doubt. "The concert was just fantastic. Those few hours were worth it to cross the whole of Europe and spend so much money. It was a very special night that I'll keep in my head forever."

During the break in writing, Rothers continued to work with Hannah Stobart on the long, long-awaited sequel to Wishing Tree's *Carnival of Souls*. Releasing a near-complete track called 'Hollow Hills', he said, "It's a good indication of where parts, at least, of the album are going."

Once back at the Racket Club, with some 18 songs having emerged, Marillion felt ready to record. "The process has so far been painless and uplifting – I hate writing, so this is quite something for me to say," commented H. With so much material, the tough bit was deciding which songs to include. Rather than running with what all agreed to be the best songs, the band chose tracks with a common musical thread – those with "a strong sense of melody that reflects the mood," explained Pete. The selection process was contentious to say the least, confirmed Mark, "There were definitely some promises that if we didn't put a track on this album it would go on the next one."

Following the sense of escape pervading *Marbles*, and given the dual pressures of world affairs and personal trauma, the final selection of songs yearned to get away from it all. Said Mark, "You can pretty much divide the album into two." So 'Last Century For Man', 'A Voice from The Past', 'Most Toys' and 'The Wound' reflected the state of the world, while 'Thank You Whoever You Are', 'The Other Half' and, indeed, the title track 'Somewhere Else', penned on that fateful Christmas night, were more personal reflections. The gentler 'Faith' was added as a counterpoint – "The end was quite bleak so we thought we needed something to give people a bit of a lift," said Mark. "A bit like on *Brave* – it did a similar job, a bit of optimism at the end."

By August, backing tracks were nearly done and overdubs were just starting. "Mike wanted to use natural sounds and real instruments, so a lot of the parts are played on a real instrument as opposed to a mock-up on a keyboard," said Pete. This included Mark playing a harmonium. The process continued across the autumn, with just a few breaks for Los Trios or H-Natural dates to break the rhythm. Christmas came and went, and before anyone expected, another year had passed. But the album was nearly done.

As the recording process dragged on, the Racket Records team were far from idle, organising the biggest convention the band had seen – this time completely booking out Center Parcs Port Zélande, in the Netherlands. The fact that two years had gone past without an album to show this didn't spoil things for fans. Said fan Laura Warrick, "I loved the fact it was just us Marillion people at the camp. We played pool to Marillion, shopped to Marillion, bowled to Marillion, ate our breakfast listening to Marillion, and wound down after the gigs to Marillion. I mean, how cool is that!" As well as playing *This Strange Engine* in its entirety, a highlight was a covers show, including versions of 'Accidents Will Happen' by Elvis Costello (Said Mark, "I find his voice annoying but I like songs with interesting chord structures; I thought I would like it better with H singing!") and Britney Spears' 'Toxic' – with the singer in pigtails and all! Said H, "I think she heard about it, as she shaved her head about two days later!" The Saturday night also included a marriage proposal between Asad Rahman and Olivia Lorge on the main stage. The pair had just started the Cambodia Landmine Kids College Fund, a charity to help Cambodian children who had suffered landmine-related injuries get an education.

And then, quite suddenly, it was release time. No pre-order was planned for *Somewhere Else*, explained Mark. "It's like borrowing money from a friend. If you do it once or twice that's OK, do it more than that and you could start to strain the friendship. There was a bit of disagreement, but we decided not to do it." Unexpectedly, this invoked a backlash from the fans as well. "That surprised the hell out of me. A lot of fans were disappointed – they like being part of the process," said Pete. Agreed Ian, "It's that fans are buying into the whole Marillion concept – the family thing." As a solution, a pre-order version (plus a DVD) was made available by Townsend Records, in a deal which meant that money was (once again) available for marketing and promotion.

A single, the "call to deliberate innocence" 'See It Like A Baby', was released on March 26 as download-only. Said H, "Imagine you'd never seen a tree before, imagine you'd never smelt coffee before..." By this point, downloads counted as much as physical releases in the charts, a factor the band were keen to push in emails to fans. Despite best efforts, the single only reached Number Nº45 in the UK charts – many fans simply didn't want to buy a digital download. "Don't be unhappy – it has got us some radio play, which we wouldn't have got if the single wasn't scheduled for release," said the band.

As for the album, the band and Mike were pretty pleased with the overall result – with its stripped down approach, more textural guitars and diverse musical styles, it was, all agreed, quite unlike anything they had every done before. Said Rothers, "You don't want to listen to a new record and think, 'That's exactly what I expected,' because that would be very, very dull!" Concurred

H, "It is one of the strongest we've ever made – right up there with *Afraid Of Sunlight*, which was hitherto my favourite album." The Mike Hunter experiment was measured a resounding success. "I can't emphasise enough how much of a contribution he's made," said Mark. "I think the songs are more direct, and have more energy than on *Marbles* – this comes straight in with a bang from the first song." Musician Mike had only one disappointment: "My ukulele skills have, as yet, remained untapped..."

The band eventually settled on a cover (following several attempts) after a meeting between H and Carl Glover in a lift. Carl happened to have a photo he'd taken on holiday, which became the one. Only afterwards did the band find out that it was very similar to a Weather Report album – said Mark, "In the end we just said, 'It doesn't matter, we like it so we're going to use it!'" The album went on general release two weeks after the single. "It's one of our best albums EVER!" said the usual missive, but in-house, the band were more considered. "I don't have any expectations," said Mark. "I'm not expecting to sell millions of copies; it would be nice to sell more than the last one. We have a lot of fans, and if they like it, that's good enough."

The critics, at least, were not disappointed. *Classic Rock* called it "a terrific album from a singular band", while *Q* commented that it was "abreast of the times". *Uncut's* Stephen Dalton said, "Some tracks chime and soar like Coldplay. Others are just a post-rock whimper away from Radiohead... Marillion deserve a fair hearing."

Unfortunately however, when the album reached the ears of Marillion's hard core, initial reactions were not particularly positive. "*Somewhere Else* is one of the few times I have been distinctly underwhelmed by a Marillion album. It does nothing for me I'm afraid," said fan Gary Hardman, reflecting the views of many. "It got quite a hostile reaction from some of the fans," said Ian. "I thought there were some great tracks. I was really surprised when some people were quite critical about them." Reacted Mark, "One of the really annoying things was that people were posting reviews virtually assassinating us within days of it coming out. Fine if you don't like it, but have enough respect to at least give the album a couple of weeks before you go and slag it off."

With the benefit of hindsight, the failure of *Somewhere Else* to immediately inspire fans came down to three factors, not least that it was in the shadow of the stellar *Marbles* in its full, deluxe pre-order glory. Says Swedish fan Peter Tornberg, "*Marbles* was always going to be a tough act to follow. *Somewhere Else* suffered from that... it felt like something less." Agrees Anthony Craig, "One disc in a standard jewel case does feel like an anti-climax after the deluxe

Marbles edition and maybe that does influence your feelings on the album."

A second factor was the very different sonic approach that had been selected for the songs, both in production and arrangements. And finally, there was *that* song, 'Most Toys', more the musical equivalent of Surströmming than Marmite. Remarked forum member 'hillviewdavid', "The trouble was I disliked that song more than any other offering Marillion have ever recorded and it completely distorted my view of the album." Says Pete Manning, "Along with 'Thankyou...', 'Most Toys' just seemed like a throwaway pop song that was out of place on a Marillion album."

Hindsight's a wonderful thing, and many fans have grown to enjoy the album – even if they have to skip a track or two. "I have come to really love it. It is as close to *Marbles* as one can get and not be *Marbles*," says fan Steve Craig. Says forum member Jim, "I love the immediacy of it; a rare thing with Marillion."

Fan Jason Cobley found the song 'Faith' particularly moving. "My daughter had just been delivered by caesarean, which didn't go as planned – she had to be rushed straight into the Special Care Baby Unit, tiny and porcelain white," he explains. Following a harrowing period of waiting – "We were told that it was touch and go" – Jason headed home, by himself. "I don't know exactly whether I went home that day or the next, or how long I went without sleep, but I switched onto auto-pilot. The CD in the car player was Marillion; I didn't really listen, until 'Faith' started. I had to pull over before I reached the first junction as suddenly there was something in the song that said everything. I still can't quite articulate what that did to me, but the tears came in great sobs. At the same time, it gave me the strength I needed. In the tough days ahead, it was partly that song that sustained me." All turned out well – Jason's daughter recently celebrated her eighth birthday. "She's fit and well. Her favourite Marillion song is 'See It Like A Baby'," he says.

Whatever the fans' initial reactions, the album reached number 24 in the UK charts, number 18 in Holland and generally did "sell more than the last one" across Europe. A second single was released in June, 'Thank You Whoever You Are' with 'Circular Ride', 'Say the Word' and 'Toxic' as B-sides across three versions. Again with an eWeb push, it reached number 15 in the UK and the band's highest ever position – number 6 – in Holland. Whether the reactions were just down to a core of more vocal fans or a general consensus, we will never know – but no damage had been done to the band's overall trajectory.

The one person who really should have known better than read fan comments was Mike himself. "He's the sort of bloke who goes on the forums and reads everything," said Ian. "We all told him he really shouldn't, we knew he would get upset." And get upset he did. "I've got very thin skin and only remember the negative things," said Mike. "The rise of the Internet forum means that, whereas in the past if your record got panned it was by six or seven mags. Now you can have hundreds of people telling you how shit they think it is over a longer period of time. It makes a miserable bastard like me all the more miserable."

KEEPING THE FAITH

Marillion's increasing popularity inevitably meant more touring, to venues old and new. The first date of the tour, April 14 was at the Tercentenary Hall in Gibraltar, a location predicated by events instigated by long-time fan and local dignitary Fabian Vinet. "At the time I was the Minister for Heritage, Culture, Youth and Sport, and I contacted Lucy Jordache with a proposal," says Fabian. First he invited Steve Hogarth as a judge of the Miss Gibraltar pageant, held that year at Saint Michael's Cave – "A genuinely stunning, beautiful cave with a 400-seat in-built auditorium and great acoustics. In short, the type of venue an H-natural gig was perfectly suited for. The plan, cunning or otherwise, was for H to visit the cave, fall in love with it and want to perform there. On 8th September, that's exactly what happened!"

Following the success of the H-natural date, Fabian co-ordinated promoters and sponsors to enable Marillion to come to the Rock. Continues Fabian, "Concerts from major international acts were an unusual occurrence and (usually heavily subsidised) one-offs – the biggest by far having been Elton John in 2004 to commemorate 300 years of British Gibraltar. On April 14 2007 not only did the *Somewhere Else* tour kick off in my hometown, but this was the first time that the Rock had been a stop in any major act's touring schedule. Without realising it, Marillion had made history. Recalls Fabian, "It was a truly special experience and one I will never forget. My favourite band, enjoyed by a crowd of over 1,300, in my little hometown. I'd never have thought it possible."

In the knowledge that many fans would attend multiple shows, the band changed the set list every night – even Frenchie, the tour manager, chose the songs on one occasion. "We had to rehearse as if we were planning a convention with lots of songs in our heads and take extra guitar basses, more pedals and so on," says Pete. For H it offered a release: "I personally had been frustrated for years at the lack of spontaneity in our show but changing things around was technically troublesome because we use so many sounds. The weekends have helped because Mark was forced to programme so much music, bit by bit the library of available sounds grew so that he could call songs up much more easily."

The benefits were not lost on fan Mariusz Krause: "My colleagues asked why the hell I wanted to go and see Marillion in 16 different places? Attending so many gigs, you can always make a judgement about the best gig, the best set list, the best crowd, the best mood of the band. But the biggest advantage is that you meet your friends from all over Europe." An unexpected bonus was driving Rothers from Poznan to Warsaw. "When Steve opened the car door, I realised I hadn't turned off the CD – his brilliant solo in 'Born to Run' resounded around. 'This is going to be fun,' he said with a laugh. Well, we had a lot of fun during this trip, arriving at the venue in Warsaw ONE minute before the sound check!"

The initially disappointing fan reaction to *Somewhere Else* was negated by the tour. Says Pete, "The album is a strong album. The proof of this is in the strength of the tour and reaction to live shows when we played that material." Agreed 'Elephant' Alex in the forum, "The songs seemed to come to life in a live setting. It really clicked when the band released the *Somewhere in London* DVD. I was listening to the album the other day and really don't know why I had any doubts."

With troubles global, personal and creative moving into the past, Marillion were riding on the crest of a wave. "Every gig has been amazing, even when I don't think we've played that well, people's reactions have been incredible," said Ian. Agreed Pete, "I have been really surprised by how different this tour feels compared to the last few tours as I remember them. There is a real empathy between us on stage and you lovely people, which I haven't picked up on before in the same way."

Speaking of the past, Fish himself had attended Marillion's Glasgow show, following which he approached his old colleagues with a proposition – would they like to play a song with him at the Aylesbury 'Hobble on the Cobbles' event that August? "It would have been odd to say no," said Pete, despite having said "over my dead body" some ten years before! Ian, Pete, Mark and Rothers felt it might dispel any myths and besides, it sounded fun.

Off stage, H had been finding his own catharsis was not yet completely done, however. "Steve had to see a doctor in Holland because he had some mind problems," said Mark. "Even though he was a real medical doctor, he said, 'Just read this book.' The volume in question was Eckhart Tolle's *The Power of Now* – and at its heart contained a similar message to the *Marbles'* lyric 'Don't Hurt Yourself'. "It just says, 'Stop caring about the past, the past is gone, forget it, it's not important. Don't worry about the future too, it hasn't happened.'"

Following Eckhart Tolle's advice to "live for the moment", as the tour came to a close H headed back on the road in his H-natural guise. "I'd paid the tax bill and didn't need the money anymore, but I discovered that I quite enjoyed doing it," he remarked. The first date was back at La Tulipe in Montreal. Once again, the ovation was rapturous – but this time, it was all for him. "It was a while before everybody calmed down and let him sing!" recalls fan Michel Drolet. Said H, "It knocked me sideways. I had been conscious for many years of having, to some extent, inherited the success I've had with Marillion. A horse was already running, and we switched riders: Fish got off, I got on. So it was difficult to assess how much of the excitement in the audience was for me, or was there already." It was a good moment to receive such unanimous confirmation.

'Hobble on the Cobbles' took place on August 26, uniting the 'old' band with Fish for the first time in 19 years. Said Mark, "It was weird. He stayed the evening beforehand at my house, it was nice to see him and talk about the old days." While all agreed it was fun, it still left a bit of a funny aftertaste. Said Pete, "He did quite well out of it but we see it as a negative thing – you can't live in the past. We've done it now, that's kind of as far as I want to take it." Despite comments to the contrary by all involved, to outsiders it offered an opportunity for misinterpretation, thought Mark, "Fish casts a really long shadow, especially for people who aren't regular listeners." H may not have thought that much of it either, but still, it was a vestigial demon put to rest.

With not much happening in the studio, the summer offered a time to reflect. On September 13, Mark and Angie had a baby boy, while Rothers continued work on Wishing Tree. All involved continued to wonder about the fan reaction to *Somewhere Else*. Says Pete, "I was mostly concerned about Mike and the upsetting time he went through. It was very unfair and unjust." At the time, however, it was simply onward and upward. "We've got most of the next album ready to go, we're going to be releasing it in spring 2008," said Mark in an interview. "Well, it's mostly finished!" Or was it?

SOMEWHERE ELSE

Marillion's 14th album saw a break with what many had imagined was now an established way of working. Unlike the *Marbles* and *Anoraknophobia*, there was no pre-order campaign for *Somewhere Else*. The shortest album released since 1998's *Radiat10n*, it was also notable for its stripped-back production style. Many critics seemed to respond well to this change, yet the reception among the fans was less good. Others cited too much repetition in the choruses as a weakness and one song in particular came in for a bit of a kicking.

The album opens strongly with 'The Other Half', a *Revolver*-era Beatles-tinged song of, well, two halves. H does well to come up with a fresh way of dealing with this rather than saying "you complete me"... The song begins with Hogarth intoning lines about mystical, aerial signs and astrological markers over a vamped chord sequence and some snappy drumming from Ian. A jazzy piano arpeggio introduces the second part of the song, with H swearing he has changed. It isn't hard for a familiar listener to join some dots between this, some of the other tracks on the album and more than a couple from the past. A fantastic bluesy Rothery solo caps things off nicely.

The album's first single, 'See It Like A Baby', starts off rather promisingly with some intriguing chords that give way to a darkly grooving verse with something of 'Cathedral Wall' about it, and a lyric about trying to see the world like a young 'un. The repetitive chorus drew a fair amount of ire from certain sections of the fan base, though that's hardly unique to *Somewhere Else*. It's a song that benefits greatly from being turned up loud enough for the bass to rattle your chest.

It's not clear why the first two words in second single 'Thankyou Whoever You Are' run together, but Steve Hogarth insists that this is correct. The song itself is a piano-led ballad that isn't a million miles away from 'Fantastic Place' territory. Steve Rothery doesn't have a great deal to contribute apart from his exquisite solo, and Mark Kelly's string sounds dominate the chorus. It all sounds like it's trying a bit too hard to pull the strings. Lyrically, however, it's a rather nice piece about celebrating the moment with that special person.

Without question one of the least well-received songs Marillion have ever released, 'Most Toys' was inspired by the footer of an email sent to H by his new partner, Linette. Opening with the chorus, the song is extremely straightforward by Marillion's standards. Unfortunately, it's not punky enough to cut it on those terms, and it's not melodically interesting enough for the majority of the fan base. Mark Kelly has stated the song was not up to scratch either.

If the album isn't consistently strong until this point, the title track does much to redeem it. A story of guilt and the damage it does, this lament is heart-rendingly stark and plaintive. When Hogarth reveals his barely disguised personal indiscretions in a nursery rhyme pastiche and then refers to his marriage as "here's one I broke earlier", his sense of regret is all too apparent. The second half of the song deals with the aftermath, being separated from those he most needs to be with. It doesn't matter that it's more than a little self-indulgent: his sense of disgust when he examines his own behaviour, as the band turn up the self-loathing – Ian battering around his kit, Rothery peeling out notes of despair

– create one of the most powerful and cathartic pieces in their arsenal.

The band invoke the spirit of a man murdered on 'A Voice From The Past'. At the time, the band members were keen supporters of 'Make Poverty History' and it is all too apparent how it informs this track. Over a mournful bass, tinklings of piano, military drums and choice bluesy phrases, Hogarth compares the state of the world to the hopeful optimism captured by John Lennon's 'Imagine' some 30 years before the song was recorded and wonders why the hell we *still* haven't managed to get to grips with the issues he had raised. During the extended build-up to a searing guitar solo, Hogarth implores us to embrace a common humanity and do something to help. Five years on we're seemingly no closer, and the song cannot help but make you feel guilty. 'No Such Thing' is an unusual number. A catalogue of things that supposedly don't exist, the song begins with a repeating chimed guitar motif and Hogarth's heavily phased vocal. The introduction of Kelly's keyboards and Mosley's drums reminds the listener of the *Afraid Of Sunlight* B-sides 'Icon' and 'Live Forever'. Many cited a similarity with Black Sabbath's 'Planet Caravan', and the assertion is not without merit. Towards the last third of the song, the tempo increases and injects a little more energy into this languid blues.

In the rock canon, few songs attempt to use a fern as a metaphor for how pain grows and festers. The first half of 'The Wound' is a welcome injection of aggression into a largely quite restrained and melancholic album. Kelly's Hammond organ sounds and Pete's throbbing bass drive the song until the breakdown at the halfway point, where it builds up again into the bastard child of the play-out of 'This Is The 21st Century' and Massive Attack's 'Angel', though regrettably lacking the bass punch of the latter.

Penultimate number 'The Last Century For Man' postulates that indifference and apathy have triumphed and that our collective demise is our just desserts. Whether Hogarth actually believed that to be true or (as seems more likely from the "If you're not outraged, you haven't been paying attention" line) that it offers a bitterly ironic wake-up call to the state of the world, it was another track that attracted some negative comments. Many were objecting to the lines about the USA, which was seen to be a bit of a soft target.

Closing track 'Faith' strongly (and deliberately) invokes The Beatles' 'Blackbird'. The song had been premiered at the 2003 Marillion Weekend in a simpler arrangement, which many preferred to the album version, though both have their champions. Much like 'Made Again' at the end of *Brave*, 'Faith' is something of a palate-cleanser. Mike Hunter devised a pastoral orchestration for the final part of the song, which some fans feel didn't improve on the earlier version.

The cover is based upon Carl Glover's holiday photograph of a coin-operated public telescope against a startlingly blue sky. The striking image was drawn from a collection the designer had amassed over a number of years.

18

Recording Happiness Is The Road

As October approached, it was time to start looking at the new album. Despite the *Somewhere Else* feedback, the band felt confident about working with Mike Hunter who, having been encouraged to stop reading the forums ("No one is that bullet-proof!" laughs Ian), was more determined than ever to prove himself. Says Pete, "I think he decided to go out of his way to show what he could do with us and our music." In parallel with his time with Marillion, somehow he was also managing to squeeze in a music degree. "He's been itching to get his teeth into something more highbrow," laughed H.

Kicking off a regular routine, at the start of the process Mike asked each band member to bring in a song to discuss, as a musical show-and-tell. "Some of the elements of other people's music contain things that they wouldn't ever entertain in their own work," he explained. "I didn't want anyone to feel embarrassed to try anything." Super Furry Animals, Ian Dury, System of a Down and The Shangri-Las – nothing was out of bounds. Said Mark, "It's just getting us away from Marillion tunnel vision."

With a catalogue of seemingly near-finished music, all agreed that following the collection of songs that was *Somewhere Else*, it was time for something more cohesive – "A bit of a journey," said Mark. Rothers suggested each member work on a track at home and bring it in, further broadening the boundaries by removing the 'peer approval' element from creativity. One piece to come directly out of this process was a piano crescendo that became known as 'Liquidity'.

Once again the idea of an EP was mooted – explains H, "We say we'll do EPs for every album and then decide against it. I think it's just a way of depressurising…" The band eventually decided an album made more financial sense, returning to the special edition pre-order idea. Went the eWeb, "You will once again be acting as part of our global family record company, without us having to resort to the headaches which happen when we get into bed with "blokes in suits". We did it before, and it felt good." The band were sufficiently confident to announce a double album from the outset. "The writing process was prolific, it seemed a shame to put a stop to that while the light was shining brightly," explained Ian.

Two weeks later and with thousands of orders in, it was back to business as usual: jamming in the mornings and rehearsing in the afternoons. With the financial pressure off, the band were once again free to go where the music went. "It allows you to experiment a bit more - you can encompass everything," said Pete.

Speaking of experiment, H wasn't the only band member to be getting natural, artistically speaking. Back in June, Rothers had headed to the Academy of Contemporary Music in Guildford to talk about his experiences of working in music. Then, in early November, he took to the Bose Stand at Music Live to demonstrate the use of effects pedals. As he explains, "We were set to play an acoustic set at Harrods that was going have a Bose system as the main PA. I started talking to Andy Rigler, the Pro Audio representative at Bose about the specification of the L1, which we tried when we did an acoustic set at HMV in Cambridge. Andy lent me a system for my guitar clinics and in return I appeared on the Bose stand at the NEC." One such clinic was at the Oxford Guitar Gallery. "It's good to talk about how my playing has evolved and what I think sets me apart from other players… to have that one-to-one interaction with the audience like that is a great thing," he said.

A short series of Christmas dates provided an opportunity to play a couple of new songs. "One of the reasons I wanted to tour was to bring out 'Real Tears For Sale' – a thank you to the fans for pre-ordering," said Pete. 'Circular Ride' was tried as well, but quickly dropped, being considered a bit too low key. Fan Ian Atkins went to The Forum performance on December 5, having not seen the band play live since 1997. "It's a bit like bumping into an old girlfriend, to not only find you're still in love but that she's even more beautiful than she was," he remarked.

By January 2008, in now-familiar fashion the album was dividing in two with a number of thematic tracks, then several that didn't seem to fit. Reported Ian, "Mike thinks that we are going through a very productive phase, he tells us that every time we jam something magical happens." The continued use of technology fitted the band and Mike's evolving, jam-based production style, explained Pete: "In the past we would take something we liked and develop it musically in the room with the five of us … what's happening now is that some ideas are being developed in the computer." Concurred Mark, "We've turned jamming into a fine art – it's evolution through natural selection."

Equally familiar was how the band reported the album was "taking longer than expected" – extending the pre-order deadline to the end of February. "We're not struggling for ideas – we're struggling with time to finish it all," said Mark. The name of the album was finally announced on March 12 – *Happiness Is The Road*, with its two volumes – the introspective *Essence* and more objective *The Hard Shoulder*. The former was a concept disc, explained H, "about spirituality, the meaning of life, why are we all here, what's truly beautiful, what's worth getting out of bed for in the morning…" The aim was to make *Essence* a "stream of consciousness" – kicking off with the ultrasound heartbeat of H's little boy, Emil. "It literally starts with a birth," said Mike, who used a free-flow technique for some tracks , notably 'Wrapped Up In Time' which saw H composing melodies and even lyrics on the spot. Meanwhile, *The Hard Shoulder* was more of a collection of songs – said Pete, "What was left over."

By the end of April, the band were working on overdubs – again, the new production approach bore fruit. "I've been trawling through jam ideas to see if any of them could be added as incidental music," commented Pete. Confirmed Steve R, "The more of the original magic you can use, the better." One thing would never change, however – Ian could relax and enjoy the show. "This is one of my most favourite times of the whole recording process; all the drums are finished and the boys are beavering away, adding their magic," he said. A final overdub came from competition-winning fan Dawn Roberts, who added a finger cymbal sound just before the line, "choose life, choose living". Said Ian, "She was very nervous – she only had to do one 'ting', but getting it in time is something else when you've got headphones on and ten people staring at you!" Given that the album was being recorded at a higher bit and sample rate than previously (24 bit and 96 kHz), fans were also asked whether they wanted an "Ultimate Edition" – 4 vinyl LPs, a 5.1 surround sound mix and all the artwork trimmings, numbered and autographed by the band. Priced at £150, the idea was shelved following fan feedback. "Thank you for your honesty!" said the eWeb, but the recording quality was not lost on the final CD. "It's probably the best-sounding record we've ever made," said Rothers. "Even when it's dithered down to 16 bit for CD it still retains some of that extra clarity."

By June 20 it was at the mix-down stage, and then it was done. Mike had proved his worth in more ways than one. "It's extremely likely we'll work with him again," said H. "He's a very light-hearted guy, very funny." Said Mark, "You can almost see the confidence of our relationship grow over time so that the last few songs to be recorded were more adventurous, like 'Essence', 'Happiness Is The Road', 'Asylum Satellite' and 'The Man From The Planet Marzipan'." A bit like 'Fantastic Place' two albums before, 'Essence' was a late winner, said Mike, "I'm very proud of that track, it really came off. Not everybody liked it until late in the process, which doesn't make it easy as you are trying to convince people to continue to work on it."

Another track that scraped in was 'Half Empty Jam', which ended up as a 'hidden' track on the end of *Essence*. "It deserved to be heard," said H. Expanded Mike, "Everybody loved it at first, but nobody wanted to do it in the end – which is why it's hidden." A couple of songs didn't make the cut, including 'Soul Singer' – "We got halfway through putting it together and got a bit stuck," said H – as well as 'Grin And Bear It', "It's a lyric I wrote for my daughter Sofi while I was splitting up with her mother. A recognition of her pain and to let her know it would all be all right. It could have been a lovely, simple, little ditty and it nearly was. Binned in the end by the "not epic enough" quality-control department. It may yet turn up somewhere…"

With Carl Glover in Tokyo and therefore too busy to work full time on the artwork, the job was handed to Spaniard Antonio Seijas, a Marillion fan and artist who had sent a portfolio of his work to the Racket Club. "He produced so many images… two or three a day at one point, I don't think he was sleeping," said H. These included the cover, which was an instant hit. "It appealed to all five of us at the same moment, so while we were all there, we thought we'd better grab it."

Los Trios played a couple of sets on the Bose stand at the British Motor Show on July 23. And then it was show time.

SEEING IT LIKE A BABY

Continuing the spirit of experiment, the band had made various attempts to create a video using fan input. A first request came in autumn 2006, with a follow-up email in the spring. "Use your imagination – remember, the best things in art are often happy accidents!" While a great many fans sent clips, the band found they couldn't do that much with them. "The experiment was a bit of a failure, but it was good of people to try," said Mark. Undaunted, the band stepped up the game in July 2008 with a full-fat video competition to go with a single release of 'Whatever Is Wrong With You'. The prize was £5,000 cash for the most views on YouTube. At the beginning of September (and perhaps recognising the Internet's propensity for vote stuffing), another £5,000 was added as a spot prize, which was won by fan Marco Allegri. An additional benefit, of course, was that Marillion were splashed all over the video site – fan David Esquivel's Lego-based video eventually reached over 700,000 views.

As *Happiness Is The Road* was sent for mastering, even with the pre-orders the stark question was: how to release the album? Fan base or no fan base, Marillion were faced with the same, growing challenge as any other artist: illegal downloads. Like the two albums before it, copies of *Somewhere Else* had started to appear on Internet file-sharing sites within hours of the album's release, and the impact on general CD sales had been, in a word, staggering. "In Holland, CD sales dropped from 25,000 to 7,000 or 8,000. The same number of people have your music but only one in three have paid for it," said Rothers.

Various options were considered including giving the album away for free or on a Radiohead-style, pay-what-you-like basis. "We were sure that some people would like to buy it anyway," said Mark, keeping one eye on the still-expanding list of fan email addresses. In the end, the band settled on a two-pronged strategy, the first prong of which was to release a version on September 10 (a month before the official release date), via P2P network Music Glue, incorporating a video message asking for an email address and enticing the listener to buy the retail album. "While we don't condone illegal file-sharing, it's a fact of life. We want to know who our file-sharing fans are. If they like our new album enough, we want to persuade them to pay something for it, or at least come and see us on tour."

The band collated 8,000 new email addresses from the exercise; unexpected but equally beneficial was the amount of media attention – not least landing the band a slot on Sky TV's *Ditto Music Live* show. "We received more coverage in Europe than we have had in years," said Pete. Not all pre-ordering fans were happy, however. "We paid a year in advance but you're giving it away to everyone BEFORE we even get a copy," said one disgruntled aficionado. Replied Mark, "We agonised over this decision, knowing that some people would see it as a kick in the teeth. Did you know that *Anoraknophobia* and *Marbles* were available on the Internet weeks before pre-orders were sent out?"

The second prong of the release strategy was to make *Happiness* available exclusively from Marillion.com. "We wanted to see if people would buy it directly from us rather than the shops," said Mark. Agreed Rothers, "Retail just wasn't viable financially – we aren't going to sell so many albums this way, but these days it's a case of working out how we can survive – the best solution was to sell as much as possible direct to our fans."

The answer to Mark's question was easy to measure – only about a third wanted to buy online. "If we have learned anything from the last 15 years, it's to listen to our fans," said Mark. "Loads of you are telling us that you simply want to go into your local shop and buy our CD. Not a download, not from iTunes, and not from Amazon." Early the following year, Marillion announced that EMI would be making the album available at retail outlets across Europe – an offer to which the Marillos had readily agreed. In conclusion, the dual-pronged strategy had succeeded in one way above all others, in that it illustrated there would be no easy answers to the download problem. "I am now firmly on the side of 'piracy is a bad idea,'" said Mark.

While a few critics marked down the album as being too introspective and leaving some parts – particularly Rothers – too low in the mix, *Happiness Is The Road* was much better received than its predecessor – "By the fans, most importantly," said Mark. Says forum member RobEastUSA, "Two great discs, one incredible album. Soothing, rousing, inspiring masterpiece - I don't own anything better." Many fans agreed that it made more sense to view each of the two discs on their own merits. "*Essence* disc is amongst the best music the band has come up with, absolutely fantastic. *The Hard Shoulder* is a bit hit-and-miss…" says fan Ian Walford. Agrees forum member Shoggz, "I think *Essence* is a fabulous run of tunes and would easily place it in my top 5 Marillo albums."

While *The Hard Shoulder* lagged behind *Essence* in terms of fan feedback, it still had its share of positive feedback. "*The Hard Shoulder* is more of a basket of a mixed emotions, but it's still a powerful collection of great songs," says forum member Hillviewdavid. Agrees Dave Cooper, "I do like albums that are a bit unhinged or wilfully eclectic, and *The Hard Shoulder* is definitely all of those things. You've got a very themed album, and one that really is all over the place, and I find they work together very well as a pair for just that reason."

One fan, Dutch musician Egbert Derix, was inspired enough to make some music of his own, kicking off a Marillion-based project called *Paintings In Minor Lila* – with unexpected results. "I recorded a string arrangement for 'This Train Is My Life' and sent it to Steve Hogarth, just to share it with him. Steve liked my arrangement and suggested to do the narration himself. Wow…I gratefully accepted his offer and we came up with an original, beautiful and intense version of 'Train'. Having Steve on my album is a true gift and it made me think about how special it would be if Fish would do a version of one of my favourite Marillion songs. So I made a piano and string quartet arrangement of 'Pseudo Silk Kimono', the first Marillion song I heard as a 16-year-old boy. I sent my arrangement to Fish, told him about Steve's narration of 'Train' and asked if he would also consider it. Without any hesitation he offered to do it. It was deeply emotional to hear his voice in combination with my piano-playing and string arrangement. What it means to me to have these two men contribute to my first solo album goes beyond words."

H managed to squeeze in a few H-natural dates (including a performance of 'Estonia' in Rome with Riccardo Romano on mandolin – "Un momento indimenticabile per chi ha avuto il piacere di assistere," wrote a fan, "An unforgettable moment for those who had the pleasure of attending").

Then *Happiness* hit the road on November 8 at the Ironworks in Inverness, before heading south and then into Europe, with a few weeks back in Oxfordshire for the holiday season. Once again, the increased media attention had a positive impact on the audiences. Said Mark, "The Berlin promoter told us that there were twice as many people than were there when we played the same venue a year ago." Each date of the tour was recorded, with the result made available for download the following day.

Two Weekends were played in 2009: the first in Holland in March, and the second in Montreal a month later. Following what was now a tradition, *Seasons End* was played in its entirety. If conventions offered any measure of the band's popularity, it looked like Marillion had never had it so good. "We have never known anything quite like the atmosphere of affection, good humour and raw energy you people seemed so happy to put together," said H of Port Zélande, which was followed swiftly by a similar vibe in Montreal. "We all had tears in our eyes on more than one occasion, so thank you all for the emotion. How we top our two weekends is hard to imagine," he continued. An outing of Los Trios in Bologna, a full-band festival in Sweden, a couple of H-natural dates and then, on June 13, a final, rescheduled date of the *Happiness Is The Road* tour at the Winter Palace of Sport in Sofia, Bulgaria offered the cherry on the icing on the cake.

Then it was back to the studio. But not in that way!

HAPPINESS IS THE ROAD

Marillion's 15th album came out in October 2008, although a month earlier the band took the unusual step of trying to stop piracy by flooding the peer-to-peer networks with special versions of the files. The album itself is split into two distinct discs; *Essence*, a concept piece and *The Hard Shoulder*, a more diverse collection.

Essence is based on a book recommended to Hogarth during the *Somewhere Else* tour called *The Power of Now* by New Age author Eckhart Tolle. It is an extraordinarily confessional album, providing a real insight into the psyche of the singer.

In prologue piece 'Dreamy Street', Hogarth imagines himself free of doubt and pain, and living in the moment. It's a close-miked piece over some piano, with the faintest ghosts of some Kelly atmospheres in the background before leading into 'This Train Is My Life', an instant Marillion classic. Opening with Steve Rothery's chiming arpeggios, the song is both a metaphor and a description of the life of a band on the road and the loneliness experienced living disconnected from real life. The song comes into its own with the "So take my hand" section, Hogarth offering his thanks to his partner for understanding his life and sharing the journey. A marvellous Rothery solo caps things off nicely.

'Essence' is a plea to grasp the nettle and experience life directly, warning of the distractions from the real thing in a life lived vicariously. Like the previous track, it builds subtly and gradually, paying off when Rothery's guitar break gives way to a euphoric, soul-tinged mantra. The 'choose life, choose essence' line deliberately apes the iconic closing speech in Irvine Welsh's *Trainspotting*.

'Wrapped Up In Time' was unfairly overlooked upon the album's release, yet it is a sublime and moving piece of work, with its lyric about mourning a high point of Hogarth's career. There are some subtle electronica influences on the early part of the song, and some lovely piano playing going on throughout.

The instrumental 'Liquidity' is Mark Kelly's baby. An ethereal piece that is not a million miles from Sigur Rós, it is based on some glacial piano figures with ambient textures drifting in and out behind. Key is the restraint in never tipping into something bombastic.

'Nothing Fills The Hole' is an odd one. A rather well-executed soul pastiche about the emptiness of the consumer mentality (with a great Motown chorus and the tambourines appropriately loud in the mix), the last minute-and-a-half is patently the low-key introduction to the next track, 'Woke Up', which is a nodding acquaintance of 'Runaway' from *Brave*. Putting aside niggles about why the track is needlessly cut in two, the second piece is a nice mid-tempo rocker. The album definitely required an injection of a bit of rock at this point, quite Who-ish in the verses with some great swirls of Leslie'd Hammond organ to push along the Beatles-y choruses. Maybe it's the tabla drums at the end, but the track is reminiscent of 'Cage' from H's *Ice Cream Genius* solo album.

'Trap The Spark' starts with Hogarth singing about living in the moment rather than spending one's efforts trying to preserve these moments in amber. He uses the highest parts of his vocal range for much of this song, something that not all fans particularly like, but it's put to good use here. Note how the lyrics deliberately evoke the 'Genie' line about opening the box and the 'I have lost the Earth' line from 'Fantastic Place'.

'State Of Mind' caused a ripple of excitement when the *Happiness* track listing was first announced, but this isn't a cover of the Fish solo track. A Phil Collins vocal melody is in there somewhere, however. Noteworthy are Mark Kelly's keys for their 'Estonia'-like quality on the verses and Ian Mosley's superb snare work on the lush choruses. A bit of what might be slide guitar from Mr Rothery takes us to a near-euphoric outro with some great drumming.

While the title track takes a while to get going, the lyrics are rather lovely, saying that each new day is a new opportunity. Layers of keys give way to an effective bassline and stabs of off-beat guitar as Hogarth relates meeting the man who set him on the path to happiness by introducing him to Tolle's book, and presents a summary of its philosophy. As Mark Kelly commented, you don't have to subscribe to New Age beliefs to understand the idea that satisfaction isn't to be found in the destination, but that 'happiness is the road'. 'Happiness is the ro-ad...', repeat to fade.

The album should probably end there, but after a short silence, there's the dreaded 'bonus track'. 'Half Full Jam' is (unsurprisingly) a jammed piece over which Hogarth sings some lyrics from the album, plus some related ideas. A couple of minutes in, the band have started to riff more heavily than elsewhere on the album and Ian seems intent on smashing his kit to bits. It provides a little more of the rock for what is, for the most part, a pretty unrocking album, but it's hard to see where it could have really gone, and it doesn't say anything that hasn't already been said.

The Hard Shoulder is a much more eclectic collection of songs. In fact, many of them had been knocking around in one form or another for quite a while, and it's probably fair to say that the second disc suffers from a bit of an identity crisis. Having said that, it's also true that had the band not elected to make a double album, it's unlikely that all of these songs would have made their way into the light.

'Thunder Fly' enters like the illegitimate offspring of 'Ticket To Ride' and 'Daydream Believer' in the middle of a psychedelic bender. Mark does a sterling job of evoking an acid-haze and Pete's constantly moving bassline drives the song along nicely. Lyrically, it uses annoying summer flies as a metaphor for a particularly irritating type of girlfriend, a perhaps unkinder Marillion lyric than we're used to.

'The Man From Planet Marzipan' is a weird one. Pete's slap bass is the key to the slightly off-kilter start of the song that's ostensibly about an alien. More deeply, the song seems to be about feeling out of phase with the rest of the human race and its often casually stupid ways of behaving. The track's quirkiness allows the band to indulge in all sorts of experiments, with little burbles of electronica bubbling through all the time. Mark Kelly has remarked that the vocal reminded him of Ian Dury.

Rothers' heavily chorused guitar brings in 'Asylum Satellite #1', but it would be foolish to ignore yet more fabulous bass work from Pete. At nearly ten minutes, it's the longest track on the album, and concerns an orbiting space station where banished dissidents and troublemakers look back at the Earth. Like the preceding song, it suggests a sense of disenfranchisement and confusion at contemporary society. The section starting 'Next thing y'know...' is one of the most affecting things the band have done, laden with pathos. Topping it off is an extended guitar wig-out, before dropping back a notch for the end.

Back on Earth once more, 'Older Than Me' is a gently moving ballad about a man rejecting society's attitudes to women with younger partners. The song was from the *Somewhere Else* sessions, but was kept off because another track already occupied a similar niche.

'Throw Me Out' also dates from the previous album. Over the ticking of a clock and a harmonium, H delivers what we might imagine as an autobiographical lyric of his marriage coming to an end - and it's as uncomfortable as can be. The string stabs in the later part of the song give way to Mr Peter Trewavas's recording debut on the clarinet, and the backing "aaah"s at the end feature the whole of Racket Records - girlfriends, children, mates, passing tramps - and then, despite being a cheery, upbeat shuffle number, one can't help but suspect from the lyrical clues that 'Half The World' is addressed to the same person as the preceding song. H has described it as "a really positive, affectionate lyric. I don't write many, wishing someone well." It has a vibe not completely removed from 'Enlightened', on *Marillion.com*.

Lyrical celebration of quirkiness 'Whatever Is Wrong With You' is a straightforward rock song that functions much as 'You're Gone' on *Marbles*. It's got a hooky chorus with great power chords and Garbage-esque keyboards. It's followed by 'Especially True', a song about America, cultural relativism and, it would seem, things that might happen between people on planes. Another track left over from the *Somewhere Else* sessions, it opens with a nice guitar figure before settling into a relatively sparse verse, followed by a strong melodic chorus. The end is surprisingly heavy, with Pete and Ian locking down a tight groove over which Rothers can cut loose.

'Real Tears For Sale' is a song about the dangers of selling your real life in songs and trying to keep up the emotional authenticity. Sinead O'Connor has a key role in the cautionary tale, but it's pretty obvious who it's really about. The track had been around in a different form since the *Marbles* days, but was musically reworked for *Happiness*. Over the repeated harp-like motif, bass pedals and Ian's tom work, the build-up at the end is fabulous. A classic Rothery solo ends the album on an emotional high.

Working with photography, photo-manipulation and illustration, Spanish artist Antonio Seijas produced a substantial number of moody, enigmatic and engaging images for each song. The strikingly iconic satellite image that graces the front cover wasn't specifically conceived as such, however; it was just one of the many images submitted.

19

Less is More, More or Less

The fact was, the band were knackered. Little remained in the coffers, and there was hardly any material banked. All knew that the last album would be difficult to follow, and the prospect of heading back and starting the recording process all over again left the Marillos cold. Lyrically speaking, while H had a new relationship, a new child and a more positive outlook, he had left little unsaid across the four hours of music and lyrics that made up *Marbles*, *Somewhere Else* and *Happiness Is The Road*. "Sometimes I feel I have nothing left to say," he remarked.

"I know," suggested someone, "How about we do an acoustic album?" The fivesome jumped at the chance, setting a target for an autumn release. Said Rothers, "It's six or nine months where we don't have to think about the next studio album." Nobody was happier with the idea than Steve H – "It is a fantastic relief, it means I can just enjoy being a musician and a singer." As the musicians were waiting for their equipment to come back from Sofia, they started to think about how it might work. "The original idea was to strum through some songs in a similar way to Los Trios," said Rothers. Added H, "At the beginning I was worried we would make a record that was bland..." No chance.

It all seemed so straightforward, at the start. Each member proposed three or four ideas for songs, which were put to the vote. "Any that we multi-voted for got accepted right away," explains Pete. "We got a list out of that and then decided to do two or three days of quick knocking through the songs to see if they would work." The initial rule was that if a song wasn't working the band would quickly move on – but before long, the band were inadvertently back in jamming mode. "I know Mike was tearing his hair out, saying, 'We haven't got time for this!' It is hard sometimes, to get us all concentrating on the same idea at once..."

Before long, everyone was into the idea that songs had to be sufficiently different to merit their inclusion. Said Pete, "A lot of our songs are a work in progress, so being able to have another look at a song and give it a makeover is a really good thing." This included songs that weren't obviously acoustic, such as 'Interior Lulu'. As the band worked on new arrangements, the Racket Club was beset by a mini heat wave, recalls H: "It was really hot, in the high 20s, and we were all twirling around – I almost fainted working 'Quartz' out."

In parallel, the fivesome started to look at what instruments to use: this snowballed equally quickly. Pete borrowed a glockenspiel and xylophone from Mike, H bought a new dulcimer, Ian picked up some African drums and temple blocks ("I haven't used those since the Steve Hackett days,") and Mark, well... "There's a church organ I'm bidding for on eBay at the moment. It's not huge –

big enough though." To nobody's surprise, he won the auction. "That bloody church organ, it was like a 300-piece Airfix kit!" said Ian. "You've got to admire his passion – there were no plans, no glue, he just built it. I quite admire that enthusiasm, he's just nuts. In a nice way." With balalaika, harmonium, autoharp and dulcitone in tow, the stage was set. Laughed H, "We're like a room full of mad professors!"

Only Rothers retained a sense of normality. "He is reserving the right to plug in if necessary..." said Mark. Agreed Steve, "I think a lot of people would miss that, if there was no electric on there at all." Above all, he was hankering to play with a prototype of his "Steve Rothery model" signature guitar, made by Jack Dent Guitars in North Carolina. "He's got some very clever ideas about guitar construction, how the neck's mounted to the body, with a continuous piece of wood pretty much throughout the length of the guitar. This gives incredible clarity, sustain and tone," he expounded. He also brought a mandolin and a "really, really beautiful" guitar given to him by the Portuguese fan club.

The main challenge was how to actually play some of the instruments, particularly for Pete and H. Said Mark, "It's a bit like the Monkees – at the start they couldn't play anything, but by the end they were reasonably good." Mike also played on some tracks. "If you see credits for people you have never heard of, that's probably him!" In the end, Mark couldn't actually use his organ – not as such. "When it was moved it was all completely out of tune," he explained. "I didn't have time to sort it out so I sampled it and retuned the samples. It's a shame – when it was in tune it sounded great."

The acoustic arrangements enabled H to inject more emotion into his vocals. "I'm not competing with a wall of noise," he said. "'Go!' is so incredibly sparse, as is 'Out Of This World', they're so quiet instrumentally that I'm really naked singing them, which means I'm finding them quite difficult technically. I'm having to sing in falsetto, or so quietly that the voice is on the edge of being off, or sometimes the notes stop altogether – there is just not enough air going across the tubes to make sounds."

A 'new' song for the album was 'It's Not Your Fault' – "A lullaby for grown-ups", according to H, based on his experiences of a few years before and which had lain unused since the *Somewhere Else* sessions. The challenge for H was to recreate the emotions he was feeling at the time, to make the song work. "So I tried to put myself back in that place," he said.

Before anyone knew it, the album was done. "We did the whole thing in a couple of months – quick for us," said Mark. Commented Rothers, "It's going to surprise quite a few people. Mike's done an amazing job sonically; the wider array of instruments has made the whole thing a lot more quirky and interesting." Following the early October release, the Marillos headed straight out on a stripped-back tour, with a set list padded out with historically acoustic numbers. "Anything to put off writing another album," said Ian, who took a much-reduced kit – "A normal-sized one," joked Mark. Said Ian, "It's definitely a challenge playing quietly... I'll probably need sedatives, but I'm sure I'll adapt." A couple of songs, like 'Fantastic Place' and 'See It Like A Baby', were kept for the tour – "They weren't necessarily right for an album," said Mark.

Venues were as quirky as the set list, from theatres in Holland to a cave in Cornwall. Mark, who hadn't shared the Los Trios experience, had his eyes opened to the appetite for Marillo-acoustic. "I am surprised how well the acoustic stuff has been going down," he said. Two dates stood out – the Victoria Theatre in Oslo, when the audience got the better of the band – "I felt like I was riding a horse in a race that suddenly turned left and ran off the track, down the road and through town," laughed H. Then came Tallinn, Estonia, where the song of that name was inevitably in the set list. Said H, "Everyone stood up like they were standing for the National Anthem. They didn't clap and go crazy. It was just their way of acknowledging what their countrymen had been through because it was such a national disaster. It wasn't like they stood up for us, they just all stood up."

As the tour came to a close, all agreed they had done the acoustic thing. "It was a pleasant change – but pretty sedate," said Rothers. "We've had enough of that – enough of sitting down on a stool, playing music for a couple of hours in very nice classical music venues. It's time for a little bit more rock and roll."

20

You Never Knew Power, Did You?

2010. The dawn of a new decade and, in principle, a new album. Conscious of their ever-hungry fan base, the band had started to collate new ideas as they prepped for the *Less Is More* tour. Said Rothers, "We were jamming every day before we started rehearsals." As the year began, it was time to face the music – and lyrics. H had little in terms of material, or for that matter life experiences he hadn't already covered. "It's going to be quite a challenge because he's used an awful lot of what we've had on the shelf," continued Rothers. "He needs to go traveling the world for six months."

Still, nobody was in a desperate rush. "We talked ourselves out of heading straight into the studio," said Ian. Numerous opportunities to procrastinate presented themselves: at the end of January, Rothers made a special trip to the US to collect his Jack Dent guitars from Winston Salem. To make the most of the trip he booked in a guitar clinic at the Dog Ear Tavern in New York, letting the others off the hook for a little longer. But the studio couldn't be avoided forever.

Following a few sessions at the Racket Club (occasionally affected by bouts of man-flu), the band headed to Portugal for a fortnight to get the creative juices flowing. "A great house and a vineyard, near a place called Lousada," says Ian. "They just weren't prepared for a band, though. It was a bit too regimented – we had to eat at certain times." Another fly in the ointment was H himself, who was in the process of buying a house – and his girlfriend Linette was ill, back in Blighty. "Writing came to a pretty abrupt stop," said Ian. "H said it was like Alcatraz, you couldn't escape. I think it would have been best if Steve just hadn't come out."

It wasn't all wasted effort, but quite clearly the band, and particularly the singer, weren't yet able to just turn on the tap. "We'd just got to a place where we didn't know where to go or what to do," said Pete. "I don't think we realised how burnt-out and sick of each other we were, not as friends but as musical partners. We needed some fresh air." On return, the band decided to take the pressure right off. A second trip to Italy took place, with expectations kept low. Continues Pete, "More came out of that than we thought would – then we spent quite a lot of time just knocking around ideas and progressing with other stuff."

There was plenty to get on with: gigs to perform, live recordings to mix and master, more guitar clinics for Rothers in France, Greece and back in the US, another couple of outings for H-Natural around H's birthday, some Transatlantic tour dates for Pete... "Truth be known, we should have had some proper time away from each other, but we didn't," said the bassist. As spring turned to summer, festival rehearsals brought the band back together. The players tried out some tentative jams, with Mike taking the outputs and turning them into arrangements – a softly-softly approach which proved to be what was needed. "There is a real enthusiasm again," Pete remarked.

Festival season offered a timely reminder of what it was all about. Rock in Rio in Spain, High Voltage in the UK, then Ex Prog in Italy, Rock Legend in Poland and Loreley in Germany – the band's first time back for 24 years. High Voltage was a high point despite a battery pack failing on Pete's bass. Said Mark, "It's the first time we've been to a festival where we feel like we belong. We're not heavy enough for heavy metal and we're not poppy enough for pop... we're not that proggy either, so hopefully we'll fit in." Fan Liz Medhurst was there: "Being a festival, people would naturally dip in and out and all acts had to work hard to keep their audience engaged. Marillion had the reunion of Emerson, Lake and Palmer to contend with but there was no mass exodus. They did themselves and the festival proud."

The festivals offered the hard core a much-needed dose of Marillion but equally, fans were missing the Marillion family atmosphere. Fan Darren Newitt, who was at the "World Premiere screening" of *Less Is More* (recorded at London's Cadogan Hall the previous year), caught the mood. "The show was great, but it was not just about a brilliant screening of a performance, the music or meeting the band. It was also great to meet up with fellow fans again... they truly are a splendid lot."

And a patient lot. While the Marillos felt ready to get back into the studio at last, they didn't want to blow any enthusiasm they felt. "We have decided to continue the process without stressing, with the intention of making our next album when we feel we're ready and not until," said H. "Love means never having to say 'Where's the new f***ing album gone then?'" Most of November was taken up with a series of dates in Germany supporting Deep Purple ("It's good to have a bit of room to move again, on these big stages," said H. "Deep Purple are very pleasant chaps,"). And then, as sure as autumn turns to winter, the gates closed on another year. At least the boys felt a bit more resourcefulness and creativity than a year before.

To keep ideas flowing, the band perfected the idea of 'drive-thru jams'. "We come in for an hour, jam, and leave Mike to the mind-numbing job of listening to every noise we make in search of the good moments," said H. Funnily enough, the model was looking increasingly similar to that preferred by Dave Meegan – but with Mike's musical knowledge built in. Following the *Less Is More* acoustic experience, Rothers was testing out a tube amp brought back from the US – an Oldfield Marquis 15: "It has a vintage sound similar to a Vox amplifier from the 1960s." By March he was also playing with some new effects pedals. "You can never have too many toys," he remarked. In other words, business as usual had returned.

The fan base finally had its opportunity for mingling, music and mayhem as the biennial convention season rolled back round. With dates in Holland, Montreal and the UK, the 2011 Marillion Weekend events offered both a release of tension and a timely reminder of what it was all about. The weekend was particularly special for fans Mark Kennedy and Vanessa De Vries. Explains Mark, "Getting all our friends to the Netherlands was proving to be tricky, so we had an idea – get married at the Marillion Weekend in Port Zélande when they would all be there anyway." Marillion's Lucy Jordache was up for the idea, then the pair had another brainwave. "We'd met a Dutch registrar who we really liked and would travel to marry us, but we also thought it would be amazing if we could arrange for Steve Hogarth to take our vows. I pestered Lucy again, she got in touch with H and luckily the reply came back saying that he'd be honoured. We wanted to surprise our guests though, so we kept it to ourselves. So, on the Saturday, sixty guests turned up at The Market Dome, we had a wonderful wedding ceremony and H officiated. Unforgettable."

Swap the Band was back, with Rick Armstrong's cousin Kali singing 'Afraid Of Sunlight'. Explains Rick, "She'd sung 'Waiting To Happen' at the 2005 convention in Minehead, and then performed again at Montreal in 2011, both of which went down extremely well, according to all reports. The reaction in Montreal, in particular, was amazing. Since I was the 'supplemental guitarist' in both of those performances, I can attest to the fantastic crowd reactions. I completely understand why people do that for a living." Typically, while Port Zélande had been a blast, it was at Montreal once again that the fans blew the roof off. Said H, "I have never witnessed a vibe like it, for us, or any other band ever. We're very blessed and indebted."

Once back at Racket, inspiration finally started to flow – helped by mixing up studio sessions with playing with ideas at home – said Rothers, "My home studio has turned into an Aladdin's cave of guitars, amplifiers and effects pedals. Having the five amazing guitars that Jack Dent has built for me really helped as well." Before long, the strange engine had been well and truly kick-started. "It's like having an old vintage car and cranking the handle in the morning and trying to get it going; there's a lot of noise and smoke," continued Steve. "That's what we're like for the first year, but then it all kicks off. The difficulty is stopping..."

Like-minded musical ideas were collated, ordered and arranged, then linked to words and themes emerging from H's own, reinvigorated consciousness. "I think if what you've written comes from a place where you were moved and if being moved is what led you to write in the first place, the chances are that what you write will move other people," said H. Not least, a stream of lyrical consciousness about the city that seemed to get Marillion more than any other. "The vibration of the shows when we've gone to Montreal has been incredible. I thought it would be nice to let 'em know we know that and it's precious to us."

"Something Arabic today," commented H in his diary, intriguingly referring to a folder of musical ideas that married perfectly with some lyrics he had written about a child's view of life on the Gaza Strip. The words pulled no punches, and nor were they supposed to. "I wanted to go over there but was told it's almost impossible to get into Gaza without a visa, which is almost impossible to get. Getting out is a good deal harder than getting in," he said. The goal wasn't Israel-bashing, however – indeed, he was careful to speak with people on both sides of the wire, to ensure he portrayed the situation accurately. "You've got to keep coming back to the perspective of a child growing up there," he continued. Added Ian, "Steve was very concerned about it when he first broached the subject, but the more we worked on it, and the more people he spoke to, it just grew and turned into this incredible thing. Sometimes you've got to speak up, really, haven't you?" Agreed Steve Rothery, "In a way, it's the most important song we've ever written."

In early October and with a hat full of music, the band headed to Peter Gabriel's "uncompromisingly comfortable" Real World studios at Box, near Bath. Said Pete, "It is the ultimate shed in the garden for musicians. It's got everything. Very state-of-the-art." The goal was to pick out ideas that all five players could get behind, and turn them into something resembling songs. The extra-large studio room could accommodate both band and producer, which fitted well with Mike's hands-on approach. "The drum kit can get a bit loud at times, spilling over into the guitar and vocal mics, but it's worth it, especially when we need to talk a lot about what we are doing," said Pete. By the end of the week, a dozen ideas had been distilled into songs, one of which – 'Sounds That Can't Be Made' – was a cert for the album's title. Finally (and with much relief all round), the band had found its mojo.

In November the band toured, co-headlining with Saga. After Christmas, following brief stops from H performing H-Natural in Barcelona and Paris, the six fellows decamped to Real World once again to finish off pieces that could be finished off, and develop ideas that still needed developing. Said Pete, "We were on the home stretch and we decided to treat ourselves. Anything that helps the band enjoy what they do." The first three days were spent finalising one, longish song, said Pete, "There was lots of playing through passages, changing a note in a chord here and there, or reshaping sections." Defeat was nearly snatched from the jaws of victory as the tinnitus Mark had picked up on a prior holiday to Thailand turned out to be something more serious – Sudden Sensorineural Hearing Loss (SSHL). "Despite this, it was a very productive week," he said.

As the calendar turned, it was clear that the end of the process was nearing: the band had 8 songs that "deserved" to be on the album. Not least 'Sky Above The Rain' – "One of those special songs," remarked Pete. Another clear winner was the title track, on which Rothers felt free to experiment. "It's an invitation to go as weird as you can get," he said. The end couldn't come too quickly for H: "This could be one of the best albums we've ever made," he said. "But we're in this mind-numbingly difficult stage of arranging the songs and picking holes in them, which gets me down a bit. I just have to summon the patience to put up with the arguments over whether something should be in F minor 7."

By the end of May the drums were done and the rest of the band were finishing their overdubs, sometimes at home. "Working on headphones so that I can have the windows open and listen to birds singing in between takes. Bliss," said H. Rothers wasn't so lucky: "In my garage studio, I spent a lot of the last two days dealing with technical hell. It really is *Sounds That Can't Be Made* day today! Apparently the sun's shining outside..."

Time was running out and there was a stateside tour to be done, the dates for which couldn't be postponed. Two nights had been planned in each of three major cities – New York, Chicago and Los Angeles – with different set lists each night, and then a smattering of dates across North America. The tour had proved an organisational and financial nightmare, with costs of transport, crew and, explained Mark, "30% withholding tax to the US government – on the income, not the profit!" Said H to the *Ottawa Citizen*, "It actually might be cheaper to put you guys on a few jumbo jets and fly you to the UK. I'm not joking."

Following a last rush of recording effort ("I worked non-stop at home for many days right up to the time we left, singing harmonies, playing bits of guitar and VST keyboard sections," said Pete), Mike remained at the Racket Club to continue mixing while H, Mark and Rothers squeezed in final overdubs between shows. "I've done bits and pieces of guitars. Mark is doing some keyboards and Steve Hogarth is finishing some vocals," said Steve R. Continued Pete, "*Sounds That Can't Be Made* is an apt title in some ways." "Or the *Sleep That Can't Be Had* tour!" laughed Rothers. Fans who attended the shows were treated to two new songs – 'Power' and 'Lucky Man' – the first songs on the album to be completed.

Although traveling on a tour bus was exhausting at times and despite the tour plague ("which lingered for a bit," said Pete, who succumbed in New York), the audiences more than made up for it. "The first night in New York along with the first night in Chicago, the second night in LA and the final show at the Fillmore in San Francisco are some of the best concerts I think we've ever played," said Rothers. Agreed Mark, "I can honestly say that this North American tour was the most enjoyable tour we have done over there EVER!"

One of the Chicago shows was particularly moving for US fan Mike Kuntz, who had been a fan since 1982. "When the North American 2012 tour was announced I was unable to commit to tickets as my son Justin (our only child) was sick. My son did not get better and went on hospice care, dying on February 26, 2012, six months to the day before his 18th birthday; my Mom died the day after his funeral. In May, I started thinking about going but had no tickets. The Saturday show was sold out and I thought if I did go it could only be with my wife, who had never seen the band. She always stayed home with our son and I went alone, but she had no reason to stay home this time." A call-out to a certain guardian angel in rural Oxfordshire was all it took, and Mike and his wife were soon heading to Chicago. "Before the show I asked H to dedicate a song to my son Justin. He asked what song and I said any song. Then at the show he did it – dedicating 'Estonia' to Justin – my wife and I both cried. The weekend in Chicago was very helpful to the journey we are on."

It was an upbeat band that returned to the UK at the end of June. "The US government made us jump through hoops to come and play, and at one stage I was wondering if it was worth the humiliation and aggravation," said H. "But the reaction from the fans was right up there with the best vibrations we've had, and I include the conventions in that. So many people shook us by the hand and thanked us for coming as if we'd actually rowed the Atlantic to get there. (But that's another song..)"

In the meantime, momentum was building. On July 17 Marillion released another new song to YouTube – "Power" – and the band left Mike at Racket once again while they headed for Europe and worked on final bits and pieces from the road. Says H, "It all got finished the day before the cut. We were recording right up to the deadline. On tour, after tour, at home, in hotel rooms. You name it." A month later, in parallel with sending the album for mastering, a teaser video was uploaded to YouTube. As the album was booked for release in September, the work started some two years before was finally complete.

Sounds That Can't Be Made had been a creative struggle, but the band were delighted with both their own resilience and the result. "Most bands burn out after a few albums, so to come up with something as strong as this after 17 albums says a lot for the chemistry between us, never mind the talent of the individuals," said Rothers. Equally, the band knew they had been right to trust working with Mike. "I subscribe to the theory that it took a while for Mike to fully realise what is special about this band. He did so by mixing a lot of our live stuff, watching the videos for weeks on end whilst doing so. I now think he has a better idea of where our strengths are than any of us," said H. As remarked Ian a couple of years before, "It is always the same – working with a producer or anyone new always seems to take three albums." This, the third album in the Mike series, showed just how far the relationship had come.

Reviews were effusive, from both critics and fans. "It only takes one listen to 'Gaza', the album's opening epic, to realise there's something different about this album," wrote Dom Lawson in *Prog Magazine*. "Above all, it dares to connect on a profound emotional level... All notions of predetermined style melt away amid a sustained, celebratory rush of wonderful, life-affirming sound." Added Jim Bryant at *The V2 Journal*, "Even after multiple listens it reveals hidden gems throughout. It's well worth listening through headphones, only then do the layers unravel a little through the sonic landscape that Mike Hunter has created through what is his best production yet."

Despite being strongly discouraged from doing so by Lucy Jordache on the Marillion forum, members could be forgiven for posting reviews within minutes of spinning the disc. "Can I be the first to say: WOW" said Fertzy, who set the scene for a barrage of beautiful feedback. "Fantastic after a few goes," said Blue Devil. Added Signase, "The album blew me away – the vibe, the power inside the music is simply overwhelming." Said the band in an eWeb, "We honestly can't remember getting such amazing feedback to an album in all our years together." Said Mr Lazland, "What struck me immediately on first listen is the sheer quality of the production. The band have never sounded better. Mark is soaring, whilst Rothers is back on fire." "It is such a relief to hear Rothery back," said Kevman28.

Marillion didn't get the feedback all their own way, of course – the main cause of controversy was the 17-minute 'Gaza', which tested some fans' loyalty to the limit, particularly those few who felt the song attacked Israel. "Gutted and empty," said one. For the majority, however, the song did what it set out to do and H, while sympathetic, remained unrepentant. "The more I spoke to people in Gaza, much as I can sympathise with Israel's "tied hands" in terms of resolving any kind of peace since Hamas took over in Gaza, the more we all felt that the lyric was not a condemnation of Israel, but a condemnation of a child's situation."

Despite last minute complications with international postage services (the band made the album available for download for those whose special edition pre-orders were stuck in the post), it was an upbeat Marillion that headed to South America in October 2012, riding a continuing wave of adulation for a band still in its prime.

SOUNDS THAT CAN'T BE MADE

Marillion's 17th album took a while to arrive but even with the extended gestation time, the band were working up to the wire. Steve Hogarth has remarked that the final few days of making the album were so stressful that he couldn't face listening to the finished CD. And yet, when it arrived, *Sounds That Can't Be Made* was quickly hailed as being up there with the band's best work.

Starting with a heavy and portentous groove, 'Gaza' is the heaviest song Marillion have ever recorded. When the music explodes like a drone attack, Steve Rothery's harrowing, atonal guitar screams are similar to those of King Crimson's Adrian Belew, yet his second solo, towards the end of the piece is among his most melodic. The song incorporates a number of Arabic-sounding melodies that help transport the listener to the dust of Middle East conflict. The song is told from the position of a child growing up amid the chaos, squalor and horror and while it reports the child's plight, it also acknowledges wrong doings on each side of the conflict. Hogarth has stated his hope that it will make people read up on Gaza for themselves.

Very much in musical contrast, the title track is a song about magic and metaphysics. Steve Hogarth has described it as being about trying to move someone without actually touching them. There is something of the Blue Nile and The Waterboys about the piece that is constructed around some wonderful keyboard riffing from Mark Kelly. The 'aurora borealis' section at the end is utterly wonderful.

'Pour My Love' has been described by band members as sitting somewhere between Prince, the Isley Brothers and Todd Rundgren and it's not hard to see what they mean. This affecting tale of love for someone dying clearly bears the influence of these artists; Prince's 'Money Don't Matter' certainly seems to be a touchstone. Away from the sound of the track, the song is interesting for having a John Helmer lyric, his first since *Marillion.com* over a decade earlier – not a new lyric, but one that Hogarth had collected and held on to.

'Power' had been mentioned by the band as long ago as *Marillion.com* and they'd tried a version of it during the *Marbles* sessions. The version on

Sounds retained the lyrics but the music was completely new. Sound-wise, the track is a classic Marillion rocker with at least some DNA from 'You're Gone' or 'Whatever Is Wrong With You'. It concerns the true nature of power and how it's not about force. The stand out performance goes to Mr Trewavas's funk bass work.

The 14-minute 'Montréal' is substantially based on extracts from H's diary, set to music. The source material for the lyrics gives an unusual travelogue feel to the song that moves through a number of different musical sections. Mark Kelly deserves special praise for his judicious use of interesting sonic themes, providing a distinct, atmospheric backdrop to each one.

'Invisible Ink' needs to be on a shortlist for the quirkiest Marillion song of all time. Hogarth paints a picture of a man who leaves notes written in invisible ink on his lover's pillow, but who doesn't have the courage to tell her how to read them. Built around the curious vocal tune and the child-like tinkling bells of the main melody, the song really shouldn't work but, somehow, it does. Hogarth has revealed that when he first heard Ian's drums kick in, it made him want to dance about the room.

Straight ahead rock song 'Lucky Man' has more than a little in common with 'Three Minute Boy'. The Beatles' influence is clearly apparent on this number, about having everything you want in life and realising it's not all about material trappings. For some, it lacked a little something, but others clamoured (in vain) for its release as a single.

Set-closer 'The Sky Above The Rain' uses an omniscient narrator to dissect a relationship in which love is still present but desire has gone. This intimate portrait of communication breakdown, repressed feelings and the flame of hope is uncomfortable and affecting. The band manages to render these emotions sensitively but without bombast. Steve Rothery is particularly effective, inserting a poignant bluesy phrase wherever required. Like the title track, there's something of The Waterboys' 'Big Music' in some of the string chords.

The cover is based upon a photograph of a cardioid (defined, as Wikipedia reliably tells us, as a "plane curve traced by a point on the perimeter of a circle that is rolling around a fixed circle of the same radius") made by a 3D printer. Racket Record's Simon Ward was responsible for the main image and the use of the decoded Arecibo radio wave message (first broadcast into space in 1974) on the special edition box design, with Carl Glover, Antonio Seijas, Andy Wright and Marc Bessant joining him to illustrate the individual songs in the lavish book.

THANKYOU, WHOEVER YOU ARE

At the time of writing Marillion are still on the South American leg of a worldwide tour, with dates stretching well into 2013. Another series of weekends is planned for next year, with *Radiat10n* the plat de résistance, accompanied by a remixed and re-mastered version of the album now that the album rights have reverted. Tasked with the remix, Mike Hunter's first job will be retrieving the original multi-tracks from the (potentially degraded) DAT tapes. "It will sound much better. He's a sonic wizard," says H.

And then, what next? Who knows… but nobody in the band has any intention of hanging up tools. Suggests Mark, "We're probably all in denial, thinking that we don't have to think about the future, that we've done it up to now and we will just keep going." Equally however, there is little reason to call a halt. Said Steve Hogarth recently, "The situation we're in is the holy grail. Why would you want to stop when you're free to do whatever you want?" Or, as Ian once put it, "What else am I going to be? A plumber?"

Of *course* the band would not exist without its fan base – but this is a two-way street. "The fans are what Marillion means to me," says H. "We exist because the fans believe in us, and we try to bear in mind that fact, to be honest and true and live up to it." It would be difficult to sustain such a relationship otherwise, thinks fan and film-maker Paul Rowlston, "They care about what they do; they care about who they do it for; they understand the true value of their fans. It's the perfect symbiotic relationship – made possible because, each in their own unique way, the five members of the world's best band™ are some of the world's best people."

Today Marillion are more successful than ever, but the band still fly largely below the radar of the media and, therefore, the broader public. Says Pete. "I think there are people sitting at home with Coldplay, Floyd and maybe a bit of Radiohead, Keane or the Kooks and who have probably never heard of Marillion or choose not to listen to us. But if they listened to the last two or three albums they would probably love us." Fans would agree – after all, if Marillion's music is designed with any purpose at all, it is to engage the emotions. Those who get this, share the band's frustrations and remain keen to spread the good word, in the knowledge that the world would be a better place. The lack of profile means the big stadium tour may remain outside Marillion's reach, which is a shame: says Ian, "It'd be nice to have mega-media exposure, because I'd love to put on a show like Roger Waters or Pink Floyd. I'd love to blow up the drum kit at the end of the gig!"

All the same, however, the band have created a substantial legacy – more than 14 million records sold; 17 studio albums released, 8 of which achieved UK Top 10 positions; 24 UK singles; and gigs played to well over 3 million people. "In the 30 years we've been going, we've achieved far more than we expected – and we're having fun doing it. Lots of bands are very jealous of us," says Pete. So well they might be – it's one heck of a portfolio, making it all the more surprising that Marillion do not have more recognition. "The true reckoning will come when the band no longer exists for whatever reason... I'd like to think that in years to come there'll be a re-evaluation of our worth," says Rothers.

On the upside, having such a solid body of work does mean the band can afford to be objective, even when accolades are spread. As remarks Steve H about the band's most recent album, "The acclaim is wonderful, but that doesn't make it a better album – it just means more people are getting off on it. Give 'em all time, I say, and then someone can decide where the gold is in 50 years time." He has a point, and it's an important one – whatever the future holds, the perseverance of Marillion over the decades means nobody is going to be resting on their laurels. Says Rothers, "I don't know how many albums we have left in us. However many it is, we'll try to make each one of them as special as possible. You maybe realise you're not always going to be doing this and that you've got to enjoy it... and savour each moment."

Deconstruct the magic that is Marillion and you are left with five fellows who have, collectively, seen so much of life that there really is no going back. Says Pete, "I made a pact with myself after I joined: if I ever didn't enjoy being in the band any more or found I was doing it for the wrong reasons, I would gracefully step down. This is because I love music too much to be cheapening respect and love of it. Put me down for another twenty then!"

With the pact between Marillion and their audience holding as strong as ever, you can put the global fan base down for another twenty as well.

Happiness is the road.

Repeat to fade.

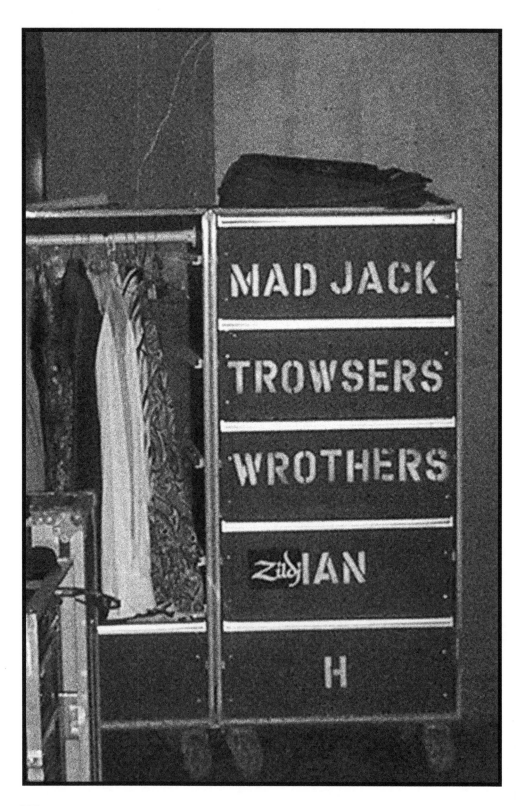

WE'RE THE BAND

Marillion are no ordinary bunch of fellows, and how could they be? Who would choose a life that alternates time on the road, far away from family and friends in cramped buses, airport lounges and hotel rooms, with time in and out of the studio under intense pressure to produce yet another sixty minutes of music? "We don't write songs because we've got to do an album, we do an album because we've got something to say," says Pete, but there can be no more intense, team-building experience than working as a band. Every note, every chord and drum beat needs to tightly bind with each other. In writing and recording, a delicate dance is performed as one person's evolving ideas are accepted, rejected or built upon by the others.

For the outsider, writing and performing involves a strange magic, as if music comes from nowhere in an inspired, near-final form. Viewed from within, magical moments may happen but there is no magic formula. *Fugazi* was a strain on the band, *Misplaced Childhood* needed a rethink, and the writer's block at the start of the band's fourth album was a deciding factor in the break-up. *Holidays In Eden* was another difficult conception, as was Marillion's most recent release, *Sounds That Can't Be Made*. While the financial and managerial freedom of the past decade has given the band the time they wanted to be truly creative, this doesn't make the process any easier.

HAPPY ALCHEMY

The initial stage of any album is to try out some ideas and see what feels right. "It's about having a feel," says Pete. "We want to make music that makes people feel alive." No wonder inspiration doesn't come easy, considering the constant push to move in new musical directions. "It's harder every time not to repeat ourselves," comments Rothers. Adds Ian, "We're up for experimenting a lot more now, but because we're older, we're guilty of being a bit too careful sometimes. But you don't want to write the same album every time." Agrees H, "I'm always striving to say something more important than the songs I hear everywhere. The higher you aim, the harder it is to hit the target."

If there is any magic, it happens when the band get together and jam. Put five musicians into a room, each with a parcel of ideas, and let them bounce a riff, a beat, a chord sequence off each other. Comments H, "Every idea is welcome, we have no rules." The band know enough about one another to let jamming deliver the material, however long it takes. Continues H, "We jam for weeks and record it all. Most of it is rubbish, but every now and then there will be a happy accident."

It was perhaps Dave Meegan's work on *Brave* and *Afraid Of Sunlight* that turned the jamming habit into an art form. While *Brave* involved many individual sessions, *Afraid Of Sunlight* saw the whole band recording together, with Dave picking out the best takes (a process Mike Hunter has embraced and enhanced with the use of multi-track recording). Recalls Steve Rothery, "Dave would take all his favourite moments, and not always the most technically perfect live parts." The artistic, if not commercial, success of both albums firmly cemented this approach, helped by the use of digital technologies such as DAT and minidisc, Petri dishes upon which happy accidents can grow. Says Pete, "At around about tape six or seven, the good ideas start to come. We take the best things and put them on compilations. We sometimes end up with compilations of compilations, or supercomps."

More recently, with the advent of digital technologies the band has been recording more and more at home. Said Mark, "I tend to do all the keyboards at home, for two reasons – to avoid wasting people's time, I'd rather do it at home and then present to the band for approval or not when I'm happy with it. The other reason is that Mike Hunter can be recording guitars, or vocals." In parallel H is working on lyrics, matching metaphors from his life and experience with the mood of the music. "The lyrics could be five years old, and the music could be new," says H. "I like to write words that mean three things - something obvious, something metaphorical and something hidden, that you'd have to know me to know what it is." John Helmer still provides the occasional words, notes H, "He's not too precious about what I do with them. We meet up a couple of times a year and get drunk and talk about the meaning of life and what have you. It's a very odd co-writing relationship."

Finally, the band decide what is good and what is not. "We tend to write one song at a time, and we never even know how that's going to turn out until it's evolved on its own," says Pete. Naturally, this can be a contentious area – of course the band argues, particularly if one band member's ideas are being rejected out of hand. "We work according to a certain pattern, in which each band member has his say in choosing the songs," H explains. As they are chosen, the structure of the album starts to form. In the past, near-complete songs would be arranged and then recorded as demos. "I help with arranging more than the real writing. I can interpret what other people do sometimes easier than they can remember what they did," says Pete. "It's not until you record something that it gets defined," says Pete.

With today's technologies however, some 'happy accidents' make their way directly onto the final album. Whatever the process, a producer helps considerably: he has many roles, from recording engineer to arranger and peacemaker. Explains Steve Rothery, "With so many creative people, it is good to have another person involved who can make the best of what's there and who can get us to focus attention." In other words, explains Dave Meegan, "They get into such a state they can't physically enjoy making an album without a producer." Chris Neil agrees, "Somebody has to drive the bus. The producer provides a musical shoulder to cry on, taking all their aspirations and helping to take them on to the goal."

Is it any wonder then that the band refuse to define their musical style? Not that they won't, but they can't. "You never know how something is going to come out until it's recorded, mixed and finished," says Ian. As French fan Ed Wood puts it, "I always buy a Marillion album without knowing what will be on it, and I buy it with confidence built up over the years." Fan and Web Holland activist Jeroen Schipper concurs: "The best element of Marillion is how they keep changing themselves in their musical style and don't hang on to something successful. Every new album is a surprise."

BUT IS IT PROG?

The term 'progressive' has traditionally had something of a bad reputation. Many bands jumped on the prog bandwagon at the height of the '70s, but very quickly jumped off when they thought the pomp and ceremony had had its day. The genre never went away, however: notes Mark Kelly, "There were two dozen bands with pub status, several had their roots in the '70s like The Enid, Twelfth Night and Pendragon, but none had any success to speak of." Then along came Marillion who picked up a couple of hit singles, and suddenly there was a ready-made new wave of British prog. "All the bands were dragged into the limelight, *Kerrang!* started talking about it, but the reality was it was all total bollocks!" Mark frowns.

At the outset, Marillion were unashamedly progressive despite being uncomfortable with the label, not least because it was an immediate turn-off to both music journalists and public. Of course, other bands were most definitely prog. "IQ, Solstice and so on, they all seemed too derivative. In hindsight we were too," admits Mark. Even as late as 1986, band members would continue to confirm Marillion's prog status. "It's always been progressive rock," Steve Rothery proclaimed. Trouble is, Marillion were never just about prog alone. As

Pete explains, "Marillion was borne out of several bands, many of which weren't prog bands - The Beatles, The Who, Led Zeppelin. We all have similar record collections, and less than half of the records are prog. Me and Steve Rothery share a liking for James Bond themes by John Barry."

When Steve Hogarth joined, it appeared the band would lose the reference altogether. "He was much more anti-prog," remembers Mark. "He tried to get us to move in other directions, the technique he used was, 'Why-not-give-it-a-try?'" H hated genre labels even more than his forebear, as they imposed unspoken limitations. As he remarked, "I'd love to think Marillion is progressive rock, in the sense that it's experimental, it doesn't work necessarily with a three-minute format and it's not derivative. If progressive is derivative, it's a contradiction in terms." Indeed, if *Holidays In Eden* succeeded at anything it was in remodelling Marillion as a straightforward rock band. Its backlash, *Brave* was a return to progressive type, this time with H in concurrence.

At the end of the day, while the term 'progressive' is not harmful, how people use it can be. H sums things up: "We're not on a mission to be re-categorised, but we drag this progressive rock label like a lot of chains. We don't really see music as falling into categories. What is commercial? It is something which sells. Did *Brave* sell? It sold more copies than *Marillion.com*, so it must have been more commercial, wouldn't you say?" The problem isn't so much with the prog label, as complacency, says H, "It's the path of least resistance. If the five of us went into a room and did what comes easiest and simplest, we'd probably make a prog album."

Fans tend to fall into one of three camps - Marillion are unashamedly prog and should be proud of it; Marillion's music is far too diverse to suffer a label such as prog; and, never quite understood what all the fuss was about in any case. Perhaps one would do well to follow Mark Kelly's lead: "I ask journos, 'What do you mean by prog? Answer me that and I'll tell you if we are or not.'" Over the years, the label has diminished in its negative connotations and indeed is even seeing a resurgence in popularity. The band remain unphased, says Ian, "Years ago we always were scared about upsetting people, 'Oh we can't go into that area of music, it's not done...' but these days, I suppose we just don't care anymore."

PLAYING LIVE

"I love everything about touring. I love being out on the road, I love playing to everyone, I love being on stage, I love sleeping on the bus, I love being a bit fitter, I love the divine exhaustion and (ahem) I love being admired. I think I'm a bit of a circus person at heart," says H, expressing a sentiment that drives many an artist. Following the stasis of the studio, the thought of hitting the road is a welcome one. "Once we've been in the studio for six-seven months writing and then three months recording, I'm thinking, *I'm going to be out on the road in a couple of weeks - great!*" comments Mark. And it's a necessity. "For this band the concerts are probably the most important thing," says Ian. "We've always been known as a live band and everybody still feels the same, we just want to get out there and tour."

Trouble is, for each couple of hours in the limelight, there's weeks of preparation, rehearsal, travel, sound checks, and waiting. Waiting. Waiting for trains and planes. Waiting to go places. Waiting to get there. Waiting to get back. Waiting in the dressing room for a gig to start. "Touring is made up of two distinct experiences. The first is playing live to an audience, which I love. The second is all the travelling and hanging around that you have to do. All that feels like such a waste of your life," says Rothers. Concurs Ian, "It was Charlie Watts of the Rolling Stones who said, 'We've been together for 20 years... 5 years playing music, and 15 years hanging about.'"

PREPARATION

For most gigs, everything starts with the set list. Explains Steve Hogarth, "We all have different agendas, for instance, Ian wants to play songs that have different drumming, not 4/4 all the time. I can imagine how tedious that must get." Then the band need to make the songs work. Says Ian, "If it's a new album, if there's a fade out we have to work out a proper ending or a segue." Adds Steve R, "We write it as it comes and worry about it later." For some in the band, this means repetitive practising and re-arranging, for others hours of programming and sequencing. Laughs Rothers, "It takes Mark longer than he expects to programme his keyboards, so out of two weeks we end up with about three days to rehearse." Singing is no easy ride either, as emotions are difficult to fake, even in rehearsals. Explains H, "I sing the lyrics with a lot of passion, and if one of the band makes a mistake, I'm in the middle of all these emotions and then have to start all over again, it's very frustrating."

Alongside rehearsals, the band have to get booked in. When Marillion were at their pinnacle of mainstream popularity they used booking agents, but in these independent days co-manager Lucy Jordache handles the bookings herself. A few weeks before a tour is to start, the band contact a tour manager and bookings are turned into actions. "My job is transport, hotels, guest lists and general dogsbody," laughs Tim Bricusse, past tour manager. The band own their own equipment, but everything else (such as PA equipment, sound and lighting rigs) is usually hired. Says old hand Paul Lewis, "A month would be nice but all the arrangements could be turned around in a week if need be. The only restriction on this would be if any visas are required, which takes things out of our hands."

Leaving home is not always a pleasant experience. "Missing your family, that's probably the most difficult thing," remarks Steve Rothery. Before leaving for Mexico, August 31 1994, he wrote in his diary, "I climbed into the back of the car feeling I'm to blame for the misery of the people I love." Finally, the band unite with crew and it's time to climb aboard the bus, the plane, whatever. Different members of the band have different experiences of the tour bus: Ian can never sleep, for example, whereas H can think of nothing better. "I love lying on one of these little bunks late at night, drifting in and out of sleep and knowing that when I wake up I'll be in another city."

For the band, arrival at venues involves checking into a hotel, taking a shower and going for a walk before waiting for the sound check. Meanwhile the tour manager is making sure that everything is in place in the run-up to the gig. "I've done most venues before, so I know what to do in advance," remarks Tim. "I compile a book for the whole tour, covering each venue, transport details, hotels, rider arrangements (which are sent to the promoters so they know what to expect) and so on. Every venue is different." The load-in follows a set process, explains Paul Lewis: "It starts with loading in the lights and getting them off the ground so that the other equipment can be loaded underneath. Then it would be the PA and monitors and finally the back line. While the back line is being set up we would normally do any interviews to get them out of the way before the sound check. Around 4.30 the sound check would start and that would take 15 minutes to an hour-and-a-half, depending on whether there are any problems with the sound. Around 6pm the band and crew sit down to dinner, after which a few may go back to the bus to relax or watch a movie. 7.30 doors open and the opening act would normally go on about 7.45 - 8.30 giving us an hour to change over the equipment for Marillion to start at 9.00, usually playing for two hours including the encore after which the whole process is done in reverse with the truck doors closing at about 1.30am."

Before the main set comes the support act, which will either have bought on to - or have been invited to join - the tour. Laughs H, "We prefer solo support artists, they don't take up much space. Seriously, support bands are technically a pain in the arse, as they will always compromise your own sound. Most of all we like people who put out a good vibe - we just don't need it otherwise." Prospective support acts are actively encouraged to send a CD, says Lucy Jordache. "Marillion have discovered many great groups this way. It offers independent bands an invaluable leg up and insight into touring, and a chance for these bands to play to thousands of people." And what about the main act? "Fortunately, Marillion are an easy band to manage, they don't want much pampering," comments Tim. "Some acts are more demanding, the types who want the blue M&M's taken out (or only the blue ones left in?) I mean honestly; they'll all go back home and eat any colour."

Musically speaking, the first few dates of a tour will inevitably be less polished. "The first two weeks for me is like playing squash for the first time after laying off for a year," says Ian, "I just feel like I've been run over a couple of times! It's quite a physical thing to play the drums." For H, things can go the other way. "When you're in the middle of the tour the high notes become harder to sing," he remarks. "Certain songs are so hard to sing technically so it detracts from the enjoyment because there's so much responsibility to come up with the intensity of the performance." As the tour progresses, set lists will be changed, swapping songs in and out to suit the audience, the mood, the timing. "Eventually you end up with a structure of songs that works, but even then we still swap songs in and out just as we feel," comments Mark. Adds H, "It's quite important that we vary the show from one night to the next, because so many of our fans come to many of our shows, and then complain."

The important part of a successful tour is to keep it fun. Comments Tim Bricusse, "It's a very close, claustrophobic experience, so if anyone isn't happy - the band, the management, the crew - it rubs off on everyone. Everyone has off days, that's why it's important that everyone gets on." Eventually, the time out of time that is touring comes to a close. "Adapting to a normal life can be difficult," remarks Rothers. "It's reality - you know, you've got to cut the lawn and pay the bills."

ATMOSPHERE FRIENDLY

Waiting to go on stage is a bit like standing on the teleport deck of the Starship Enterprise. One minute, there's a small group of people in their own protected environment. Seconds later, they are transported into the heart of the new world. The adrenaline rush is inevitable. Remembering a stadium gig in Sao Paolo, H recalls, "As we went on, I don't know whether they were camera flashes or people flashing their lighters or something, but there was a very bright light flickering right the way round the stadium and this enormous noise. It was like the greatest excitement and the greatest terror happening simultaneously!" Then it's into position and the mix of careful orchestration, intra-band chemistry and the artistic muse takes over.

It's a very different experience to perform live compared to in the studio. "When we play live, I concentrate on the music and make sure I get it right and in time," says Mark. Timing is everything – Marillion don't play with a click track but occasionally lean on gadgets such as "Mr Blinky", a metronome used for 'This Strange Engine'. Says Ian, "There were a few complaints (of speeding up) so we put Mr Blinky there as a rough guide.

Hand signals provide liaison with technicians and front of house engineers. Explains engineer Privet Hedge, "I try as much as possible to recreate the general mix of the album, but performances and arrangements change. Steve Rothery may play four different guitar parts on an album track but only one part live." The vocals are one of the hardest things to mix, due to the spillage of sound into the vocal mikes from the other instruments. Continues Priv, "If the singer has a weak voice, you're knackered. Steve H does not, thank heavens, 'cos they're loud up there!"

Mistakes are more acceptable live, as they will be hidden in the overall mix, and add a certain spark to the performance. "It's very cool to fuck up, it's very cool to get things wrong if you overcome them in a good-humoured, gentlemanly way," says Pete. Though he adds, with a barely perceptible sideways glance, "If you see someone raging and throwing stuff at the poor techs, well that's a bit of a shameful display of behaviour really." Acceptable maybe, but this is why recording a live performance can be particularly dicey. Remarks H, 'On the one hand, you are thinking, 'I better be good,' and, 'I better sing in tune' because it's being recorded. But on the other hand, you don't want it to inhibit you or constrain your performance."

Many factors determine a successful show, including the venue. Comments H, "I've often come off stage thoroughly depressed from a gig to find people coming back going, 'That was an amazing gig - didn't you feel the vibe?' and I'm like, 'What vibe?'" Happily, such occasions are in the minority. "The atmosphere the crowd generates at each show is just not really like any other band you might see," says Mark. "It still makes my pulse race." Adds H, "I would give up touring only at the point of a gun. When a man is tired of touring, he is tired of life."

IT'S A RACKET

One of the biggest decisions Marillion have had to make was whether to run their own affairs. Already, on Steve Hogarth's arrival, a number of initiatives were being considered that would give the band more independence. In particular, Racket Records and the Racket Club. Perhaps the hardest thing for a label-independent band such as Marillion is to marry the need for creative output with the fact that they are a business, with cash flow, bank accounts, salaries, marketing budgets and all the horrible paperwork that goes with it. As Steve Hogarth says, "We're in business to make money, otherwise we're not here next year." But this is not at any cost.

Racket Records was originally set up by John Arnison as a direct response to bootleggers releasing live recordings at exorbitant prices. "The bootlegs were expensive and really crap quality," remarks John. First the band had to get the go-ahead from EMI - "We explained how we wanted to sell live recordings of a tour to the fan club only - they limited the figure to no more than a few thousand a year, and it kind of grew from there." The first Racket CD was *Live At The Borderline*, a recording made at the Web UK convention on May 4 1992.

Racket was never set up to be a label in its own right, but opportunism led to signing artists such as John Wesley for his first album, *Under A Red And White Sky*. Recalls Wes, "John Arnison said to me, we're bringing you on tour, let's sell some records!" It also helped that Mark, Ian and Steve R were all involved in the album's production. Another early signing was Mike Hunter's ambient mix of Marillion samples, *River*. "Arnison being ever one to spot an opportunity said, 'Let's knock up a thousand!'" says Mike. "Years later, people would come up to me and say, 'Did you know, my missus used it to give birth to?'"

A few months after the label was started, Steve Rothery came up with the idea of the band having their own place for equipment storage and rehearsals. "We could save a fortune - until that time we'd been storing our equipment at Nomis studios in London and going away to expensive residential studios to write." The band opted for a place he had found in Buckinghamshire, with Steve Hogarth and his family moving up from Windsor to be close. As the Racket Club opened its doors for the writing sessions of *Brave* in November 1992, it quickly became obvious what an asset it would be. "We realised the biggest cost was recording. We had to rent a writing studio, then go away and record, it all cost money," explains John Arnison. Commented Pete, "It was not a glamorous affair by any standard, but the freedom we had to go in at any time and work on ideas helped make it a good environment."

Steve Rothery suggested EMI paid for some equipment that the band had acquired. "We'd used it to record various live B-sides around *Holidays In Eden* time," explains Rothers. Mike Hunter was brought in as engineer. "I kipped on the studio floor," says Mike. "I can play bass, drums and piano so, if they knocked it on the head at about 7.30, I would spend the evenings practising on their instruments. I was happy as a pig in shit!" Ian remembers how the band clubbed together to raise some cash so Mike could buy a car. "It was an old Vauxhall, he had it for about an hour before it blew up."

By 1994 the Racket Club had outgrown its original location, moving lodgings and gaining some new equipment for the recording of *Afraid Of Sunlight*. As the band left EMI immediately afterwards, the Racket Club became an essential facility. When Mike Hunter moved back up to Liverpool (he claimed it was too far to travel every Saturday to watch Everton play), the band found a replacement in the shape of Stewart Every, who had worked with Dave Meegan at Maison Rouge. Racket's next employee was American Erik Nielsen in 1997 - first as Mark's keyboard technician and then website manager. Racket Records was still very much a cottage operation, he recalls, "Stewart Every was packing a few CDs every day, and popping down to the village post office to stick the stamps on." All soon changed, when the tour fund showed the band the powder keg they were sitting on. The next two Racket releases really lit the touch paper: first *Tales From The Engine Room* was initially sold only over the Web; then another live CD, *Piston Broke*, was released to capitalise on the demand for live performances. As a result, Stewart was spending all of his time packing CDs and taking them to the post office. This posed a bit of a problem, as he was supposed to be acting as engineer.

When John Arnison and the band went their separate ways in 1998, management tasks were passed to Rod Smallwood at Sanctuary. "He heard we were without a manager so he approached us," says Mark. "He looked after us for a year or so, then he got too busy with Iron Maiden, so we stopped using him." Meanwhile, the band started to take over the administration and what was a label became a business. "I'd been going once a year with John to see the bank manager," explains Ian. "When John left, I went in with Mark, and somehow at that meeting I ended up being the person who signed the cheques." Ian was the logical choice as the money man. "I guess I'm quite good at moving money around, and making it last if there's not much of it," he says. "He's very meticulous," comments Mark. "He's very tight!" laughs Erik.

Shifting to a commercial operation was a major learning experience. A great source of ideas was Mark, comments Steve H, "It's his vision that has led us to the degree of self-sufficiency that we now have." Steve Rothery also picked up a number of lessons from his Dorian Music, set up to release music from The Wishing Tree as well as Jadis, Mr So & So and Iris. Having suffered issues around staffing and bad payers, Steve eventually decided that his talents lay elsewhere. "I thought, *I'm a musician, I don't want to spend my whole time chasing money.*" In the process, he also gained a deeper understanding of his industry: "For example, how record companies and radio stations are dominated by quick profit thinking, that all the bands who are marginal and who aren't mainstream are pushed to one side." With such experience added to the mix, before long the Marillion collective realised that they knew as much as anybody else. Remarks Ian, "None of us are businessmen, but we're doing just as good a job as anyone ever did for us."

In 2000, the volume of work once again exceeded available resource, so Racket went recruiting. First in was Lucy Jordache, who built up her initial role of promotional responsibilities to take on the job of agent and band management. "She's always been into the band and done great stuff with EMI, so we just offered her a job," says Mark. Added Ian at the time, "Lucy's been on a massive learning curve, she's coped brilliantly." Marketing a non-mainstream band like Marillion has long been an uphill struggle – "It's the whole us-against-the-world thing," said Ian. Confirmed Steve Rothery, "People don't realise that in the US you need at least a couple of hundred thousand dollars to get a song on the radio. That doesn't make it a hit. You pay the independent plugger to plug your record. And that's it. To be honest, we don't play that game." Why should they, and how could they? "To be fair to radio," comments Steve H, "it does generally take us three minutes to get to the chorus!"

Promoting Marillion is a case of striking a careful balance between preaching to the converted and growing the fan base, ignoring the reviews and acting on feedback, going it alone and using the infrastructure of the major labels. "It's been a difficult trek, because we see ourselves as artists," remarked H. "By nature we don't like the idea of promoting ourselves." Of course, the more interactive nature of the socially networked world has played into Marillion's hands. Continues H, "The thing about the Internet is that we can reach people one to one, and it feels more natural and real, rather than the usual promotional activities that bands get up to."

Also recruited in August 2000 was Colin Price, a long-time Marillion fan who had spent 15 years managing a warehouse for the Oxford University Press. Says Erik, "Colin had a trial by fire – almost as soon as he arrived, we went on tour and left him to it." "Some days, I can't believe I'm here," remarked Colin, "but other days I can believe I'm here - it's a lot of hard work." One of Colin's tasks was to make the packaging area more usable and efficient. "The main area used to be above the studio in the loft and could only be accessed by a huge ramp. Sliding boxes of shirts and CDs up and down was hazardous to say the least, not to mention Mad Jack Kelly hurtling downwards at a hundred miles per hour towards you!"

The Racket Club has been a second home to the band and a work place for all their employees, not to mention a place that has gained almost mythical status in the hearts and minds of the fans. Over time Lucy has built on her initial promotional role to take on the job of agent and band management, building a team of like-minded individuals – Stephanie Bradley, Rich Lee, Simon Ward and the occasional assistant. And meanwhile, the band are better able to run their own affairs than they have ever been. "We've managed to keep the boat afloat very well, thanks to Lucy's forward thinking and Ian's brilliant accounting (he'd make a better Chancellor than anyone since I've been alive - there'd have been no credit crunch!)," says H. "It's a fine line though, between keeping the band solvent and compromising the quality of what's released. Hopefully we've stayed on the right side of that so far, but I'm constantly advising caution..." Past Racket team members have moved on to work with other artists – Erik works with Elton John and James Blunt, and Colin Price has performed guitar tech duties for Iron Maiden and Keane. "Looking back I think the huge risks we took and what we achieved within Racket Records set the band up ever since on a smooth course for the remainder of their career," says Colin.

Not bad for a money-saving idea.

ENOUGH OF A FREAK?

Marillion have an audience many bands would die for. As the band evolved and some fans dropped away, a new audience has developed to provide a consistent, continuous backbone of strength that has supported the band through thick and thin, over the years becoming more family than fan base. Where do they come from, these fans? Why do they do it? And indeed, how do they do it? And how has the band responded over the years?

From international fan clubs to internet forums and email lists, no stone is left unturned when it comes to how band and fans communicate and interact. Things were not always so rosy, as band, management and fan club all learned how best to engage the fans. Fate is not without a sense of irony, as a low point of the fan club mirrored a peak in the band's early career. It took another ten years for Marillion to recognise fully what a great asset they had, since which point they have not looked back.

WHERE ARE THEY ALL COMING FROM?

Early on, the band realised that their non-mainstream style would need more than a few gigs and a catchy tune to build an audience. Growth by popular vote – the approach typical of '60s and '70s gigging acts - was not the easy route, but it was the most logical. And, for numerous reasons, it worked: Marillion were developing a loyal following even before Fish joined, which stepped up a level when the big man arrived. It was a rare person who could resist the urge to clap when Fish said 'Clap,' or sing when he said 'Sing.'

The music itself was a major factor: it was good, tight and above all, different. Remarks Canadian fan Miles Macmillan, "They were playing a style of music at that time that no one else was playing. It was cool to be into a band that not a whole lot of people knew about." Early fan Dave Rogers comments, "I liked these guys as players, and the songs themselves struck a chord with my male angst, borne of a society that did not seem to care about its youth. In the eyes of many, these really were the days of Market Square Heroes." Peter Gifford agrees, "It felt special and was very exciting to be involved at the start of something. I felt like I was getting in on the ground floor of something new."

Even as the band headed towards the limelight they recognised that the audience was a key element of their strategy to prove something, against the odds. "It was us against the world," remarks John Arnison. Fish's complex lyrics and Mark Wilkinson's detailed covers layered new qualities on top of the music. Recalls fan Miles Macmillan, "They were putting a great deal of work into their concepts and not just slapping together a bunch of tunes." Together with the live show, such elements formed the basis of something that people could really believe in.

KEEPING THE FAITH

The spread-the-word attitude of the early days has been a mainstay throughout Marillion's history. Writes Rick Collins, a fan back in 1983, "This strange desire I have to share the news that I've found something amazing and I'm concerned that no-one else seems to see it... it seems so scary when you listen to born-again Christians and hear that same strange excitement." When the band spread their wings beyond the shores of Britain, this mood of sharing extended first to Germany, Holland and the Nordic countries, crossing the Atlantic with the release of *Misplaced Childhood*.

The euphoria was severely dented in late 1988, however. When Fish left the band the audience split as well, as fans felt forced to declare their allegiance to Fish or the remaining four players. Some found it difficult to see beyond the front man, however good Marillion's collective musical output might have been. Says Pendragon's Peter Gee, "Many felt that without Fish, Marillion were as good as dead." History shows that both parties did manage to pick up where Fish-era Marillion left off: the 'new guy' won over many die-hard fans, succeeding on the strength of his incredible voice and devotion to the cause.

Outside of the hard core, however, Marillion's popularity waned. Whatever the band tried, they could not slow the slide downhill as more casual fans moved on to pastures new. The three albums after *Afraid Of Sunlight*, following the band's departure from EMI, were considered Marillion's wilderness years, made before the band left record labels behind and reached out to their audience on their own terms.

Marillion.com, its liner covered with passport pictures of devoted fans from around the world, represented a new covenant between band and audience. With its follow-up, *Anoraknophobia* in 2001, Marillion did more than discover a new way to fund an album: they relit the fires of their fan base. The message was that, whatever happened in the future, band and fans would be in it together.

Today's fans are a just reward for the decades of hard graft on the part of the band. Marillion have a truly global fan base, with its members coming from as far afield as Brazil and Japan, as well as the more familiar haunts of Northern Europe. "Wherever we have fans, they're in it up to their necks," says Mark

Kelly. For some reason that nobody has ever managed to fathom, none are as devoted as the Dutch. Says H, "The Netherlands has always been a very passionate following."

Not that the location matters that much - fans will come wherever the band decide to play. "I'm amazed and moved by how far people are willing to travel," remarked H. The distance poses the obvious difficulties to further-out pockets of fans. "It's very difficult being a Marillion fan in South America or the Caribbean," comments fan Carmen Julia Quintero. "You practically miss all the concerts, which you can not afford to go to every time, call it time or call it money." But some will manage to make the journey: when the first candlelit dinner with Marillion was announced in Oswestry, the band were amazed not just because of the numbers of people who wanted to attend but also the distances they were prepared to cross.

Marillion fans include teenagers and grandparents, DJs and schoolteachers, barristers and exotic dancers. One-time dancer Heidi Huff became a fan when a suitor gave her a tape of Marillion songs. "'Just For The Record' caught me," she says, "It reminded me of my father." Heidi had a wide repertoire of songs that she used in her act, from 'Lady Nina' to 'Three Minute Boy' (puts a new spin on that one). "That was my way to spread some Marillion joy to the world. It worked!" comments Heidi. With fans like these, you can be sure that the hard core will remain as strongly devoted as ever.

WHAT KIND OF A FAN?

All fans are equal, but some fans are more equal than others... tour followers, for example, who travel the country (or the world!) to see their band perform. Explains Simon Clarke, "You bump into people at gigs and get chatting, they say, 'Are you going to so-and-so-place?' and the whole thing snowballs." An infamous tour-follower called Rob the Vending Machine would hitchhike across the USA, according to another US fan, Bubba. "He smelled real bad, but he knew everything about Marillion and lived on the road in truck stops. He was wild!" From the fan's perspective, travelling to gigs is a lot of fun. "It's an escape from the job, a chance to catch up with people and enjoy the music," comments fan Judith Mitchell.

After the followers come the collectors, who locate and purchase every item of music and memorabilia they can find, however obscure. At the end of a gig, collectors ask for plectrums, drum sticks, set lists... "I've never understood the set lists," laughs Racket Records' Colin Price. "People get hyped, the atmosphere at the front gets so intense." For every obsessive fan, there will always be another who is more obsessive, more diligent. Confided Erik Nielsen, "There's a list of about ten true obsessives that we know, but they're harmless. If the band ever stopped we'd have serious problems however."

From time to time fans will try to step over the line - or at least try to determine whether a line exists. Occasionally, a fan will discover the location of the Racket Club for example, as Colin recalls. "We had a forces guy stationed nearby, well he just turned up. He said, 'Hello; just thought I'd pop in,' and then he was gone again. For every fan that appears, there are a thousand that ask, 'I'm over for a holiday, could I just come over and say hello?' The answer is always a polite, yet firm, 'No.'"

How do band members feel about this level of obsession? Over the years the band's understanding has gone from acceptance through understanding to genuine affection. "We don't really understand it, but for some reason people either live for us or don't like us at all. There aren't many people who just think we're OK. The vibe is so rare and precious, it surprises us - it's a bigger deal than a bit of music." The relationship goes both ways – "I think the fact that the band members are so obviously genuine has a lot to do with the loyalty they engender," says fan John Deveraux. Agrees John Helmer, "Marillion are extremely down to earth - I admire that about them."

On occasion fans will get up to japes – such as Richard Loveridge, who played tracks from the *Less Is More* album from the top of the fourth plinth in Trafalgar Square, on September 1 2009. Or they will record music which reflects their love of the band, as did Egbert Derix in 2012. The Marillos will help out if they feel they can – testing which songs were "plinth-suitable", or in Egbert's case, contributing directly to the album.

Indeed, the relationship can only work if band and fans exist in harmony, thinks sociology lecturer and Marillion fan Martin Johnes, "Fandom is about developing a sense of identity and belonging. This can cause dilemmas for people who like the unfashionable. After all, self-esteem matters. It matters to Marillion and it matters to the fans. No one likes our band so we make a joke and virtue out of being 'fashion unconscious' and claim that the band are only prevented from world domination (or at least critical appreciation) by media prejudice. The band have done the same with their embracing of the anorak."

The fun extends to tribute bands, often set up by fans who are talented musicians in their own right – with names such as Stillmarillion, Misplaced Neighbourhood and Skyline Drifters, which first 'formed' in the late 1990s and have played on frequent occasions since, including the infamous 2001 Garden

Party at Stourbridge Rock Café. "A proper venue with a stage and lights," laughs Drifters (and also Also Eden) front man Rich Harding. "It was an awesome gig to play. It's a great privilege to play such wonderful music with a brilliant bunch of people, for an appreciative audience."

Ultimately, thinks fan Nathan Vines, it's the whole package that matters: "Marillion are different; they have soul in their music, as well as passion and meaning - qualities lacking in many new acts. There is something magic present, a chemistry that is so special to many: 'This band has turned me into what I have become.'" And, with fans like Carmen Julia Quintero, the devotion looks set to continue: "I cannot conceive a day without listening to Marillion or without learning something new about them. It is like the oxygen you need to breathe every day. They are poets, they are lifesavers, inspirational speakers, a motivation to go on without minding the terrifying world around." Enough said!

TWISTING TO TALES

A direct collaboration between fans and band came about when Jersey-based producer and long-time Marillion fan Mark Daghorn first approached John Arnison in April 1996 with the idea of producing a remixed version of *Afraid Of Sunlight*. "I had bought *Market Square Heroes* the day before playing my first gig," says Mark D. "I regarded *Afraid Of Sunlight* as one of the best albums I had ever heard, and the idea of doing new versions of some of those songs excited me beyond anything I can possibly explain!" When requested to send some material, Mark posted a copy of his recently completed *African Mission* album, produced in collaboration with trance mixer (and, in his own words, " a long time secret prog-head") Marc Mitchell, under the moniker The Positive Light.

African Mission ended up in Steve Hogarth's car without him having any idea who it was. "It's not the ordinary kind of trance, it's far deeper," said Steve. Following a number of telephone calls, Steve Rothery invited Mark Daghorn to the Racket Club that November. "I don't think I've ever been as nervous," wrote Mark. He needn't have worried - the band agreed to the pair remixing a couple of tracks from the virtually complete *This Strange Engine*. Mark returned to the Channel Isles triumphant, with vocals and guitar parts from 'Estonia' and A' Man Of A Thousand Faces' in his back pocket.

'Estonia' was remixed in Marc's basement over the Christmas break: "I remember thoughts of vengeful Marillion fans wanting to hurt me; and that

God somehow managed to get the duck-billed platypus together." By January, Mark returned to the mainland with the result. Said H, "We all loved it. And so the experiment was born." "Many management and record company meetings later," according to Mark, the pair got the thumbs up. "We did 'Memory Of Water' next," remembers Mark. Marc recalls how his first child Malachi was conceived during the recording of the track. "It took 6 weeks to complete - 120 tracks of mood-setting music evolving over 4 different sections." That's the track, not the child!

Back in the basement, Marc mixed and Mark produced what Marc considers "Some of my most diverse and best work." Comments Mark, "I think 'Strange Engine' and 'Estonia' are superb, mainly because H's lyrics were just so damn good and painted big pictures for us to work with." Unfortunately, artistic differences and mounting delays eventually caused the pair to break off relations, leaving Mark to finish the album with Tony Turrell, a partner in Mark Daghorn's other project, The Silent Buddhas. "The first fruit of my labours with Mark was 'Eighty Days'," recalls Tony. "We went on to do other remixes of 'Memory Of Water' under our own project name."

Tales From The Engine Room was mastered at Abbey Road Studios by Peter Mew, (also busy with the Marillion remasters series) and finally released on June 22 1998. It was, notably, "The first time that a rock band had an entire album remixed by one remix team." The band loved the album. "It's very impressive - particularly sympathetic to the lyrical feelings," said H. Mark Daghorn had 20 vinyl copies of 'Memory Of Water' pressed and distributed to trance DJs including Paul Oakenfold. Recalls Mark, "The idea was to get grass roots interest in the track as a club single and then release it with the additional mixes." According to Finnish fan Robin Lauren, it became a personal favourite of club DJs, "who between them made it one of the anthems of both the Ibiza scene and New York's The Factory." Paul Oakenfold even called up Mark to say he was playing it. The additional releases didn't happen however – casualties of the changing label situation.

Hard core fans greeted the remix album with interest and scepticism in equal measure. A few were even "devoid of prejudice" as hoped for in H's liner notes. Robin Lauren surmises, "*Tales From The Engine Room* is a weird baby. It's not a (traditional) prog album, it's not a rock album. It's a dance album. I'm not into the dance scene, but I know what I like, and I like this album." "I thought it was superb, and a good way of alerting people to the new Marillion," thinks fan Simon Hoban. "'Estonia', and in particular 'One Fine Day' are better than the originals, and almost prophetic of what Marillion came to do themselves with the dub influences on *DotCom* and *Anorak*." *Tales* offered hope to those quarters of the fan base who had been disappointed with *This Strange Engine*, thinks fan Joe Griffin. "To this day I'm actually more familiar with Tales than I am with *This Strange Engine*. I still prefer the *Tales* version of 'Memory Of Water'." Mark Donald concurs: "I was dubious before hearing it but I think they improved some tracks. Trippy music from my fav band - what more could I ask for?"

The remix experienced no whitewash, however. "The only thing bearable to listen to is 'Estonia'," comments Marc Roy. Adds Bernard Koops, "The whole Positive Light album was something I feared for a long time. I listened to it twice, and now it's gathering dust." Recalls "quite polar" Liam Birch, "'Estonia' was a quick favourite, 'Eighty Days' also sat well with me, giving me a flavour of World Cup Soccer music. 'One Fine Day' and 'This Strange Engine' are okay, if not a bit thin and 'Memory Of Water' is kicking a dead cow when he's down. And don't get me started on 'Face 1004'!" The press were similarly sceptical, seeing the album as a premeditated attempt at reinvention. Quoth the *Dutch Progressive Rock Pages*, "Seemingly they thought that changing the music altogether and targeting the result at the club audiences is the way to ensure themselves of new fans? Who are they kidding?"

One track in particular would go on and on, namely Tony Turrell's Big Beat Mix version of 'Memory Of Water'. "I enjoy that," says Ian, who translated the drum-based track into a full-blown live performance, "It's got a bit of energy. I like stuff that gets you between the eyes." The fans liked it too: "Fantastic!" expounds Rick Collins. Bernard Koops (who was not too comfortable with the album version) comments, "With the integration of this track into the *Radiat10n* tour, my admiration for Marillion was renewed. To play this mix with original instruments as up-tempo as the mix is astounding. I don't believe Marillion have any other song which they play this fast."

HOPE FOR THE FUTURE

Alongside the tour fund, one of the fans' most coordinated efforts was the release of a tribute album, started by Jon Epstein and his then-wife Cathleen in 1998. "It occurred to us that there were quite a few musicians on Freaks, and quite a few popular bands that were into Marillion," recalls Jon. "We spoke about it quite a bit with Fish and Mark before we did it. As I recall Fish was fairly indifferent, H was, well, H, and Mark was into it in a big way."

As demos rolled in, Cathleen and Jon set about putting together an album.

"The response was pretty interesting," says Cathleen, "Some of the demos were amazingly good and some were eye-bulgingly appalling!" Jon also approached a number of better-known artists to participate but unfortunately they wanted payment, and this was to be a charity record (the band and Fish had waived their rights to royalties). Meanwhile, the pair were faced with that age-old difficulty of finding a record deal, before eventually deciding to do it themselves. Jon spoke to fan Gina Achord, at the time working for Surgeland Records as product marketing manager. "Of course, I said yes," remarks Gina.

When Jon and Cathleen found themselves unable to complete the project, they handed the reins over to Gina: "I knew nothing about all the workings and legalities of pressing a CD. Just contacting publishers and waiting to hear back took several months." Marillion were not the only supporters of the charity project, recalls Gina, "Michael Gardiner was a great help with legal matters and offered to help free of charge; the wonderful Carl Glover at Bill Smith Studios agreed to do the artwork free of charge; and Scott Jones and Larry P. Sipes at Bernie Grundman Mastering mastered the CD at no cost. Steve Hogarth had said 'Bernie Grundman is God's own engineer,' so just hearing that made me happy."

Gina was to find the biggest problem had nothing to do with publishers or royalties, but the selection process. Initially the tracks were put online and to the vote, but following the online equivalent of "ballot box stuffing", Gina asked a number of long-time fans and friends to make the decision instead: "I believe I lost a lot of friendships..." Not Alan Walker, who had recommended Interplast as the charity, as well as submitting a number of songs including 'Out Of This World'. "Gina was an absolute joy to work with," he commented.

One contributor was fan Joe Griffin, "My brother Pete picked 'Going Under'. He wanted to make something different from the original, and had been listening to quite a lot of David Bowie's _Earthling_. So he was very into the drum and bass style, and very much into digitally cut-up guitars and vocals. When we were done we submitted the track, and found the deadline had been extended so I started 'Just For the Record'. I was able to use an old drum track of Pete's, lopping off the last eighth note to create a 7/8 drum loop and recruiting my ex-bass player to come in and jam a part out. An interesting side note - Pete told me he heard that when the CD was played for Marillion, Mark Kelly said the Braintree 'Going Under' was better than the original. Don't know whether that's true but it certainly is rewarding if it is." The final result also included songs from John Wesley and Tracey La Barbera (who had sung backing vocals for Wes).

Gina laboured on – the project still required financial backing, for which Gina contacted an old friend, Derek Sivers at CDBaby.com, who set up a pre-order page: "I figured out how much money it would take to press 1,000 CDs, and announced that it was in the hands of the fans. If I received enough money for pre-orders, the CD would be able to be released. Luckily it did!" Then it was just a case of sending the CD for manufacture, and awaiting the results. "I was very pleased with the outcome," remarks Gina. "It took nine months or so from the time I started. I definitely felt like I had given birth to this CD when the boxes arrived on my doorstep."

The *Dutch Progressive Rock Pages* paid tribute to Gina "for the wonderful work she has done," and as for the songs, "Half of the music is good, the other half isn't, at least not if we keep in mind that this is supposed to be a tribute. If you're a big Marillion fan it's still worth checking out!" Fan opinions were equally divided. "I really liked it," says Marc Roy. "A good mix of totally reworked songs, some very faithful renditions and some new twists on familiar themes. 'Beautiful' by Tracy La Barbera is simply breath-taking - sounds like it was written for her."

How did the band feel? "There's some interesting stuff on there," says Steve Rothery, non-committally. H commented, "Obviously it is flattering if someone wants to do it, that's a good feeling. The only way a tribute album could be interesting for me is if an artist I really admire was involved in it, but there aren't that many. If Joni Mitchell sat down and played 'Estonia', I really would like to hear it."

REACHING OUT

From the very beginning, Marillion have actively nurtured a relationship with their fans. Things started simple, with handwritten notes listing forthcoming gigs and contact phone numbers. As the band became more popular, photocopied newsletters gave way to a more professional format; in parallel, the fan club itself emerged, evolved and adapted to meet the needs of band and fans, providing a focal point but also inserting a fan-friendly comfort zone between the two parties.

Throughout its life, the club has used all possible channels of communication, from flyers and phone numbers in the beginning, to the global reach of today's Internet. Since its creation in 1969 the Internet has become a part of life, its impact felt across the globe as a conduit for all kinds of communications including, for some, discussion of their favourite band. At first email and Usenet news were used to share opinions, then interactive communications such as IRC chat evolved. Finally, in the early '90s, the Internet found its 'killer app' in the form of the World Wide Web.

We all know that Marillion have a unique relationship with their fans, but it is with the Web that they managed to be truly ground-breaking.

AN INTERNATIONAL WEB

Marillion's fan club evolved rather than being created. Mick Pointer's girlfriend Stef Jeffries was first to take up promotional duties, passing the baton to fan Tim Hollings when she became too busy. Early newsletters consisted of a handwritten, photocopied sheet with the occasional illustration provided by whoever wanted to draw it. Stef eventually took over from Tim, continuing even after Mick left the band. "She carried on for about a year," says Mick. "That made for a nice, healthy atmosphere!"

When Stef left in 1983 another fan, named Angie, took over and held the post until 1987 – so it appeared. "When the real Angie left, we kept the name," says John Arnison. Angie was helped by various people including John himself, and his assistant Ann Lawler. By the time of 'Incommunicado', Angie was in reality Patsy Smith, who was then replaced by a (female) New Zealander called Bernie. When she went back to the Antipodes, the name 'Bernie' remained and Jo Rothery, Steve's wife took over. Says Steve, "It was such a shame - people wrote saying they wanted to meet him at gigs!" Jo managed to keep up the momentum for five years before throwing in the towel.

For many years the fan club offered little more than a communications channel. "Fan clubs weren't as much of a tool as they are now," remarks John, but by 1994 it was clear that more could be done. The task of growing the fan club beyond an information source fell to fans Bonnie Alberts and Wayne Kensett, who quickly accepted the offer of assistance from long-time fan Lucy Jordache. Andy Rotherham was recruited the same year, then James Fishwick met the team at the launch party for *Afraid Of Sunlight* and he too was recruited. "I was conned!" he laughs. Rob Crossland's involvement kicked off as he helped typeset the magazine for Bonnie and Wayne. And thus, The Web team came into existence.

"It was all pretty low-tech," recalls helper Mark Nelson: "In those days, all the membership records were held on index cards. All the address labels were handwritten, with the amount of labels giving the indication of when your membership renewal was due. If an address change happened mid-membership, it meant more labels. It was enough to make you weep tears of gratitude when some kind soul actually included their own pre-written labels."

Across the pond, the Web North America started life as an informal structure during the *Holidays In Eden* period, as organiser Dan Sherman explains, "There was a need to strengthen the communication between the band and American fans, as the fan base was growing due to a radio promotion from IRS records." Dan started the Web USA with his wife Dana, which was formally adopted during the *Brave* tour. As Steve H commented, "We're very pleased with the job that Dan does, and we're happy to remain close to him. He's easy to work with, and never gets in the way of our work. He's a gentleman."

From the outset however, John Arnison's goal was for fan clubs to provide an air gap. "John used to have a problem with the fans - they always wanted much more than he wanted to give," says Pete Trewavas. Concurs Andy Rotherham, "The idea was that if the fan club sank, then the band wouldn't be liable." This was not ideal – the resulting breakdowns in communication culminated in an unforgivable error in 1997, that members were not informed about the tour fund. They could neither donate nor, as a result, gain access to the much-coveted, limited edition CD.

When Marillion took the reins in 1998, the fan club was one of the first things to change. After some enquiries, a team was drawn up to include Andy Rotherham and James Fishwick, Rob and Alexis Crossland, Simon Clarke and Vicki Harding. "I answered the phone and it was Mark Kelly," says Andy, who recalls a meeting at the Racket Club a week or so later. "When we went, it was all very surreal. H sat down between myself and Vicki, asked who everyone was and we got down to business."

The Web US also became a casualty of the band's Castle years and the absence of promotion that came with it. "We were left with only a few hundred members, producing a magazine better than any of the European ones," says Dan. Finally, in spring 1998 Dan and Dana decided to call it a day. "I feel we left amicably, I turned over the database and every dollar left in the bank account." A gent to the end.

Over the years a number of fan clubs sprung up in other countries, including Blue Angel in France, Real to Read in Italy, and organisations in Spain, Germany and Holland. Over time these have been subsumed into international arms of The Web, each running its own affairs. Marillion fan clubs in Europe often have a wider remit than with many bands. "The clubs are involved in organising gigs, particularly in Germany and Spain," said Racket Records' Erik Nielsen. "They find the venues, they know them better than we do."

While the personnel has continued to change over the years, the core Web team has continued pretty much in the same vein, distinguished by its commitment to helping the band and their fans work in harmony. Replacing the hand-written notes is a full-colour quarterly magazine, that much has changed – but the current team - Andy, Anne, Fraser, Jim, Lynne, Pete, Simon and Stuart - work as tirelessly as ever.

THANK GOD FOR THE INTERNET

For tech-savvy Marillion fans, life before the World Wide Web meant using the UUCP protocol as a primal form of electronic communication. Here is the first recorded news item on the Internet concerning Marillion, which is typical of its era.

Newsgroups: net.music Subject: Another Genesis ??
Posted: Fri Jul 1 18:49:21 1983 GREAT! FANTASTIC! EXCELLENT!
A new group just hit the US from England, and they are a great relief from the commercial blues.
Who is it you ask????
Its Marillion - Script for a jester's tear. They may be a genesis rip off but their damn good at it. In fact they are much better that the current genesis.
The singer named Fish, has a voice some where between Gabriel and Collins.
At times he sound almost like Gabriel.
The band has an early genesis sound but with an 80's twist.
I would rate this album a 8 on the 1 - 10 scale. (only the WALL gets a ten because of its perfection).

Eventually Marillion gained sufficient fans to deserve their own news feed: alt.music.marillion, which was reputed to be not for the faint-hearted. When email arrived on the scene it yielded a different, more direct form of fan communication. Fan Graham Orndorff started the Freaks mailing list in 1990 but, bizarrely, when he lost interest and withdrew from the scene, nobody could leave. As fan, early subscriber and Marillion FAQ authority Jeroen Schipper noted, "(Un)subscribing was no longer possible as it was not automated but done by Graham himself. This runaway list went on for quite a while, but died a slow death."

In September 1992, Ken Bibb started a new Freaks list at bnf.com, moved in August 1994 to arastar.com. It was about this time that Mark Kelly was introduced to the list by fan Miranda Benson. "She phoned the studio at Parr

Street while we were recording *Brave*," says Mark. "How she knew we were there, I don't know. She asked me if I knew about the Freaks list and offered to show me some printouts. A couple of months later I subscribed. They didn't know that band members were reading it." Eventually the temptation to post a message became too much to resist, and Mark became a regular contributor. "I lurked for about two years, then one day I decided to blow my cover," he said. "I don't even remember why, I'm sure someone said something outrageous that I felt I needed to address or something…" Indeed, one of Mark's posts prompted a response from Jeff Pelletier and catalysed the 1997 USA tour fund. Other active posters have included Steve Rothery, Fish, Mark Wilkinson and John Wesley.

By the late 1990s the Freaks list had become an invaluable resource for information and discussion. Max Rael remarks, "In 1999 I happened to look up Marillion on the Internet… a quick look around the site led to me joining the Freaks list just to see what it was like. Everyone was talking about the new album *Marillion.com* so I went out and got it." Recalls fan Mike Rengel, "I stumbled across the Freaks list and found out that I'd just missed a US tour, and that something called a 'tour fund' was winding down. I stayed on Freaks and I haven't looked back." For offshore fans, like John Stevens in Bermuda, Freaks was a lifeline: "Bermuda is a bit of a cultural backwater if your tastes run anything to the right or left of mainstream." At the height of Freaks, it was possible to win a most frequent poster crown – held at one point by Bruno Galli, who posted 93 messages in one month. "I got flamed a lot for that," he laughs.

Freaks is no longer the online community for fans of Marillion and Fish. Initially replaced by Yahoo! group FishFans for fans of Fish (the clue's in the name) and The Opium Den for the 'current line up' of Marillion, the world of social networking and Marillion's own online forum have largely replaced what was an essential piece of the Marillion jigsaw. Leaving the last word to US fan Mike Stoor, "I got a computer in the Spring of 1998 and first order of business was subscribing to Freaks. Not only could I keep up with the news in both camps, I could order without relying on the pathetic music stores in Minnesota. It was about this time I fired off a drunken thank-you to Freaks for the camaraderie signing off with 'Thank God for the Internet', still waiting for the credit on that one."

FROM THE WEB TO WEB

As well as getting the hang of email lists, by the mid-'90s the band were also starting to grasp the potential of the wider Internet. As Jeroen Schipper (who registered the Marillion.com domain in December 1996) recalls, "The first band member I talked to about it was Mark Kelly. He already saw its importance and supported me in setting up the first Web Online website. He provided me with info and other stuff like sound samples from his keyboards. That helped a lot in making the site a success." As the band were building up to leaving the Castle label, the need to engage with fans drove greater interest: the following year, Erik Nielsen was recruited to build a 'proper' Web site, first registering Marillion.co.uk and then taking over Marillion.com. "The band wanted to call the next album *Marillion.com* when *Radiat10n* came out," explains Erik."

Marillion's Web site has gone through several incarnations since this time, and the rest of the world has had plenty of time to catch up both with the site and the spirit it represents. In a review of the album *Marillion.com* a journalist commented, "Marillion have embraced the Internet not as new technology, which it isn't, but as new culture, which it still is." Marillion remain at the forefront, adopting each new wave of Web-based technology as it happens, from Myspace and YouTube to Twitter and Facebook. "Without the Internet, the future of the band is less sure," notes Mark Kelly. A sobering thought... Thank God indeed.

SOLO IN THE GAME

While Marillion have achieved a great deal, they remain a close-knit, yet disparate, set of personalities each with their own stories. Fish and Mick, Ian and Mark, Pete, Rothers and H are all inextricably linked with the Marillion story. Where did they come from, what led them to decide on a life of music and how have they spent their time outside the band?

FISH

The big man, the charismatic Scot, the poet, the hero, the assassin – Fish has been called many things. In 1984 he described himself as a hedonist, attracted to the fringe activities of life, "The human magpie collecting things, collecting experiences," unconfident and yet always ready with his mouth, "I'm a vicious bastard with my tongue!" Restless, never comfortable stuck in any one place, yet still yearning for the predictability of home, Fish's story was never going to be the path of least resistance.

A gawky, shy lad whose vocal prowess was overshadowed by his inability to toe the line, Dalkeith-born Derek William Dick was not an obvious candidate for the role of charismatic front man. When his peers found him unable to swagger in the appropriate manner at school, they ridiculed him for his size. Eventually he learned to deal with the abuse through humour. "It's the Les Dawson thing," he commented. "There were a lot of people laughing at me and I was really hurt, so I learnt that if you can turn that and make them laugh with you, you conquer them with a smile."

Neither was school an appropriate seed-bed for the poetry that would make him famous. "I felt very self-conscious when I wrote anything down," he remarked. "I felt as though I was betraying something." Still, he loved to sing, joining the school choir and debuting with two solos at Donaldson's School for the Deaf. "I sang 'Ye Banks And Braes' and 'St. Lucia'," he recalled. "I was fired for not attending rehearsals. I still have the same problem!"

At home, Derek's musical journey was boosted when he picked up The Kinks' 'Lola' at a jumble sale. "I immediately fell in love with the lyrics and the ability to tell a story through song," he said. When he wasn't off watching his football team, Hibernian FC, he was listening to the prog giants Genesis and King Crimson, in parallel with more mainstream T-Rex, Elton John, Deep Purple and Paul McCartney. "I never felt part of any tribe and I could get a kick out of Led Zeppelin as much as Carole King," he later remarked.

At 18 Derek turned his back on education, trying a variety of jobs (notably with the Forestry Commission) before recognising his path lay elsewhere. It was in this phase that he gained his nickname, as he made maximum use of the bath facilities offered by a landlady. "She only allowed me one bath a week and on any other night I had to pay an extra 20 pence. On my 'free' night I used to stay in the bathroom for up to two hours," he recalled. A visiting friend coined the name: "He asked if I was some sort of fish and as I moved on and into different town and professions, the name stuck. With a real name of Derek William Dick, it quickly became necessary to find a nickname."

While confidence was not his strong point, the man known as Fish gained enough courage to indulge his passion for singing. He'd also started to consider acting, but "I quickly found it was easier to get a singing job than an acting job!" While still a forestry worker, he failed an audition for Not Quite Red Fox, whose bassist/vocalist had been approached in March 1980 to replace a chap called Doug Irvine in some Aylesbury band. Finally, at the age of 22, Fish joined a covers band called Blewitt and moved down to Galashiels, much to the chagrin of his parents who had hoped for a sensible future for their son.

Blewitt's set included material from Steely Dan and the Average White Band, a good mix for Fish's broad tastes. His first night at the Golden Lion was below par, however. Stage nerves led to alcohol-based calming measures, and Fish took the floor a bit the worse for wear. "I threw up over my all-white outfit of Indian cotton shirt and flared trousers as soon as the gig finished." He nearly got the boot, but not for his behaviour. "We should have sacked him. He sung really bad that night," commented guitarist Frank Usher, who helped Fish develop his vocal capabilities. "He kept on pushing," recalls Fish.

With confidence increasing, Fish headed for an audition with the Stone Dome Band in Retford, Nottinghamshire. As soon as he got the gig he gave up his job and moved down, initially staying with bassist Diz Minnitt's parents. The pair quit shortly afterwards, moving to the potentially more lucrative Cambridge. They spent a few months living at a girls' hall of residence ("I remember thinking it strange that no-one minded" says Diz), going to less-than-welcoming parties including a formal dinner with both Fish and Diz in full face makeup ("To wind up the hoi polloi," according to Fish), and attempting to form a band before eventually retreating north of the border.

As the pair moved to Ettrick Bridge and signed on, they managed to convince a holiday cottage-owner that they were a band called Sirius. "Fish said we needed somewhere to write over the winter," smiles Diz. Fish returned to Blewitt that November and played a total of 15 gigs; in the meantime, they got on with their hard-up, depressing lives. "We felt completely isolated. Our lifestyle got so totally out of sync, we went to bed at 5am and got up at 5pm," says Diz. There was the occasional, surreal high point – such as when the hapless pair were transporting a PA system to Edinburgh and had to pick up a load of cuddly toy penguins. "We popped in on a mate on the way back and skinned up... later we were trying to drive home in a weird state with a truck full of penguins!"

Eventually, however, Fish and Diz realised they'd reached the very bottom. 'We have to do something', said Fish, before heading out to buy a copy of *Musicians Only*. One ad was for a vocalist/bassist and included an Aylesbury phone number, which Diz was quick to call. "I was almost salesman-like, it just felt absolutely right." The pair sent a tape with Fish singing in Blewitt and Diz playing with the Stone Dome Band. "He sang the 'Guards of Magog' section from 'Supper's Ready', a couple of Yes tracks, something by Peter Gabriel and a version of 'Garden Party'," recalls Diz. In the return post, Mick sent 'Lady Fantasy' and 'Close'.

It was like coming home. Fish's first reaction to Steve Rothery's fretwork was, "Fuck, this guitarist is brilliant!" Unabashed, the vocalist set about working one of his existing lyrics around the piece, which he titled 'The Web'. Following a final gig with Blewitt, supporting Alexis Korner in Melrose on December 13 1980, Fish and Diz sold up, signed off and, on New Year's Eve, drove south once again. Notes Fish, "We decided, 'This is what we have to do.' We burned our bridges behind us."

And that was that. Until, some eight years later, Fish found himself independent of a band once again.

SO HERE I AM ONCE MORE

When Fish quit Marillion, many thought it was the end both of his career and the band he left behind. Yet there was more to the man than one musical entity. Almost immediately following the split, he and his wife Tamara relocated from Gerrards Cross to Scotland, a decision helped along when his parents found an old farmhouse in Haddington. Spittalrig Farm had a number of outbuildings suitable for use as a rehearsal rooms; furthermore it was cheap, freeing Fish of any debts and leaving him enough to live on while he got a musical team together.

First to arrive was keyboard player Mickey Simmons, who Fish had met through fellow Buckinghamshire resident, Mike Oldfield. "Bringing an awareness of melody and hook-lines, Mickey guided me down the first avenue of solo creations," Fish remarked. Close friend and engineer Andy Field also stuck with the singer. Things were still open enough between Fish, Rothers and Ian for him to ask the pair if they wanted to participate. "Steve quite rightly turned my offer down, as did Ian, as they felt that for us to be working together so soon would be detrimental to both our new careers," Fish commented.

With John Cavanagh, a senior EMI executive, agreeing to become manager, in November 1988 Fish went on the hunt for a producer. First choice was Chris Kimsey but he was tied up with the Rolling Stones (with *Steel Wheels*). In the end Fish selected Jon Kelly, who had worked with The Damned and Kate Bush. According to fan Andy McIntosh, "What tipped the balance was his work with Deacon Blue." Recording began in May 1989 at the Townhouse Studios in London. "In retrospect I don't think Chris would have been the right man," Fish commented later, "I needed to get away from the Marillion connection."

By August the album was complete. Mark Wilkinson produced the cover, not least because it was already started - the artwork had been planned for Marillion's fifth studio album. Says Mark, "I had dealt with Fish 99% of the time on the Marillion cover designs - it seemed natural to carry on that relationship." Although the album was ready, EMI held back on its release as Marillion's album had just been finished. Explains Fish, "EMI didn't want to go head to head; they thought my profile was bigger so they asked us to put the release back a few months."

The hiatus gave Fish and Mark Wilkinson a chance to see the cover for Marillion's new album. It was never the intention to insult the artist or his icons, according to Mark Kelly, "We merely wanted to show some continuity with the past, while showing that we were moving on." From Mark Wilkinson's perspective, his imagery was being trashed: a clown sinking in a pond and a jester vanishing in the sand, with a solitary magpie feather floating down. It didn't take long to add some subtle enhancements to his own artwork. Scrapped next to the hill was a white Porsche (Steve Rothery drove one), while around the fire sat two tramps, with the faces of Kelly and Arnison. "It was mischievous... but so was having my clown from *Fugazi* drowning in a muddy pool," says Mark Wilkinson, for whom the water has long passed under the bridge. Nether was Mark Kelly too amused, at the time. "I thought, bloody cheek!" he says. "I told EMI I wanted all the albums destroyed." A compromise was reached, with the next batch having the tramps' faces painted out.

With the album *Vigil In A Wilderness Of Mirrors* finished, Fish quickly booked a series of dates in his homeland. "I hadn't been on the road for a while, I wanted to get out there and do a pub tour," he says. "Financially it was a fucking disaster, but in terms of confidence-boosting it was immense." He performed with Robin Boult and Frank Usher, with whom he still had good relationships. Says Robin, "Playing the solo stuff was great, but playing the Marillion stuff was different, it felt like being in a covers band but not." Adds Fish, "The costumes were terrible. People said we looked like extras from *Blake's Seven*, I came across it on satellite and cringed." The tour was a boost for the fans, preparing the ground for the album and two singles.

'State Of Mind' was released on October 16, reaching No. 32 in the UK charts. Fish's Christmas single, 'Big Wedge' followed it up but fans had to wait until January 29 to buy the album. Despite, or perhaps because it was a departure from Fish's immediate past, it was generally well received. Steve Rothery described the album as, "Interesting, if a little poppy for my tastes." The follow-up single 'A Gentleman's Excuse Me', was released on March 11, achieving a respectable 30th position. The tour proper also started in March; on July 9, Fish played to a packed audience at The Royal Albert Hall.

Attending the Royal Concert Hall gig in Nottingham on March 31, were fan Andy McIntosh and his then-fiancée, Lesley. "It was the first time I'd managed to get Lesley to come to a gig – it was her very first gig of any kind. The show was a couple of months before we were due to be married and, unbeknown to Lesley, I had written to Fish and asked if he could dedicate a song," he says. "The set had a good mix of old and new and everyone was enjoying the show, but as it went on without the dedication I was beginning to get a little disappointed. The main set ended with 'Heart Of Lothian' and the band left the stage to thunderous applause. After a few minutes the band returned and Fish had a bit of paper clutched in his hand. He introduced the first encore and checking with his bit of paper dedicated 'Cliché' to us. Fish had asked whereabouts in the hall we were and I'd sheepishly raised my hand only to find that we were instantly 'bathed in the spotlight's glare'. Apart from going beetroot red with embarrassment it was great to hear the best wishes for our coming wedding and the rest of the encores seemed to float by."

Among the acknowledgements on the *Vigil* album cover was a thank you to Marillion, "for showing me the hill". But it was a false summit. Not only had he kicked off legal action against his former cohorts ("It was like getting divorced with four women at the same time"), he was also being held in breach of contract by EMI due to a bluff, intended to shock the record company into submission. The resulting injunction prevented Fish from releasing albums for almost a year; he went AWOL for the duration of the case, which he eventually lost due to lack of funds. "I had to leave the table, tail between my legs and a huge legal bill to follow," recalled Fish. He was also advised to settle with his ex-band mates.

Coupled with what was "an over-ambitious tour" with musicians being paid session rates and the on-going work to turn the farm's outhouses into a fully-fledged studio. Fish was broke again, and broken.

EXILE IN THE WILDERNESS

Despite the feelings of "defeat and betrayal" that accompanied the failed court cases, the only way was up. While seemingly productive talks with a new label, Polydor, had not yet resulted in that all-important signing, at least he did have a recording studio. Chris Kimsey's name was in the frame again, with the slight complication that Chris had also been tapped to produce *Holidays In Eden*. Working on both projects was not an option: "To have the albums stamped with the same production would destroy two years work on both parts," commented Fish. In the end, time was the decider. Chris had a live album to produce for the Stones in February 1991, Marillion had booked the slot before, and Fish's material was planned for late April. "Marillion still hadn't enough songs, in Chris's opinion, to start as they intended in January," recalls Fish. "This time the Stones schedule came in my favour - a neat coincidence."

Chris brought engineer Thomas Stiehler with him to Spittalrig, recreating the *Misplaced Childhood* production team from five years before. Unfortunately however, the success of Berlin was still too fresh. "Chris tried to work like he did with *Misplaced Childhood*," explains Thomas – not, looking back, a good idea. Says Chris, "Musically, I missed Marillion. In hindsight I was trying to make a Marillion album."

The new studio was plagued with problems and the album itself didn't quite gel - the songs drew on a mixture of styles but, according to Fish, "never got into a particular groove or locked into a direction." Still *Internal Exile* came together and, with a deal freshly inked with Polydor, was released to a still-expectant audience. On board was David Munns, previously responsible for marketing Marillion at EMI. "His enthusiasm is infectious and his belief in me as an artist is undeniable!" Fish wrote. The new label didn't live up to expectations, however: "They rushed the album out with my acquiescence, resulting in a fractured promotion campaign and disappointing sales." Indeed - its first single, 'Internal Exile', made the top 40 for one week only.

An exacerbating factor was the sentiment of the album. The Scottish nationalism already rising during Fish's Marillion days was well and truly at the fore, says Thomas Stiehler, "Some people said that Fish went too Scottish, the English companies didn't like it." Neither did many fans. "It just didn't sell," commented Fish. To add insult to injury, the tour to accompany the album was, simply "Disastrous!" according to Fish. "The UK promoter [Bandstand] went bankrupt just as it was about to kick off." It was an inauspicious start for the new production manager known only as Yatta.

Feeling both financially and creatively at a low ebb, Fish returned to the idea he'd had in 1985: recording the songs of others seemed to be more achievable than developing new material. "It was one of those moments, like when a coyote gets his leg caught in a trap, something I had to do," he remarks. Somehow Fish managed to convince Polydor and the covers album *Songs From The Mirror* was recorded in summer 1992.

Sadly, during the recording, Andy Field finally passed away. The funeral saw a brief reunion with old band members. "I was quite cut up, he was a great bloke and we'd had some fantastic times together," says Pete. Adds Ian, "Up until that point, I'd never been around death; he was my drum roadie, crew boss. Andy was very old school, he showed people respect.'"

Songs From The Mirror bombed on its release in January 1993, leaving a crater most would not have attempted to crawl out of. The record deal was over; Mickey Simmonds went to work with Mike Oldfield ("He paid better than I could," says Fish); and John Cavanagh was laid off. "It was a pretty bleak period," says Fish. Indeed, he even went as far as saying that recording the album, "...was the worst decision I have ever made."

All was not lost, however. The accompanying tour made a profit, and Fish had started to find some creative acorns, mainly rooted in his cynical feelings towards the music industry. Furthermore, *Songs From The Mirror* had enabled a catharsis. "The album was a turning point for me as an artist," Fish commented. "By delving into my past and the influences that had made me what I was, I rediscovered myself and the magic that had brought me here in the first place."

LABEL FREE

Whoever held the key to Fish's success, it was becoming all too clear that it wouldn't be a record executive. Following a session with a spirit medium who "passed on a message from my grandfather," Fish decided to form a record company – called Dick Brothers, after his forebears' motor business. Even as plans for the next album were taking shape, five "official bootleg" releases were made, including *Uncle Fish And The Crypt Creepers*. According to Fish, these were aimed at providing an income and, he said, "A quality alternative to the illegal bootlegs that plagued my career."

By the time *Suits* came into being, the cynical tone of the subject matter had been tempered. Failure was not an option. "There was a lot of pressure because I was using the Dick Brothers name," says Fish. Back on board was *Songs* producer James Cassidy, who co-wrote many of the songs. One of James's previous projects, *War Of The Worlds* was having a little too much influence, comments Fish, "I didn't yet have the maturity to know when to stop. 'Jumpsuit City' goes on far too long."

Two months before the release of *Suits* came live album *Sushi*, supported immediately by a tour including a 14-date HMV in-store promotion - Fish resorting to his skills as a promoter, to ensure the bills could be paid. The touring paid off, not least enabling Fish and his band to rehearse the new material. "Touring led to a tightness in the band not often found in a session musician-based outfit," Fish recalls. *Suits* was released May 16 1994, followed by more dates, both electric and acoustic.

Indeed, with the follow-up release of two 'Best Of' albums in 1995, *Yin* and *Yang*, Fish managed to stay on the road for nearly two years. However in this period no new words were written, no music was considered or performed apart from the back catalogue. It was in 1996 that Fish once again found his muse, following a tour of Bosnia playing to the UNIFOR troops. Everything Fish had ever written about the horrors of war, from 'Forgotten Sons' to 'Fugazi' and 'White Russian' was brought to life in those few short weeks. "I had to get the experiences onto paper, or crack up through the intensity," Fish recalls.

Soon after, he was back in the studio recording what was to become *Sunsets On Empire*. Fish had been introduced to Steven Wilson, lead singer of Porcupine Tree and a mixer and producer in his own right. Steven explains, "Fish contacted me through our mutual publishing company Hit And Run/Charisma. He had heard some of my albums and was actually more interested in what I was doing with No-Man (using break beats and trip hop rhythms but combining them with rock)." Despite what Fish described as a healthy friction, the pair co-wrote a number of songs that earned the label "progressive nouveau" as they brought Fish bang up to date.

Fish was delighted with the overall result, widely lauded as a return to form. "A lot of people have been saying it's the best thing I have done so far," he remarked. Despite an 18-month, 115-date promotional tour of 22 countries including the USA, and a number of favourable reviews, the album didn't make the money it was expected to make and the tour made a major loss. "It was an absolute fucking nightmare," Fish commented.

Fish remained determined to succeed. The breakthrough came in May 1997, when Miles Copeland invited him to participate in a song-writing retreat with 23 others, at Château Marouatte in France - the same haunt where Marillion had recorded *Brave*. "I was at my lowest point and it gave me the incentive to get up and do it again." Fish met a number of established songwriters, such as Sam Brown and Liz Antwi (who later sang the backing vocals on a version of 'Just Good Friends'). "The whole Marouatte session gave me the chance to flex my muscles, it was like a songwriter's gym," reflected Fish. With six songs (including 'Incomplete', 'Tumbledown' and 'Chasing Miss Pretty') and "a sackful of confidence," he returned to base.

Dick Bros was struggling. "It had no expertise whatsoever. We were just relying on luck and taking gambles," he said. On his return from France, Fish closed the label and residential studio business and signed a deal with Roadrunner for a new album – *Raingods With Zippos*. The album was notable for its collaborations - with Mickey Simmonds, Steven Wilson and Robin Boult, Rick Astley and Paul Thorn – and culminated in the 25-minute, epic highlight, 'Plague Of Ghosts', based on a 20-minute "ambient piece" written by Tony Turrell and Mark Daghorn. Claiming it to be the track of which he was most proud in his entire career, Fish boasted, "It's as valid to a 14-year old dance music fan, as to the fans of the old Marillion prog stuff."

With the Roadrunner deal settled the album was released in April 1999. "Easily the best thing I have ever done, the reviews were fantastic!" Fish remarked. Difficulties with Roadrunner led to Fish once again setting out on his own, but by now he was more in control. "There's a change in me now," he commented. "Before, I think my life revolved around our music. Now I think the music revolves around my life."

Touring the album wasn't any easier, however. "Just about everything that could go wrong did go wrong. The production manager was lying in hospital and they were talking about amputating his arm because of a blood infection, and I was laid up with a viral infection for six weeks. There were Fisher Price PA systems. But I had to keep going," he said. Not helping, in Fish's own words, was his home situation – his marriage to German model Tamara Nowy was being blown towards the rocks.

Still, the number of positives in Fish's life was increasing. Having lost his acting cherry back in 1991 (in the BBC thriller *Jute City*), he landed roles in The Bill and, excitingly, *The Young Persons Guide to Becoming a Rock Star*. While joking, "I'm glad I'm not depending on it for a living," it was nonetheless a more central part of his life. He was also using his gift of the gab to good effect as a DJ, presenting a show every Sunday evening on Scotland's Radio Forth. "Jay Crawford was a good friend, he'd been after me to do a rock show for years," says Fish.

And meanwhile, relations were thawing with his old band. On April 9 1999, when Steve Rothery turned up at a Fish gig it was only a matter of time before he got up to play. The song was 'Sugar Mice', says Steve, "I'd heard about his range problems, but I couldn't just play it in a different key. He did an OK job though - at least as good as he was on the *Clutching* tour!"

The topic of a reunion gig was even discussed, having been rejected at the time EMI released the *Best Of Both Worlds* compilation back in 1997. Recalled Fish, "Arnison came back to me and said, 'Come out without your band; Marillion'll learn some of your solo stuff.' I declined because it'd look like I was going back to Marillion." Once again, Fish proposed a two-band solution, with each playing a set before some joint material. "If it worked maybe we could write an album together, not even calling it Marillion, just elevating ourselves together. But the band answer was no," he said.

SO FELLINI

With the creation of his new record label Chocolate Frog Records, Fish once again took matters into his own hands. Former Marillion support John Wesley was recommended by Mark Daghorn, who produced Wes's second album *The Emperor Falls*. "Mark found out Fish was looking for a guitar player," remembers Wes. "Fish called up Mark Kelly and Steve Rothery, they said, 'Go for it,', so Fish called me up and I was hired." The album was recognised as progressive – but not in that way. "Keeping up with all those nonce bands regurgitating all that stuff from the '70s? Not my scene," he remarked. "*Fellini Days* is taking the light and shade, sampling the dramatic Federico Fellini stuff, taking blues and putting it next to Spanish guitar, using Mexican trumpets..."

A fan convention in Haddington accompanied the release in the autumn of 2001, followed by a worldwide tour covering venues across Europe and South America. "How can one describe a weekend like this?" said fan Andreas Dahl of the convention. "Monks Muir, the den of iniquity, the home of debauchery, Tikifour... no five star suite in the world can match this place. Andy's party tent, the pleasure dome, the scene of felonious karaoke, experienced drinking, uncountable cheers, perfumed cigarettes and lurkers in shadows. The beach party, a dream fulfilled, the vision I've had in my head for most of the year materialised and the result exceeded my wildest imaginations. The gigs, my first time at St Mary's, a magical venue, send shivers down my spine. The dancing beams of the Fidra lighthouse; I now know exactly what Fish means. Watching a video EP in a certain singer's TV room, singing along and miraculously not being thrown out. The stars, can't forget the stars, the sky was magnificent, the veil of the Milky Way for all to see. Fish walking sombrely amongst the gravestones..."

Fish played over a hundred gigs across 2001 and 2002, interspersed with acting credits for TV and film appearances. Notable for a clutch of reasons was his role as 'Old Nick' in the film *Nine Dead Gay Guys*. "I was scared that I'd be stereotyped as a six foot five, drunken, hard man jock, so I might as well get typecast as a great big gay!" he said. While the film didn't do so well at the box office, it sold out its Cannes premiere and won Festival Prize at Montreal's 'Just For Laughs' comedy film festival.

By 2003 it was time to go back to the studio. Released in December 2003, the album *Field of Crows*, based on looking back at a neglected battlefield, was seen to symbolise an artist who had found a new musical groove. "This is the record that sees him become an artist fully equipped for the modern age," said *Classic Rock*'s Malcolm Dome. A European tour followed, taking Fish through to the summer – but he still found time to appear in John Maybury's film *The Jacket* alongside Keira Knightley and Kris Kristofferson.

Together with back-catalogue releases such as the *Curtain Call* box set, all should have been going very well indeed – had it not been for the back-office misdemeanours of Fish's administrative assistant. As the sorry tale of Kim Waring unfolded, Fish calculated losses amounting to tens of thousands of pounds – not to mention the knock-on effects on disgruntled fans not receiving their merchandise. "On *Field of Crows* there was a discrepancy of over 1700 albums unaccounted for and on *Curtain Call* there were 100 units missing," he said. In December 2005 he successfully sued his former employee for £68,000 plus £100,000 in damages. "No money can compensate for the damage and the hurt she has caused to me and my daughter. I feel foolish and betrayed but a lot wiser for the experience and can only apologise to the fans for having backed this person."

Once again, Fish shook himself off and carried on. Having toured *Misplaced Childhood* on both sides of the Atlantic to celebrate its twentieth anniversary in 2005, he headed out again in 2006 before setting down with Steve Vantsis to write a new album, *13th Star*, which was released in September 2007. Originally touted as a love letter to his fiancée, Heather Findlay, when the marriage was called off that June, Fish put all of his hurt into what is generally seen as his best work in years. "Quite simply, this is a work of art... and if you want a shorter description then I can think of only one word. Masterpiece," wrote fan and reviewer Dean Pedley. And, wrote Colin Somerville in *The Scotsman*, "Fish has finally made an album to eclipse Marillion's finer moments and easily the best of his solo career."

Today's Fish is older, undoubtedly wiser and yet still treading the lines of paradox. He has won awards for his *Fish on Fridays* radio show on Planet Rock, another movie – *Electric Man* – is complete, and following a scare about a growth on his throat (it was benign), his voice is sounding better than ever. Following a highly successful convention in Leamington in 2009 a repeat is planned, at which fans will be treated to an outing of the ultimate epic – 'Grendel'. And meanwhile, a new album *Feast Of Consequences*, again on the theme of war, is nearing completion.

Perhaps the most intriguing news came back in 2009, when Fish announced he would be releasing his autobiography. "It's going to be an interesting read, that's for sure," he said. "I have always liked writing. People forget that I'm not a musician, I am a lyricist." The big man certainly has a story to tell. On July 17 2012 Fish opened the market square in Galashiels, into the pavement of which had been carved the lyrics to the 1985 hit 'Kayleigh'. "Do you remember the cherry blossom in the market square?" they asked. Fish might still be trying to write that love song, but his words will be preserved for all time.

STEVE HOGARTH

Steve Hogarth (not the name on his birth certificate, but what he's always been called) caught the music bug early. "I was in a choir when I was a kid. I'd always loved to sing, especially on my own in echoey places. I'd stay behind after school sometimes and sing in the corridors of the empty school to myself for the sheer joy of hearing it," he said. His epiphany came in 1973 when, at the age of 17, he went to see his first gig, Deep Purple at Sheffield City Hall, on the *Machine Head* tour. "It was inspirational. I went from really loving the music, to actually wanting to be one of the people on the stage," he remarked. "This is what I should do! What's the point of doing anything else?" A few weeks later, he talked his parents into getting a piano.

Steve attended Danum Grammar School for boys in Armthorpe. A suburb of miners' town Doncaster, Armthorpe was a stronghold of leader Arthur Scargill. "Doncaster was conservative, as in with entrenched views of how to fit in with 'normal' working class fashions and prejudices," says Steve. "I was being beaten up on a fairly regular basis – I used to wear a lot of pink even in those days." Steve's early musical tastes were diverse, including a measure of prog. "I was a big fan of Yes, I think Yes's best album was *The Yes Album*; it was my favourite because it was raw. I loved *Nursery Cryme* and *Foxtrot*... but that was a long time ago." While at school, Steve participated in his first band, The Last Call.

When Steve left school he went to study Electrical Engineering at Trent Polytechnic (now Nottingham Trent University). In the third year, while working for a wire-drawing company in Doncaster, Steve and some mates formed a band called Harlow who used to tour the local working men's clubs. "We steadfastly refused to play covers, it used to get us into all sorts of trouble," said Steve, describing when the band played to an audience of fishermen. "I was in the toilets and this huge bloke came in and pulled a very large hunting knife on me, saying, 'Do 'Delilah'!' He said if we didn't, we'd regret it." Of course, the first song in the next set was 'Delilah', despite Steve only knowing the first verse. "Once we started, all these fishermen just took over and finished the song by themselves..."

An incident during a gig on a cruise ship almost spelt the end of Steve's playing career. "One night, about 3 o'clock in the morning, the bass player decided to murder the drummer and attacked him with a broken glass. The rest of the band tried to prevent the drummer's demise, and it turned out that I got very badly cut up," he recalls. "There wasn't a doctor so I was stitched up by a Swedish sailor. He saved my life. The glass severed the tendon in my thumb. It took two years of surgery, physiotherapy and pain to get it going again. My hands were constantly bandaged. Later, I saw the funny side; I used to bandage my fingers on stage for nostalgia."

Harlow folded in 1980 when the band's plans to go to London ground to a halt, as the guitarist's girlfriend didn't want him to move. Steve had been offered a full-time job with the wire-drawing company, but he decided to go to London anyway. "I thought, *If I take this job, that's it, you can nail the lid down on my coffin.*"

GOING EUROPEAN

At the same time as Steve Hogarth and his girlfriend moved into a flat in Shepperton, a new-wave band called Motion Pictures were also heading south. "We just jumped in a van," smiles guitarist, Colin Woore, who travelled down from Glasgow with bassist Ferg Harper, drummer Geoff Dugmore and keyboard/vocalist Alan Dalgleish. When Alan left after just a few months, the band advertised in *Melody Maker* and (given that his own band, renamed The Neutrinos, had folded) Steve was quick to respond. The fellows hit it off and the newly-named Europeans set about getting into the lights. They played "streamlined rock affected by punk," according to Carl Glover, who saw them in Maidstone. While Steve started on keyboards and backing, he quickly progressed to sharing vocal duties with the others. "I remember they liked a song called 'Going To Work' and Ferg said, 'Why don't you sing it?' He was always very relaxed, he was more interested about getting out of rehearsals and going to clubs than stressing too much about the music."

The Europeans acted as John Otway's backing band for one album (*All Balls And No Willy*, referring to John's old partner Wild Willy Barrett) and one tour. Explains Colin, "We'd done some session work for them, they liked us enough to use us on the album, then they offered us the chance to tour it." Not wanting to become John Otway's band, the foursome proposed playing silhouetted behind a curtain with John in front. In addition they played a complete support set as the Europeans, loaned the PA and did a lot of the roadie work. "We were absolutely knackered," says Colin, who put a tea towel and top hat on his head to appear like John's old partner. "Wild Willy would magically appear, it was hysterical!"

The Europeans signed with A&M Records in 1982, immediately heading to the Townhouse studio in London to work on their debut. Recording moved to The Manor in Oxfordshire ("Richard Branson was there at the time," says Colin), before returning to the Townhouse, where Tony Childs and Kiki Dee recorded additional vocals. It was here that Steve first met Dave Gregory of XTC. Says Dave, "I met him in the canteen. In those days, he wore these little white bandages on his fingers, even at the breakfast table, which I thought a bit strange. But he was very chatty and friendly, and instantly likeable."

The October 1983 release of *Vocabulary*, with artwork by Daevid Western, was quickly followed by a live album, recorded at London's Dingwalls that December. Explains Colin, "The band were playing really well live, but the spirit never got captured on the studio album. Our management, Mark Thompson realised this and so did A&M, so we said, 'Let's do a live album.'" Despite the *NME* saying the album sounded like "a coal-scuttle full of vomit", the cut-price release managed to sell 100,000 copies.

The next, and sadly final Europeans album was *Recurring Dreams*, recorded in 1984. Things did not go well from the start, as Ferg was in hospital - arriving at a gig with "raging flu", he had imbibed a combination of aspirin, beer and Jack Daniels to get him through. He managed the concert, but at the cost of a ruptured stomach. "It led to me collapsing in Baker Street station a day later," remembered Ferg. "As I crawled home, little did I know I was actually bleeding to death inside." Another bassist, Steve Greetham was hastily pulled in to fill the gap.

Recurring Dreams was recorded at Rockfield Studios and Crescent Studios in Bath, with producer David Lord, himself fresh from working on *Peter Gabriel 4*. In Bath Steve Hogarth bumped into Dave Gregory once again. Recalls Dave G, "They bought a bass amp from us." The album was mixed at Sarm East, Dave Meegan's old haunt. "We had a lot of mutual friends," remarks Dave M. "I rented a flat from Geoff Dugmore's ex-girlfriend. Steve Hogarth was round once when I was out - he broke my CD player!"

Sadly, *Recurring Dreams* was not the commercial success everyone had hoped for. "It really captured the essence of the band," says Colin; concurs Steve, "It was much better than *Vocabulary* on the whole." Little did the players know however, that Derek Green, then-head of A&M who was "right into it," was looking to leave the label. "He resigned the day before the release," says Colin. "There was no promotion, no single." Eventually the band released their own single, offering a double A-side free giveaway to the shops. Such endeavours failed to raise the band's profile, and the Europeans never really recovered.

Even as the band floundered, all the while owing £20,000 to A&M, offers came in for individuals but not for the unit as a whole. "Geoff was being offered fantastic tour deals with big-name bands, and our manager came to us and said people were interested in a Hogarth/Woore collaboration," says Colin. Adds Steve, "No one wanted to split but, the way I saw it, there was no viable alternative. It still feels like I betrayed Geoff and Ferg, and maybe I should have stuck it out for a year longer. The irony is that the Europeans had never sounded better." Whatever: they were no more. "I was devastated," remarked Geoff. "This band had been my life since the age of 10 and now it was taken away. You have to grow up fast in these situations."

HOW WE LIVE

In the hiatus between the Europeans and what would eventually become How We Live, Steve and Colin both took up singing lessons with Tona De Brett, who has taught everyone from All Saints to Ozzy Osbourne. Steve was told thathe didn't really need the lessons, explains Tona, "If a voice is really good, frankly I like to leave it alone." Steve had his own reasons for going along for three lessons at least: "I fell a little bit in love with the singing teacher, who appeared about 80!"

Following some showcase performances, the pair eventually signed to CBS using the name Jump The Gun, changing it to How We Live shortly afterwards. The new album, *Dry Land* was recorded back in Bath in late 1986, with David Lord again at the helm. Various items of equipment were borrowed from local performers including Peter Gabriel and Dave Gregory: recalls Dave, "David Lord called and asked if he could borrow our Mellotron for a project he was working on, How We Live. I said, 'Sure, if you collect it, bring it back and do all the lifting and carrying.' So a van pulls up and out jumps the driver, with Steve H." As Dave wouldn't accept payment, Steve bought him a bottle of whisky. "We sort of became chums at that point," says Steve.

Just as *Dry Land* was being released in January 1987, disaster stuck again. CBS was getting ready to sell up to Sony, and the axe fell for any new signings that had yet to make a profit. How We Live carried on for a while but the pair eventually went their separate ways. Steve's disillusion with the music business, together with the arrival of his first child, made him nearly ready to throw in the towel. "I planned to become a postman or something," said Steve. "We put the house on the market, we were going to move up North, live the quiet life."

Just prior to Christmas 1988, a chance remark by Steve to his publisher Alan Jones at Rondor would change the course of events. "I bounded into the place and said, 'Can anyone think of anything for me to do?' – I really meant, like a bit of typing – and Alan said, 'Well, do you know Marillion are looking for a singer?'" Steve was aware of Marillion, but wouldn't have classed himself as a fan. "I had a copy of *Misplaced Childhood* somewhere, but it wasn't what I put on every day." In any case, Steve and Alan sent off a tape including 'Kingdom Come', 'Games in Germany' and 'Dry Land'.

After sending the tape, Steve and his wife went to Derbyshire to look for houses. No wonder that he was initially reluctant, when Marillion's call came. "I thought they were a bunch of hippies who knitted their own shoes and stuff. The last thing I wanted was to be back on centre stage. I'd also had a call from Matt Johnson [of The The] about playing piano on his *Mind Bomb* tour. I quite fancied that, I would have a lot less responsibility and I could get back into enjoying playing, just what I needed after a couple of years of being signed to CBS. It took quite a few phone calls for them to even persuade me to turn up." As it happened, a mutual friend of both Steve and Ian, Darryl Way, set him on the right track.

ICE CREAM GENIUS

A few years into Steve's time with Marillion, he felt the need for an alternative release valve for his art. "I had introduced a couple of lyrics and musical ideas that I was convinced were very strong, but that the band didn't want to pursue," he told Robert Lewis of *AMZ* magazine. "Those ideas get stuck in your creative tubes and get in the way." "He saw it as an opportunity to do the things we wouldn't let him do," laughs Mark Kelly. At the time, Steve was keen to be judged on his own merits. "In my mind, rightly or wrongly, any success I've had with Marillion, to some extent I've inherited. I'm very conscious of that."

Steve spent much of the 1995 Christmas break working on his compositions, before contacting friends and admired fellow musicians for help. Having first approached Steven Wilson as producer ("He was about to produce Fish's album so I thought perhaps it's not such a good idea…"), he asked Dave Gregory for advice. Says Dave, "I suggested Craig Leon, with whom I'd worked the previous year, and thought Steve would like." Craig's credits included everyone from The Ramones to The Bangles and he, in turn, introduced Steve to the Eurythmics' Clem Burke and Chucho Merchan.

In the meantime, Steven Wilson had played H's demos to ex-Japan virtuoso soundsmith (and Porcupine Tree bandmate), Richard Barbieri. "I've been a fan ever since I heard Japan's *Tin Drum* in the early '80s," said Steve H. "He liked the demos – particularly 'The Deep Water' which was very much his sort of thing. I invited him to add his distinctive colours to my album and he came on board."

The album was recorded at The Racket Club, with vocals added at Chris Rea's Sol Mill studios (previously owned by Jimmy Page). "It was a spooky little room we were working in, and yet very, very comfortable. Like working in an old gentlemen's club," recalls Steve. Mixing took place at Van Morrison's Woolhall studios in Somerset. According to Dave Gregory, "Craig has a number of snappy phrases for any given situation, often abbreviated to '(I scream) Genius!' for good stuff, or 'Torture' for the not-so good." As a joke, Steve wrote 'Ice Cream Genius' on the tape box for the album. 'Genius' seemed appropriate as each person seemed to have a long and proven musical heritage. Following a break for the *Made Again* tour in April, *Ice Cream Genius* was completed on July 20 1996.

After a turbulent previous year, H described the album as "a reflection of someone with an unsettled mind, trying to laugh at himself a little bit, and figuring out what makes him and other people tick." This was the key to the variety of songs on the album, from the melodic 'Better Dreams', through more poppy tracks like 'Until You Fall', the straight rock of 'You Dinosaur Thing' and the downright weird 'Cage'. US fans were treated to a sublime final track, 'The Last Thing', left off the UK release as Craig wasn't sure it fitted with the rest of the album.

The album was to be released through Castle in the UK and Europe, and on the Resurgence label in the USA. Douggie Dudgeon, who had originally brought the band to Castle, was tapped for the A&R. But, just before the release, Douggie left Castle to form Snapper Music. "The whole project was effectively abandoned," said Steve. "I found out by accident during a conversation at Steely Dan's Wembley Arena show. I was devastated. He did the original deal and we worked together on it for months. He didn't even call me to say he was quitting. Once again the rug had been pulled from beneath me by record company politics - he's never spoken to me since. Nice people in the music business!"

THE H BAND

The February 1997 release of *Ice Cream Genius* was accompanied by a mini-tour covering London, Paris, Amsterdam and Cologne. The aptly-named H-band consisted of the players on the album, plus guitarist Aziz Ibrahim who Steve met through Forge Studios owner Phil Beaumont. Explains Phil, "We had a covers band called Total Chaos, Aziz was with us and we were going to play at the Boars Head in Oswestry. Steve was up in Liverpool, they'd just finished recording, he gave me a call and I said 'Why don't you come down?'" Steve H was immediately impressed by Aziz's unique style. "My music doesn't fit into a category," says Aziz. "I call it Asian Blues - no-one's created a shelf for that." Steve remarked, "Aziz can make a Les Paul sound like a sitar or a koto, and then a full-on Les Paul rock guitar. He has this great chemistry with Richard Barbieri and I regret not meeting him until it was too late for him to be involved in the record."

A second outing came in 1999, when H was invited to perform at the Festival of Hope in Geneva. John Wesley and, interestingly, Fish were also on the list. "It was only at a late stage that I heard Fish was doing it," says H. "I felt a bit, not nervous, but I didn't want to end up sitting at a table with him all night, with him bending my ear. Of course I did end up sitting at a table with him all night, but we had a great time." The encounter culminated in a joint performance, explains H, "Wes rounded up people to sing backing vocals on 'Hope For

The Future', Fish says 'I'll sing on it, will you return the favour?', and I said, 'If you're sure, then yes I will.' I don't think it was premeditated, it just sort of happened."

Fan Judith Mitchell remembers the event. "Hogarth was first up, doing a short solo set with some local musicians for backing. 'Easter' was the opener, Fish was watching from the wings. Halfway through 'Hope For The Future', he was joined by some familiar backing singers: his wife Sue, Wes and Fish. The song broke into a series of repeated choruses with everyone cheering at the end and huge hugs onstage," recalls Judith. Then it was Fish's turn. "Fish's reception was like a conquering hero returning - it was so loud! The last sections of 'Plague Of Ghosts' saw them offstage and I screamed my head off for more, along with everyone else. The wait was only a few minutes, but seemed like a lifetime. Back came Fish to introduce the band and his new friend Steve Hogarth. 'Lavender' was the result, Fish singing the verses and Hogarth joining in the choruses and also singing the 'Blue Angel' section. The reception as they left the stage was magnificent."

When Steve was asked back the following year, he decided to reform his band of geniuses but as Clem and Chucho had commitments elsewhere, Mike Wilson (of Texas) stepped in on drums, and Derek "Jingles" Jhingoree (who played with Howard Jones and Gabrielle) on bass. The gig, on May 27 2000, was a tremendous success. In his infamous diary , Steve H wrote, "I can't believe how much the musicians have put into this venture. Everyone involved is doing the show for expenses only. It's meant many hours of work just to arrive at this point. It's a great feeling to have a band of this calibre entering into the spirit of it and playing purely for pleasure."

The players had no regrets. "It was pretty cool," says Dave Gregory, "certainly our biggest crowd." Agrees Jingles, who had just finished a four year stint with BBMak in the United States, "I was earning great money but I was not happy, I was feeling drained. This was like a holiday." After that, recalled H, "The boys said, 'Why don't we do another one?' So I called a chum, Billy Manning, who was running Dingwalls and he said we could come and play there." The gig, on August 8, was another win. "It was terrific - everyone even got paid."

While at Dingwalls, fan and Web Holland staffer Natasja Gravendahl suggested playing again, this time in her country. "She sort of convinced me it could make sense, despite my initial reticence," said H. The show took place in Utrecht on Halloween night. When Mike Wilson couldn't make it, he put H in touch with drummer Andy Gangadeen. "Andy defies all conventional wisdom, he looks, plays and is like no-one I have met. When I saw him on TV playing

SEPARATED OUT ... REDUX

with Massive Attack I never imagined I'd someday have him in my band. I'd have done a back flip if I'd known!"

In the summer of 2001 the H-band played two "unmissable" gigs at Dingwalls, according to fan Heloise Brown. The audience was treated to an array of covers, including, 'I Don't Remember', 'Dream Brother' and 'Life On Mars'. There were two complete sets to learn – Dave Gregory, who helped choose the sets, commented, "I've never worked so hard. Steve does have a habit of giving us too much to learn in too short a time." Agrees Jingles, "It was a nightmare!" Aziz is sanguine – "That's just graft, that is." A surprise guest was Colin Woore, H's old partner in crime, playing 'Working Town' from the re-released How We Live album, *Dry Land*.

All the players derived enormous pleasure from the H-band experience. "I've gained a wealth of musical knowledge," says Aziz. "Even though you think your tastes are diverse, it's a shock when you meet someone whose tastes really are." For Dave Gregory, the gigs provided welcome opportunities to play live. "Having spent so much time away from it, I do get incredibly nervous nowadays, make that terrified!" says Dave. "But a friendly audience can make all the difference." Agrees Jingles, "Every gig is different. The reason why I took this gig and stuck with it is the people. No band has ever given back what I get from this one."

The next outing of the H-band was in Autumn of 2003. Pete Trewavas came along for musical support – "It was a pleasure to join Steve and his merry band. I had a thoroughly good time as we travelled from city to city in a big blue bus," he said. The idea of recording another H-band album has always been there, but time is the issue. "Marillion is a very hungry animal," says H. "Everybody always asks me, 'Are you going to do another H-band album?' The answer is always 'Yes,' – but I thought it would be eight years ago."

NOT THE WEAPON...

Of all the musicians Steve Hogarth worked with during the H-band sessions, he particularly hit it off with Richard Barbieri. "We got to know each other and realised that although we're quite different characters, we get along really well. We joke that we're long-lost brothers – there's a feeling between us," he said. The feeling was mutual – and both parties felt they should do something together. "I always wanted to do something where we were equally involved in a project," said Richard who made the initial approach. Recalls Steve, "I remember where I was when his email arrived: Starbucks in Leeds. From that day forward it was

358

on my mind fairly constantly."

Richard already had a number of soundscapes in development – each a swirling mass of auditory themes drawing on Richard's experiences. "It was like painting pictures on a landscape," he says. "I had a definite imagery for every piece of music. It can be nature, imagery, everyday sounds... often ideas that are going through my head." He suggested that Steve added his own lyrical and vocal magic on top – of course, the singer jumped at the chance. "I was desperately keen, I didn't want to drop dead without having worked on an album with Richard Barbieri. It was a fantastic creative opportunity."

As each piece of music emerged, Richard sent it over to Steve who burned it to CDs and listened in the car. Immediately clear was that it would require a very different vocal approach. "I didn't want my voice to get in the way sonically," he said. As he drove he threw a few words together on his iPhone, capturing inspiration when it came. Says Richard, "There were no instructions, no specific sections of songs in which to do anything, just basically, whatever he wanted." Some lyrics, like "Somewhere under all that shit" didn't quite make the grade however.

By 2010 the pair finally kicked off a recording process, with Richard sending over mixes and H recording lyrics over the top. "We had a stark division of labour," said H. "I set up a little studio in the top of my house and had a lot of fun recording all of these voices and dreaming up the melodies. We didn't work together in the same room – we just met four or five times to swap files. It was a really good way of working, it's an interesting and liberating process to work alone without the paranoia of anyone else's presence."

Eventually, songs like 'Red Kite' started emerging. "I heard 'Red Kite' like a landscape – I could see a wider horizon, and because I was driving around I was influenced by my journeys," says H, who watched red kites swoop and soar from his car. "The idea of a bird being part of the landscape, separate and observing..." On some occasions, like 'Crack', H already had material to hand. "I had a lyric I'd been developing for years but never managed to get to work with anything, about obsessive love – being so obsessed with another human being that you smother them and drive them away – and you know you are doing it. It might have happened to me in the past and I've certainly been victim of it..."

Gently, gently, H added vocal mixes to the music. "Some of the songs worked better spoken than sung so I simply spoke them. 'Only Love' is, for instance, more a piece of vocal theatre than a song. I'm imagining a cast of characters while I'm singing – a Shaman, a preacher, a philosopher, a section of ghosts, a narrator..." Meanwhile, Richard waited, nervously, to find out whether H had managed to get what he was trying to achieve with his music. "I was unsure I wanted a vocal on 'Lifting The Lid' at all but eventually I sent it over," he said. H's approach was equally tentative – "I wanted to get involved in this without taking up too much room," he said. It worked, says Richard, "It's probably my favourite piece."

By the summer of the following year, the pair had created a good proportion of the music that would become *Not The Weapon... But The Hand*. "It sounds like nothing I've ever heard," said H. "There's much in this album which is about the juxtaposition of darkness and light... like a Vermeer, or a Rembrandt. Is it too weird? Well, everyone to whom I have played the demos has been knocked out. These people are my kids, girlfriend, and a small circle of mates (mostly 'cool farmers' and their wives...)."

With the local vote in the bag, the pair headed to the studio to finalise the recording, adding elements from other musicians, including Dave Gregory who contributed string arrangements, guitar and bass – "To have his input, his musical instincts, it was nice to have him involved as well," said Richard. The album was mixed by Mike Hunter ("I'm ever grateful," says H) just before Christmas 2011, and it was put on general release at the end of February the following year.

The option to tour some of the material remains. "Some of the music may sound quite minimal but it's not that easy to make that happen on stage," says Richard. "We need to think about the arrangements and how to do it, but we'd like to try."

MARK KELLY

Born in Dublin in 1961 to an Irish father and English mother, Mark's family moved to Essex when he was four years old, first to Hornchurch, then Romford. "My mother basically said, 'I'm going back to England, I've had seven children, I don't want any more," he said. "I grew up in quite a rough area. My schooling didn't start off very well. Firstly having an Irish accent and secondly I couldn't read. I used to hang around with the thugs and louts, but I wasn't as thick as the rest of them! If I had gone to a better school I probably wouldn't have ended up in a band."

While his first musical influences came from his parents ("They were quite young, into a lot of rock music – bands like Led Zeppelin, Pink Floyd, Free," he says), Mark spent most of his early teenage years painting and drawing ("I was a big fan of Da Vinci,") before discovering music for himself at the age of fifteen. "I did have a good art teacher at school, he used to lend me his albums," he said. His musical moment of truth came when he heard Rick Wakeman's *Journey To The Centre Of The Earth* – from that moment on, he wanted to be a keyboard player. "I thought, *Yes, that's the instrument for me.*" Mark persuaded his Mum to buy a transistor Hammond Everett Organ for £185. "I paid her back five pounds per week from my Saturday job," he says. "It was a big thing with a tiny little keyboard, it didn't sound very good. Eventually I took a saw to it - inside it was just an empty cabinet."

Mark spent the next four years working through Rick Wakeman's entire repertoire, first on his Hammond, then a Farfisa and a Kawai synthesizer ("I couldn't afford a Mini-Moog!"). He joined a band in his last year at school (which was when the Hammond-chopping took place, "It was too big to take to rehearsals!"). Under the continued mentoring of his art teacher, Mark headed to Art College in Bath but he already knew that music was his thing. "I had sort of lost interest, the music had taken over," he said. He hoped for greater success in the second year, but alas, he wasn't even offered a place. "I re-applied and they refused me. I hadn't been to any History Of Art lectures... the lady who interviewed me was the History of Art lecturer. She said, 'I should have known you, why haven't we met?'"

On his return to Essex, Mark went to college to study electronics, immediately looking for bands. Initially he joined an ensemble called Spilt Grass, before forming Chemical Alice with Jack Grigor on Bass and Dave Weston on guitar. The band got a regular slot at the Electric Stadium at Chadwell Heath, where that November he bumped into the band that had recently lost its 'Sil'. Mark's first impressions were mixed. "I thought, *Interesting music, weird singer, wearing a priest's outfit, big bare feet on stage – rather strange*, but the music was good," he says.

Which was enough for him. He checked with his college tutor – "I said I wanted to go and join a rock band and if it didn't work out could I come back in a year's time? The tutor agreed, so I thought I would give it a year. I did honestly think I'd just see what happens – it really appealed to me but I didn't think it would get us anywhere."

PRODUCTION CREDITS

Until recently, Mark's solo career was marked more by a series of production slots than collaborations. His first came in 1991, when he produced John Wesley's first album, *Under A Red And White Sky*. He hadn't meant to play keyboards on the album, but as he recalls, "It was a case of having to."

In the gap following *Afraid Of Sunlight*, Mark put himself forward to produce Jump's fourth album. Vocalist John Jones remembers, "We did a Marillion fan club show at the Skoolhouse in June 1994. It went down quite well and we had a chat afterwards about our next album." Mark recalled, "I thought they were maybe a bit prog, but they didn't fit into the typical '70s prog rock pigeon hole." A few months later, says John, "The phone rang and a voice said, 'Hi, this is Mark Kelly. That new album, how about me producing it?'"

John invited Mark to see the band again that October, at the Captain Cook in Acton. "We really hit it off," says John. At the time, Jump were running a rehearsal studio in High Wycombe, and Mark turned up a few times to help out on pre-production. "I'd listen in to the writing process and provide some thoughts on the arrangements, and they would listen, take some ideas up or think about it." After a few months the band had about 15 songs, and work moved to the Racket Club. "It was a novelty to us not to have to worry about recording costs," says John.

Recording started on Good Friday 1995 and finished a few weeks later. As John reminisced, "Marillion's flight cases, a candlestick on the piano and a good area for soccer outside. Yes, the studio's fine." Most of the songs were complete so it was a case of "getting the parts down," arranging and mixing them. Mark selected songs to come up with a balanced album, even dropping one and requesting a new one with a better fit. Mark was keen to keep his musical involvement to a minimum, adding a bit of keyboard to 'Val Addiction' – "I didn't really want to try and muscle in on it," he explained.

COUNTING TO NUMBER 33

The whereabouts of Mark's much-mooted solo project remain unknown. In 1996, he initiated a project based on Dante's *Inferno* – planning a mainly instrumental album, with John Helmer providing a few lyrics to be sung by John Jones. "It's a bit dark. In fact I'm beginning to think I shouldn't devote the entire album to *Inferno*, as it might be a bit heavy going," he wrote. The project was referenced on various occasions over the years, right up to 2002 when he said, "I have built a small home studio to start work on an album of my own music. All previous attempts to produce a solo album have ground to a halt with me feeling unhappy with the results. So far, this time things are progressing nicely. I won't start taking orders yet, but watch this space..." Watch the fans did, but in the end it was Mark himself who announced that the idea was canned.

Fast forward to January 2011 and a conversation with Andy Ditchfield, lead singer of prog band Dee Expus. "I asked him whether he was interested in playing on a track called 'Maybe September'," says Andy. Says Mark, "I thought, *Hmm, pretty good.* I said I would look at it when I had some spare time. By May I was contacted by the main man, Andy, saying, 'Where's my bloody piano track?'" So one rainy afternoon, Mark sat down and worked out a piece of piano music. "Within half an hour of playing around with it I had come up with a part I was happy with. In fact, I was really enjoying myself, so I was somewhat relieved when Andy liked it too and pleased when he asked me if I would like to play on some more of the album."

Communicating via Skype and Dropbox, the pair collaborated until the length of the title track was too much for the technology to cope with. "I invited him down for the weekend. To be honest we didn't get a huge amount of work done but became firm friends over a few too many pints." By the end of the summer Mark headed north to finish things off and somehow became a fully-fledged member of the band, agreeing to join the ensemble on tour.

On December 3 2011, the band held an album launch party for *King Of Number 33* in the north of England. As bad luck would have it, shortly afterwards Mark was diagnosed with SSHL (Sudden Sensorineural Hearing Loss) and had to back out of the tour. But the band did end up supporting Marillion on their 2012 UK dates – no small consolation prize!

PPL AND FAC

Outside of playing music, Mark has been taking an increasing interest in industry affairs, not least co-founding the Featured Artists Coalition – an organisation set up to promote the interests of artists such as Marillion. As Mark said on his 40th birthday, "To me, the music industry has got nothing to do with creating music, just the business of recording, distributing and selling it. Computers and the Internet in particular herald the end of the music industry." While all stakeholders were struggling with the changes, Mark determined to take a more proactive role.

Over the past 10 years his involvement has grown – he is now on the board of the UK rights organisation PPL, and in July 2011, he had to give a keynote speech to the Westminster Media Forum. "I was more nervous standing in front of that audience then when we've played to 50,000 people. It must be something about having a bunch of keyboards to hide behind," he said.

IAN MOSLEY

Probably the least changed, or indeed changeable of band members past and present, Ian was always more musician than rock star. He was born into a musical household – his Dad was a violin soloist, at one time playing in six orchestras at the same time in theatres across London's West End. From an early age Ian wanted to play the drums, taking his lead from the complex rhythms of '60s jazz. "I was into Duke Ellington, Count Basie, Buddy Rich, then I went through the jazz/rock fusion thing. Those bands heavily influenced me," he recalls.

Ian's teenage years were spent at Abbotsfield School in Ickenham, where in 1966 the music teacher (named Mr Bean!) set the seal on Ian's future career by inviting him to join the school's jazz orchestra. Ian was determined to be the best drummer he could possibly be. "At seventeen, I was obsessed with technique. I just wanted to be able to play faster than anybody else. I used to practise with my eyes shut, one beat on every drum."

When he left school in 1968, Ian immediately joined a band called Walrus. He filled out his time and paid the bills with theatre work, within a year replacing Peter Wolf in the West End musical *Hair*. He also washed cars for a few weeks after he came back from a tour, at The Roundbush Garage, opposite the Roundbush Pub in the hamlet of Roundbush. Recalls Ian, "The boss of the garage came out one day and said, 'You don't give a toss about this, do you?' 'Not really,' I replied. 'That's fine, carry on!'"

The next four years involved mainly session work – "Whoever called, I would do the job," he said – including a film appearance as a drummer in *The Romantic Englishwoman*, starring Michael Caine and Glenda Jackson. His first big break came in 1974 when he was approached to join Darryl Way's Wolf, with John Etheridge and (of course) Darryl Way. The career of a drummer is rarely a bed of roses, however. When Ian's time with Darryl Way came to an end in 1976, he found himself mixing session work with destitution, before being offered a post two years later with the Gordon Giltrap Band. "None of these projects were 'real' bands, as the whole responsibility was on the solo artists' shoulders," he recalled. "It seemed that the only way in the '80s that you could join a 'real' band was if a member died."

In 1980 Ian took a position with Steve Hackett, a role he held for three years – which overlapped with the formation of that "neo-prog" band, Marillion. Ian remembers the after-gig signing sessions, where fans would raise the comparison between Genesis and Marillion. "People asked me and Steve Hackett what we thought," recalls Ian. "I'd never heard of Marillion, but being a true professional I said, 'Yeah, they're great!'"

Following Ian's tenure with Steve Hackett began a chain of events which led, eventually, to Marillion's door. "At the end of the tour I thought I'd buy a *Melody Maker*, something I rarely did but I just wanted to catch up a bit," he remembers. "I saw this advert, 'Marillion need drummer.' Well, I thought, *This is too much of a coincidence!* I thought, *I must know someone in the Marillion camp...*" Ian found that Paul Crockford, who used to work with Steve Hackett, also knew John Arnison. "I called him and said, 'Paul, recommend me, send flowers.'"

First time round, timing was not in Ian's favour – his next booking was a drum clinic tour for Zildjian and Yamaha. "John phoned asking if I could come for an audition, but there was no way I could, I was in the middle of this tour." Ian returned two days later to be told the job had been taken, but that wasn't the end of the story. Says Ian, "A few weeks later, John called again. He said 'Ian, the boys are in Monmouth writing *Fugazi*, they've just sacked the drummer, could you go up and just help?' He asked me where I lived and I said Tring, near Aylesbury. He told me that was where the band was from - it was spooky."

While Ian had even lied about his age to get the gig ("I was 30 but I told them 29!" he laughs), he was soon to find out what John had meant by 'boys'. While Mark and Fish were up in Monmouth already, Pete and Steve were still at home so Ian suggested he drive them to Wales. "I went to Pete's house and when I came to the door I thought, *He's so young...* I thought the same about Steve."

CROSSING THE DESERT

Twelve years later, in early 1996 a French guitarist called Sylvain Gouvernaire was staying at Ian's UK flat in Aylesbury. Explains Ian, "Steve Rothery had invited him over, he said, 'Sylvain needs somewhere to live.'" As he was living in Florida at the time, Ian was quite happy to loan his flat – only to find himself sharing with Sylvain a few weeks later, when his marriage to then-wife Wanda broke up.

Sylvain had come to Britain to develop some musical ideas based on leftovers from his time in a band called Arrakeen. Says Sylvain, "The ideas were often generated by events in my life or moods I was in, or short impressions from a film, or a book, or a walk in the mountains, anything that impresses me, really..." Initially it was Pete who was interested in getting involved but, with Ian finding himself at an unexpected loose end, it seemed only logical to join in." I could hear it coming through the wall – that's when I thought, *Let's do something*." says

Ian, who suggested that they decamped to the studio: "The Racket Club was empty and we had all this equipment lying around. I said it would be criminal if it wasn't being used."

"I was amazed to have the luck of working with some of my very favourite musicians. They were both very excited by the project," says Sylvain. "Ian and Pete played extremely well - they're so used to playing together it's magic. 'Train de Vie' and most of 'Crossing The Desert' were inspired by jamming along with Ian; I used some of his amazing drum patterns as the starting point. Pete was like reading Ian's mind, guessing his fill-ins advance." Adds Pete, "I was enhancing what was already played, without knowing exactly what Sylvain wanted. There was none of the usual structure, no fitting around vocals, so I could let rip!" Ian described the sessions as, "A bit Clouseau – whenever I suggested a break for a cuppa, Sylvain started a discussion on, 'Why it is not a good time for me to stop right now...'"

Mixing took a little longer than anyone had expected. "Sylvain spent months, much to the dismay of Ian," laughs Pete. As far as Sylvain was concerned it was worth it - "I am very proud of the result," he says. The project still lacked a name: "Ian wanted it to be called 'Sylvain Gouvernaire', but I wanted to see the album with the name of the project. Finally I chose 'Iris', the name of the messenger between the ancient gods of Greek mythology. I liked the symbols attached to this name and its multiple interpretations."

Crossing The Desert was released on the Racket Records label on April 22 1996, the same date that the *Made Again* tour kicked off. Science fiction artist Danny Flynn, who had bumped into H in an artists' materials shop, provided the artwork. For Ian, it was a welcome antidote to re-crossing the Atlantic.

POSTMANKIND

While *Crossing The Desert* was instigated by others, *Postmankind* was Ian's own idea, a return to his jazz roots in collaboration with saxophonist Ben Castle. Ben was leader of big band The Big Blue, as well as son of musician and TV celebrity, the late Roy Castle. Ben had first seen Marillion play at the Milton Keynes Bowl on June 28 1985, when he was 12. While he once lived in the same village as Ian and Fish, serendipity came in France. As he recalled, "I was playing a lot of drums, when by sheer coincidence I met Ian at Nice airport. When we got back to England Ian gave me a lift home, and we stayed in touch."

A few years later, Ben happened to be playing in Wolverhampton on the same night as Marillion. His gig finished early, so he made his way to the Marillion gig. "We met and I said to him, 'Do you fancy doing something?'" says Ian. Ben came to the Racket Club with a head full of ideas and his friend Mark, who was to play keyboards. "Pete and I had done the backing tracks, then he came down and added the brass section. He had all these amazing arrangements, I thought, *If I'd known he was going to do that, I would have tried harder!"*

The album was structurally esoteric, to say the least, a reflection of the 'anything goes' attitude that pervaded the studio sessions. In a *Web* interview Ian mentioned, "The thing I've noticed throughout the whole process of recording this album so far, is that it has been extremely enjoyable. Everybody is just having a bloody good time. Hopefully this will be reflected in the finished project, however trying to describe the music is like trying to glue down smoke, it is so diverse."

Once the main structures were in place, Ian made some calls to colour in some gaps with guitar. Answering in the affirmative were Steve Rothery, John Etheridge and even Ian's old colleague Steve Hackett. "Steve was a real inspiration," says Ian. "I'd played 'Someday In May' to a couple of guitarists; he was the one who said, 'I'll have a go at this.' I loved what he did on it."

The project was finished in early 2001, with final mixes by Steve Wilson at his own studio, No Man's Land. The cover involved Racket Records' own Colin Price, packaged in brown paper and packing tape, a fitting end to an enjoyable ride. "It was really good fun," says Ian. "We might do something again at some time. I'd like it to have more guitars than brass next time, but if Ben could be involved then great."

MICK POINTER

Mick Pointer, the man who dropped the 'Sil' from Silmarillion, was quick to recognise that there was more to life than the production plant. "We were all lining up to be cannon fodder at the local car factory," he says of his time at the local secondary school, in the village of Long Crendon near Brill, Buckinghamshire. Recognising that anything had to be better than that, Mick left school at 16 and went to college. "My brother was a carpenter, some courses came up so I did an apprenticeship."

Three years into his course, Mick was re-introduced to old classmate Martin Butler, who had started a band called Stockade with his brother, Clive. "The guy doing drums had a really crappy drum kit. I went and bought one, a week later I was the drummer 'cos I had a better kit!" laughs Mick. Things were fine for 18 months, but then Clive left the band, and Martin started to have greater aspirations. "He said he wanted to be a pop star, and sort of vanished," says Mick, who was left to look for other people to play with.

Mick also took some lessons on the flute. "I'm no flute player, I just thought it might give me a better chance," he explains. When the neighbour's daughter's boyfriend (a drummer), said he was leaving a band called Electric Gypsy, Mick auditioned for the job and started Marillion on its journey. He remained on good terms with Martin Butler, a factor that proved important 15 years later when he found himself, once again, without a gig.

THE LONG ROAD TO ARENA

Disillusioned following his departure from Marillion, Mick intended to turn his back on the music business altogether. "I don't think I even listened to music," says Mick, who picked up his old trade as a kitchen designer and fitter. 12 years passed before an unsuspecting fan put Mick back on the road again. He explained, "This fan called Richard Jordan phoned up; he said, 'I've been trying to track you down, I'm a mad Marillion fan and I love all the early Marillion stuff. There are thousands of people around that would really love to hear this again, so why don't you do an album?'"

It so happened that old mate Martin Butler knew Pendragon keyboardist Clive Nolan and he introduced the pair. "That was really the catalyst for getting things moving," says Mick. "Clive was a proper musician, his take on music was totally refreshing." The meeting led to not only Mick picking up his sticks again, but also the creation of a new record label, a trick Clive had learned through Pendragon's Toff Records. By November 1994, the pair were writing. "We wanted to get the album completely intact before we started introducing other people to it," recalls Mick.

Arena was formed with singer John Carson from Asia, Cliff Orsi on bass, and session guitarist Keith More. When Steve Rothery found out about the project, he offered his support as well. "I did it as a favour," says Steve. "He was booted out of Marillion - it was a small recompense." Steve was sent a track with vocals, drums and keyboard, and the message, "As soon as the vocals finish, put the solo in." Steve recorded two solos for the band to choose from. "He did a brilliant job," Mick commented.

Released in 1995, Arena's debut incorporated one backward glance. "When we split, I suggested to Doug that every time somebody leaves, we should get rid of a bit of the name, that's why 'Sil' went. The album is called *Songs From The Lion's Cage* because by the time I left, we'd have been left with 'Lion'. My little joke!" Both album and band were well-received - Arena achieved Best New Band and Best New Album categories in the 1996 Classic Rock Society awards. In the first of many line-up changes, John Carson left shortly before the ceremony, so Mick quickly found Paul Wrightson as replacement.

Several albums and personnel changes followed, including *The Cry* (again featuring Rothers, on 'Only Child'), The Visitor and Immortal. On April 2 2000, the band released its second live album, *Breakfast In Biarritz*, recorded the previous year at the Amsterdam Paradiso.

The line-up of Arena remained the same across 1999-2011 – with John Mitchell on guitar, bassist Ian Salmon, vocalist Rob Sowden and the irrepressible Mick Pointer. *Contagion*, was released in 2003, followed by *Pepper's Ghost* in 2005 and *The Seventh Degree of Separation* in 2011, accompanied by a pan-European tour. Says Mick, "I want to do it for the enjoyment - that's why I got into it in the first place."

STEVE ROTHERY

Steve Rothery was, in his own mind, late picking up the guitar. "I was just too busy doing other stuff, although I did have a guitar when I was about eleven," he said. "Always wanted to play it. I thought it was such a cool, magical thing." It was Alan Freeman's Saturday night rock show that piqued Steve's interest, when he was 15. "He played this wonderful music such as Pink Floyd, Genesis, Camel, Led Zeppelin, Yes and King Crimson. I started to develop this feeling for music." He finally got the bug listening to *Wish You Were Here* sitting on a beach by his hometown, Whitby. I thought, *This is what I want to do with my life – to create something that magical."*

A year later Steve acquired a clone Stratocaster before graduating to a Yamaha SG2000, and set about emulating his new heroes. "One of the most inspiring things I heard was 'The Knife' by Genesis. Certain players were really good at conveying emotion in their playing, not simply blues rock but they had a more melodic sensibility. My favourite players, like Dave Gilmour, Andy Latimer and Steve Hackett had this ability to make their guitar something more, more special."

That was that – he was hooked, learning through books and listening to his favourite players. "School kind of went out the window. Not that I was doing badly all of a sudden, but I just didn't fancy an academic career," he said. He left at 16 and took a job as a van driver, largely because anything else would have wasted valuable practice time. "When I went to see careers advisers, they'd ask me, 'What are you going to do with your life?' and I'd answer, 'I'm going to be a guitarist in a rock band.' They'd fall about laughing."

Eventually, with old school mate Edwin Hart, he joined a band called Purple Haze. "Jimi Hendrix was one of his biggest influences," confirms fan and chronicler Claus Nygaard. Steve's first gig was the Queen's 25th Jubilee in 1977. "It was a kind of street party with a low key introduction. But the band I was in was so bad that people would actually stop to see what it was they were hearing. Fortunately no one ever threw tomatoes."

When Steve saw the Marillion ad in *Melody Maker* a year later, he was a lot more practised – "All the people I was in bands with had gone to art college or university, while I did nothing but play guitar," he said. To the guitarist, it was a dream waiting to come true. "I sensed the possibility of something happening, it was worth giving everything up for." So he did, quitting his job, jumping in the car and earning his own place in rock history.

WISHING WELL

Since the early days, Steve has jumped at offers of guest appearances, playing with Sylvain Gouvernaire's old band Arrakeen, as well as John Wesley and Jadis, "Friends whom I wanted to give a little push." In August 1993, in parallel with the completion of *Brave*, Steve produced and remixed US band Enchant's debut album, *Blueprint Of The World*. Doug Ott and Paul Craddick were both Marillion fans, who had first seen the band play at The Cabaret in San Jose. Enchant's album had been partially produced and engineered by Paul Schmidt, and now the band needed help to finish it. When the opportunity came, they were delighted when Steve accepted the opportunity to help out.

Steve quickly earned the nickname 'The Compiler', due to his systematic approach to recording: capture each section a few times, select the best parts of each, assemble the resulting fragments into a completed section and move on. "They're good friends which makes it all the more fun to be working with them," Steve commented. Doug and Paul reciprocated: "He's been a real inspiration, an all round great guy!" With five of the nine tracks produced by Steve, the CD was released in October 1993.

Following his work with Mick Pointer for Arena's debut album *Songs From The Lion's Cage*, Steve was keen to pursue some musical ideas of his own. A few years before, he had met producer Miles Copeland, who wanted the guitarist to record an instrumental album for his music-only No Speak label. Says Steve, "He offered me a considerable sum of money." While the project never happened (the label itself folded after only three years), Steve got to thinking about making such an album himself. Converting his garage into a studio ("I was one of the first users of Digital Design ProTools in the country," he said), one of his first recordings was 'Winter Trees', which became the B-side of the 'Hollow Man' single.

It wasn't long before Steve had enough material to make a whole album. Having moved on from the instrumental album idea, he approached John Helmer for some lyrics and started looking for a singer. Steve's original plan was to work with Julianne Regan from All About Eve. "John Arnison approached their management, but they weren't really interested," remembers Steve. The second try was for the singer in Hit And Run stable mates, The Escape Club. "Her voice reminded me of Annie Haslam of Renaissance, but I didn't like her attitude. I thought, *Life's too short!*"

The breakthrough came on May 16 1994, when friends introduced 19-year-old Hannah Stobart to Rothers at the Colston Hall, Bristol, following a *Brave* gig. A few conversations later, Hannah professing her love for singing. "I said that I was a far better singer than I was guitar player," she says. "He wanted to hear my voice and insisted that I send him a recording." Hannah sent a tape, which included covers of the Irish folk song 'She Moved Through The Fair' and Tori Amos's 'Me And A Gun'. The demos were pretty raw – "Me singing a capella in my bedroom," laughs Hannah – but they hit the spot. Says Steve, "I finally found what I had been looking for, for years: vocal purity."

Steve and Hannah took the opportunity to produce a number of demos at his home, the first of which (which later turned up on the remaster) was 'She Moved Through The Fair'. Most of the album was written and recorded across a two-week period in the first months of 1996 – though the song 'Evergreen' had its origins alongside the recording of *Clutching At Straws*, parts of 'Midnight Snow' date from *Holidays In Eden* and 'Nightwater' was based on a jam at the time of Steve Hogarth's audition – "He found the lyrics too gothic," says Rothers. Enchant's Paul Craddick played drums and Pete Trewavas contributed a bass line; Steve's wife, Jo added backing vocals.

Naming the project 'The Wishing Tree' after a film by Russian director Tengiz Abuladze, "about a community on the eve of revolution," Steve knew only too well that perfectionism was not an option - not only was his day job pretty demanding, but Jo was also heavily pregnant. "At one given point I decided that the album was finished and it had to be released," says Steve. With one last heave, he finished the rough mix at 6 o'clock one Sunday morning. With perfect timing, just 21 hours later, another series of pushes saw the arrival of

Steve's son. "Every time the phone rang, we thought, 'This Is It,' " recalled Stewart Every.

Carnival Of Souls was released in September 1996 on Steve's new Dorian Music label. Steve had been looking for distribution channels a couple of years previously, when he was talking to Mick Pointer and his then-partner, Mandy about Arena's label, Verglas Records. Mick and Mandy offered to 'sign' The Wishing Tree but shortly afterwards, Mick split up with Mandy. All the same she offered to set up a similar distribution operation for Steve, which he called Dorian Music.

Following the release, The Wishing Tree made a couple of appearances on Italian TV, followed by an acoustic showcase organised by Marillion's Italian fan club, Real To Read. A new Wishing Tree album was quickly mooted, and Steve still fancied doing an instrumental album. "There's still tons of material I haven't used," he said at the time. In the event however, a whole decade would pass before he started, in August 2006. Time was ever the factor – "I spend as many hours as I can spend doing it without getting divorced," he laughed. "It's a slow process as I'm pretty much doing everything (writing, engineering and playing all the instruments apart from the drums)."

Twelve months later, Steve headed to California to record vocals with Hannah and her husband, Paul Craddick (see what they did there). The pair had bought a mountain cabin, which appeared the perfect setting for writing and recording. "I was looking forward to the peace and quiet while we worked on the last few tracks," said Steve. "Unfortunately one of their neighbours had decided to dig up their swimming pool during my stay and we were greeted most days to the sound of bulldozers shattering the tranquillity." Somehow, the ensemble managed to remain productive.

The album dragged on. By July 2008, Steve was able to report again, "In any spare time I have, I'm slowly moving forward with the new album. I really hope to have it finished by the end of the summer, it's driving me a little crazy!" It was not to be - *Ostara* was eventually released as a download in early 2009, so fans could hear the album before it was played live at the imminent convention. "We think it has been worth the wait," said the pair, with a palpable sigh of relief.

PETE TREWAVAS

Pete found himself drawn to music from his earliest childhood. "It's something I was charmed with – a gift, one of those things that just happened," he said. "Even before I picked up an instrument I was able to understand music, which seemed odd. It's hard for me to understand why other musicians don't get that sometimes, for me its as simple as walking." Having been entranced by the Beatles' performance at Shea Stadium ("I saw it on the BBC when I was about seven," he says), the young Pete would pick apart Beatles songs to understand the chord structures, "Some would seem so simple but there was always one chord that I would think, *What does it do?* because it doesn't do what it's supposed to." Pete's Dad ("A complete muso") catalysed his growing interest. "He would play me stuff like Glenn Miller, and say, 'That's good, isn't it?', then he'd play Artie Shaw and Benny Goodman and say, 'Now that's *really* good'..."

By the age of twelve, Pete had picked up a bass guitar. "I came to the conclusion that most bass players weren't very good," he says. "That might have been a bit harsh but there wasn't much music I couldn't pick up and play, so I started to listen more to my Dad's jazz records and Yes, Genesis, King Crimson and Caravan. Then, of course, very muso stuff came along like Maravishnu Orchestra and Weather Report, etc., but I found that for playing I most enjoyed bass with strong melody amongst the rhythms, à la McCartney."

Having moved from Middlesbrough at an early age, Pete went to The Grange secondary school in Aylesbury, where he became mates with fellow fledgling performer Robin Boult. As soon as they were able, the pair formed a band. "I wanted to play in front of people. I wanted to hear the roar of the crowd and feel the thrill." says Pete. "There was Robin, Mark Marsh, John Hill and me; it was just a Hawkwind type band. We played the school assembly - it proved so popular we were asked to put on lunchtime shows for everyone."

Pete won his first bass guitar ("A Fender Mustang bass, converted to fretless, not a brilliant idea really,") in a raffle at the local music shop, staffed by a young Bradley Bowey. "It was 'Free 'n' Easy Music' at the bottom of Aylesbury High Street," he recalls. Pete was never sure if the raffle was rigged, but it was not the case – continues Bradley, "I was told at the time that it was a genuine win by my friend the shop owner." Sadly, Pete didn't make as much use of the guitar as he might have liked. "I loaned it to a friend, who sold it."

On leaving school, Pete and Robin joined a band called Manantus, followed by the prog combo, Orthi. "Terrible songs, bad, long solos," remembers Robin, "But we were playing proper gigs for the first time, especially Friars supports." Also in the band was Malcolm Allen. "He was the first musician I knew who went on to do quite big things, like getting a recording contract. I thought, if he can do it then so can I," says Pete. Orthi used to rehearse in Long Marston Village Hall, and were voted best local band three years in a row, at Friars. It was in this time that Pete had his first brush with the Marillion family tree. "Doug

Irvine was my roadie," he laughs. Meanwhile, Pete found a job as an apprentice TV engineer.

Orthi were soon to fold, explains Robin, "We had some great times and a reasonable local following, but the band never had any proper sense of direction or concept and eventually it came to a halt." Pete and Robin worked through a number of bands, including The Robins, Heartbeat, Tamberlane ("I was playing bass and singing as well, it was a bit of a tall order," says Pete), The Cameras (who played at the Marquee) and finally Red Stars. Robin left to work with singer-songwriter John Wilson. ("Mari Wilson's brother," says Robin, "Although at that point Mari hadn't had any hits.")

Pete's first real break came on January 1 1981, when he joined Haircut 100-style band The Metros: he was given the stage name Pete True. The band released an EP that proved so popular it had to be re-pressed. Flushed with success, they tried their luck in New York. It didn't work, but Pete did have the pleasure of supporting Duran Duran. "Because they looked good on *Top Of The Pops* we all assumed they couldn't play," says Pete. "In fact it was a good gig with the songs coming across really well." Pete maintained his interest in Haircut 100 until he joined Marillion, when he claimed he didn't like them anymore. "It's a good job our fans aren't as fickle," Tim Hollings wrote in *The Web*.

TRANSATLANTIC

Two years after Messrs Rothery and Hogarth appeared with Dream Theater at Ronnie Scott's on January 31 1995, Mike Portnoy was speaking to H about whether he could use the tapes from the gig. At the same time, asked Mike, would Pete be interested in playing bass on a solo project he was planning? Explains Mike, "My love for Marillion and respect for Pete as a (very underrated) player put him on the top of my list. I also remembered when we played with them back in 1989, at Marillion's sound check, Pete was fiddling with some bits of Yes's *Close To The Edge* and that stuck with me. I remember thinking, *Seems this guy has good taste.*"

Pete was not only unsure about leaving his band for a while, but also concerned about his own competence and style. "I had various conversations with Mike about what he wanted and if I was right for the project. He assured me that he wanted me to do my thing as he liked my melodic approach, which was reassuring," he says. With the addition of Neil Morse from Spock's Beard and Roine Stolt from Nordic band The Flower Kings, the line-up was complete. "I liked the idea of two Americans and two Europeans working together. It adds to the music immensely and brings a charm to the whole thing."

Initially planned for June 1998, the "Portnoy Project" was pushed back to January 1999 due to various commitments. The entire project (and Pete!) nearly came to an abrupt end, when the bassist was hit by a car while on his bicycle – he ended up in hospital with a suspected fractured spine and a pin through his leg. "I thought it would probably go on without me," says Pete. "However, I got a message from Mike saying, 'Get better soon,' and that the project would be put back till the summer for me to recover. I cannot tell you how much that meant to me at that particular time. I was very depressed and wondering if I would ever walk properly again. That one thing really helped me keep my strength."

Eventually, with Pete back on his feet and with diaries matching, the four managed to get together in the summer of 1999. Pete remarked, "It was a bit of a supergroup. I felt privileged to be in the same room as them." The album was to be unashamedly Prog. Says Pete, "I think if you're going to be progressive there's only two ways to do it, one of which is to say, 'Look, this is what we really love about progressive music and we don't care what anyone else thinks!'" For Pete it offered a creative release of tension, as he could go where the mood took him. "I'm allowed to play like whoever I want to be and no-one's looking down at me, saying, 'Don't you think that's a bit old?' or 'Don't you think that's a bit derivative?' It was absolutely, very self-indulgent!"

All the same, the recording process was lightning quick. "We recorded the bass and drums in about a week," remembers Pete. "Mike is a scary bloke and he likes everything to be done as quickly as possible." It helped that Neal and Roine already had some song ideas: "We decided to work on one of Neal's songs first - it ended up over 30 minutes long, which we really like." At the end of the recording sessions, everyone took away a copy of the tapes and added sounds and instruments as they saw fit. "Some of them got used and some of them didn't, 'cos we were all recording blind the moment we left the studio."

The final album was mixed by Rich Mouser (who had worked with Spock's Beard) and a second mix was done by Roine. Explains Pete, "Roine had recorded some overdub guitar tracks that were left off Rich's version." In the end the players went with the Mouser mix. Pete was delighted with the result: "It's totally retro, I make no bones about it!"

The generally positive reception to the album *SMPTe* on its release in 2000 meant that a short tour was inevitable. This took place during a break in the recording of *Anoraknophobia*: Pete played six shows in seven days, ranging from the massed hordes of Nearfest to a handful of people in Boston. "It was a back-to-basics, spit and sawdust busman's holiday for me," says Pete. "I even set my own gear up and took it down again at Nearfest, which was dangerous, but not as frightening as doing your first show ever in front of a full house of prog fanatics, after rehearsing for two and a half days."

By January 2001 a second album was underway, recorded at the Dark Horse studio in Nashville, itself once used by Yes. "It is very cool, some kind of cross between the Addams Family house and an old fort," said Pete. The once-again high-octane process resulted in *Bridge Across Forever*, which was released on October 8, again with a suitably proggy cover by Per Nordin. While the first album was very much a progressive release of tension, the second showed itself to be more considered. "It's definitely more rounded and listenable," comments fan Adrian Holmes.

At the time of recording, Pete had been trying to entice Mike and Neil over to play Europe: "Obviously Roine and I would like to, but the Americans are a bit reluctant. I think it's the weather." Eventually the tour went ahead and the supergroup were determined to make the most of it, squeezing in 11 dates in England, France, Germany, Holland and Italy between November 9-21 2001. The musicians rehearsed at The Fruit Farm near Oxford, a converted apple barn also used by Radiohead (allegedly, where *OK Computer* was written).

The players reunited in Nashville after the 2009 Marillion weekend to record a new album, *The Whirlwind*, the title track based on a 49-minute Neal Morse piece. "We decided to approach it like an overture to a piece of classical music and go through a variety of themes that would occur and re-occur throughout the song," said Pete. End to end the process took ten days – "a phenomenal amount of work – non-stop and fast and furious like all Transatlantic things are." The album was released in October 2009. Live dates inevitably followed, and a live album and DVD followed a year later.

So, how did Pete's melodic approach pan out? "I love playing with the guy," says Mike Portnoy. "Pete has got (hands down) the most melodic sensibilities of anybody I have ever played with."

KINO

The Kino project emerged from a conversation between Pete and Thomas Weber, who was running Transatlantic's German record label. Pete suggested a collaboration with John Beck, and Thomas remarked how John was already planning to work with John Mitchell. Said Pete, "I think Thomas is hoping for some radio-friendly hits, but the end result will probably be more of a muso thing." With a background like Pete's, how could it be anything else?

By June 2003 some plans had firmed up – starting with recording a version of Kevin Gilbert's 'Loser's Day Parade', with John Mitchell, John Beck and Steve Hughes, for a tribute album. Following the exercise, Pete had been testing ideas with the two Johns and with ex-Porcupine Tree drummer Chris Maitland. "I probably have the best part of two albums worth of songs," said Pete. "Ideally it will be folk-based with a couple of rocky things for good measure."

From start to finish the whole project took about three years – "There were lots of conversations about whether it would ever get finished," says Pete. "We could never find John Beck, he seemed to disappear but he was on tour in America and it was hard to track him down." For want of a name it became known as 'The Arm Band' - "It is NOT our intention to keep the name," insisted Pete. Following a fan poll, the name of Kino was selected and, eventually, *Picture* was released in February 2005.

While the music was as much mainstream as muso in the end, it didn't get the recognition it deserved. "It's a shame it hasn't gone a bit more mainstream," said Pete. "Everybody picked up on the fact that John Beck's from It Bites, and I'm from Marillion, and they kind of put two and two together and made five. Once you've got that progressive pigeonhole, a lot of other areas of music won't touch you with a bargepole."

Still, Kino were well received by those who heard them, both on disc and at the handful of dates played across 2005. Fan Marc Hughes was at the Borderline on November 16, where he heard Pete perform the vocals for 'Won't Fall Down'. "Pete has a great voice for this material and he thanked the audience for letting him sing," said Marc.

As always, a follow-up is yet to emerge. Said Pete in Feb 2009, "We nearly did some writing together, and then we didn't – that's the story of side projects."

EDISON'S CHILDREN

With Pete's uncanny ability to sniff out a potential collaboration, it was almost inevitable that he should run into heavy metal musician (retired) Eric Blackwood, who had volunteered his van to transport equipment between Marillion gigs – quite an ask given that this was the US Los Trios tour. Eric had started out in a metal band called Crimson Steele – he recalls, "We did a lot of hard but good music, like Manowar and Queensrÿche, Dio and Rainbow..." After a varied musical career in a number of bands, he decided to turn his back on the scene for a while. "I was burnt out from it all," he says on his move into film music props and Special FX – hence the van.

It was as Eric was line-checking Rothers' guitar rig ready for a sound check that Pete walked out from back stage. "I did an old song from my Blackwood and Foti days," he said. "Pete heard me jamming, singing this song and he began playing on H's keyboard." Afterwards, Pete suggested the pair worked on something together, to which Eric readily agreed. "I didn't really believe him," he says. "But he kept bringing it up."

A missed transfer from New York to Nashville, on a subsequent Transatlantic tour left Pete at a loose end, at which point Eric held him to his word. "I phoned up Eric and told him I was in New York for the evening and he came and got me - we hung out until the next evening," recalls Pete of the day the pair spent in Sandy Hook, New Jersey. "He always had a guitar with him and I picked up a guitar and we started jamming. He played me a song of his and I thought that we should really work together." "Yes, we should," replied the American – but real progress had to wait until Pete was next over, again with Transatlantic. Says Pete, "We got together and started demoing some songs and they kind of took off from there."

Emerging from Pete's prog/melodic sensibilities and Eric's more mainstream rock approach was a "psychedelic project" which became known as Edison's Children. "There was a nice marriage in the middle," said Pete. "We also both love playing lead; he is a great lead player and I'm a frustrated lead player so it's great to be playing around with that too. It was a lot of fun." Eric wrote most of the lyrics with Pete adding a few English-isms, and even found himself singing lead vocals on a couple of the songs. Said Eric, "Pete has got a great voice so with Edison's Children I really wanted him to showcase his vocals."

A couple of years of file-swapping later, in 2011 Pete was able to take some extra time following the Marillion Weekend in Montreal. "I spent three weeks," said Pete. "Eric hired a place and we got the bare bones of the album together. After my summer holiday in Florida, I went up to Ocean Pines near Washington and we finished it." The final album included contributions by Rothery, Mosley, Hogarth, Kelly and others, and a couple of mixes from Robin Boult, one of which, 'A Million Miles Away (I Wish I Had A Time Machine)' was being touted as a potential single.

Said Pete, "As a project it has been exciting, enlightening and downright frightening. Sometimes all at once which is pretty scary!" Following a "lead-in' single ('Dusk') on November 11 2011, the album *In The Last Waking Moments* was released a week later. Nobody could have expected the events of 6 months later, when 'A Million Miles Away' was released – 6 weeks in the US top 40 - and counting.

What of the future? Says Eric, "We certainly feel that Edison's Children could make some big waves in the music world and so far it has done very well. As long as it gives us an excuse to hang out and goof about under the guise of "work", I think it could continue indefinitely."

DISCOGRAPHY

STUDIO ALBUMS
Script For A Jester's Tear (1983)
Fugazi (1984)
Misplaced Childhood (1985)
Clutching At Straws (1987)
Seasons End (1989)
Holidays In Eden (1991)
Brave (1994)
Afraid Of Sunlight (1995)
This Strange Engine (1997)
Radiat10n (1998)
Marillion.com (1999)
Anoraknophobia (2001)
Marbles (2004)
Somewhere Else (2007)
Happiness Is The Road (2008)
Less Is More (2009)
Sounds That Can't Be Made (2012)

SINGLES
'Market Square Heroes' (1982)
'He Knows, You Know' (1983)
'Garden Party' (1983)
'Punch And Judy' (1984)
'Assassing' (1984)
'Kayleigh' (1985)
'Lavender' (1985)
'Heart Of Lothian' (1985)
'Lady Nina' (1986)
'Welcome To The Garden Party' (1986)
'Incommunicado' (1987)
'Sugar Mice' (1987)
'Warm Wet Circles' (1987)
'Freaks' (Live) (1988)
'Hooks In You' (1989)
'The Uninvited Guest' (1989)
'Easter' (1990)
'Cover My Eyes (Pain & Heaven)' (1991)
'No One Can' (1991)
'Dry Land' (1991)
'Sympathy' (1992)
'The Great Escape' (1994)
'The Hollow Man' (1994)
'Alone Again In The Lap Of Luxury' (1994)
'Beautiful' (1995)
'Man Of A Thousand Faces' (1997)
'80 Days' (1997)
'These Chains' (1998)
'Between You And Me' (2001)
'You're Gone' (2004)
'Don't Hurt Yourself' (2004)
'The Damage' (Live) (2004)
'You're Gone' (Remix Single) (2005)
'See It Like A Baby' (2007)

'Thankyou Whoever You Are' (2007)
'Whatever Is Wrong With You' (2008)

LIVE ALBUMS (INCLUDING RACKET RELEASES)
Real To Reel (1984)
The Thieving Magpie (1988)
Live At The Borderline (1992)
Live In Caracas (1993)
Live In Glasgow (1993)
Made Again (1996)
Marillion Rochester (1998)
Piston Broke (1998)
Unplugged At The Walls (1999)
Zodiac (1999)
Anorak In The UK (2002)
Brave Live 2002 (2002)
Marbles Live (2005)
Popular Music (Marillion Weekends 2002-2003) (2005)
Marbles By The Sea (Marillion Weekend 2005) (2005)
Smoke/Mirrors (Marillion Weekend 2005) (2006)
Friends/Family (Marillion Weekend 2007)
Early Stages: The Official Bootleg Box Set 1982-1987 (2008)
Happiness Is Cologne (2009)
Happiness On The Road (Download) (2008, 2009)
Live From Loreley (2009)
Recital Of The Script (2009)
Less Is More Live (Download) (2009)
The Official Bootleg Box Set, Volume 2: 1990-1994 (2010)
Tumbling Down The Years (2010)
Size Matters (2010)
Live From Cadogan Hall (2010)
Keep The Noise Down (Download Sampler) (2010)
Live In Montreal (2010-2011)
Sounds Live (2012)

COMPILATION ALBUMS
Brief Encounter EP (1986)
B'Sides Themselves (1988)
A Singles Collection (1992)
The Best Of Both Worlds (1997)
The Singles '82-88' (2000)
The Singles '89-95' (2002)
The Best Of Marillion (2003)
Warm Wet Circles (2003)

VIDEOS
Recital of the Script (1983)
Grendel/The Web Video EP (1984)
1982-1986 The Videos (1986)
Live from Loreley (1987)
From Stoke Row to Ipanema (Documentary) (1990)

A Singles Collection (In US *Six of One,*
Half-Dozen of the Other) (1992)
Brave: The Film (1995)
Shot in the Dark (2000)
EMI Singles Collection (2002)
Brave Live 2002 (2002)
A Piss-Up in a Brewery (2002)
Before First Light (2003)
Christmas in the Chapel (2003)
Marbles on the Road (2004)
Wish You Were Here (2005)
Colours and Sound (Documentary) (2006)
Bootleg Butlins (2007)
Something Else (2007)
Somewhere in London (2007)
This Strange Convention (2009)
M-Tube Video Sampler (2010)
Out of Season (2010)
Live at Cadogan Hall (2010)
Holidays in Zélande (2011)
Live in Montreal (2011)
Best.Live (2011)
A-Z (2012)

RACKET RECORDS RELEASES(NON-LIVE)

The Making Of Brave (1995)
Tales From The Engine Room (1998)
marillion.co.uk (Sampler) (2000, 2002, 2005)
Crash Course - An Introduction To Marillion
(2001, 2002, 2004, 2006, 2007, 2008, 2012)
AWOL (Solo projects sampler) (2002)
View From The Balcony (Front Row Club sampler) (2003)
Remixomatosis (2004)
A Handful Of Marbles (Compilation Sampler) (2005)
Playing Away (Solo projects sampler) (2012)
From Dusk 'Til Dot – The Making Of series:
ReFracted (2001) (Afraid Of Sunlight)
Another DAT At The Office (2001) (This Strange Engine)
Fallout (2002) (Radiat10n)
Caught In The Net (2002) (Marillion.com)
Unzipped (2006) (Anoraknophobia)

SOLO/COLLABORATIONS (CURRENT LINE-UP)

STEVE HOGARTH

Ice Cream Genius (1997)
Live Spirit: Live Body (2002)
H Natural Selection (2010)
Not The Weapon But The Hand (with
Richard Barbieri) (2012)

MARK KELLY

DeeExpus – *The King of Number 33*
(as band member) (2012)

IAN MOSLEY

Iris – *Crossing The Desert* (with
Sylvain Gouvernaire) (1996)
Postmankind (with Ben Castle) (2001)

STEVE ROTHERY

The Wishing Tree - *Carnival Of Souls* (1996)
The Wishing Tree - *Ostara* (2009)

PETE TREWAVAS

Transatlantic - *SMPT:e* (2000)
Transatlantic - *Bridge Across Forever* (2001)
Transatlantic - *The Whirlwind* (2009)
Transatlantic - *Live In America* (2001)
Transatlantic - *Live In Europe* (2003)
Transatlantic - *Whirld Tour 2010: Live In London* (2010)
Kino – *Picture* (2005)
Edison's Children - *In The Last Waking Moments...*
(with Eric Blackwood) (2012)

FISH - STUDIO AND LIVE ALBUMS

Vigil In A Wilderness Of Mirrors (1990)
Internal Exile (1991)
Songs From The Mirror (covers album) (1993)
Suits (1994)
Yin And Yang (1995)
Sunsets On Empire (1997)
Kettle Of Fish (88-98) (1998)
Raingods With Zippos (1999)
Fellini Days (2001)
Field Of Crows (2004)
Bouillabaisse (2005)
13th Star (2007)

MICK POINTER/ARENA – STUDIO AND LIVE ALBUMS

Songs From The Lion's Cage (1995)
Pride (1996)
Welcome To The Stage (live) (1997)
The Visitor (1998)
Immortal? (2000)
Breakfast In Biarritz (live) (2001)
Contagion (2003)
Live & Life (live) (2004)
Pepper's Ghost (2005)
The Seventh Degree Of Separation (2011)